THE NEW
PALGRAVE

MARXIAN
ECONOMICS

THE NEW
PALGRAVE

MARXIAN
ECONOMICS

EDITED BY

JOHN EATWELL · MURRAY MILGATE · PETER NEWMAN

W. W. NORTON & COMPANY

NEW YORK · LONDON

© The Macmillan Press Limited, 1987, 1990

First published in
The New Palgrave: A Dictionary of Economics
Edited by John Eatwell, Murray Milgate and Peter Newman
in four volumes, 1987

The New Palgrave is a trademark of
The Macmillan Press Limited

First American Edition, 1990

ISBN 0-393-02735-X

ISBN 0-393-95860-4   PBK

W. W. Norton & Company, Inc.
500 Fifth Avenue
New York, NY 10110

W. W. Norton & Company, Ltd.
37 Great Russell Street
London WC1B 3NU

Printed in Hong Kong

1   2   3   4   5   6   7   8   9   0

Contents

Contents

General Preface

The books in this series are the offspring of *The New Palgrave: A Dictionary of Economics*. Published in late 1987, the *Dictionary* has rapidly become a standard reference work in economics. However, its four heavy tomes containing over four million words on the whole range of economic thought is not a form convenient to every potential user. For many students and teachers it is simply too bulky, too comprehensive and too expensive for everyday use.

By developing the present series of compact volumes of reprints from the original work, we hope that some of the intellectual wealth of *The New Palgrave* will become accessible to much wider groups of readers. Each of the volumes is devoted to a particular branch of economics, such as econometrics or general equilibrium or money, with a scope corresponding roughly to a university course on that subject. Apart from correction of misprints, etc. the content of each of its reprinted articles is exactly the same as that of the original. In addition, a few brand new entries have been commissioned especially for the series, either to fill an apparent gap or more commonly to include topics that have risen to prominence since the dictionary was originally commissioned.

As *The New Palgrave* is the sole parent of the present series, it may be helpful to explain that it is the modern successor to the excellent *Dictionary of Political Economy* edited by R.H. Inglis Palgrave and published in three volumes in 1894, 1896 and 1899. A second and slightly modified version, edited by Henry Higgs, appeared during the mid-1920s. These two editions each contained almost 4,000 entries, but many of those were simply brief definitions and many of the others were devoted to peripheral topics such as foreign coinage, maritime commerce, and Scottish law. To make room for the spectacular growth in economics over the last 60 years while keeping still to a manageable length, *The New Palgrave* concentrated instead on economic theory, its originators, and its closely cognate disciplines. Its nearly 2,000 entries (commissioned from over 900 scholars) are all self-contained essays, sometimes brief but never mere definitions.

Apart from its biographical entries, *The New Palgrave* is concerned chiefly with theory rather than fact, doctrine rather than data; and it is not at all clear how theory and doctrine, as distinct from facts and figures, *should* be treated in an encyclopaedia. One way is to treat everything from a particular point of view. Broadly speaking, that was the way of Diderot's classic *Encyclopédie raisonée* (1751–1772), as it was also of Léon Say's *Nouveau dictionnaire d'économie politique* (1891–2). Sometimes, as in articles by Quesnay and Turgot in the *Encyclopédie*, this approach has yielded entries of surpassing brilliance. Too often, however, both the range of subjects covered and the quality of the coverage itself are seriously reduced by such a self-limiting perspective. Thus the entry called '*Méthode*' in the first edition of Say's *Dictionnaire* asserted that the use of mathematics in economics 'will only ever be in the hands of a few', and the dictionary backed up that claim by choosing not to have any entry on Cournot.

Another approach is to have each entry take care to reflect within itself varying points of view. This may help the student temporarily, as when preparing for an examination. But in a subject like economics, the Olympian detachment which this approach requires often places a heavy burden on the author, asking for a scrupulous account of doctrines he or she believes to be at best wrong-headed. Even when an especially able author does produce a judicious survey article, it is surely too much to ask that it also convey just as much enthusiasm for those theories thought misguided as for those found congenial. Lacking an enthusiastic exposition, however, the disfavoured theories may then be studied less closely than they deserve.

The New Palgrave did not ask its authors to treat economic theory from any particular point of view, except in one respect to be discussed below. Nor did it call for surveys. Instead, each author was asked to make clear his or her own views of the subject under discussion, and for the rest to be as fair and accurate as possible, without striving to be 'judicious'. A balanced perspective on each topic was always the aim, the ideal. But it was to be sought not *internally*, within each article, but *externally*, between articles, with the reader rather than the writer handed the task of achieving a personal balance between differing views.

For a controversial topic, a set of several more or less synonymous headwords, matched by a broad diversity of contributors, was designed to produce enough variety of opinion to help form the reader's own synthesis; indeed, such diversity will be found in most of the individual volumes in this series.

This approach was not without its problems. Thus, the prevalence of uncertainty in the process of commissioning entries sometimes produced a less diverse outcome than we had planned. 'I can call spirits from the vasty deep,' said Owen Glendower. 'Why, so can I,' replied Hotspur, 'or so can any man;/ But will they come when you do call for them?' In our experience, not quite as often as we would have liked.

The one point of view we did urge upon every one of *Palgrave*'s authors was to write from an historical perspective. For each subject its contributor was asked to discuss not only present problems but also past growth and future prospects. This request was made in the belief that knowledge of the historical development of any theory enriches our present understanding of it, and so helps to construct better theories for the future. The authors' response to the request was generally so positive that, as the reader of any of these volumes will discover, the resulting contributions amply justified that belief.

John Eatwell
Murray Milgate
Peter Newman

Preface

Marxian ideas are alive and (reasonably) well in anthropology, in history, in philosophy and in sociology. In economics, though not quite dead, they are certainly not in good health. Yet economics lies at the very core of the Marxian approach. For despite the broad sweep of its analysis, which seeks to encompass all the forms of social and economic organization, Marxism is pre-eminently a theory of capitalism, and hence of an economic system in which production and distribution are organized by a generalized process of exchange. If it is even to begin to provide a coherent explanation of the operations of such a system, Marxian economics must provide a theory of how prices (rates of exchange) are determined, since prices are the signals which guide economic action in a market economy.

The labour theory of value, a remarkably powerful tool with which to link the process of exchange to the social character of production, to the nature of work and exploitation and to broader questions of social organization, is at once a strength and a fatal weakness. A strength because the proposition that commodities exchange at rates determined by the quantity of labour embodied in their production leads to the clear demonstration that profits and the competitive rate of profit are determined by surplus value, that is by the hours worked over and above the needs of reproduction of the labour force. A weakness, because the proposition that commodities will tend to exchange at their labour values is false.

There have been many attempts to put matters right.

Some have emphasized the 'qualitative' power of the labour theory of value and denied the relevance of any quantative exchange relationship. But a 'theory of value' which fails to explain what determines the rates at which commodities exchange is not only an abuse of language, it also eschews any explanation of how a fundamental characteristic of capitalism actually works. Others have pursued the often elaborate algebra of the 'transformation problem', attempting to show that results obtained by using the labour theory of value may be reproduced in an economy of normal competitive prices without losing either their content or their precision. Yet others have grafted Marxian concepts and language onto the neoclassical theory of value and distribution.

A somewhat different approach, which builds on Marx's own discussion of the relationship between labour values and competitive prices (prices of production), is to be found in the generalization by Piero Sraffa of earlier approaches by Dmitriev and Bortkiewicz. In *Production of Commodities by Means of Commodities*, Sraffa demonstrates that it is indeed possible to determine competitive rates of exchange using the data which Marx used – the conditions of reproduction of commodities, the real wage and the fact that in a competitive capitalist economy the surplus is distributed as a general rate of profit.

This solution, regarded by some as the starting point of a fundamental rehabilitation of Marxian economics, is not widely favoured by Marxists. It circumvents any use of the labour theory of value, and accordingly appears to some to weaken the central Marxian chain of exploitation–surplus–profit.

A satisfactory solution to the problem of a coherent theory of value and distribution would release Marxian ideas on crises, growth, imperialism, the social and economic evolution of forms of production, and so on, into the mainstream of economics. It is the discussion of these ideas which forms the bulk of this volume. The often uncomfortable messages they bear will always make their survival difficult. It will only be possible if the ideas are demonstrably practical, in the sense of providing useful insights into economic behaviour and helpful answers to the pressing questions of the day.

The strength of Marxian analysis derives from the forging of coherent links between economics, history, sociology and philosophy. The very scale of the enterprise is unique and enduring. That part of it which comprises Marxian economics is painfully controversial. But the numerous declarations of its demise have been exaggerated.

The Editors

Karl Marx

ERNEST MANDEL

Karl Marx was born on 5 May 1818, the son of the lawyer Heinrich Marx and Henriette Pressburg. His father was descended from an old family of Jewish rabbis, but was himself a liberal admirer of the Enlightenment and not religious. He converted to Protestantism a few years before Karl was born to escape restrictions still imposed upon Jews in Prussia. His mother was of Dutch-Jewish origin.

LIFE AND WORK

Karl Marx studied at the *Friedrich-Wilhelm Gymnasium* in Trier, and at the universities of Bonn and Berlin. His doctoral thesis, *Differenz der demokritischen und epikurischen Naturphilosophie*, was accepted at the University of Jena on 15 April 1841. In 1843 he married Jenny von Westphalen, daughter of Baron von Westphalen, a high Prussian government official.

Marx's university studies covered many fields, but centred around philosophy and religion. He frequented the circle of the more radical followers of the great philosopher Hegel, befriended one of their main representatives, Bruno Bauer, and was especially influenced by the publication in 1841 of Ludwig Feuerbach's *Das Wesen des Christentums* (The Nature of Christianity). He had intended to teach philosophy at the university, but that quickly proved to be unrealistic. He then turned towards journalism, both to propagandize his ideas and to gain a livelihood. He became editor of the *Rheinische Zeitung*, a liberal newspaper of Cologne, in May 1842. His interest turned more and more to political and social questions, which he treated in an increasing radical way. The paper was banned by the Prussian authorities a year later.

Karl Marx then planned to publish a magazine called *Die Deutsch-Französische Jahrbücher* in Paris, in order to escape Prussian censorship and to be more closely linked and identified with the real struggles for political and social emancipation which, at that time, were centred around France. He emigrated to Paris with his wife and met there his lifelong friend Friedrich Engels.

1

Marx had become critical of Hegel's philosophical political system, a criticism which would lead to his first major work, *Zur Kritik des Hegelschen Rechtsphilosophie* (1843, A Critique of Hegel's Philosophy of Right). Intensively studying history and political economy during his stay in Paris, he became strongly influenced by socialist and working-class circles in the French capital. With his 'Paris Manuscripts' (*Oekonomisch-philosophische Manuskripte*, 1844), he definitely became a communist, i.e. a proponent of collective ownership of the means of production.

He was expelled from France at the beginning of 1845 through pressure from the Prussian embassy and migrated to Brussels. His definite turn towards historical materialism (see below) would occur with his manuscript *Die Deutsche Ideologie* (1845–6) culminating in the eleven *Theses on Feuerbach*, written together with Engels but never published during his lifetime.

This led also to a polemical break with the most influential French socialist of that period, Proudhon, expressed in the only book Marx would write in French, *Misère de la Philosophie* (1846).

Simultaneously he became more and more involved in practical socialist politics, and started to work with the Communist League, which asked Engels and himself to draft their declaration of principle. This is the origin of the *Communist Manifesto* (1848, *Manifest der Kommunistischen Partei*).

As soon as the revolution of 1848 broke out, he was in turn expelled from Belgium and went first to France, then, from April 1848 on, to Cologne. His political activity during the German revolution of 1848 centred around the publication of the daily paper *Die Neue Rheinische Zeitung*, which enjoyed wide popular support. After the victory of the Prussian counter-revolution, the paper was banned in May 1849 and Marx was expelled from Prussia. He never succeeded in recovering his citizenship.

Marx emigrated to London, where he would stay, with short interruptions, till the end of his life. For fifteen years, his time would be mainly taken up with economic studies, which would lead to the publication first of *Zur Kritik der Politischen Oekonomie* (1859) and later of *Das Kapital*, Vol. I (1867). He spent long hours at the British Museum, studying the writings of all the major economists, as well as the government Blue Books, Hansard and many other contemporary sources on social and economic conditions in Britain and the world. His readings also covered technology, ethnology and anthropology, besides political economy and economic history; many notebooks were filled with excerpts from the books he read.

But while the activity was mainly studious, he never completely abandoned practical politics. He first hoped that the Communist League would be kept alive, thanks to a revival of revolution. When this did not occur, he progressively dropped out of emigré politics, but not without writing a scathing indictment of French counter-revolution in *Der 18. Brumaire des Louis Bonaparte* (1852), which was in a certain sense the balance sheet of his political activity and an analysis of the late 1848–52 cycle of revolution and counter-revolution. He would befriend British trade-union leaders and gradually attempt to draw them towards international working class interests and politics. These efforts culminated in the creation of the International Working Men's Association (1864) – the so-called First International – in which Marx and Engels would play a leading role, politically as well as organizationally.

It was not only his political interest and revolutionary passion that prevented Marx from becoming an economist pure and simple. It was also the pressure of material necessity. Contrary to his hopes, he never succeeded in earning enough money from his scientific writings to sustain himself and his growing family. He had to turn to journalism to make a living. He had initial, be it modest, success in this field, when he became European correspondent of the *New York Daily Tribune* in the summer of 1851. But he never had a regular income from that collaboration, and it ended after ten years.

So the years of his London exile were mainly years of great material deprivation and moral suffering. Marx suffered greatly from the fact that he could not provide a minimum of normal living conditions for his wife and children, whom he loved deeply. Bad lodgings in cholera-stricken Soho, insufficient food and medical care, led to a chronic deterioration of his wife's and his own health and to the death of several of their children; that of his oldest son Edgar in 1855 struck him an especially heavy blow. Of his seven children, only three daughters survived, Jenny, Laura and Eleanor (Tussy). All three were very gifted and would play a significant role in the international labour movement, Eleanor in Britain, Jenny and Laura in France (where they married the socialist leaders Longuet and Lafargue).

During this long period of material misery, Marx survived thanks to the fiancial and moral support of his friend Friedrich Engels, whose devotion to him stands as an exceptional example of friendship in the history of science and politics. Things started to improve when Marx came into his mother's inheritance; when the first independent working-class parties (followers of Lassalle on the one hand, of Marx and Engls on the other) developed in Germany, creating a broader market for his writings; when the IWMA became influential in several European countries, and when Engels' fiancial conditions improved to the point where he would sustain the Marx family on a more regular basis.

The period 1865–71 was one in which Marx's concentration on economic studies and on the drafting of *Das Kapital* was interrupted more and more by current political commitments to the IWMA, culminating in his impassioned defence of the Paris Commune (*Der Bürgerkrieg in Frankreich*, 1871). But the satisfaction of being able to participate a second time in a real revolution – be it only vicariously – was troubled by the deep divisions inside the IMWA, which led to the split with the anarchists grouped around Michael Bakunin.

Marx did not succeed in finishing a final version of *Das Kapital* vols II and III, which were published posthumously, after extensive editing, by Engels. It remains controversial whether he intended to add two more volumes to these, according to an initial plan. More than 25 years after the death of Marx, Karl Kautsky edited what is often called vol. IV of *Das Kapital*, his extensive critique of other economists: *Theorien über den Mehrwert* (Theories of Surplus Value).

Marx's final years were increasingly marked by bad health, in spite of slightly improved living conditions. Bad health was probably the main reason why the final version of vols II and III of *Capital* could not be finished. Although he wrote a strong critique of the Programme which was adopted by the unification congress (1878) of German social democracy (*Kritik des Gothaer Programms*), he was heartened by the creation of that united working-class party in his native land, by the spread of socialist organizations throughout Europe, and by the growing influence of his ideas in the socialist movement. His wife fell ill in 1880 and died the next year. This came as a deadly blow to Karl Marx, who did not survive her for long. He himself died in London on 14 March 1883.

HISTORICAL MATERIALISM

Outside his specific economic theories, Marx's main contribution to the social sciences has been his theory of historical materialism. Its starting point is anthropological. Human beings cannot survive without social organization. Social organization is based upon social labour and social communication. Social labour always occurs within a given framework of specific, historically determined, social relations of production. These social relations of production determine in the last analysis all other social relations, including those of social communication. It is social existence which determines social consciousness and not the other way around.

Historical materialism posits that relations of production which become stabilized and reproduce themselves are structures which can no longer be changed gradually, piecemeal. They are modes of production. To use Hegel's dialectical language, which was largely adopted (and adapted) by Marx: they can only change qualitatively through a complete social upheaval, a social revolution or counter-revolution. Quantitative changes can occur within modes of production, but they do not modify the basic structure. In each mode of production, a given set of relations of production constitutes the basis (infrastructure) on which is erected a complex superstructure, encompassing the state and the law (except in a classless society), ideology, religion, philosophy, the arts, morality, etc.

Relations of production are the sum total of social relations which human beings establish among themselves in the production of their material lives. They are therefore not limited to what actually happens at the point of production. Humankind could not survive, i.e. produce, if there did not exist specific forms of circulation of goods, e.g. between producing units (circulation of tools and raw materials) and between production units and consumers. *A priori* allocation of goods determines other relations of production than does allocation of goods through the market. Partial commodity production (what Marx calls 'simple commodity production' or 'petty commodity production' – '*einfache Waren-produktion*') also implies other relations of production than does generalized commodity production.

Except in the case of classless societies, modes of production, centred around

4

prevailing relations of production, are embodied in specific class relations which, in the last analysis, overdetermine relations between individuals.

Historical materialism does not deny the individual's free will, his attempts to make choices concerning his existence according to his individual passions, his interests as he understands them, his convictions, his moral options etc. What historical materialism does state is: (1) that these choices are strongly predetermined by the social framework (education, prevailing ideology and moral 'values', variants of behaviour limited by material conditions etc.); (2) that the outcome of the collision of millions of different passions, interests and options is essentially a phenomenon of social logic and not of individual psychology. Here, class interests are predominant.

There is no example in history of a ruling class not trying to defend its class rule, or of an exploited class not trying to limit (and occasionally eliminate) the exploitation it suffers. So outside classless society, the class struggle is a permanent feature of human society. In fact, one of the key theses of historical materialism is that 'the history of humankind is the history of class struggles' (Marx, *Communist Manifesto*, 1848).

The immediate object of class struggle is economic and material. It is a struggle for the division of the social product between the direct producers (the productive, exploited class) and those who appropriate what Marx calls the social surplus product, the residuum of the social product once the producers and their offspring are fed (in the large sense of the word; i.e. the sum total of the consumer goods consumed by that class) and the initial stock of tools and raw materials is reproduced (including the restoration of the initial fertility of the soil). The ruling class functions as a ruling class essentially through the appropriation of the social surplus product. By getting possession of the social surplus product, it acquires the means to foster and maintain most of the superstructural activities mentioned above; and by doing so, it can largely determine their function – to maintain and reproduce the given social structure, the given mode of production – and their contents.

We say 'largely determine' and not 'completely determine'. First, there is an 'immanent dialectical', i.e. an autonomous movement, of each specific superstructural sphere of activity. Each generation of scientists, artists, philosophers, theologists, lawyers and politicians finds a given *corpus* of ideas, forms, rules, techniques, ways of thinking, to which it is initiated through education and current practice, etc. It is not forced to simply continue and reproduce these elements. It can transform them, modify them, change their interconnections, even negate them. Again: historical materialism does not deny that there is a specific history of science, a history of art, a history of philosophy, a history of political and moral ideas, a history of religion etc., which all follow their own logic. It tries to *explain* why a certain number of scientific, artistic, philosophical, ideological, juridical changes or even revolutions occur at a given time and in given countries, quite different from other ones which occurred some centuries earlier elsewhere. The *nexus* of these 'revolutions' with given historical periods is a *nexus* of class interests.

Second, each social formation (i.e. a given country in a given epoch) while being characterized by predominant relations of production (i.e. a given mode of production at a certain phase of its development) includes different relations of production which are largely remnants of the past, but also sometimes nuclei of future modes of production. Thus there exists not only the ruling class and the exploited class characteristic of that prevailing mode of production (capitalists and wage earners under capitalism). There also exist remnants of social classes which were predominant when other relations of production prevailed and which, while having lost their hegemony, still manage to survive in the interstices of the new society. This is, for example, the case with petty commodity producers (peasants, handicraftsmen, small merchants), semi-feudal landowners, and even slave-owners, in many already predominantly capitalist social formations throughout the 19th and part of the 20th centuries. Each of these social classes has its own ideology, its own religious and moral values, which are intertwined with the ideology of the hegemonic ruling class, without becoming completely absorbed by that ideology.

Third, even after a given ruling class (e.g. the feudal or semi-feudal nobility) has disappeared as a ruling class, its ideology can survive through sheer force of social inertia and routine (custom). The survival of traditional *ancien régime* catholic ideology in France during a large part of the 19th century, in spite of the sweeping social, political and ideological changes ushered in by the French revolution, is an illustration of that rule.

Finally, Marx's statement that the *ruling* ideology of each epoch is the ideology of the ruling class – another basic tenet of historical materialism – does not express more than it actually says. It implies that other ideologies can exist side by side with that ruling ideology without being hegemonic. To cite the most important of these occurrences: exploited and (or) oppressed social classes can develop their own ideology, which will start to challenge the prevailing hegemonic one. In fact, an ideological class struggle accompanies and sometimes even precedes the political class struggle properly speaking. Religious and philosophical struggles preceding the classical bourgeois revolutions; the first socialist critiques of bourgeois society preceding the constitution of the first working-class parties and revolutions, are examples of that type.

The class struggle has been up to now the great motor of history. Human beings make their own history. No mode of production can be replaced by another one without deliberate actions by large social forces, i.e. without social revolution (or counter-revolution). Whether these revolutions or counter-revolutions actually lead to the long-term implementation of deliberate projects of social reorganization is another matter altogether. Very often, their outcome is to a large extent different from the intention of the main actors.

Human beings act consciously, but they can act with false consciousness. They do not necessarily understand why they want to realize certain social and (or) political plans, why they want to maintain or to change economic or juridical institutions; and especially, they rarely understand in a scientific sense the laws of social change, the material and social preconditions for successfully conserving or changing such institutions. Indeed, Marx claims that only with the discovery of the main tenets of historical materialism have we made a significant step forward towards understanding these laws, without claiming to be able to predict 'all' future developments of society.

Social change, social revolutions and counter-revolutions are furthermore occurring within determined material constraints. The level of development of the productive forces – essentially tools and human skills, including their effects upon the fertility of the soil – limits the possibilities of institutional change. Slave labour has shown itself to be largely incompatible with the factory system based upon contemporary machines. Socialism would not be durably built upon the basis of the wooden plough and the potter's wheel. A social revolution generally widens the scope for the development of the productive forces and leads to social progress in most fields of human activity in a momentous way. Likewise, an epoch of deep social crisis is ushered in when there is a growing conflict between the prevailing mode of production (i.e. the existing social order) on the one hand, and the further development of the productive forces on the other. Such a social crisis will then manifest itself on all major fields and social activity: politics, ideology, morals and law, as well as in the realm of the economic life properly speaking.

Historical materialism thereby provides a measuring stick for human progress: the growth of the productive forces, measurable through the growth of the average productivity of labour, and the number, longevity and skill of the human species. This measuring stick in no way abstracts from the *natural* preconditions for human survival and human growth (in the broadest sense of the concept). Nor does it abstract from the conditional and partial character of such progress, in terms of social organization and individual alienation.

In the last analysis, the division of society into antagonistic social classes reflects, from the point of view of historical materialism, an inevitable limitation of human freedom. For Marx and Engels, the real measuring rod of human freedom, i.e. of human wealth, is not 'productive labour'; this only creates the material pre-condition for that freedom. The real measuring rod is leisure time, not in the sense of 'time for doing nothing' but in the sense of time freed from the iron necessity to produce and reproduce material livelihood, and therefore disposable for all-round and free development of the individual talents, wishes, capacities, potentialities, of each human being.

As long as society is too poor, as long as goods and services satisfying basic needs are too scarce, only part of society can be freed from the necessity to devote most of its life to 'work for a livelihood' (i.e. of forced labour, in the anthropological/sociological sense of the word, that is in relation to desires, aspirations and talents, not to a juridical status of bonded labour). That is essentially what represents the freedom of the ruling classes and their hangers-on, who are 'being paid to think', to create, to invent, to administer, because they have become free from the obligation to bake their own bread, weave their own clothes and build their own houses.

Once the productive forces are developed far enough to guarantee all human

7

beings satisfaction of their basic needs by 'productive labour' limited to a minor fraction of lifetime (the half work-day or less), then the material need of the division of society in classes disappears. Then, there remains no objective basis for part of society to monopolize administration, access to information, knowledge, intellectual labour. For that reason, historical materialism explains both the reasons why class societies and class struggles arose in history, and why they will disappear in the future in a classless society of democratically self-administering associated producers.

Historical materialism therefore contains an attempt at explaining the origin, the functions and the future withering away of the state as a specific institution, as well as an attempt to explain politics and political activity in general, as an expression of social conflicts centred around different social interests (mainly, but not only, those of different social classes; important fractions of classes, as well as non-class social groupings, also come into play).

For Marx and Engels, the state is not existent with human society as such, or with 'organized society' or even with 'civilized society' in the abstract, neither is it the result of any voluntarily concluded 'social contract' between individuals. The state is the sum total of apparatuses, i.e. special groups of people separate and apart from the rest (majority) of society, that appropriate to themselves functions of a respressive or integrative nature which were initially exercised by all citizens. This process of alienation occurs in conjunction with the emergence of social classes. The state is an instrument for fostering, conserving and reproducing a given class structure, and not a neutral arbiter between antagonistic class interests.

The emergence of a classless society is therefore closely intertwined, for adherents to historical materialism, with the process of withering away of the state, i.e. of gradual devolution to the whole of society (self-management, self-administration) of all specific functions today exercised by special apparatuses, i.e. of the dissolution of these apparatuses. Marx and Engels visualized the dictatorship of the proletariat, the last form of the state and of political class rule, as an instrument for assuring the transition from class society to classless society. It should itself be a state of a special kind, organizing its own gradual disappearance.

We said above that, from the point of view of historical materialism, the immediate object of class struggle is the division of the social product between different social classes. Even the political class struggle in the final analysis serves that main purpose; but it also covers a much broader field of social conflicts. As all state activities have some bearing upon the relative stability of a given social formation, and the class rule to which it is submitted, the class struggle can extend to all fields of politics from foreign policy to educational problems and religious conflicts. This has of course to be proven through painstaking analysis, and not proclaimed as an axiom or a revealed truth. When conducted successfully, such exercises in class analysis and class definition of political, social and even literary struggles becomes impressive works of historical explanation, as for example Marx's *Class Struggles in France 1848–50*, Engels' *The German Peasant*

War, Franz Mehring's *Die Lessing-Legende*, Trotsky's *History of the Russian Revolution*, etc.

MARX'S ECONOMIC THEORY – GENERAL APPROACH AND INFLUENCE

A general appraisal of Marx's method of economic analysis is called for prior to an outline of his main economic theories (theses and hypotheses).

Marx is distinct from most important economists of the 19th and 20th centuries in that he does not consider himself at all an 'economist' pure and simple. The idea that 'economic science' as a special science completely separate from sociology, history, anthropology etc. cannot exist, underlies most of his economic analysis. Indeed, historical materialism is an attempt at unifying all social sciences, if not all sciences about humankind, into a single 'science of society'. For sure, within the framework of this general 'science of society', economic phenomena could and should be submitted to analysis as specific phenomena. So economic theory, economical science, has a definite autonomy after all; but it is only a partial and relative one.

Probably the best formula for characterizing Marx's economic theory would be to call it an endeavour to explain the *social economy*. This would be true in a double sense. For Marx, there are no eternal economic laws, valid in every epoch of human prehistory and history. Each mode of production has its own specific economic laws, which lose their relevance once the general social framework has fundamentally changed. For Marx likewise, there are no economic laws separate and apart from specific relations between human beings, in the primary (but not only, as already summarized) social relations of production. All attempts to reduce economic problems to purely material, objective ones, to relations between things, or between things and human beings, would be considered by Marx as manifestations of mystification, of false consciousness, expressing itself through the attempted reification of human relations. Behind relations between things, economic science should try to discover the specific relations between human beings which they hide. Real economic science has therefore also a demystifying function compared to vulgar 'economics', which takes a certain number of 'things' for granted without asking the questions: Are they really only what they appear to be? From where do they originate? What explains these appearances? What lies behind them? Where do they lead? How could they (will they) disappear? *Problemblindheit*, the refusal to see that facts are generally more problematic than they appear at first sight, is certainly not a reproach one could address to Marx's economic thought.

Marx's economic analysis is therefore characterized by a strong ground current of *historical relativism*, with a strong recourse to the genetical and evolutionary method of thinking (that is why the parallel with Darwin has often been made, sometimes in an excessive way). The formula 'genetic structuralism' has also been used in relation to Marx's general approach to economic analysis. Be that as it may, one could state that Marx's economic theory is essentially geared to the discovery of specific 'laws of motion' for successive modes of production. While

9

his theoretical effort has been mainly centred around the discovery of these laws of motion for capitalist society, his work contains indications of such laws – different ones, to be sure – for precapitalist and postcapitalist social formations too.

The main link between Marx's sociology and anthropology on the one hand, and his economic analysis on the other, lies in the key role of *social labour* as the basic anthropological feature underlying all forms of social organization. Social labour can be organized in quite different forms, thereby giving rise to quite different economic phenomena ('facts'). Basically different forms of social labour organization lead to basically different sets of economic institutions and dynamics, following basically different logics (obeying basically different 'laws of motion').

All human societies must assure the satisfaction of a certain number of basic needs, in order to survive and reproduce themselves. This leads to the necessity of establishing some sort of equilibrium between social recognized needs, i.e. current consumption and current production. But this abstract banality does not tell us anything about the concrete way in which social labour is organized in order to achieve that goal.

Society can recognize all individual labour as *immediately social labour*. Indeed, it does so in innumerable primitive tribal and village communities, as it does in the contemporary *kibbutz*. Directly social labour can be organized in a despotic or in a democratic way, through custom and superstition as well as through an attempt at applying advanced science to economic organization; but it will always be immediately recognized social labour, inasmuch as it is based upon *a priori* assignment of the producers to their specific work (again: irrespective of the form this assignation takes, whether it is voluntary or compulsory, despotic or simply through custom etc.).

But when social decision-taking about work assignation (and resource allocation closely tied to it) is fragmented into different units operating independently from each other – as a result of private control (property) of the means of production, in the economic and not necessarily the juridical sense of the word – then social labour in turn is fragmented into private labours which are not automatically recognized as socially necessary ones (whose expenditure is not automatically compensated by society). Then the private producers have to exchange parts or all of their products in order to satisfy some or all of their basic needs. Then these products become commodities. The economy becomes a (partial or generalized) market economy. Only by measuring the results of the sale of his products can the producer (or owner) ascertain what part of his private labour expenditure has been recognized (compensated) as social labour, and what part has not.

Even if we operate with such simple analytical tools as 'directly social labour', 'private labour', 'socially recognized social labour', we have to make quite an effort at abstracting from immediately apparent phenomena in order to understand their relevance for economic analysis. This is true for all scientific analysis, in natural as well as in social sciences. Marx's economic analysis, as presented in his main books, has not been extremely popular reading; but then, there are not yet so many scientists in these circumstances. This has nothing to do with any innate obscurity of the author, but rather with the nature of scientific analysis as such.

The relatively limited number of readers of Marx's economic writings (the first English paperback edtion of *Das Kapital* appeared only in 1974!) is clearly tied to Marx's scientific rigour, his effort at a systematic and all-sided analysis of the phenomena of the capitalist economy.

But while his economic analysis lacked popularity, his political and historical projections became more and more influential. With the rise of independent working-class mass parties, an increasing number of these proclaimed themselves as being guided or influenced by Marx, at least in the epoch of the Second and the Third Internationals, roughly the half century from 1890 till 1940. Beginning with the Russian revolution of 1917, a growing number of governments and of states claimed to base their policies and constitutions on concepts developed by Marx. (Whether this was legitimate or not is another question.) But the fact itself testifies to Marx's great influence on contemporary social and political developments, evolutionary and revolutionary alike.

Likewise, his diffused influence on social science, including academic economic theory, goes far beyond general acceptance or even substantial knowledge of his main writings. Some key ideas of historical materialism and of economic analysis which permeate his work – e.g. that economic interests to a large extent influence, if not determine, political struggles; that historic evolution is linked to important changes in material conditions; that economic crises ('the business cycle') are unavoidable under conditions of capitalist market economy – have become near-platitudes. It is sufficient to notice how major economists and historians strongly denied their validity throughout the 19th century and at least until the 1920s, to understand how deep has been Marx's influence on contemporary social science in general.

MARX'S LABOUR THEORY OF VALUE

As an economist, Marx is generally situated in the continuity of the great classical school of Adam Smith and Ricardo. He obviously owes a lot to Ricardo, and conducts a running dialogue with that master in most of his mature economic writings.

Marx inherited the labour theory of value from the classical school. Here the continuity is even more pronounced; but there is also a radical break. For Ricardo, labour is essentially a *numeraire*, which enables a common computation of labour and capital as basic elements of production costs. For Marx, *labour is value*. Value is nothing but that fragment of the total labour potential existing in a given society in a certain period (e.g. a year or a month) which is used for the output of a given commodity, at the average social productivity of labour existing then and there, divided by the total number of these commodities produced, and expressed in hours (or minutes), days, weeks, months of labour.

Value is therefore essentially a social, objective and historically relative category. It is social because it is determined by the overall result of the fluctuating efforts of each individual producer (under capitalism: of each individual firm or factory). It is objective because it is given, once the production of a given commodity is finished, and is thus independent from personal (or collective) valuations of customers on the market place; and it is historically relative because it changes with each important change (progress or regression) of the average productivity of labour in a given branch of output, including in agriculture and transportation.

This does not imply that Marx's concept of value is in any way completely detached from consumption. It only means that the feedback of consumers' behaviour and wishes upon value is always mediated through changes in the allocation of labour inputs in production, labour being seen as subdivided into living labour and dead (dated) labour, i.e. tools and raw materials. The market emits signals to which the producing units react. Value changes after these reactions, not before them. Market price changes can of course occur prior to changes in value. In fact, changes in market prices are among the key signals which can lead to changes in labour allocation between different branches of production, i.e. to changes in labour quantities necessary to produce given commodities. But then, for Marx, values determine prices only basically and in the medium-term sense of the word. This determination only appears clearly as an explication of *medium and long-term price movements*. In the shorter run, prices fluctuate around values as axes. Marx never intended to negate the operation of market laws, of the law of supply and demand, in determining these short-term fluctuations.

The 'law of value' is but Marx's version of Adam Smith's 'invisible hand'. In a society dominated by private labour, private producers and private ownership of productive inputs, it is this 'law of value', an objective economic law operating behind the backs of all people, all 'agents' involved in production and consumption, which, in the final analysis, regulates the economy, determines what is produced and how it is produced (and therefore also what can be consumed). The 'law of value' regulates the exchange between commodities, according to the quantities of socially necessary abstract labour they embody (the quantity of such labour spent in their production). Through regulating the exchange between commodities, the 'law of value' also regulates, after some interval, the distribution of society's labour potential and of society's non-living productive resources between different branches of production. Again, the analogy with Smith's 'invisible hand' is striking.

Marx's critique of the 'invisible hand' concept does not dwell essentially on the analysis of how a market economy actually operates. It would above all insist that this operation is not eternal, not immanent in 'human nature', but created by specific historical circumstances, a product of a special way of social organization, and due to disappear at some stage of historical evolution as it appeared during a previous stage. And it would also stress that this 'invisible hand' leads neither to the maximum of economic growth nor to the optimum of human wellbeing for the greatest number of individuals, i.e. it would stress the heavy economic and social price humankind had to pay, and is still currently paying, for the undeniable progress the market economy produced at a given stage of historical evolution.

The formula 'quantities of abstract human labour' refers to labour seen strictly as a fraction of the total labour potential of a given society at a given time, say a labour potential of 2 billion hours a year (1 million potential producers, each supposedly capable of working 2000 hours a year). It therefore implies making an abstraction of the specific trade or occupation of a given male or female producer, the product of a day's work of a weaver not being worth less or more than that of a peasant, a miner, a housebuilder, a milliner or a seamstress. At the basis of that concept of 'abstract human labour' lies a social condition, a specific set of social relations of production, in which small independent producers are essentially equal. Without that equality, social division of labour, and therefore satisfaction of basic consumers' needs, would be seriously endangered under that specific organizational set-up of the economy. Such an equality between small commodity owners and producers is later transformed into an equality between owners of capital under the capitalist mode of production.

But the concept of the homogeneity of productive human labour, underlying that of 'abstract human labour' as the essence of value, does not imply a negation of the difference between skilled and unskilled labour. Again: a negation of that difference would lead to the breakdown of the necessary division of labour, as would any basic heterogeneity of labour inputs in different branches of output. It would then not pay to acquire skills: most of them would disappear. So Marx's labour theory of value, in an internally coherent way, leads to the conclusion that one hour of skilled labour represents more value than one hour of unskilled labour, say represents the equivalent of 1.5 hours of unskilled labour. The difference would result from the imputation of the labour it costs to acquire the given skill. While an unskilled labourer would have a labour potential of 120,000 hours during his adult life, a skilled labourer would only have a labour potential of 80,000 hours, 40,000 being used for acquiring, maintaining and developing his skill. Only if one hour of skilled labour embodies the same value of 1.5 hours of unskilled labour, will the equality of all 'economic agents' be maintained under these circumstances, i.e. will it 'pay' economically to acquire a skill.

Marx himself never extensively dwelled on this solution of the so-called *reduction problem*. This remains indeed one of the most obscure parts of his general economic theory. It has led to some, generally rather mild, controversy. Much more heat has been generated by another facet of Marx's labour theory of value, the so-called *transformation problem*. Indeed, from Böhm-Bawerk writing a century ago till the recent contributions of Sraffa (1960) and Steedman (1977), the way Marx dealt with the transformation of values into 'prices of production' in *Capital* Vol. III has been considered by many of his critics as the main problem of his 'system', as well as being a reason to reject the labour theory of value out of hand.

The problem arises out of the obvious modification in the functioning of a

13

market economy when *capitalist* commodity production substitutes itself for *simple* commodity production. In simple commodity production, with generally stable technology and stable (or easily reproduceable) tools, living labour is the only variable of the quantity and subdivision of social production. The mobility of labour is the only dynamic factor in the economy. As Engels pointed out in his Addendum to *Capital* Vol. III (Marx, *g*, pp. 1034–7), in such an economy, commodities would be exchanged at prices which would be immediately proportional to values, to the labour inputs they embody.

But under the capitalist mode of production, this is no longer the case. Economic decision-taking is not in the hands of the direct producers. It is in the hands of the capitalist *entrepreneurs* in the wider sense of the word (bankers – distributors of credit – playing a key role in that decision-taking, besides entrepreneurs in the productive sector properly speaking). Investment decisions, i.e. decisions for creating, expanding, reducing or closing enterprises, determine economic life. It is the *mobility of capital* and not the mobility of labour which becomes the motive force of the economy. Mobility of labour becomes essentially an epiphenomenon of the mobility of capital.

Capitalist production is production for profit. Mobility of capital is determined by existing or expected profit differentials. Capital leaves branches (countries, regions) with lower profits (or profit expectations) and flows towards branches (countries, regions) with higher ones. These movements lead to an equalization of the rate of profit between different branches of production. But approximately equal returns on all invested capital (at least under conditions of prevailing 'free competition') coexist with unequal proportions of inputs of labour in these different branches. So there is a disparity between the direct value of a commodity and its 'price of production', that 'price of production' being defined by Marx as the sum of production costs (costs of fixed capital and raw materials plus wages) and the average rate of profit multiplied with the capital spent in the given production.

The so-called 'transformation problem' relates to the question of whether a *relation* can nevertheless be established between value and these 'prices of production', what is the degree of coherence (or incoherence) of the relation with the 'law of value' (the labour theory of value in general), and what is the correct quantitative way to express that relation, if it exists.

We shall leave aside here the last aspect of the problem, to which extensive analysis has recently been devoted (Mandel and Freeman, 1984). From Marx's point of view, there is no incoherence between the formation of 'prices of production' and the labour theory of value. Nor is it true that he came upon that alleged difficulty when he started to prepare *Capital* Vol. III, i.e. to deal with capitalist competition, as several critics have argued (see e.g. Joan Robinson, 1942). In fact, his solution of the transformation problem is already present in the *Grundrisse* (Marx, *d*), before he even started to draft *Capital* Vol. I.

The sum total of value produced in a given country during a given span of time (e.g. one year) is determined by the sum total of labour-inputs. Competition and movements of capital cannot change that quantity. The sum total of values equals the sum total of 'prices of production'. The only effect of capital competition and capital mobility is to *redistribute* that given sum – and this through a redistribution of surplus value (see below) – between different capitals, to the benefit of some and at the expense of others.

Now the redistribution does not occur in a haphazard or arbitrary way. Essentially value (surplus-value) is transferred from technically less advanced branches to technologically more advanced branches. And here the concept of 'quantities of socially necessary labour' comes into its own, under the conditions of constant revolutions of productive technology that characterize the capital mode of production. Branches with lower than average technology (organic composition of capital, see below) can be considered as wasting socially necessary labour. Part of the labour spent in production in their realm is therefore not compensated by society. Branches with higher than average technology (organic composition of capital) can be considered to be economizing social labour; their labour inputs can therefore be considered as more intensive than average, embodying more value. In this way, the transfer of value (surplus-value) between different branches, far from being in contradiction with the law of value, is precisely the way it operates and should operate under conditions of 'capitalist equality', given the pressure of rapid technological change.

As to the logical inconsistency often supposedly to be found in Marx's method of solving the 'transformation problem' – first advanced by von Bortkiewicz (1907) – it is based upon a misunderstanding in our opinion. It is alleged that in his 'transformation schemas' (or tables) (Marx, *g*, pp. 255–6) Marx calculates inputs in 'values' and outputs in 'prices of production', thereby omitting the feedback effect of the latter on the former. But that feedback effect is unrealistic and unnecessary, once one recognizes that inputs are essentially data. Movements of capital posterior to the purchase of machinery or raw materials, including the ups and downs of prices of finished products produced with these raw materials, cannot lead to a change in prices and therefore of profits of the said machinery and raw materials, on sales which have already occurred. What critics present as an inconsistency between 'values' and 'prices of production' is simply a recognition of *two different time-frameworks* (cycles) in which the equalization of the rate of profit has been achieved, a first one for inputs, and a second, later one for outputs.

MARX'S THEORY OF RENT

The labour theory of value defines value as the socially necessary quantity of labour determined by the average productivity of labour of each given sector of production. But these values are not mathematically fixed data. They are simply the expression of a *process* going on in real life, under capitalist commodity production. So this average is only ascertained in the course of a certain time-span. There is a lot of logical argument and empirical evidence to advance the hypothesis that the normal time-span for essentially modifying the value of commodities is the business cycle, from one crises of over-production (recession) to the next one.

15

Before technological progress and (or) better (more 'rational') labour organization etc. determines a more than marginal change (in general: decline) in the value of a commodity, and the crisis eliminates less efficient firms, there will be a coexistence of firms with various 'individual values' of a given commodity in a given branch of output, even assuming a single market price. So, in his step-for-step approach towards explaining the immediate phenomena (facts of economic life) like prices and profits, by their essence, Marx introduces at this point of his analysis a new mediating concept, that of *market value* (Marx, *g*, ch. 10). The market value of a commodity is the 'individual value' of the firm, or a group of firms, in a given branch of production, around which the market price will fluctuate. That 'market value' is not necessarily the mathematical (weighted) average of labour expenditure of all firms of that branch. It can be below, equal or above that average, for a certain period (generally less than the duration of the business cycle, at least under 'free competition'), according to whether social demand is saturated, just covered or to an important extent not covered by current output plus existing stocks. In these three cases respectively, the more (most) efficient firms, the firms of average efficiency, or even firms with labour productivity below average, will determine the market value of that given commodity.

This implies that the more efficient firms enjoy *surplus profits* (profits over and above the average profit) in case 2 and 3 and that a certain number of firms work at less than average profit in all three cases, but especially in case 1.

The mobility of capital, i.e. normal capitalist competition, generally eliminates such situations after a certain lapse of time. But when that mobility of capital is impeded for long periods by either unavoidable scarcity (natural conditions that are not renewable or non-substitutable, like land and mineral deposits) or through the operation of institutional obstacles (private property of land and mineral resources forbidding access to available capital, except in exchange for payments over and above average profit), these surplus profits can be frozen and maintained for decades. They thus become *rents*, of which *ground rent* and *mineral rent* are the most obvious examples in Marx's time, extensively analysed in *Capital* Vol. III (Marx, *g*, part 6).

Marx's theory of rent is the most difficult part of his economic theory, the one which has witnessed fewer comments and developments, by followers and critics alike, than other major parts of his 'system'. But it is not obscure. And in contrast to Ricardo's or Rodbertus's theories of rent, it represents a straight-forward application of the labour theory of value. It does not imply any emergence of 'supplementary' value (surplus value, profits) in the market, in the process of circulation of commodities, which is anathema to Marx and to all consistent upholders of the labour theory of value. Nor does it in any way suggest that land or mineral deposits 'create' value. It simply means that in agriculture and mining less productive labour (as in the general case analysed above) determines the market value of food or minerals, and that therefore more efficient farms and mines enjoy surplus profits which Marx calls *differential* (land and mining) *rent*. It also means that as long as productivity of labour in agriculture is generally below the average of the economy as a whole (or more correctly: that the organic composition of capital, the expenditure in machinery and raw materials as against wages, is inferior in agriculture to that in industry and transportation), the sum total of surplus-value produced in agriculture will accrue to landowners + capitalist farmers taken together, and will not enter the general process of (re)distribution of profit throughout the economy as a whole.

This creates the basis for a supplementary form of rent, over and above differential rent, rent which Marx calls *absolute land rent*. This is, incidentally, the basis for a long-term separation of capitalist landowners from enterpreneurs in farming or animal husbandry, distinct from feudal or semi-feudal landowners or great landowners under conditions of predominantly petty commodity production, or in the Asiatic mode of production, with free peasants.

The validity of Marx's theory of land and mining rents has been confirmed by historical evidence, especially in the 20th century. Not only has history substantiated Marx's prediction that, in spite of the obstacle of land and mining rent, mechanization would end up by penetrating food and raw materials production too, as it has for a long time dominated industry and transportation, thereby causing a growing decline of differential rent (this has occurred increasingly in agriculture in the last 25–50 years, first in North America, and then in Western Europe and even elsewhere). It has also demonstrated that once the structural scarcity of food disappears, the institutional obstacle (private property) loses most of its efficiency as a brake upon the mobility of capital. Therefore the participation of surplus-value produced in agriculture in the general process of profit equalization throughout the economy cannot be prevented any more. Thereby absolute rent tends to wither away and, with it, the separation of land ownership from entrepreneurial farming and animal husbandry. It is true that farmers can then fall under the sway of the banks, but they do so as private owners of their land which becomes mortgaged, not as share-croppers or entrepreneurs renting land from separate owners.

On the other hand, the reappearance of structural scarcity in the realm of energy enabled the OPEC countries to multiply the price of oil by ten in the 1970s, i.e. to have it determined by the oilfields where production costs are the highest, thereby assuring the owners of the cheapest oil wells in Arabia, Iran, Libya, etc. huge differential minerals rents.

Marx's theory of land and mineral rent can be easily extended into a *general theory of rent*, applicable to all fields of production where formidable difficulties of entry limit mobility of capital for extended periods of time. It thereby becomes the basis of a *marxist theory of monopoly and monopoly surplus profits*, i.e. in the form of cartel rents (Hilferding, 1910) or of technological rent (Mandel, 1972). Lenin's and Bukharin's theories of surplus profit are based upon analogous but not identical reasoning (Bukharin, 1914, 1926; Lenin, 1917).

But in all these cases of general application of the marxist theory of rent, the same caution should apply as Marx applied to his theory of land rent. By its very nature, capitalism, based upon private property, i.e. 'many capitals' – that is, competition – cannot tolerate any 'eternal' monopoly, a 'permanent' surplus profit deducted from the sum total of profits which is divided among the capitalist class as a whole. Technological innovations, substitution of new products for old ones including the fields of raw materials and of food, will in the long run reduce or eliminate all monopology situations, especially if the profit differential is large enough to justify huge research and investment outlays.

MARX'S THEORY OF MONEY

In the same way as his theory of rent, Marx's theory of money is a straightforward application of the labour theory of value. As value is but the embodiment of socially necessary labour, commodities exchange with each other in proportion to the labour quanta they contain. This is true for the exchange of iron against wheat as it is true for the exchange of iron against gold or silver. Marx's theory of money is therefore in the first place a *commodity theory of money*. A given commodity can play the role of universal medium of exchange, as well as fulfil all the other functions of money, precisely because it is a commodity, i.e. because it is itself the product of socially necessary labour. This applies to the precious metals in the same way it applies to all the various commodities which, throughout history, have played the role of money.

It follows that strong upheavals in the 'intrinsic' value of the money-commodity will cause strong upheavals in the general price level. In Marx's theory of money, (market) prices are nothing but the expression of the value of commodities in the value of the money commodity chosen as a monetary standard. If £1 sterling $= \frac{1}{10}$ ounce of gold, the formula 'the price of 10 quarters of wheat is £1' means that 10 quarters of wheat have been produced in the same socially necessary labour times as $\frac{1}{10}$ ounce of gold. A strong decrease in the average productivity of labour in gold mining (as a result for example of a depletion of the richer gold veins) will lead to a general depression of the average price level, all other things remaining equal. Likewise, a sudden and radical increase in the average productivity of labour in gold mining, through the discovery of new rich gold fields (California after 1848; the Rand in South Africa in the 1890s) or through the application of new revolutionary technology, will lead to a general increase in the price level of all other commodities.

Leaving aside short-term oscillations, the general price level will move in medium and long-term periods according to the *relation* between the fluctuations of the productivity of labour in agriculture and industry on the one hand, and the fluctuations of the productivity of labour in gold mining (if gold is the money-commodity), on the other.

Basing himself on that commodity theory of money, Marx therefore criticized as inconsistent Ricardo's quantity theory (Marx, *h*, part 2). But for exactly the same reason of a consistent application of the labour theory of value, the quantity of money in circulation enters Marx's economic analysis when he deals with the phenomenon of *paper money* (Marx, *c*).

As gold has an intrinsic value, like all other commodities, there can be no 'gold inflation', as little as there can be a 'steel inflation'. An abstraction made of short-term price fluctuations caused by fluctuations between supply and demand, a persistent decline of the value of gold (exactly as for all other commodities) can only be the result of a persistent increase in the average productivity of labour in gold mining and not of an 'excess' of circulation in gold. If the demand for gold falls consistently, this can only indirectly trigger off a decline in the value of gold through causing the closure of the least productive gold mines. But in the case of the money-commodity, such overproduction can hardly occur, given the special function of gold of serving as a universal reserve fund, nationally and internationally. It will always therefore find a buyer, be it not, of course, always at the same 'prices' (in Marx's economic theory, the concept of the 'price of gold' is meaningless. As the price of a commodity is precisely its expression in the value of gold, the 'price of gold' would be the expression of the value of gold in the value of gold).

Paper money, banks notes, are a *money sign* representing a given quantity of the money-commodity. Starting from the above-mentioned example, a banknote of £1 represents $\frac{1}{10}$ ounce of gold. This is an objective 'fact of life', which no government or monetary authority can arbitrarily alter. It follows that any emission of paper money in excess of that given proportion will automatically lead to an increase in the general price level, always other things remaining equal. If £1 suddenly represents only $\frac{1}{20}$ ounce of gold, because paper money circulation has doubled without a significant increase in the total labour time spent in the economy, then the price level will tend to double too. The value of $\frac{1}{10}$ ounce of gold remains equal to the value of 10 quarters of wheat. But as $\frac{1}{10}$ ounce of gold is now reprsented by £2 in paper banknotes instead of being represented by £1, the price of wheat will move from £1 to £2 for 10 quarters (from two shillings to four shillings a quarter before the introduction of the decimal system).

This does not mean that in the case of paper money, Marx himself has become an advocate of a quantity theory of money. While there are obvious analogies between his theory of paper money and the quantity theory, the main difference is the rejection by Marx of any *mechanical automatism* between the quantity of paper money emitted on the one hand, and the general dynamic of the economy (including on the price level) on the other.

In Marx's explanation of the movement of the capitalist economy in its totality, the formula *ceteris paribus* is meaningless. Excessive (or insufficient) emission of paper money never occurs in a vacuum. It always occurs at a given stage of the business cycle, and in a given phase of the longer-term historical evolution of capitalism. It is thereby always combined with given ups and downs of the rate of profit, of productivity of labour, of output, of market conditions (overproduction or insufficient production). Only in connection with these other fluctuations can the effect of paper money 'inflation' or 'deflation' be judged, including the effect on the general price level. The key variables are in the field of production. The key synthetic resultant is in the field of profit. Price moments are generally epiphenomena as much as they are signals. To untwine the tangle, more is necessary than a simple analysis of the fluctuations of the quantity of money.

Only in the case of extreme runaway inflation of paper money would this be otherwise; and even in that border case, *relative* price movements (different degrees of price increases for different commodities) would still confirm that, in the last analysis, the law of values rules, and not the arbitrary decision of the Central Bank, or any other authority controlling or emitting paper money.

MARX'S THEORY OF SURPLUS-VALUE

Marx himself considered his theory of surplus-value his most important contribution to the progress of economic analysis (Marx, *l*; letter to Engels of 24 August 1867). It is through this theory that the wide scope of his sociological and historical thought enables him simultaneously to place the capitalist mode of production in his historical context, and to find the root of its inner economic contradictions and its laws of motion in the specific relations of production on which it is based.

As said before, Marx's theory of classes is based on the recognition that in each class society, part of society (the ruling class) appropriates the social surplus product. But that surplus product can take three essentially different forms (or a combination of them). It can take the form of straightforward unpaid surplus labour, as in the slave mode of production, early feudalism or some sectors of the Asiatic mode of production (unpaid *corvée* labour for the Empire). It can take the form of goods appropriated by the ruling class in the form of use-values pure and simple (the products of surplus labour), as under feudalism when feudal rent is paid in a certain amount of produce (produce rent) or in its more modern remnants, such as sharecropping. And it can take a money form, like money-rent in the final phases of feudalism, and capitalist profits. Surplus-value is essentially just that: the *money form of the social surplus product* or, what amounts to the same, the money product of surplus labour. It has therefore a common root with all other forms of surplus product: unpaid labour.

This means that Marx's theory of surplus-value is basically a *deduction* (or residual) *theory of the ruling classes' income*. The whole social product (the net national income) is produced in the course of the process of production, exactly as the whole crop is harvested by the peasants. What happens on the market (or through appropriation of the produce) is a distribution (or redistribution) of what already has been created. The surplus product, and therefore also its money form, surplus-value, is the residual of that new (net) social product (income) which remains after the producing classes have received their compensation (under capitalism: their wages). This 'deduction' theory of the ruling classes' income is thus *ipso factor* an exploitation theory. Not in the ethical sense of the word – although Marx and Engels obviously manifested a lot of understandable moral indignation at the fate of all the exploited throughout history, and especially at the fate of the modern protelariat – but in the economic one. The income of the ruling classes can always be reduced in the final analysis to the product of unpaid labour: that is the heart of Marx's theory of exploitation.

That is also the reason why Marx attached so much importance to treating *surplus-value as a general category*, over and above profits (themselves subdivided into industrial profits, bank profits, commercial profits etc.), interest and rent, which are all part of the total surplus product produced by wage labour. It is this general category which explains both the existence (the common interest) of the ruling class (all those who live off surplus value), and the origins of the class struggle under capitalism.

Marx likewise laid bare the economic mechanism through which surplus-value originates. At the basis of that economic mechanism is a huge social upheaval which started in Western Europe in the 15th century and slowly spread over the rest of the continent and all other continents (in many so-called underdeveloped countries, it is still going on to this day).

Through many concomitant economic (including technical), social, political and cultural transformations, the mass of the direct producers, essentially peasants and handicraftsmen, are separated from their means of production and cut off from free access to the land. They are therefore unable to produce their livelihood on their own account. In order to keep themselves and their families alive, they have to hire out their arms, their muscles and their brains, to the owners of the means of production (including land). If and when these owners have enough money capital at their disposal to buy raw materials and pay wages, they can start to organize production on a capitalist basis, using wage labour to transform the raw materials which they buy, with the tools they own, into finished products which they then automatically own too.

The capitalist mode of production thus presupposes that the producers' *labour power has become a commodity*. Like all other commodities, the commodity labour power has an exchange value and a use value. The exchange value of labour power, like the exchange value of all other commodities, is the amount of socially necessary labour embodied in it, i.e. its reproduction costs. This means concretely the value of all the consumer goods and services necessary for a labourer to work day after day, week after week, month after month, at approximately the same level of intensity, and for the members of the labouring classes to remain approximately stable in number and skill (i.e. for a certain number of working-class children to be fed, kept and schooled, so as to replace their parents when they are unable to work any more, or die). But the use value of the commodity labour power is precisely its capacity *to create new value*, including its potential to create more value than its own reproduction costs. Surplus-value is but that difference between the total new value created by the commodity labour power, and its own value, its own reproduction costs.

The whole marxian theory of surplus-value is therefore based upon that subtle distinction between 'labour power' and 'labour' (or value). But there is nothing 'metaphysical' about this distinction. It is simply an explanation (demystification) of a process which occurs daily in millions of cases.

The capitalist does not buy the worker's 'labour'. If he did that there would be obvious theft, for the worker's wage is obviously smaller than the total value he adds to that of the raw materials in the course of the process of production. No: the capitalist buys 'labour power', and often (not always of course) he buys it at its *justum pretium*, at its real value. So he feels unjustly accused when he is said to have caused a 'dishonest' operation. The worker is victim not of vulgar theft but of a social set-up which condemns him first to transform his productive capacity into a commodity, then to sell that labour power on a specific market (the labour market) characterized by institutional inequality, and finally to content himself with the market price he can get for that commodity, irrespective of whether the new value he creates during the process of production exceeds that market price (his wage) by a small amount, a large amount, or an enormous amount.

The labour power the capitalist has bought 'adds value' to that of the used-up raw materials and tools (machinery, buildings etc.). If, and until that point of time, this added value is inferior or equal to the workers' wages, surplus-value cannot originate. But in that case, the capitalist has obviously no interest in hiring wage labour. He only hires it because that wage labour has the quality (the use value) to add to the raw materials' value more than its own value (i.e. its own wages). This 'additional added value' (the difference between total 'value added' and wages) is precisely surplus-value. Its emergence from the process of production is the precondition for the capitalists' hiring workers, for the existence of the capitalist mode of production.

The institutional inequality existing on the labour market (masked for liberal economists, sociologists and moral philosophers alike by juridical equality) arises from the very fact that the capitalist mode of production is based upon generalized commodity production, generalized market economy. This implies that a propertyless labourer, who owns no capital, who has no reserves of larger sums of money but who has to buy his food and clothes, pay his rent and even elementary public transportation for journeying between home and workplace, *in a continuous way* in exchange of money, is under the *economic compulsion* to sell the only commodity he possesses, to wit his labour power, also on a continuous basis. He cannot withdraw from the labour market until the wages go up. He cannot wait.

But the capitalist, who has money reserves, can temporarily withdraw from the labour market. He can lay his workers off, can even close or sell his enterprise and wait a couple of years before starting again in business. The institutional differences makes price determination of the labour market a game with loaded dice, heavily biased against the working class. One just has to imagine a social set-up in which each citizen would be guaranteed an annual minimum income by the community, irrespective of whether he is employed or not, to understand that 'wage determination' under these circumstances would be quite different from what it is under capitalism. In such a set-up the individual would really have the economic *choice* whether to sell his labour power to another person (or a firm) or not. Under capitalism, he has no choice. His is forced by economic compulsion to go through that sale, practically at any price.

The economic function and importance of trade unions for the wage-earners also clearly arises from that elementary analysis. For it is precisely the workers' 'combination' and their assembling a collective resistance fund (what was called by the first French unions *caisses de résistance*, 'reserve deposits') which enables them, for example through a strike, to withdraw the supply of labour power temporarily from the market so as to stop a downward trend of wages or induce a wage increase. There is nothing 'unjust' in such a temporary withdrawal of the supply of labour power, as there are constant withdrawals of demand for labour power by the capitalists, sometimes on a huge scale never equalled by strikes. Through the functioning of strong labour unions, the working class tries to correct, albeit partially and modestly, the institutional inequality on the labour market of which it is a victim, without ever being able to neutralize it durably or completely.

It cannot neutralize it durably because in the very way in which capitalism functions there is a powerful built-in corrective in favour of capital: *the inevitable emergence of an industrial reserve army of labour*. There are three key sources for that reserve army: the mass of precapitalist producers and self-employed (independent peasants, handicraftsmen, trades-people, professional people, small and medium-sized capitalists); the mass of housewives (and to a lesser extent, children); the mass of the wage-earners themselves, who potentially can be thrown out of employment.

The first two sources have to be visualized not only in each capitalist country seen separately but on a world scale, through the operations of international migration. They are still unlimited to a great extent, although the number of wage-earners the world over (including agricultural wage labourers) has already passed the one billion mark. As the third source, while it is obviously not unlimited (if wage labour would disappear altogether, if all wage labourers would be fired, surplus-value production would disappear too; that is why 'total robotism' is impossible under capitalism), its reserves are enormous, precisely in tandem with the enormous growth of the absolute number of wage earners.

The fluctuations of the industrial reserve army are determined both by the business cycle and by long-term trends of capital accumulation. Rapidly increasing capital accumulation attracts wage labour on a massive scale, including through international migration. Likewise, deceleration, stagnation or even decline of capital accumulation inflates the reserve army of labour. There is thus an upper limit to wage increases, when profits (realized profits and expected profits) are 'excessively' reduced in the eyes of the capitalists, which triggers off such decelerated, stagnating or declining capital accumulation, thereby decreasing employment and wages, till a 'reasonable' level of profits is restored.

This process does not correspond to any 'natural economic law' (or necessity), nor does it correspond to any 'immanent justice'. It just expresses the inner logic of the *capitalist* mode of production, which is geared to profit. Other forms of economic organization could function, have functioned and are functioning on the basis of other logics, which do not lead to periodic massive unemployment. On the contrary, a socialist would say – and Marx certainly thought so – that the capitalist system is an 'unjust', or better stated 'alienating', 'inhuman' social system, precisely because it cannot function without periodically reducing employment and the satisfaction of elementary needs for tens of millions of human beings.

23

Marx's theory of surplus-value is therefore closely intertwined with a *theory of wages* which is far away from Malthus's, Ricardo's or the early socialists' (like Ferdinand Lassalle's) 'iron law of wages', in which wages tend to fluctuate around the physiological minimum. That crude theory of 'absolute pauperization' of the working class under capitalism, attributed to Marx by many authors (Popper, 1945, et al.), is not Marx's at all, as many contemporary authors have convincingly demonstrated (see among others Rosdolsky, 1968). Such an 'iron law of wages' is essentially a demographic one, in which birth rates and the frequency of marriages determine the fluctuation of employment and unemployment and thereby the level of wages.

The logical and empirical inconsistencies of such a theory are obvious. Let it be sufficient to point out that while fluctuations in the supply of wage-labourers are considered essential, fluctuations in the demand for labour power are left out of the analysis. It is certainly a paradox that the staunch opponent of capitalism, Karl Marx, pointed out as early as in the middle of the 19th century the potential for wage increases under capitalism, even though not unlimited in time and space. Marx also stressed the fact that for each capitalist, wage increases of other capitalists' workers are considered increases of potential purchasing power, not increases in costs (Marx, *d*).

Marx distinguishes two parts in the workers' wage, two elements of reproduction costs of the commodity labour power. One is purely physiological, and can be expressed in calories and energy quanta; this is the bottom below which the wage cannot fall without destroying slowly rapidly the workers' labour capacity. The second one is historical–moral, as Marx calls it (Marx, *i*), and consists of those additional goods and services which a shift in the class relationship of forces, such as a victorious class struggle, enables the working class to incorporate into the average wage, the socially necessary (recognized) reproduction costs of the commodity labour power (e.g. holidays after the French general strike of June 1936). This part of the wage is essentially flexible. It will differ from country to country, continent to continent and from epoch to epoch, according to many variables. But it has the upper limit indicated above: the ceiling from which profits threaten to disappear, or to become insufficient in the eyes of the capitalists, who then go on an 'investment strike'.

So Marx's theory of wages is essentially an *accumulation-of-capital theory of wages* which sends us back to what Marx considered the first 'law of motion' of the capitalist mode of production: the compulsion for the capitalists to step up constantly the rate of capital accumulation.

THE LAWS OF MOTION OF THE CAPITALIST MODE OF PRODUCTION

If Marx's theory of surplus-value is his most revolutionary contribution to economic science, his discovery of the basic long-term 'laws of motion' (development trends) of the capitalist mode of production constitutes undoubtedly his most impressive scientific achievement. No other 19th-century author has been able to foresee in such a coherent way how capitalism would function, would develop and would transform the world, as did Karl Marx. Many of the most distinguished contemporary economists, starting with Wassily Leontief (1938), and Joseph Schumpeter (1942) have recognized this.

While some of these 'laws of motion' have obviously created much controversy, we shall nevertheless list them in logical order, rather than according to the degree of consensus they command.

(a) *The capitalist's compulsion to accumulate*. Capital appears in the form of accumulated money, thrown into circulation in order to increase in value. No owner of money capital will engage in business in order to recuperate exactly the sum initially invested, and nothing more than that. By definition, the search for profit is at the basis of all economic operations by owners of capital.

Profit (surplus-value, accretion of value) can originate outside the sphere of production in a precapitalist society. It represents then essentially a *transfer of value* (so-called primitive accumulation of capital); but under the capitalist mode of production, in which capital has penetrated the sphere of production and dominates it, surplus-value is currently produced by wage labour. It represents a constant *increase in value*.

Capital can only appear in the form of *many capitals*, given its very historical–social origin in private property (appropriation) of the means of production. 'Many capitals' imply unavoidable competition. Competition in a capitalist mode of production is competition for selling commodities in an anonymous market. While surplus-value is produced in the process of production, it is *realized* in the process of circulation, i.e. through the sale of the commodities. The capitalist wants to sell at maximum profit. In practice, he will be satisfied if he gets the average profit, which is a percentage really existing in his consciousness (e.g. Mr Charles Wilson, the then head of the US automobile firm General Motors, stated before a Congressional enquiry: we used to fix the expected sales price of our cars by adding 15% to production costs). But he can never be sure of this. He cannot even be sure that all the commodities produced will find a buyer.

Given these uncertainties, he has to strive constantly to get the better of his competitors. This can only occur through operating with more capital. This means that at least part of the surplus-value produced will not be unproductively consumed by the capitalists and their hangers-on through luxury consumption, but will be accumulated, added to the previously existing capital.

The inner logic of capitalism is therefore not only to 'work for profit', but also to 'work for capital accumulation'. 'Accumulate, accumulate; that is Moses and the Prophets', states Marx in *Capital*, Vol. I (Marx, *e*, p. 742). Capitalists are *compelled* to act in that way as a result of competition. It is competition which basically fuels this terrifying snowball logic: initial value of capital → accretion of value (surplus-value) → accretion of capital → more accretion of surplus-value → more accretion of capital etc. 'Without competition, the fire of growth would burn out' Marx, *g*, p. 368).

(b) *The tendency towards constant technological revolutions*. In the capitalist mode of production, accumulation of capital is in the first place accumulation of productive capital, or capital invested to produce more and more commodities. Competition is therefore above all competition between productive capitals, i.e. 'many capitals' engaged in mining, manufacturing, transportation, agriculture, telecommunications. The main weapon in competition between capitalist firms is cutting production costs. More advanced production techniques and more 'rational' labour organization are the main means to achieve that purpose. The basic trend of capital accumulation in the capitalist mode of production is therefore a trend towards more and more sophisticated machinery. Capital growth takes the dual form of higher and higher value of capital and of constant revolutions in the techniques of production, of constant technological process.

(c) *The capitalists' unquenchable thirst for surplus-value extraction.* The compulsion for capital to grow, the irresistible urge for capital accumulation, realizes itself above all through a constant drive for the increase of the production of surplus-value. Capital accumulation is nothing but surplus-value capitalization, the transformation of part of the new surplus-value into additional capital. There is no other source of additional capital than additional surplus-value produced in the process of production.

Marx distinguishes two different forms of additional surplus-value production. *Absolute surplus-value* accretion occurs essentially through the extension of the work day. If the worker reproduces the equivalent of his wages in 4 hours a day, an extension of the work day from 10 to 12 hours will increase surplus-value from 6 to 8 hours. *Relative surplus-value* accretion occurs through an increase of the productivity of labour in the wage-goods sector of the economy. Such an increase in productivity implies that the equivalent of the value of an identical basket of goods and services consumed by the worker could be produced in 2 hours instead of 4 hours of labour. If the work day remains stable at 10 hours and real wages remain stable too, surplus-value will then increase from 6 to 8 hours.

While both processes occur throughout the history of the capitalist mode of production (viz. the contemporary pressure of employers in favour of overtime!), the first one was prevalent first, the second one became prevalent since the second half of the 19th century, first in Britain, France and Belgium, then in the USA and Germany, later in the other industrialized capitalist countries, and later still in the semi-industrialized ones. Marx calls this process the *real subsumption* (subordination) *of labour under capital* (Marx, k), for it represents not only an economic but also a physical subordination of the wage-earner under the machine. This physical subordination can only be realized through social control. The history of the capitalist mode of production is therefore also the history of successive forms of – tighter and tighter – control of capital over the workers inside the factories (Braverman, 1974); and of attempts at realizing that tightening of control in society as a whole.

The increase in the production of relative surplus-value is the goal for which capitalism tends to periodically substitute machinery for labour, i.e. to expand the industrial reserve army of labour. Likewise, it is the main tool for maintaining a modicum of social equilibrium, for when productivity of labour strongly increases, above all in the wage-good producing sectors of the economy, real wages and profits (surplus-value) can both expand simultaneously. What were previously luxury goods can even become mass-produced wage-goods.

(d) *The tendency towards growing concentration and centralization of capital.* The growth of the value of capital means that each successful capitalist firm will be operating with more and more capital. Marx calls this the tendency towards growing concentration of capital. But in the competitive process, there are victors and vanquished. The victors grow. The vanquished go bankrupt or are absorbed by the victors. This process Marx calls the centralization of capital. It results in a declining number of firms which survive in each of the key fields of production. Many small and medium-sized capitalists disappear as indepedent business men and women. They become in turn salary earners, employed by successful capitalism firms. Capitalism itself is the big 'expropriating' force, suppressing private property of the means of production for many, in favour of private property for few.

(e) *The tendency for the 'organic composition of capital' to increase.* Productive capital has a double form. It appears in the form of *constant* capital: buildings, machinery, raw materials, energy. It appears in the form of *variable* capital: capital spent on wages of productive workers. Marx calls the part of capital used in buying labour power variable, because only that part produces additional value. In the process of production, the value of constant capital is simply maintained (transferred *in toto* or in part into the value of the finished product). Variable capital on the contrary is the unique source of 'added value'.

Marx postulates that the basic historic trend of capital accumulation is to increase investment in constant capital at a quicker pace than investment in variable capital; the relation between the two he calls the 'organic composition of capital'. This is both a technical/physical relation (a given production technique implies the use of a given number of productive wage earners, even if not in an absolutely mechanical way) and a value relation. The trend towards an increase in the 'organic composition of capital' is therefore a historical trend towards *basically labour-saving technological progress.*

This tendency has often been challenged by critics of Marx. Living in the age of semi-automation and 'robotism', it is hard to understand that challenge. The conceptual confusion on which this challenge is most based is an operation with the 'national wage bill', i.e. a confusion between wages in general and variable capital, which is only the wage bill of productive labour. A more correct index would be the part of the labour costs in total production costs in the manufacturing (and mining) sector. It is hard to deny that this proportion shows a downward secular trend.

(f) *The tendency of the rate of profit to decline.* For the workers, the basic relation they are concerned with is the rate of surplus-value, i.e the division of 'value added' between wages and surplus-value. When this goes up, their exploitation (the unpaid labour they produce) obviously goes up. For the capitalists, however, this relationship is not meaningful. They are concerned with the relation between surplus-value and the *totality* of capital invested, never mind

27

whether in the form of machinery and raw materials or in the form of wages. This relation is the *rate of profit*. It is a function of two variables, the organic composition of capital and the rate of surplus-value. If the value of constant capital is represented by c, the value of variable capital (wages of productive workers) by v and surplus-value by s, the rate of profit will be $s/(c + v)$. This can be rewritten as

$$\frac{s/v}{(c + v)/v} + 1$$

with the two variables emerging ($(c + v)/v$ obviously reflects c/v).

Marx postulates that the increase in the rate of surplus value has defiinite limits, while the increase in the organic composition of capital has practically none (automation, robotism). There will be a basic tendency for the rate of profit to decline.

This is however absolutely true only on a very long-term, i.e. essentially 'secular', basis. In other time-frameworks, the rate of profit can fluctuate under the influence of countervailing forces. Constant capital can be devalorized, through 'capital saving' technical process, and through economic crises (see below). The rate of surplus-value can be strongly increased in the short or medium term, although each strong increase makes a further increase more difficult (Marx, *d*, pp. 335–6); and capital can flow to countries (e.g. 'Third World' ones) or branches (e.g. service sectors) where the organic composition of capital is significantly lower than in the previously industrialized ones, thereby raising the average rate of profit.

Finally, the increase in the *mass of surplus-value* – especially through the extension of wage labour in general, i.e. the total number of workers – offsets to a large extent the depressing effects of moderate declines of the average rate of profit. Capitalism will not go out of business if the mass of surplus-value produced increases 'only' from £10 to 17 billion, while the total mass of capital has moved from £100 to 200 billion; and capital accumulation will not stop under these circumstances, nor necessarily show down significantly. It would be sufficient to have the unproductively consumed part of surplus-value pass e.g. from £3 to £2 billion, to obtain a rate of capital accumulation of 15/200, i.e. 7.5%, even higher than the previous one of 7/100, in spite of a decline of the rate of profit from 10 to 8.5%.

(g) *The inevitability of class struggle under capitalism.* One of the most impressive projections by Marx was that of the inevitability of elementary class struggle under capitalism. Irrespective of the social global framework or of their own historical background, wage-earners will fight everywhere for higher real wages and a shorter work day. They will form elementary organizations for the collective instead of the individual sale of the commodity labour power, i.e. trade unions. While at the moment Marx made that projection there were less than half a million organized workers in at the most half a dozen countries in the world, today trade unions encompass hundreds of millions of wage-earners spread around the globe. There is no country, however, remote it might be, where the introduction of wage labour has not led to the appearance of worker's coalitions.

While elementary class struggle and elementary unionization of the working class are inevitable under capitalism, higher, especially political forms of class struggle, depend on a multitude of variables which determine the rapidity with which they extend beyond smaller minorities of each 'national' working class and internationally. But there too the basic secular trend is clear. There were in 1900 innumerably more conscious socialists than in 1850, fighting not only for better wages but, to use Marx's words, for the abolition of wage labour (Marx, *i*) and organizing working class parties for that purpose. There are today many more than in 1900.

(h) *The tendency towards growing social polarization.* From two previously enumerated trends, the trend towards growing centralization of capital and the trend towards the growth of the mass of surplus-value, flow the trend towards growing social polarization under capitalism. The proportion of the active population represented by wage-labour in general, i.e. by the modern proletariat (which extends far beyond productive workers in and by themselves), increases. The proportion represented by self-employed (small, medium-sized and big capitalists, as well as independent peasants, handicraftsmen, tradespeople and 'free professions' working without wage-labour) decreases. In fact, in several capitalist countries the first category has already passed the 90 per cent mark, while in Marx's time it was below 50 per cent everywhere but in Britain. In most industrialized (imperialist) countries, it has reached 80–85 per cent.

This does not mean that the petty entrepreneurs have tended to disappear. 10 or 15–20 per cent out of 30 million people, not to say out of 120 million, still represents a significant social layer. While many small businesses disappear, especially in times of economic depression, as a result of severe competition, they also are constantly created, especially in the interstices between big firms, and in new sectors where they play an exploratory role. Also, the overall social results of growing proletarization are not simultaneous with the economic process in and by itself. From the point of view of class consciousness, culture, political attitude, there can exist significant time-lags between the transformation of an independent farmer, grocer or doctor into a wage-earner, and his acceptance of socialism as an overall social solution for his own and society's ills. But again, the secular trend is towards *growing homogeneity*, less and less heterogeneity, of the mass of the wage-earning class, and not the other way around. It is sufficient to compare the differences in consumer patterns, attitudes towards unionization or voting habits between manual workers, bank employees and government functionaries in say 1900 and today, to note that they have decreased and not increased.

(i) *The tendency towards growing objective socialization of labour.* Capitalism starts in the form of private production on a medium-sized scale for a limited number of largely unknown customers, on an uncontrollably wide market, i.e. under conditions of near complete fragmentation of social labour and anarchy of the economic process. But as a result of growing technological progress, tremendously increased concentration of capital, the conquest of wider and wider markets throughout the world, and the very nature of the labour organization inside large and even medium-sized capitalist factories, a powerful process of objective socialization of labour is simultaneously set in motion. This process constantly extends the sphere of economy in which not blind market laws but conscious decisions and even large-scale cooperation prevail.

This is true especially inside mammoth firms (inside multinational corporations, such 'planning' prevails far beyond the boundaries of nation-states, even the most powerful ones!) and inside large-scale factories; but it is also increasingly true for buyer/seller relations, in the first place on an inter-firm basis, between public authorities and firms, and more often than one thinks between traders and consumers too. In all these instances, the rule of the law of value becomes more and more remote, indirect and discontinuous. Planning prevails on a short and even medium-term basis.

Certainly, the economy still remains capitalist. The rule of the law of value imposes itself brutally through the outburst of economic crises. Wars and social crises are increasingly added to these economic crises to remind society that, under capitalism, this growing objective socialization of labour and production is indissolubly linked to private appropriation, i.e. to the profit motive as motor of economic growth. That linkage makes the system more and more crisis-ridden; but at the same time the growing socialization of labour and production creates the objective basis for a general socialization of the economy, i.e. represents the basis of the coming socialist order created by capitalism itself, within the framework of its own system.

(j) *The inevitability of economic crises under capitalism*. This is another of Marx's projections which has been strikingly confirmed by history. Marx ascertained that periodic crises of overproduction were unavoidable under capitalism. In fact, since the crisis of 1825, the first one occurring on the world market for industrial goods, to use Marx's own formula, there have been twenty-one business cycles ending (or beginning, according to the method of analysis and measurement used) with twenty-one crises of overproduction. A twenty-second is appearing on the horizon as we are writing.

Capitalist economic crises are always crises of *overproduction of commodities* (*exchange values*), as opposed to pre- and post-capitalist economic crises, which are essentially crises of *underproduction of use-values*. Under capitalist crises, *expanded reproduction* – economic growth – is brutally interrupted, not because too few commodities have been produced but, on the contrary, because a mountain of produced commodities finds no buyers. This unleashes a spiral movement of collapse of firms, firing of workers, contraction of sales (or orders) for raw materials and machinery, new redundancies, new contraction of sales of consumer goods etc. Through this *contracted reproduction*, prices (gold prices) collapse, production and income is reduced, capital loses value. At the end of the declining spiral, output (and stocks) have been reduced more than purchasing power. Then production can pick up again; and as the crisis has both increased the rate of surplus-value (through a decline of wages and a more 'rational' labour organization) and decreased the value of capital, the average rate of profit increases. This stimulates investment. Employment increases, value production and national income expand, and we enter a new cycle of economic revival, prosperity, overheating and the next crisis.

No amount of capitalists' (essentially large combines' and monopolies') 'self-regulation', no amount of government intervention, has been able to suppress this cyclical movement of capitalist production. Nor can they succeed in achieving that result. This cyclical movement is inextricably linked to production for profit and private property (competition), which imply periodic over-shooting (too little or too much investment and output), precisely because each firm's attempt at maximizing profit unavoidably leads to a lower rate of profit for the system as a whole. It is likewise linked to the separation of value production and value realization.

The only way to avoid crises of overproduction is to eliminate all basic sources of disequilibrium in the economy, including the disequilibrium between productive capacity and purchasing power of the 'final consumers'. This calls for elimination of generalized commodity production, of private property and of class exploitation, i.e. for the elimination of capitalism.

MARX'S THEORY OF CRISES

Marx did not write a systematic treatise on capitalist crises. His major comments on the subject are spread around his major economic writings, as well as his articles for the *New York Daily Tribune*. The longest treatment of the subject is in his *Theorien über den Mehrwert*, subpart on Ricardo (Marx. *h*, Part 2). Starting from these profound but unsystematic remarks, many interpretations of the 'marxist theory of crises' have been offered by economists who consider themselves marxists. 'Monocausal' ones generally centre around 'disproportionality' (Bukharin, Hilferding, Otto Bauer) – anarchy of production as the key cause of crises – or 'underconsumption' – lack of purchasing power of the 'final consumers' as the cause of crises (Rosa Luxenburg, Sweezy). 'Non-monocausal' ones try to elaborate Marx's own *dictum* according to which *all* basic contradictions of the capitalist mode of production come into play in the process leading to a capitalist crises (Grossman, Mandel).

The question of determining whether according to Marx, a crises of overproduction is first of all a crisis of overproduction of commodities or a crisis of overproduction of capital is really meaningless in the framework of Marx's economic analysis. The mass of commodities is but one specific form of capital, commodity capital. Under capitalism, which is generalized commodity production, no overproduction is possible which is not simultaneously overproduction of commodities and overproduction of capital (overaccumulation).

Likewise, the question to know whether the crisis 'centres' on the sphere of production or the sphere of circulation is largely meaningless. The crisis is a *disturbance* (interruption) of the process of enlarged *reproduction*; and according to Marx, the process of reproduction is precisely a (contradictory) *unity* of

31

production and circulation. For capitalists, both individually (as separate firms) and as the sum total of firms, it is irrelevant whether more surplus-value has actually been produced in the process of production, if that surplus-value cannot be totally realized in the process of circulation. Contrary to many economists, academic and marxist alike, Marx explicitly rejected any Say-like illusion that production more or less automatically finds is own market.

It is correct that in the last analysis, capitalist crises of overproduction result from a downslide of the average rate of profit. But this does not represent a variant of the 'monocausal' explanation of crises. It means that, under capitalism, the fluctuations of the average rate of profit are in a sense the seismograph of what happens in the system as a whole. So that formula just refers back to the sum-total of partially independent variables, whose interplay causes the fluctuations of the average rate of profit.

Capitalist growth is always disproportionate growth, i.e. growth with increasing disequilibrium, both between different departments of output (Marx basically distinguishes department I, producing means of production, and department II, producing means of consumption; other authors add a department III producing non-reproductive goods – luxury goods and arms – to that list), between different branches and between production and final consumption. In fact, 'equilibrium' under capitalism is but a conceptual hypothesis practically never attained in real life, except as a border case. The above mentioned tendency of 'overshooting' is only an illustration of that more general phenomenon. So 'average' capital accumulation leads to an over-accumulation which leads to the crisis and to a prolonged phenomenon of 'underinvestment' during the depression. Output is then consistently inferior to current demand, which spurs on capital accumulation, all the more so as each successive phase of economic revival starts with new machinery of a higher technological level (leading to a higher average productivity of labour, and to a bigger and bigger mountain of produced commodities. Indeed, the very duration of the business cycle (in average 7.5 years for the last 160 years) seemed for Marx determined by the 'moral' life-time of fixed capital, i.e. the duration of the reproduction cycle (in value terms, not in possible physical survival) of machinery.

The ups and downs of the rate of profit during the business cycle do not reflect only the gyrations of the output/disposable income relation; or of the 'organic composition of capital'. They also express the varying correlation of forces between the major contending classes of bourgeois society, in the first place the short-term fluctuations of the rate of surplus-value reflecting major victories or defeats of the working class in trying to uplift or defend its standard of living and its working conditions. Technological progress and labour organization 'rationalizations' are capital's weapons for neutralizing the effects of these fluctuations on the average rate of profit and on the rate of capital accumulation.

In general, Marx rejected any idea that the working class (or the unions) 'cause' the crisis by 'excessive wage demands'. He would recognize that under conditions of overheating and 'full employment', real wages generally increase, but the rate of surplus-value can simultaneously increase too. It can, however, not increase in the same proportion as the organic composition of capital. Hence the decline of the average rate of profit. Hence the crisis.

But if real wages do not increase in times of boom, and as they unavoidable decrease in times of depression, the average level of wages during the cycle in its totality would be such as to cause even larger overproduction of wage goods, which would induce an even stronger collapse of investment at the height of the cycle, and in no way help to avoid the crisis.

Marx energetically rejected any idea that capitalist production, while it *appears* as 'production for production's sake', can really emancipate itself from dependence on 'final consumption' (as alleged e.g. by Tugan-Baranowski). While capitalist technology implies indeed a more and more 'roundabout-way-of-production', and a relative shift of resources from department II to department I (that is what the 'growing organic composition of capital' really means, after all), it can never develop the productive capacity of department I without developing in the medium and long-term the productive capacity of department II too, admittedly at a slower pace and in a lesser proportion. So any medium or long-term contraction of final consumption, or final consumers' purchasing power, increases instead of eliminates the causes of the crisis.

Marx visualized the business cycle as intimately intertwined with a *credit cycle*, which can acquire a *relative* autonomy in relation to what occurs in production properly speaking (Marx, *g*, pp. 570–73). An (over)expansion of credit can enable the capitalist system to sell temporarily more goods that the sum of real incomes created in current production plus past savings could buy. Likewise, credit (over)expansion can enable them to invest temporarily more capital than really accumulated surplus-value (plus depreciation allowances and recovered value of raw materials) would have enabled them to invest (the first part of the formula refers to net investments; the second to gross investment).

But all this is only true temporarily. In the longer run, debts must be paid; and they are not automatically paid through the results of expanded output and income made possible by credit expansion. Hence the risk of a *Krach*, of a credit or banking crisis, adding fuel to the mass of explosives which cause the crisis of overproduction.

Does Marx's theory of crisis imply a theory of an inevitable final collapse of capitalism through purely economic mechanisms? A controversy has raged around this issue, called the 'collapse' or 'breakdown' controversy. Marx's own remarks on the matter are supposed to be enigmatic. They are essentially contained in the famous chapter 32 of volume I of *Capital* entitled 'The historical tendency of capitalist accumulation', a section culminating in the battle cry: 'The expropriators are expropriated' (Marx, *e*, p. 929). But the relevant paragraphs of that chapter describe in a clearly non-enigmatic way, an interplay of 'objective' and 'subjective' transformations to bring about a downfall of capitalism, and not a purely economic process. They list among the causes of the overthrow of capitalism not only economic crisis and growing centralization of capital, but also the growth of exploitation of the workers and of their indignation and revolt in the face of that exploitation, as well as the growing level of skill, organization and unity of the working class. Beyond these general remarks, Marx, however, does not go.

Marx was disinclined to comment at length about how a socialist or communist economy would operate. He thought such comments to be essentially speculative. Nevertheless, in his major works, especially the *Grundrisse* and *Das Kapital*, there are some sparse comments on the subject. Marx returns to them at greater length in two works he was to write in the final part of his life, his comments on the *Gotha Programme* of united German social-democracy (Marx, *j*), and the chapters on economics and socialism he wrote or collaborated with for Engels' Anti-Dühring (1878). Generally his comments, limited and sketchy as they are, can be summarized in the following points.

Socialism is an economic system based upon conscious planning of production by associated producers (nowhere does Marx say: by the state), made possible by the abolition of private property of the means of production. As soon as that private property is completely abolished, goods produced cease to be commodities. Value and exchange value disappear. Production becomes production for use, for the satisfaction of needs, determined by conscious choice (*ex ante* decisions) of the mass of the associated producers themselves. But overall economic organization in a postcapitalist society will pass through two stages.

In the first stage, generally called 'socialism', there will be relative scarcity of a number of consumer goods (and services), making it necessary to measure exactly distribution based on the actual labour inputs of each individual (Marx nowhere refers to different quantities and *qualities* of labour; Engels explicitly *rejects* the idea that an architect, because he has more skill, should consume more than a manual labourer). Likewise, there will still be the need to use incentives for getting people to work in general. This will be based upon strict equality of access for all trades and professions to consumption. But as human needs are unequal, that formal equality masks the survival of real inequality.

In a second phase, generally called 'communism', there will be plenty, i.e. output will reach a saturation point of needs covered by material goods. Under these circumstances, any form of precise measurement of consumption (distribution) will wither away. The principle of full needs satisfaction covering all *different needs* of *different* individuals will prevail. No incentive will be needed any more to induce people to work. 'Labour' will have transformed itself into meaningful many-fold activity, making possible all-round development of each individual's human personality. The division of labour between manual and intellectual labour, the separation of town and countryside, will wither away. Humankind will be organized into a free federation of producers' and consumers' communes.

There is still no complete edition of all of Marx's and Engels's writings. The standard German and Russian editions by the Moscow and East Berlin Institutes for Marxism-Leninism, generally referred to as *Marx-Engels-Werke* (MEW), do not include hundreds of pages printed elsewhere (e.g. Marx's *Enthüllungen zur Geschichte der Diplomatie im 18. Jahrhundert* [Revelations on the History of 18th-century Diplomacy]), and several thousand pages of manuscripts not yet printed at the time these editions were published. At present, a monumental edition called *Marx-Engels-Gesemtausgabe* (MEGA) has been started, again both in German and in Russian, by the same Institutes. It already encompasses many of the unpublished manuscripts referred to above, in the first place a previously unknown economic work which makes a bridge between the *Grundrisse* and Vol. 1 of *Capital*, and which was written in the years 1861–3 (published under the title *Zur Kritik der Politischen Oekonomie – Contribution to a Critique of Political Economy 1861–1863* in MEGA II/3/1–6, Berlin Dietz Verlag, 1976–82). Whether it will include all of Marx's and Engels's writing remains to be seen.

In English, key works by Marx and Engels have been systematically published by Progress Publishers, Moscow, and Lawrence & Wishart, London; but this undertaking is by no means an approximation of the *Marx-Engel-Werke* mentioned above. The quality of the translation is often poor. The translations of Marx's and Engels's writings published by Penguin Books in the *Marx Pelican Library* are quite superior to it. We therefore systematically refer to the latter edition whenever there is a choice. Marx's and Engels' books and pamphlets referred to in the present text are mostly in chronological order:

(Marx *a*) *Die Deutsche Ideologie* (1846), together with Friedrich Engels.

(Marx *b*) *Manifest der Kommunistischen Partei* (1848), written in collaboration with Friedrich Engels. In English: *Manifesto of the Communist Party*, in *Marx: The Revolutions of 1848*, Harmondsworth: Penguin Books, 1973.

(Marx *c*) *Zur Kritik der Politischen Oekonomie* (1858). In English: *Contribution to the Critique of Political Economy*, London: Lawrence & Wishart, 1970; New York: International Publishers, 1971.

(Marx *d*) *Grundrisse der Kritik der Politischen Oekonomie* (written in 1858–9, first published in 1939). English edition: *Foundations of a Critique of Political Economy*, Harmondsworth: Penguin Books, 1972; New York: Random House, 1973.

(Marx *e*) *Das Kapital, Band I* (1867). In English: *Capital*, Vol. I, Harmondsworth: Penguin Books, 1976.

(Marx *f*) *Das Kapital, Band II*, published by Engels in 1885. In English: *Capital*, Vol. II, Harmondsworth: Penguin Books, 1978.

(Marx *g*) *Das Kapital, Band II*, published by Engels in 1894. In English: *Capital*, Vol. III, Harmondsworth: Penguin Books, 1981.

(Marx *h*) *Theorien über den Mehrwert*, published by Karl Kautsky 1905–10. In English: *Theories of Surplus Value*, Moscow: Progress Publishers, 1963.

(Marx *i*) *Lohn, Preis und Profit*, written in 1865. In English: *Wages, Price and Profits*, in *Marx-Engels Selected Works*, Vol. II, Moscow: Progress Publishers, 1969.

(Marx *j*) *Kritik des Gothaer Programms*, written in 1878 in collaboration with Engels. In English: *Critique of the Gotha Programme*, in *Marx-Engels: The First International and After*, Harmondsworth: Penguin Books, 1974.

(Marx *k*) *Resultate des unmittelbaren Produktionsprozesses* (unpublished section VII of Vol. 1 of Capital), first published in 1933. In English: *Results of the Immediate Process of Production, Appendix to Capital*, Vol. I, Harmondsworth: Penguin Books, 1976.

(Marx l) *Marx-Engels: Briefwechsel* (*Letters*). There is no complete English edition of the letters. Some are included in the *Selected Works* in 3 vols, published by Progress Publishers, Moscow.

(Engels): *Anti-Dühring* (1878). The chapter on economy was written by Marx, who also read all the other parts and collaborated in their final draft. In English: *Anti-Dühring*, London: Lawrence & Wishart, 1955.

BIBLIOGRAPHY

There are innumerable books and articles devoted to comments or elaborations on Marx's economic thought, or which criticize them. We list here those works we refer to in the above text, as well as those we consider the most important ones (based, needless to say, upon subjective judgement).

Baran, P.A. 1957. *The Political Economy of Growth.* London: John Calder; New York: Monthly Review Press.

Baran, P.A. and Sweezy, P.M. 1966. *Monopoly Capital.* New York and London: Monthly Review Press.

Bauer, O. 1904–5. Marx' Theorie der Wirtschaftkrisen. *Die Neue Zeit*, 23.

Böhn-Bawerk, E. von. 1896. *Zum Abschluss des Marxschen Systems.* English edn, *Karl Marx and the Close of his System*, including a reply by Rudolf Hilfdering, *Böhm-Bawerk's Criticism of Karl Marx*, ed. P.M. Sweezy, New York: Augustus M. Kelley, 1949.

Bortkiewicz, L. von. 1907. *Zur Berichtigung der grundlegenden theoretischen Konstruktion von Marx im Dritten Band des 'Kapital'.* Trans. by P.M. Sweezy as 'On the correction of Marx's fundamental theoretical construction in the third volume of *Capital*'. In Böhm-Bawerk (1949), 197–221.

Braverman, H. 1974. *Labor and Monopoly Capital: the degradation of work in the twentieth century.* New York and London: Monthly Review Press.

Bronfenbrenner, M. 1970. *The Vicissitudes of Marxian Economics.* London.

Bukharin, N. 1914. *Imperialism and World Economy.* English trans. London: M. Lawrence, 1915; New York: International Publishers, 1929.

Bukharin, N. 1926. *Imperialism and the Accumulation of Capital.* Trans. by R. Wichmann, ed. K.J. Tarbuck, London: Allen Lane, 1972; New York: Monthly Review Press.

Dobb, M. 1937. *Political Economy and Capitalism: some essays in economic tradition.* London: G. Routledge & Sons. Reprinted Westport, Conn.: Greenwood Press, 1972.

Emmanuel, A. 1969. *L'échange inégal. Essai sur les antagonismes dans les rapports économiques internationaux.* Paris: François Maspero. Trans. by B. Pearce as *Unequal Exchange: a study of the imperialism of trade*, London: New Left Books, 1972.

Grossman, H. 1929. *Das Akkumulations: und Zusammenbruchsgesetz des kapitalistischen Systems.* Leipzig: C.L. Hirschfeld.

Hayek, F.A. von. 1944. *The Road to Serfdom.* Chicago: University of Chicago Press; London: G. Routledge & Sons.

Hilferding, R. 1910. *Das Finanzkapital.* Vienna: Wiener Volksbuchhandlung. Trans. by M. Watnick and S. Gordon, ed. T. Bottomore as *Finance Capital*, London: Routledge & Kegan Paul, 1981.

Itoh, M. 1980. *Value and Crisis: essays on Marxian economics in Japan.* London: Pluto.

Kolakowsi, L. 1967–8. *Main Currents of Marxism: its rise, growth and dissolution*, 3 vols. Trans. by P.S. Falla, Oxford: Clarendon Press, 1978; New York: Oxford University Press.

Lange, O. 1963. *Political Economy*, 2 vols. Trans., ed. P.F. Knightsfiield, Oxford: Pergamon Press; Warsaw: PWN – Polish Scientific Publishers.

Lange, O. and Taylor, F.M. 1938. *On the Economic Theory of Socialism*. 2 vols, Minneapolis: University of Minnesota Press.

Lenin, V.I. 1917. *Imperialism, Last Stage of Capitalism*. Petrograd. English trans., Moscow: Foreign Languages Publishing House, 1947.

Leontief, W. 1938. The significance of Marxian economics for present-day economic theory. *American Economic Review*, Supplement, March. Reprinted in *Marx and Modern Economists*, ed. D. Horowitz, London: MacGibbon & Kee, 1968; New York, Modern Reader Paperbacks, 1968.

Luxemburg, R. 1913. *Akkumulation des Kapitals*. Trans. by A. Schwarzschild, with an introduction by J. Robinson, as *The Accumulation of Capital*, London: Routledge & Kegan Paul, 1951; Homewood, Ill: R.D. Irwin, 1956.

Mandel, E. 1962. *Traité d'économie marxiste*. Paris: R. Juillard. Trans. by B. Pearce as *Marxist Economic Theory*, 2 vols, London: Merlin Press, 1968; New York: Monthly Review Press, 1969.

Mandel, E. 1972. *Der Spätkapitalimus*. Frankfurt am Main: Suhrkamp. Trans. by J. De Bres as *Late Capitalism*, London: New Left Books. Revised edn, 1975.

Mandel, E. 1980. *Long Waves of Capitalist Development: the Marxist interpretation*. Cambridge: Cambridge University Press.

Mandel, E. and Freeman, A. (eds) 1984. *Ricardo, Marx, Sraffa*. London: Verso.

Mattick, P. 1969. *Marx and Keynes: the limits of the mixed economy*. Boston: P. Sargent.

Mises, L. von. 1920. Die Wirtschaftsrechnung im sozialistischen Gemeinwesen. Trans. by S. Adler as 'Economic calculations in the socialist commonwealth', in *Collectivist Economic Planning*, ed. F.A. von Hayek, London: G. Routledge & Sons, 1935; New York: A.M. Kelley, 1967.

Morishima, M. 1973. *Marx's Economics: a dual theory of value and growth*. Cambridge and New York: Cambrige University Press.

Nutzinger, H.G. and Wolfstetter, E. (eds) 1974. *Die Marxsche Theorie und ihre Kritik*. 2 vols, Frankfurt am Main: Campus.

Pareto, V. 1966. *Marxisme et économie pure*. Geneva: Droz.

Popper, K. 1945. *The Open Society and Its Enemies*. 2 vols, London: G. Routledge & Sons; Princeton, N.J., University Press, 1956.

Robinson, J. 1942. *An Essay on Marxian Economics*. London: Macmillan. 2nd ed, 1966; New York: St Martin's Press.

Rosdolsky, R. 1968. *Entstehungsgeschichte des Marxschen 'Kapital'*. Frankfurt am Main: Europäische Verlagsanstalt. Trans. by P. Burgess as *The Making of Marx's Capital*, London: Pluto Press, 1977.

Rubin, I.I. 1928. *Essays on Marx's Theory of Value*. Moscow. English trans., Detroit: Black and Red, 1972.

Schumpeter, J. 1942. *Capitalism, Socialism and Democracy*. New York and London: Harper & Brothers.

Steedman, I. 1977. *Marx after Sraffa*. London: New Left Books; New York: Schocken Books.

Sternberg, F. 1926. *Der Imperialismus*. Berlin: Malik-Verlag.

Sweezy, P.M. 1942. *The Theory of Capitalist Development*. New York: Monthly Review Press.

Sraffa, D. 1960. *Production of Commodities by Means of Commodities*. Cambridge: Cambridge University Press.

Tugan-Baranowsky, M. von. 1905. *Theoretische Grundlagen der Marxismus*. Leipzig: Duncker & Humblot.

Wygodsky, D. *Der gegenwärtige Kapitalismus*. Trans. by C.S.V. Salt as *The Story of a Great Discovery: How Karl Marx wrote 'Capital'*, Tunbridge Wells: Abacus Press, 1972.

Absolute Rent

EDNALDO ARAQUEM DA SILVA

Marx's work on rent was based on his studies of the statistical reports published after the Russian Agrarian Reform of 1861. The importance of the Russian case on Marx's thinking is highlighted in Engels' 'Preface' to the third volume of Marx's *Capital*, which draws a parallel between the influence of Russia's diverse land tenure system on Marx's analysis of rent and the role of England on his analysis of industrial wage-labour.

Although the economic surplus normally takes the form of profits in the capitalist system, Marx gave considerable attention to rent. In chapter XLV of the third volume of *Capital* (1894), and in his critical comments on Ricardo's theory of rent, published in *Theories of Surplus-Value* (1905), Marx introduced the concept of absolute rent as the rent paid by capitalist tenant farmers to landowners, regardless of the fertility of the rented land.

Marx (1894, pp. 760, 771: 1905, pp. 244, 392) defined absolute rent as the difference between the value of the agricultural product of the least productive land and the *general* production price, $P(g)$. Absolute rent can absorb the entire $[\text{value}-P(g)]$ difference or a proportion of this difference. In contrast, differential rent is defined as the difference between the general production price and the *individual* production price, $P(i)$. These concepts are depicted in Figure 1. By definition, absolute rent is positive even on the worst cultivated land, A, whereas differential rent is zero on A, but then becomes positive and increases with improved land fertility, B, C and D.

Marx's concept of absolute rent is based on two assumptions: (1) the agricultural organic composition of capital is lower than the average of agriculture and industry; and (2) land is cultivated by capitalist tenant farmers. Assumption (1) implies that the value of an agricultural commodity will be *above* its production price; under assumption (2), landowners will lease land only to those capitalist tenants who can pay absolute rent on the worst quality and most inconveniently located land.

In contrast to other commodities whose organic composition of capital is

39

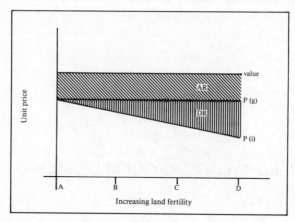

Figure 1   Marx's concept of absolute rent

lower than the average of agriculure and industry, and thus have their values
above their production prices, competition among capitalist producers does not
reduce the values of the agricultural products to their production prices. The
separation of landowners from tenant operators prevents the equalization of
profit rates in agriculture with the single rate prevailing in industry. Landowners
are therefore able to seize excess or above average agricultural profits and prevent
them from entering the process by which the average profit rate is formed (see
Marx, 1905, p. 37; Murray, 1977).

Under Marx's assumptions, the market price of an agricultural product will
include the absolute rent above the general production price.

> If the worst soil cannot be cultivated – although its cultivation would yield
> the price of production – until it produces something in excess of the price of
> production, [absolute] rent, then landed property is the creative cause of *this*
> rise in price (Marx, 1894, p. 755).

There has been some confusion as to whether the upper limit of the market
price of an agricultural product would be set by its individual value on the worst
cultivated land. Marx (1905, p. 332) himself asked: 'If landed property gives the
power to sell the product above its [production price], *at* its value, why, does
it not equally well give the power to sell the product *above* its value, at an
arbitrary monopoly price?' Echoing Marx, Bortkiewicz (1911) and, much later,
Emmanuel (1972) have also questioned why landlords limit absolute rent to the
excess of value over the production price on the worst cultivated land. They
suggest that since landowners have the power to withdraw land from cultivation
until the market price covers both the absolute rent and the production price of
the highest-cost producers, they could also charge a rent in excess of the
corresponding value. In capitalist agriculture, absolute rent has a negative impact
because it removes above average profits, a major source of capitalist technical
innovation (see Lenin, 1901, pp. 119–29).

Despite some ambiguity in Marx's formulation of absolute rent, his argument is persuasive:

Although landed property may drive the price of agricultural produce above its price of production, it does not depend on this, but rather on the general state of the market, to what degree market-price exceeds the price of production and approaches the value (Marx, 1894, p. 764, see also p. 762; Murray, 1977; Flichman, 1977).

According to Marx (1894, pp. 760, 765; 1905, pp. 244, 393), the lower composition of agricultural capital compared to that of industry 'is a *historical* difference and can therefore disappear', and so absolute rent would also tend to disappear as the productivity of agricultural labour approaches that of industry. In this case, the production price of an agricultural product would approach its value and any rent paid by the capitalist tenants would constitute a monopoly rent. The monopoly rent is paid above the value of the agricultural product, and it would thus be limited not by value, as in the case of absolute rent, but by foreign agricultural trade, competition among landowners and the consumers' budget (see Marx, 1894, pp. 758, 805, 810; 1905, p. 332).

Marx's theory of absolute rent has been by-passed by the controversy over the transformation of values into production prices, and has been little used as a conceptual device to analyse the effect of landownership on capitalist investment in agriculture or the effect of landownership on agricultural prices. Unfortunately, absolute rent has been neglected by Marxist economists, while it seems to be a favourite *bête noire* among sympathetic critics of Marx, such as Bortkiewicz (1911) and Emmanuel (1972). As a result, absolute rent has an uncertain future as a useful theoretical device, despite the fact that in many countries capitalist agriculture still largely conforms to the two basic assumptions made by Marx more than a hundred years ago.

BIBLIOGRAPHY

Bortkiewicz, L. 1911. La teoria della rendita fondiaria di Rodbertus e la dottrina di Marx sulla rendita fondiaria assoluta. In *La Teoria Economica di Marx e altri saggi su Böhm-Bawerk, Walras e Pareto*, Turin: Einaudi, 1971.

Emmauel, A. 1972. *Unequal Exchange*. New York: Monthly Review Press.

Flichman, G. 1977. *La Renta del Suelo y el Desarrollo Agrario Argentino*. Buenos Aires: Siglo Veintiuno Editores.

Lenin, V.I. 1901. The agrarian question and the 'criics of Marx'. In V.I. Lenin, *Collected Works*,Vol. V, Moscow: Progress Publishers, 1973.

Marx, K. 1894. *Capital*, Vol. III. Moscow, Progress Publishers, 1971.

Marx, K. 1905. *Theories of Surplus Value*, Part II. Moscow: Progress Publishers, 1968.

Murray, R. 1977. Value and the theory of rent: I. *Capital & Class* 1(3), Autumn, 100–122.

Abstract and Concrete Labour

ANWAR SHAIKH

The reproduction of society requires the production and distribution of the mass of products which forms the material basis of its existence. This in turn means that each society must somehow ensure that its available social labour time is regularly directed, in particular quantities and proportions, towards the specific applications needed to ensure social reproduction. As Marx points out, 'every child knows that a nation which ceased to work . . . even for a few weeks, would perish' (Marx, 1867a).

The above implies that all labour has two distinct aspects. As a part of the general pool of society's labour, it is merely one portion of the human energy available to the community. In this respect all labour is essentially the same, representing the expenditure of 'human labour-power in general' in its capacity as simply one part of the division of general social labour. This is labour as *social labour. But at the same time*, individual labour occurs in the form of a specific activity aimed at a specific result. Here it is the particular quality of the labour, its determination, etc. which is relevant. This is labour as *concrete labour*, related to the concrete result of its activity.

Although the dialectic between concrete and social labour is a necessary part of social reprduction, their inter-connection is hard to discern within societies which produce things-for-exchange (commodities), because in this case individual activities are undertaken without any apparent consideration for the necessity of a social division of labour. All useful objects now appear to be naturally endowed with quantitative worth in exchange (*exchange value*), and this apparently natural property in turn seems to regulate the actual division of labour.

It is at this point that Marx introduces two crucial questions. What precisely is a commodity? And more importantly, why does it become socially necessary to attach an exchange value to it? He begins his answer by observing that as a useful good a commodity is simply a concrete bundle of different socially desirable properties. In this respect it is similar to particular, qualitatively distinct useful objects in all social forms of organization. But as an exchangeable good, its

42

salient property is that it is treated socially as being qualitatively *identical* to every other commodity. This is manifested in the fact that when commodities are assigned differing quantities of exchange value, expressed in some common measure, they are thereby being socially regarded as qualitatively alike, all reducible to the same homogeneous measure of quantitative worth. A commodity is therefore a doublet of opposite characteristics: a multiplicity of concrete useful properties (use value) on the one hand, and a single magnitude of homogeneous quantitative worth (exchange value) on the other.

The double character of a commodity is strikingly reminiscent of the previously noted duality of labour as particular concrete labour and as general social labour. Indeed, in commodity producing society the various concrete labours 'only count as homogeneous labour when under *objectified husk*', that is, when they 'relate to one another as human labour by relating *their products to one another as values*'. The concrete labours are thus counted as social labour only when they are *valorized*, and the necessity of exchange value lies precisely in the fact that it is through this device that a society containing apparently independent private producers comes to grips with the social content of their individual labours. To answer Marx's second question, exchange value is the particular historical mode of expressing the general necessity of social labour.

The notion that exchange value is a historically specific way of accounting for social labour time does not imply that the terms of exchange of commodities always reflect the quantities of valorized social labour time that went into their respective production. Indeed, Marx distinguishes between the case in which particular useful objects are produced for direct use and only accidentally or occasionally find their way into the sphere of exchange, and the case in which goods are produced *in order* to be exchanged. In the first case, when for example otherwise self-sufficient tribes occasionally barter a few of their products, the relation between concrete labour and social labour is effectively determined within each social group, and exchange merely serves to create a temporary equivalence between the respective social labours involved. Because the objects in question are produced as useful objects and become commodities only when they enter exchange, the labours involved are valorized only in exchange itself. Moreover, since these activities do not depend fundamentally on exchange (and hence on the valorization of their labour), the precise conditions of exchange can in turn be decided by a variety of factors, ranging from broad structural influences to merely conjunctural or even accidental ones.

At the opposite extreme is the case of goods produced solely for exchange. Now, the particular labours involved are *aimed* at producing exchangeable goods, and the valorization of these labours is an intrinsic part of their reproduction. As producers of commodities, these labours create not only bundles of useful properties (use-values), but also amounts of abstract quantitative worth. In the former aspect, they are of course concrete labours; but in the latter, they are *value creating* activities whose content as social labour is manifest only in-and-through the abstract quantitative worth of their products. To emphasize this particular historical form of the duality of labour, Marx identifies that labour which is engaged in the production of commodities as being both concrete (use-value creating) labour, and *abstract* (value creating) labour.

Three further points must be briefly mentioned. First of all, Marx argues that abstract labour time not only stands behind the producton of commodities, but that the magnitudes of these labour times actually regulate the exchange relations of these commodities. To this end, he defines the quantity of abstract labour 'socially necessary . . . to produce an article under the normal conditions of production' as the (inner) *value* of the commodity, since it is the 'intrinsic measure' of the exchange value. Secondly, he distinguishes between the conditions under which the exchange relations of commodities are dependent on their (labour) values, and the conditions in which they are controlled by them. It is only in the latter instance, in which capitalism has effectively generalized commodity production, that the reproduction of society is regulated by the law of value. Lastly, he notes that once commodity production is indeed generalized, so that social labour appears only under an objective husk, then the social relation among producers is actually regulated by the mysterious value-relation between their products. In this topsy-turvy world, a social relation among persons appears in their eyes to be in fact a relation among things. This is what Marx calls the Fetishism of Commodities which is characteristic of capitalism.

BIBLIOGRAPHY

Marx, K. 1867a. *Capital*, Vol. I. 1st end, ch. 1 and Appendix to ch. 1. In *Value: Studies by Karl Marx*, trans. and ed. A. Dragstedt, London: New York Publications, 1976; New York: Labour Publications.

Marx, K. 1867b. *Capital*, Vol. I. Introdced by E. Mandel, London: Penguin, 1976, ch. 1; New York, Vintage Books, 1977.

Marx, K. 1879. Marginal notes to A. Wagner's *Textbook on Political Economy*. In *Value: Studies by Karl Marx*, trans. and ed. A. Dragstedt, London: New Park Publications, 1976; New York: Labour Publications.

Alienation

GEORGE CATEPHORES

This concept was introduced into economics from philosophy by Karl Marx, in his youthful *Economic and Philosophic Manuscripts*, written in 1844 but appearing in print only in 1932. Prior to the 1844 *Manuscripts*, alienation constituted a topic of purely philosophical speculation. Marx studied it in Hegel and Feuerbach, while present-day research claims to have observed anticipations of the idea in authors as old and as various as Jean-Jacques Rousseau, Calvin, Cicero and even Plato.

For a concept so widely used, no fully comprehensive definition seems possible. Its common element, in all authors, consists of the reference to a certain loss of self, accompanied by feelings of unhappiness or psychological *malaise*, arising from conditions of human bondage. This apart, Marx's immediate philosophical forerunners treated alienation in strikingly different manners. For Hegel, it represents a phase in the development of the Absolute Idea which, according to him, created nature by objectifying, materializing, itself and thereby losing its identity in the object of its own creation. The Idea would recover its original integrity by means of the conscious part of nature, the human being, when human history culminated, through suffering, to the point of the Absolute State (an ideal social regime defined by Hegel as totally free of alienation). In Feuerbach, on the other hand, it was not the Idea but man who became alienated, by submitting to the domination of – mainly religious – ideologies. These emanated from the human mind but were misunderstood by man to be autonomous, transcendental entities, superior to mankind. Man could get rid of elination by simply rejecting such phantoms and exercising his faculties naturally, untrammelled by religious constraints.

Marx adopted Feuerbach's materialist, or rather anthropocentric, standpoint but shifted the ground of discussion decisively from psychology to economic reality, since '... the whole of human servitude is involved in the relation of the worker to production and every relation of servitude is but a modification of this relation, (Marx, 1844, p. 280). At the same time Marx also drew inspiration from Hegel's concept of the alienated Idea which suggested to him, by analogy, the concept of alienated labour: a creative force, producing not Nature, certainly, but the man-made human environment inside which, however, man lost his identity.

This transition, from the Idea to labour, apart from constituting the beginning of the introduction of historical materialism into modern thought by Marx, transformed the whole discussion of alienation by infusing economic concreteness into the prevailing, until then, philosophical generalities. Marx enriched the concept with real content, drawn from the classical economists (Smith, Say, Ricardo) as well as from some of their early socialist critics (Moses Hess, Proudhon) and on this basis built a dense but thorough critique of capitalist society. The economic morphology of alienation that he proposed can be summarized in the following four points:

(a) In the content of private property, the producer becomes alienated from his product through the mechanism of exchange, which makes the destination of his product a matter of indifference to him. This loss of interest in one's own product is pseudo-compensated by excessive though, from a human development point of view, pointless acquisitiveness towards the products of others. Passive consumerism of this kind is fanned into rapacious greediness by the intermediation in exchange of money.

(b) Trade in commodities leads eventually to trade in human labour as a commodity. This is alienated labour in a strict sense; its ownership actually passes from the worker to a person alien to him, the capitalist employer. The worker's product follows the fate of his labour. Both arrangements offended against man's natural sense of justice, which sanctions the inalienability of the human personality and awards ownership of products to the maker rather than the non-maker of them. Having to accept such violations degrades morally both worker and capitalist.

(c) Under alienation in the sense of (b), productive labour neither expresses nor satisfies any internal human need to create. It becomes a chore imposed by others and undertaken merely as a means of satisfying needs external to the labour activity itself. Work becomes boring, charmless, unsatisfying. The worker is treated as a mere tool, whom labour de-skills if not actually damages physically or mentally.

(d) From a broader point of view, man's specificity as a natural being (what Marx called man's 'species-being') resides in his capacity to adapt nature to his needs in a conscious manner rather than suffer natural selection to adapt his own characteristics to the dictates of the environment. In humanizing nature, labour produces results that reach beyond each individual's sphere to become beneficial for others. Production is inherently a mutually supportive activity, even when not undertaken jointly. It therefore provides a crucial basis for human solidarity. Economic antagonism based on private property, on the other hand, makes individuals act at cross-purposes, frustrating each other's aims and becoming subject to arbitrary domination by their products (a fact dramatized during economic crises). Hence alienation undermines both solidarity and the capacity for purposeful interaction with the environment. It affects the very substance of the 'species-being', giving rise to feelings of loneliness, powerlessness and aimlessness that afflict human lives.

For the overcoming of alientation Marx postulated the abolition of private property in Communism, which, with overtones from Hegel's Absolute State, he described as '...the genuine resolution of the conflict between man and nature and between man and man ... between objectification and self-confirmation, between freedom and necessity, between the individual and the species' (Marx, 1844, p. 296).

The success of Marx's morphology of alienation can be gauged by the fact that, during the modern revival of the idea, social science was unable to add to the concept any important new dimensions, limiting itself to assessing, sometimes empirically, the degree of presence, in various social groups, of the characteristics of alienation listed by Marx (Blauner, 1964). Marx in 1844 was less successful in the analysis of causal links between the moral, psychological and economic aspects of capitalist society. At times he argued as if causality ran from alienation to the economy; a clearly counter-marxian view if alientation were to be seen as a mainly psychological phenomenon. Even if one accepted this interpretation, as representative of a young, immature Marx, the question would still remain: what caused alienation?

In a sense Marx spent the rest of his life trying to answer this question. In the course of his research, however, he discovered that the explanation of the main aspects of social processes in capitalism, as well as the forecast of a future downfall of the capitalist system, could be founded on strictly economic grounds, without necessarily referring to concepts imported from ethics, psychology or philosophy. He, therefore, started losing interest in alienation as a *causal explanation* of capitalist institutions; in works published during his lifetime, the relevant term is little used. He did maintain a lively interest in the psychosomatic and moral degradation (i.e. the alienation) of people, particularly of workers, as an *effect* of capitalism. But he chose to place the emphasis on the 'hard science' rather than the ethical aspect of his teaching.

In this he was followed by most of the ideologists associated with the massive political movements which, inspired by his ideas, sprang up after his death in Europe by the end of the 19th and the beginning of the 20th century. They found it practically more expedient and more convincing to stress the economic rather than the ethical flaws of capitalism. In such a climate, publication of the 1844 *Manuscripts* in 1932 (or the earlier independent rediscovery of the importance of certain aspects of alienation by Lukacs in his 1923 *History and Class Consciousness*) could not exert much influence on marxist thought.

The renaissance of interest in alienation – a most surprising intellectual event, for a concept that had lain hibernating for a whole century – came after World War II. The economic resilience of capitalism in industrially advanced countries; the desiccation of official marxist ideology, narrowly based on Marx's 'hard science'; the disillusionment caused by the persistence of hard and unequal conditions for labour in the Communist part of the world, despite abolition of private property there, all combined to lead socially critical thought to seek ethical and psychological, in addition to purely economic, underpinnings for its efforts.

In this reorientation, alienation played a central role, particularly among dissident intellectuals in Communist countries (Rudolph Bahro, Agnes Heller, István Mészáros, Rudi Supek and others) to whom it offered a marxist platform for a humanistic criticism of the regime from the inside. At the same time non-marxists adopted the idea in their analysis of the present and future of capitalism, attributing certain symptoms of alientation (boredom, loneliness, purposelessness) to the achievement of affluence rather than the persistence of social antagonism (Kahn and Wiener, 1969). Thus alienation has, to some extent, transcended its original anticapitalist, strictly marxist, character to become a more widely accepted tool for the critical study of modern industrial society, irrespective of the ownership structure prevailing in each case.

BIBLIOGRAPHY

Main works

Feuerbach, L 1841. *The Essence of Christianity*. New York: Harper, 1957.

Hegel, G.F.W. 1832. *The Phenomenology of Mind*. New York: Humanities Press, 1964.

Hegel, G.F.W. 1833–4. *The Science of Logic*. London: Allen & Unwin, 1929; New York: Macmillan, 1951.

Marx, K. 1844. *Economic and Philosophic Manuscripts of 1844*. In Karl Marx and Frederick Engels, *Collected Works*, Vol. 3, London: Lawrence & Wishart, 1975; New York, International Publishers.

Marx, K. 1857–8. *Grundrisse*. Ed. M. Nicolaus, London: Penguin Books, 1973; New York: Random House.

Other works

Althusser, L. 1965. *For Marx*. New York: Pantheon, 1970.

Bahro, R. 1978. *The Alternative in Eastern Europe*. London: New Left Books.

Blauner, R. 1964. *Alienation and Freedom: The Factory Worker and his Industry*. Chicago: University of Chicago Press.

Catephores, G. 1972. Marxian alienation – a clarification. *Oxford Economic Papers* 24(1), March, 124–36.

Elliot, J.E. 1979. Continuity and change in the evolution of Marx's theory of alienation: from the *Manuscripts* through the *Grundrisse* to *Capital*. *History of Political Economy* 11(3), Fall, 317–62.

Fromm, E. 1966. *Marx's Concept of Man*. New York: F. Ungar.

Godelier, M. 1966. *Rationalité et irrationalité en économie*. Paris: Maspero.

Heller, A. 1976. *The Theory of Need in Marx*. London: Alison & Busby; New York; St Martin's Press.

Hook, S. 1950. *From Hegel to Marx*. New York: Humanities Press.

Hyppolite, J. 1969. *Studies on Marx and Hegel*. New York: Basic Books.

Kahn, H. and Wiener, A.J. 1969. *The Year 2000*. London: Macmillan.

Lukacs, G. 1923. *History and Class Consciousness*. London: Merlin, 1971.

Mandel, E. 1967. *The Formation of the Economic Thought of Karl Marx*. London: New Left Books, 1971.

Marcuse, H. 1954. *Reason and Revolution, Hegel and the Rise of Social Theory*. 2nd edn, New York: Humanities Press.

Mészáros, I. 1975. *Marx's Theory of Alienation*. 4th edn, London: Merlin Press.

Ollman, B. 1971. *Alientation: Marx's Conception of Man in Capitalist Society*. London and New York: Cambridge University Press.

Supek, R. 1965. Dialectique de la pratique sociale. *Praxis*, No. 1.

Tucker, R.C. 1961. *Philosophy and Myth in Karl Marx*. Cambridge: Cambridge University Press.

Wood, A. 1981. *Karl Marx*. London: Routledge & Kegal Paul.

Paul Alexander Baran

PAUL M. SWEEZY

Paul Baran, the eminent Marxist economist, was born on 8 December 1910 in Nikolaev, Russia, the son of a medical doctor who was a member of the Menshevik branch of the Russian revolutionary movement. After the October Revolution the family moved to Germany, where Baran's formal education began. In 1925 the father was offered a position in Moscow and returned to the USSR. Baran began his studies in economics at the University of Moscow the following year. Both his ideas and his politics were deeply and permanently influenced by the intense debates and struggles within the Communist Party in the late 1920s. Offered a research assignment at the Agricultural Academy in Berlin in late 1928, he enrolled in the University of Berlin, and when his assignment at the Agricultural Academy ended he accepted an assistantship at the famous Institute for Social Research in Frankfurt. This experience too had a lasting influence on his intellectual development.

Leaving Germany shortly after Hitler's rise to power, Baran sought without success to find academic employment in France. He therefore moved to Warsaw, where his paternal uncles had a flourishing international lumber business. During the next few years he travelled widely as a representative of his uncles' business, ending up in London in 1938. With the approach of World War II, however, he decided to take what savings he had been able to accumulate, move to the United States, and resume his interrupted academic career.

Arriving in the United States in the fall of 1939, he was accepted as a graduate student in economics at Harvard. From there he went to wartime Washington, where he served in the Office of Price Administration, the Research and Development branch of the Office of Strategic Services, and the United States Strategic Bombing Survey, ending in 1945–6 as Deputy Chief of the Survey's mission to Japan. Back in the United States, he took a job at the Department of Commerce and gave lectures at George Washington University before being offered a position in the Research Department of the Federal Reserve Bank of New York. After three years in New York, he accepted an offer to join the economics faculty at Stanford University and was promoted to a full professorship in 1951, a position he retained until hs death of a heart attack on 26 March 1964.

Baran was not a prolific writer, but his two main books. *The Political Economy of Growth* (1957) and (in collaboration with Paul M. Sweezy) *Monopoly Capital: An Essay on the American Economic and Social Order* (1966), are generally considered to be among the most important works in the Marxian tradition of the post-World War II period.

The Political Economy of Growth is concerned with the processes and conditions of economic growth (or development, the terms are used interchangeably) in both industrialized and underdeveloped societies, with a special emphasis throughout on the ways the two relate to and interact with each other. It is at once an outstanding work of scholarship weaving an intricate pattern of theory and history, and at the same time a passionate polemic against mainstream economics. Its chief (innovative) analytical concept is that of 'potential surplus', defined as 'the difference between the output that *could* be produced in a given natural and technological environment with the help of employable productive resources, and what might be regarded as essential consumption.' (This concept presupposes Marx's 'surplus value', extending and modifying it for the particular purposes of the study in hand.) Two long chapters, totally 90 pages, apply the concepts of surplus and potential surplus to the analysis of monopoly capitalism in ways that would later be refined and elaborated in *Monopoly Capital*. Three chapters (115 pages) follow on 'backwardness' (also called underdevelopment), and it is for these that the book has become famous, especially in the Third World.

Baran begins this analysis with a question which may be said to define the focus of the whole work: 'Why is it that in the backward capitalist countries there has been no advance along the lines of capitalist development that are familiar from the history of other capitalist countries, and why is it that forward movement there has been slow or altogether absent?' His answer, in briefest summary, is as follows: all present-day capitalist societies evolved from precapitalist conditions which Baran for convenience labels 'feudal' (explicitly recognizing that a variety of social formations are subsumed under this heading). Viable capitalist societies could have emerged in various parts of the world; actually the decisive breathrough occurred in Western Europe (Baran speculates on the reasons, but in any case they are not crucial to the subsequent history). Having achieved its headstart, Europe proceeded to conquer weaker precapitalist countries, plunder their accumulated stores of wealth, subject them to unequal trading relations, and reorganize their economic structures to serve the needs of the Europeans. This was the origin of the great divide in the world capitalist system between the developed and the underdeveloped parts. As the system spread into the four corners of the globe, new areas were added, mostly to the underdeveloped part but in a few cases to the developed (North America, Australia, Japan). One of the highlights of Baran's study is the brilliant historical sketch of the contrasting ways India and Japan were incorporated into the world capitalist system, the one as a hapless dependency, the other as a strong contender

51

for a place at the top of the pyramid of power. Baran's message to the Third World was loud and clear: once trapped in the world capitalist system, there is no hope for genuine progress; only a revolutionary break can open the road to a better future. The message has been widely heard. Most of the revolutionary movements of the Third World have been deeply influenced, directly or indirectly, by Paul Baran's *Political Economy of Growth*.

The economic analysis of *Monopoly Capital* is a development and systematization of ideas already contained in *the Political Economy of Growth* and Paul Sweezy's *The Theory of Capitalist Development* (1942). The central theme is that in a mature capitalist economy dominated by a handful of giant corporations the potential for capital accumulation far exceeds the profitable investment opportunities provided by the normal *modus operandi* of the private enterprise system. This results in a deepening tendency to stagnation which, if the system is to survive, must be continuously and increasingly counteracted by internal and external factors (for an elaboration of this analysis, see MONOPOLY CAPITALISM). In the authors' estimation – not always shared, or even understood by critics – the new and original contributions of *Monopoly Capital* had to do mainly with these counteracting factors and their far-reaching consequences for the history, politics and culture of American society during the period from roughly the 1890s to the 1950s when the book was written. They intended it, in other words, as much more than a work of economics in the usual meaning of the term.

SELECTED WORKS
There is a comprehensive bibliography of Baran's writings in English in a special issue of *Monthly Review*, 'In Memory of Paul Alexander Baran. Born at Nikolaev, the Ukraine, 8 December 1910. Died at San Francisco, California, 26 March 1964', 16(11), March 1965. This also includes statements on his life and work by more than three dozen contributors, most of whom had been his friends or colleagues.

1957. *The Political Economy of Growth*. New York: Monthly Review Press. 2nd edn, with a new preface, 1962.
1966. (With P.M. Sweezy.) *Monopoly Capital: An Essay on the American Economic and Social Order*. New York: Monthly Review Press.
1970. *The Longer View: Essays Toward a Critique of Political Economy*. Edited by J. O'Neill, preface by P.M. Sweezy, New York: Monthly Review Press. This volume, which follows an outline prepared before his death by the author, brings together his most important hitherto scattered essays and reviews.

Otto Bauer

TOM BOTTOMORE

Born 5 September 1881, Vienna; died 4 July 1938, Paris. A member of a talented Jewish family and the only son of a textile manufacturer, Bauer became interested in Marxism and the 'revisionist' controversy while still in high school, and went on to study philosophy, law and political economy at the University of Vienna. He became the leader of the Austrian socialist party (SPÖ) and a prolific writer on economic and political questions. Bauer is best known for his study of nationalities and nationalism (1907), which remains the classic Marxist work on the subject, but he also wrote extensively on economics and his first major essay (1904), which brought him to the notice of Karl Kautsky, discussed the Marxist theory of economic crises. In his early writings he adopted a 'disproportionality' theory such as Hilferding expounded more fully in *Finance Capital* (1910); that is, a theory which sees the fundamental causes of crises in the 'anarchy of capitalist production', and particularly in the disproportion which regularly emerges between production in the two sectors of capital goods and consumer goods. However, in his last published book (1936) he propounded an underconsumption theory of crises which subsequently influenced the work of Sweezy. In the course of his analyses of economic crises Bauer introduced, or emphasized more strongly than other Marxist writers, such factors as the existing stock of capital, technical progress and population growth.

Bauer also discussed economic questions in a broader context in his study of the development of capitalism and socialism after World War I, of which only the first volume was published (1931). In this work he examined the rationalization of capitalist production in three spheres: technical rationalization, the rationalization and intensification of work, and the rationalization of the enterprise (especially the growth of 'scientific management'). The final part of the book dealt with the limits to capitalist rationalization revealed by the economic crisis, its consequences for the working class, which he analysed in terms of a distinction between the 'labour process' (a concept which has become central in much recent Marxist political economy) and the 'life process', and the nature of rationalization in a socialist society.

53

Besides his major studies of nationalism and of the capitalist economy Bauer published many other important essays and books: on the Austrian revolution (where he strongly opposed the idea of a Bolshevik type revolution and began to elaborate his conception of the 'slow revolution'), on violence in politics and the doctrine of 'defensive violence', on fascism, on the philosophical foundations of Austro-Marxism, and on Marxism and ethics. His work as a whole represents one of the most important and interesting contributions to Marxist thought in the 20th century. The defeat of the SPÖ in the civil war of 1934, which drove Bauer into exile, was attributed by some critics to his excessively cautious and gradualist policies; on the other hand, the social, educational and cultural achievements of 'Red Vienna' in the 1920s and early 1930s showed the effectiveness of such policies when the socialists were in power, and they have had a major influence on Austria's development since 1945.

SELECTED WORKS

1904–5. Marx' Theorie der Wirtschaftskrisen. *Die Neue Zeit* 23.

1907. *Die Nationalitätenfrage und die Sozialdemokratie.* Vienna: Wiener Volksbuchhandlung. 2nd enlarged edition with new Preface. 1924.

1923. *Die Österreichische Revolution.* Abridged English version, New York: Burt Franklin, 1925; reprinted, 1970.

1931. *Kapitalismus und Socialismus nach dem Weltkrieg.* Vol. I: *Rationalisierung oder Fehlrationalisierung?* Vienna: Wiener Volksbuchhandlung.

1936. *Zwischen zwei Weltkriegen?* Bratislava: Eugen Prager Verlag.

BIBLIOGRAPHY

Bottomore, T. and Goode, P. (eds) 1978. *Austro-Marxism.* Oxford: Clarendon Press.

Botz, G. 1974. Genesis und Inhalt der Faschismustheorien Otto Bauers. *International Review of Social History* 19, 28–53.

Braunthal, J. 1961. *Otto Bauer: Eine Auswahl aus seinem Lebenswerk.* Vienna: Wiener Volksbuchhandlung.

Hilferding, R. 1910. *Das Finanzkapital.* Vienna: I. Brand. Trans. M. Watnick and S. Gordon as *Finance Capital*, ed. T. Bottomore, London: Routledge & Kegan Paul, 1981.

Eduard Bernstein

TOM BOTTOMORE

Born in Berlin, 6 January 1850; died in Berlin, 18 December 1932. The son of a Jewish railway engineer and the seventh child in a large family of fifteen children, Bernstein grew up in a lower middle-class district of Berlin in 'genteel poverty'. He did not complete his studies at the Gymnasium and in 1866 he began an apprenticeship in a Berlin bank. Three years later he became a bank clerk and remained in this post until 1878, but he continued to study independently and for a time aspired to work in the theatre. He became a socialist in 1871, largely through sympathy with the opposition of Bebel, Liebknecht and others to the Franco-Prussian war, and strongly influenced by reading Marx's study of the Paris Commune, *The Civil War in France* (1871). In 1872 Bernstein joined the Social Democratic Workers' Party, and in 1875 he was a delegate to the conference in Gotha which brought about the union of that party with Lasalle's General Union of German Workers to form a new Socialist Workers' Party, later the Social Democratic Party (SPD). From that time Bernstein became a leading figure in the socialist movement, and in 1878, just before Bismarck's anti-Socialist law was passed, he moved to Switzerland as secretary to a wealthy young socialist, Karl Höchberg, who expounded a form of Utopian socialism in the journal *Die Zukunft* which he had founded. It was in 1878 also that Bernstein read Engels' *Anti-Dühring* which, he said, 'converted me to Marxism', and he corresponded with Engels for the first time in June 1879. After some misunderstandings with Marx and Engels, who were suspicious of his relationship with Höchberg, Bernstein won their confidence during a visit to London and in January 1881, with their support, the became editor of *Der Sozialdemokrat* (the newspaper of the SPD, established in 1879). It was, as Gay 1(52) notes, 'the beginning of a great career'.

In 1888 the Swiss government, under pressure from Germany, expelled Bernstein and three of his colleagues on the ᶜ   ᵔkrat and they moved to London to continue publication there. The   xile in England, which lasted until 1901, was crucial in the formatio. .   ..stein's ideas. He became

55

a close friend of Engels, who made him his literary executor (jointly with Bebel), and developed a stronger interest in historical and theoretical subjects, contributing regularly to Kautsky's *Die Neue Zeit* and publishing in 1895 his first major work, a study of socialism and democracy in the English revolution (entitled *Cromwell and Communism* in the English translation). Bernstein's major contributions in this study, which he later described as 'the only large scale attempt on my part to discuss historical events on the basis of Marx's and Engels' materialist conception of history', were to analyse the civil war as a class conflict between the rising bourgeoisie and both the feudal aristocracy and the workers, and to give prominence to the ideas of the radical movements in the revolution (the Levellers and Diggers), and in particular those of Gerrard Winstanley, who had been ignored by previous historians.

At the same time Bernstein established close relations with the socialists of the Fabian Society and came to be strongly influenced by their 'gradualist' doctrines and their rejection of Marxism. In a letter to Bebel (20 October 1898) he described how, after giving a lecture to the Fabian Soceity on 'What Marx really taught', he became extremely dissatisfied with his 'well-meaning rescue attempt' and decided that it was necessary 'to become clear just where Marx is right and where he is wrong'. Soon after Engels's death Bernstein began to publish in *Die Neue Zeit* (from 1896 to 1898) a series of articles on 'problems of socialism' which represented a systematic attempt to revise Marxist theory in the light of the recent development of capitalism and of the socialist movement. The articles set off a major controversy in the SPD, in which Kautsky defended Marxist orthodoxy and urged Bernstein to expound his views in a more comprehensive way, as he then proceeded to do in his book on 'the premisses of socialism and the tasks of social democracy' (1899; entitled *Evolutionary Socialism* in the English translation), which made him internationally famous as the leader of the 'revisionist movement'.

Bernstein's arguments in *Evolutionary Socialism* were directed primarily against an 'economic collapse' theory of the demise of capitalism and the advent of socialism, and against the idea of an increasing polarization of society between bourgeoisie and proletariat, accompanied by intensifying class conflict. On the first point he was attacking the Marxist orthodoxy of the SPD, expounded in particular by Kautsky, rather than Marx's own theory, in which the analysis of economic crises and their political consequences was not fully worked out, and indeed allowed for diverse interpretations (Bottomore, 1985). The central part of Bernstein's study, however, concerned the changes in class structure since Marx's time, and their implications. In this view, the polarization of classes anticipated by Marx was not occurring, because the concentration of capital in large enterprises was accompanied by a development of new small and medium-sized businesses, property ownership was becoming more widespread, the general level of living was rising, the middle class was increasing rather than diminishing in numbers, and the structure of capitalist society was not being simplified, but was becoming more complex and differentiated. Bernstein summarized his ideas in a note found among his papers after his death: 'Peasants do not sink; middle class does not disappear; crises do not grow ever larger; misery and serfdom do not increase. There *is* increase in insecurity, dependence, social distance, social character of production, functional superfluity of property owners' (cited by Gay, 1952, p. 244).

On some points Bernstein was clearly mistaken. With the further development of capitalism, peasant production has declined rapidly and has been superseded to a great extent by 'agri-business'; economic crises did become larger, at least up to the depression of 1929–33. It was his analysis of the changing class structure which had the greatest influence, becoming a major issue in the social sciences, and above all in sociology, in part through the work of Max Weber, whose critical discussion of Marxism in his lecture on socialism (1918) largely restates Bernstein's arguments. There is a more general sense in which Bernstein's ideas have retained their significance; namely, in their assertion of the increasingly 'social character' of production and the likelihood of a gradual transition to socialism by the permeation of capitalist society with socialist institutions. In a different form the same notion is expressed by Schumpeter (1942) in his conception of a gradual 'socialization of the economy'; a conception which can also be traced back to Marx (Bottomore, 1985).

One other aspect of Bernstein's thought should be noted. Influenced by the neo-Kantian movement in German philosophy and by positivism (in an essay of 1924 he noted that 'my way of thinking would make me a member of the school of Positivist philosophy and sociology') Bernstein made a sharp distinction between science and ethics and went on to argue, in his lecture 'How is scientific socialism possible?' (1901), that the socialist movement necessarily embodies an ethical or 'ideal' element: 'It is something that *ought* to be, or a movement towards something that *ought* to be.' From this standpoint he criticized in a more general way a purely economic interpretation of history, and especially the kind of 'economic determinism' that was prevalent in the orthodox Marxism of the SPD; but in so doing he cannot be said to have diverged radically from the conceptions of Marx and Engels (and indeed he cited Engels's various qualifications of 'historical materialism' in support of this own views).

Bernstein's book met with a vigorous and effective response in Rosa Luxemburg's *Sozialreform oder Revolution* (1899), and the SPD became divided between 'radicals', 'revisionists' and the 'centre' (represented by Bebel and Kautsky); and although the latter retained control Bernstein remained a leading figure in the party until 1914. But his growing opposition to the war led him to form a separate organization in 1916 and then to join the left-wing Independent Social Democratic Party of Germany (USPD) in 1917. After the war Bernstein became increasingly disillusioned with the ineffectualness of the SPD in countering the reactionary nationalist attacks on the Weimar Republic, his influence waned, and his last years were spent in isolation.

SELECTED WORKS
1895. *Cromwell and Communism*. London: Allen & Unwin, 1930.

1899. *Evolutionary Socialism*. New York: Huebsch, 1909. Reprinted, New York: Schocken, 1961.
1901. Wie ist wissenschaftlicher Sozialismus möglich? *Sozialistische Monatshefte*.

BIBLIOGRAPHY
Bottomore, T. 1985. *Theories of Modern Capitalism*. London: Allen & Unwin.
Gap, P. 1952. *The Dilemmas of Democratic Socialism*. New York: Columbia University Press.
Luxemburg, R. 1899. *Sozialreform oder Revolution*. Trans. as *Reform or Revolution*. New York: Three Arrows, 1937.
Schumpeter, J.A. 1942. *Capitalism, Socialism and Democracy*. London: Allen & Unwin, 5th edn, 1976.
Weber, M. 1918. Socialism. English trans. in *Max Weber: The Interpretation of Social Reality*, ed. J.E.T. Eldridge, London: Michael Joseph, 1970.

Bourgeoisie

J. FOSTER

The term *bourgeoisie* originally referred to the legal status of the town citizen in feudal France. In the *Encyclopédie* Diderot contrasted the political subordination of the *citoyen bourgeois* with the self-governing *citoyen magistrat* of ancient Greece. At the same time the French *bourgeoisie* (this term was first used in the 13th century) possessed certain economic and social rights, implicitly associated with the property required for trade, that distinguished it from the ordinary urban inhabitant or *domicilié* (Diderot, 1753, III, 486–9).

Something of the same concept can be found in Hegel's use of the term *bürgerliche Gesellschaft* ('civil society'). Civil society represented the legal and governmental framework required for the 'actual achievement of selfish ends', the independent sphere of activity for the economic individual. It was in contrast to what Hegel saw as the embodiment of 'absolute rationality', the State, representing the universal interest of the whole community (Hegel, 1820, p. 247).

Marx inherited, and initially used, *bourgeois* and *bürgerlich* in this restricted sense. Writing in 1842 on the opposition of the Rhineland urban estates to press freedom, he commented: 'we are faced here with the opposition of the bourgeois, not of the citoyen' (Marx, 1842, p. 168). The petty and philistine motivation of the bourgeois is contrasted with the revolutionary impulses of the wider *Tiers Etat* as defined, for instance, by Siéyes (1789). By 1843–4, however, Marx had adopted an analysis of social change in terms of economically defined class forces and consequently identified the bourgeoisie, rather than an undifferentiated *Tiers Etat*, as the revolutionary force which transformed feudal France. 'The negative general significance of the French nobility and the French clergy defined the positive general position of the immediately adjacent and opposed class of the *bourgeoisie*' (Marx, 1844, p. 185). Four years later Marx gave classic expression to this historically progressive role in the *Communist Manifesto*:

> The bourgeoisie, during its rule of scarce one hundred years, has created more massive and more colossal productive forces than all preceding generations

together . . . what earlier century had even a presentiment that such productive forces slumbered in the lap of social labour? (Marx, 1848, p. 489).

At the same time, Marx also made a historically specific redefinition of *bürgerlich* or civil society. Civil rights, far from being abstract freedoms which derived from the political character of the State, in fact expressed the material interests of a class, the private owners of capital, and it was these that ultimately determined the nature of the State. 'The political revolution against feudalism' regarded the sphere of civil society as 'the basis of its existence'. Man 'was not freed from property, he received the freedom to own property' (Marx, 1844, p. 167).

The crux of Marx's innovation was, therefore, to reconceive the terms bourgeoisie and bourgeois society in forms which anchored them to a particular mode of production. In the *Manifesto* the bourgeoisie is used as a synonym for capital ('the bourgeoisie, i.e. capital') while the 'executive of the modern state' is described as 'but a committee for managing the common affairs of the bourgeoisie as a whole' (Marx, 1848, pp. 63 and 69).

Within this usage Marx invariably presents the bourgeoisie as historically contingent and subject to 'the immanent laws of capitalist production': to the 'centralisation of capital' and the contradictions bound up in its social relationship to labour. 'One capitalist kills many. Hand in hand with this centralisation, of the expropriation of many capitalists by few, develops on an ever extending scale, the co-operative form of the labour process . . .' (Marx, 1867, p. 714–15). Accordingly, as Marx stressed in his *Eighteenth Brumaire of Louis Napoleon*, an analysis of the bourgeoisie, and of is internal 'factions' and 'interests', had to start with a concrete assessment of its particular forms of property and their changing place within capitalist production: 'upon the different forms of property, upon its social conditions of existence, rises an entire superstructure of distinct and differently formed sentiments . . .' (Marx, 1852, p. 128).

The petty bourgeoisie, for instance, represented an unstable and transitional layer between the bourgeoisie and the proletariat:

> in countries where modern civilisation has become fully developed, fluctuating between proletariat and bourgeoisie and ever renewing itself as a supplementary part of bourgeois society . . . as modern industry develops, they even see the moment approaching when they will completely disappear as an independent section of modern society and be replaced . . . by overseers, bailiffs and shop assistants (Marx, 1848, p. 509).

They represented a 'transitional class in which the interests of two classes are simultaneously mutually blunted . . .' (Marx, 1852, p. 133).

Conversely, within the bourgeoisie the centralization of capital ultimately reaches a point where management and ownership become divorced:

> the transformation of the actually functioning capitalist into a mere manager, an administrator of other people's capital and of the owner of capital into a mere owner, a mere money capitalist . . . .

Credit offers to the individual capitalist . . . absolute control over the capital and property of others . . . and thus to expropriation on the most enormous scale. Expropriation extends here from the direct producers to the smaller and medium-sized capitalists themselves . . . .

But 'instead of overcoming the antithesis between the character of wealth as social or as private wealth, the stock companies merely develop it in a new form' (Marx [1894], 1959, pp. 436–41).

Hence, in sum, Marx radically extended the significance of the concept to make the bourgeoisie that class which produced, but was itself continually modified by, the capitalist mode of production. Conversely, Marx gave a new and historically specific meaning to the term 'civil' (or *bürgerlich*) society, and argued that its endorsement of individual liberties extended only so far as they were compatible with capitalist property relations.

In the following generation a number of notable non-Marxist scholars adopted, at least in part, Marx's identification of the bourgeoisie as the class responsible for winning the social and political conditions necessary for capitalist production. But this process of wider adoption also saw a further reorientation of the concept. The new political and social institutions created by the bourgeoisie were now presented as the definitive basis for human freedom. The bourgeois character of civil society became the ultimate justification for the bourgeoisie.

Pirenne, writing in the 1890s, traced back the personal liberties of modern society to the medieval merchant bourgeoisie. It was the reliance of this class of merchant adventurers on individual enterprise and the unfettered application of knowledge that made the bourgeoisie the universal champion of 'the idea of liberty' (Pirenne, 1895 and 1925).

A little later Weber identified the origins of capitalist enterprise in the rational, resource-maximizing practices of medieval book-keeping. He then went one step further to claim that this 'capitalist spirit' was in turn derived from the doctrines of individual responsiblity and conscientious trusteeship found in early protestant theology. Parallel to this within the political sphere, Weber argued that the same doctrines also underlay the creation of representative institutions and constitutional government (Weber, 1901–2 and 1920).

In the 1940s Schumpeter extended this derivation to democracy itself: 'modern democracy is a product of the capitalist process' (Schumpeter, 1942, p. 297). To do so he redefined the essence of democracy in individual, market terms as 'free competition for a free vote' (1942, p. 271), and warned that this was likely to be destroyed unless the advance of socialism could be halted. Schumpeter's thesis has since been generalized by Barrington Moore, who has sought to demonstrate that all forms of social modernization *not* led by the bourgeoisie have produced totalitarian forms of government (Moore 1969).

This redefinition of Marx's original usage is also found in the continuing debate on the transition from feudalism to capitalism. Paul Sweezy, following Pirenne, argued that it was trade, and the role of the urban bourgeoisie as merchants, that destroyed feudalism as a mode of production. Towns and trade were alien elements that had corroded feudalism's non-market, non-exchange modes of appropriation (Sweezy, 1950). Maurice Dobb, following Marx's usage, had previously sought to show that the medieval bourgeoisie only became a revolutionary class in so far as it challenged feudalism as a mode of production (not distribution) and attempted to create a new type of exploitative relationship between capital and proletarianized labour (Dobb, 1946, p. 123; 1950). Dobb referred to Marx's own contention that the fully revolutionary overthrow of feudalism only took place when the struggle was under the leadership of the 'direct producers' rather than the merchant elite (Marx [1894], 1959, pp. 327–37).

Recently Anderson has revived this argument in a new form. Seeking the origins of the non-absolutist and democratic forms of government found in Western Europe, he argued that such institutions depended on a 'balanced fusion' between the feudalized rural remnants of Germanic society and the urban heritage of Roman *civilitas* and contract law. The role of the medieval merchant bourgeoisie within this fusion was to act as the bearer of the urban tradition (Anderson, 1974; see also Brenner, 1985).

The other major area of redefinition has been directed at the bourgeoisie in late or 'post' capitalist society. Its central feature is the claimed separation between the ownership and management of capital. If the bourgeoisie is defined by an ownership of capital that involves effective possession and control (Balibar, 1970), it is argued that in modern industrial society the actual owners of capital, the shareholders, have surrendered this to a 'new class' of corporate managers (Gouldner, 1979; Szelenyi, 1985). This concept of a managerial revolution was first popularized by Burnham (1942). It has since been developed to take account of the transnational concentration of capital. The resulting specialization of company functions has, it is argued, given executives the power to create autonomous spheres of decision-making with the result that corporate goals and strategies do not necessarily reflect the profit-maximizing interests of the nominal owners (Chandler, 1962; Pahl and Winkler, 1974).

In contrast, Marx has contended in his final writings that the growth of industrial monopoly and credit heightened the contradiction between private ownership and social labour, distorted exchange relationships and demanded systematic state intervention (Marx [1894], 1959, p. 438). Lenin later elaborated this perspective to argue that the growth of monopoly marked a new and final stage of capitalist development in which a fundamental split took place within the bourgeoisie. Utilising an analysis first made by Hilferding (1910), Lenin argued that the fusion of banking and monopoly capital, producing 'finance capital', had created a new and parasitic relationship between state power and just one section of the bourgeoisie. The result was 'state monopoly capitalism' (Lenin, 1916 and 1917). A recent variant of this analysis has used the interlocking of company directorships to argue for the existence of a controlling elite of directors exercising a strategic dominance over all capital (Aaronovitch, 1961; Useem, 1984; Scott, 1984).

BIBLIOGRAPHY

Aaronovitch, S. 1961. *The Ruling Class*. London: Lawrence & Wishart.

Anderson, P. 1974. *Lineages of the Absolutist State*. London: New Left Books.

Balibar, E. 1970. Basic concepts of historical materialism. In L. Althusser and E. Balibar, *Reading Capital*, London: New Left Books.

Brenner, R. 1985. Agrarian class structure and economic development in pre-industrial Europe. In *The Brenner Debate*, ed. T. Aston, Cambridge: Cambridge University Press.

Burnham, J. 1942. *The Managerial Revolution*. London: Putnam.

Chandler, A. 1962. *Strategy and Structure*. Cambridge, Mass.: MIT Press.

Diderot, D. 1753. *Encyclopédie ou Dictionnaire raisonné des sciences*. Paris: Briasson.

Dobb, M. 1946. *Studies in the Development of Capitalism*. London: Routledge.

Dobb, M. 1950. A reply. *Science and Society*, Spring.

Gouldner, A. 1979. *The Future of Intellectuals and the Rise of the New Class*. New York: Seabury Press.

Hegel, G. 1820. *Naturrecht und Staatswistenschaft in Grundrisse*. In *Werke* VIII, ed. E. Gans, Berlin, 1833.

Hilferding, R. 1910. *Das Finanzkapital*. Vienna: I. Brand. Trans. M. Watnick and S. Gordon as *Finance Capital*, ed. T. Bottomore, London: Routledge & Kegan Paul, 1981.

Lenin, V.I. 1916. *Imperialism: The Highest Stage of Capitalism*. In *Collected Works* XXIII, Moscow, 1964.

Lenin, V.I. 1917. *The Impending Catastrophe and How to Combat it*. In *Collected Works* XXV, Moscow, 1964.

Marx, K. 1842. Debate on the law on thefts of wood. In *Collected Works* I, Moscow: Progress, 1975.

Marx, K. 1844. Contribution to the critique of Hegel's Philosophy of Law. In *Collected Works* III, Moscow: Progress, 1975.

Marx, K. 1848. *The Manifesto of the Communist Party*. In *Collected Works* VI, Moscow: Progress, 1976.

Marx, K. 1852. *The Eighteenth Brumaire of Louis Napoleon*. In *Collected Works* XI, Moscow: Progress, 1976.

Marx, K. 1867. *Capital*, Vol. I. Moscow: Progress, 1953.

Marx, K. 1894. *Capital*, Vol. III. Moscow: Progress, 1959.

Moore, B. 1969. *The Social Origins of Democracy and Dictatorship*. London: Penguin.

Pahl, R. and Winkler, J. 1974. The economic elite: theory and practice. In *Elites and Power in British Society*, ed. P. Stanworth and A. Giddens, Cambridge and New York: Cambridge University Press.

Pirenne, H. 1895. L'origine des constitutions urbaines au moyen age. *Revue historique* 57.

Pirenne, H. 1925. *Medieval Cities: their origin and the renewal of trade*. Princeton: Princeton University Press.

Schumpeter, J. 1942. *Capitalism, Socialism and Democracy*. New York and London: Harper & Brothers.

Scott, J. 1894. *Directors of Industry: the British Corporate Network*. Cambridge: Polity Press.

Siéyes, E. 1789. *Qu'est-ce que le Tiers Etat?* Paris.

Sweezy, P. 1950. The transition from feudalism to capitalism. *Science and Society* 14(2), Spring, 134–57.

Szelenyi, I. 1895. Social policy and State Socialism. In *Stagnation and Renewal in Social Policy*, ed. G. Esping-Anderson, White Plains, NY: Sharpe.

Useem, M. 1984. *The Inner Circle*. New York: Oxford University Press.

Weber, M. 1901–2. Die protestantische Ethik und der Geist des Kapitalismus. *Archiv für Sozialwissenschaft und Sozialpolitik* 20.

Weber, M. 1920. *Gesämmelte Aufsätze zur Religionssociologie*. Tübingen: Mohr.

Harry Braverman

DAVID M. GORDON

Harry Braverman was born in 1920 in New York City and died on 2 August 1976 in Honesdale, Pennsylvania.

Born into a working-class family, he was able to spend only one year in college before financial problems forced him out of Brooklyn College and into the Brooklyn Navy Yard. He worked there for eight years primarily as a coppersmith and then moved around the United States, working in the steel industry and in a variety of skilled trades. He became deeply involved in the trade union and socialist political movements. He helped found *The American Socialist* in 1954 and worked as its co-editor for five years. After the journal ceased publication for practical reasons, he moved into publishing, working first at Grove Press as an editor and eventually as vice-president and general business manager. In 1967 he became Managing Director of Monthly Review Press, where he worked until his death.

Braverman is best known for his classic study of the labour process under capitalism, *Labor and Monopoly Capital* (1974), awarded the 1974 C. Wright Mills Award. 'Until the appearance of Harry Braverman's remarkable book', Robert L. Heilbroner wrote in the *New York Review of Books*, 'there has been no broad view of the labour process as a whole . . . .' The book was all the more remarkable because of the void it filled in the Marxian analytic tradition – a literature ostensibly grounded in the analysis of the structural effects of class conflict but persistently reticent about the actual structure and experience of work in capitalist production.

Labour and Monopoly Capital advances three principal hypotheses about the labour process in capitalist societies.

First, Braverman helps formalize and extend Marx's resonant analysis, in Volume I of *Capital*, of the distinction between labour and labour power. Braverman highlights the essential importance and persistence of managerial efforts to gain increasing control over the labour process in order to rationalize – to render more predictable – the extraction of labour activity from productive employees.

Second, Braverman argues that such managerial efforts lead inevitably to the homogenization of work tasks and the reduction of skill required in productive jobs. He concludes (p. 83) that 'this might even be called the general law of the capitalist division of labor. It is not the sole force acting upon the organization of work, but it is certainly the most powerful and general.'

Third, as a corollary of the second hypothesis, Braverman argues both analytically and with rich empirical detail that this 'general law of the capitalist division of labour' applies just as clearly to later stages of capitalist development, with their proliferation of office jobs and white collars, as to the earlier stages of competitive capitalism and largely industrial work.

The first analytic strand of Braverman's work was both seminal and crucial in helping foster a renaissance of Marxian analyses of the labour process. The second and third hypotheses have proved more controversial. There are two grounds for concern. Braverman's analysis tends to reduce the character of the labour process to essentially one dimension – the level of skill required and control permitted by embodied skills – and therefore unnecessarily compresses the *many* essential dimensions of worker activity and effectiveness in production to a single monotonic index. At the same time, there is a good reason for worrying about the simplicity of Braverman's argument of historically irreversible 'deskilling' for all segments of the productive working-class; it is quite plausible to hypothesize that for some labour segments in recent phases of capitalist development there has been a 'reskilling', as many have since called it, without in any way liberating these workers from capitalist exploitation or intensive managerial supervision.

SELECTED WORKS
1974. *Labor and Monopoly Capital*. New York: Monthly Review Press.
1976. Two comments. Special issue on 'Technology, the Labor Process, and the Working Class', *Monthly Review*, July–August.

Nikolai Ivanovitch Bukharin

DONALD J. HARRIS

Nikolai Bukharin (1888–1938) is commonly acknowledged to have been one of the most brilliant theoreticians in the Bolshevik movement and an outstanding figure in the history of Marxism. Born in Russia, he studied economics at Moscow University and (during four years of exile in Europe and America) at the Universities of Vienna and Lausanne (Switzerland), in Sweden and Norway and in the New York Public Library. While still a student, he joined the Bolshevik movement. Upon returning to Russia in April 1917, he worked closely with Lenin and participated in planning and carrying out the October Revolution. After the victory of the Bolsheviks he proceeded to assume many high offices in the Party (becoming a member of the Politbureau in 1919) and in other important organizations. In these various capacities he came to exercise great influence within both the Party and the Comintern. Under Stalin's regime, however, he lost most of his important positions. Eventually, he was among those who were arrested and brought to trial under charges of treason and was executed on 15 March 1938.

At the peak of his carer Bukharin was regarded as the foremost authority on Marxism in the Party. He was a profile writer: there are more than five hundred items of published work in his name, most of them written in the hectic twelve-year period 1916–28 (for a comprehensive bibliography, see Heitman, 1969). Only a few of these works have been translated into English and these are the works for which he is now most widely known. A brief description of the major items gives an indication of the scope and range of his intellectual interests.

The Economic Theory of the Leisure Class (1917) is a detailed and comprehensive critique of the ideas of the Austrian school of economic theory, as represented by the work of its chief spokesman Eugen von Böhm-Bawerk, but situated in the broader context of marginal theory as it had appeared up to that time. In *Imperialism and World Economy* (1917) he formulated a revision of Marx's theory of capitalist development and set out his own theory of imperialism as an advanced stage of capitalism. This was written in 1914–15, a year before

Lenin's *Imperialism*, and is credited with having been a major influence on Lenin's formulation. The theoretical structure of the argument is further elaborated in *Imperialism and the Accumulation of Capital* (1924) by way of a critique of the idea of Rosa Luxemburg, another leading Marxist writer of that time. *The ABC of Communism* (1919), written jointly with Evgenii Preobrazhensky and used as a standard textbook in the Twenties, is a comprehensive restatement of the principles of Marxism as applied to analysis of the development of capitalism, the conditions for revolution, and the nature of the tasks of building socialism in the specific context of the Soviet experience. This book, taken with his *Economics of the Transition Period* (1920), constitutes a contribution to both the Marxist theory of capitalist breakdown and world revolution on the one hand and the theory of socialist construction on the other. *Historical Materialism: A System of Sociology* (1921), another popular textbook, combines a special interpretation of the philosophical basis of Marxism with what is perhaps the first systematic theoretical statement of Marxism as a system of sociological analysis. In style much of this work is highly polemical and geared to immediate political goals. But it reveals also a versatility of intellect, serious theoretical concern and scholarly inclination. Arguably, his works represent in their entirety 'a comprehensive reformulation of the classical Marxian theory of proletarian revolution' (Heitman, 1962, p. 79). Viewed from the standpoint of their significance in terms of economic analysis, three major components stand out.

There is, first, the critique of 'bourgeois economic theory' in its Austrian version. Bukharin's approach follows that which Marx had adopted in *Theories of Surplus Value*, which is to give an 'exhaustive criticism' not only of the methodology and internal logic of the theory but also of the sociological and class basis which it reflects. He scores familiar points against particular elements of the theory, for instance, that utility is not measurable, that Böhm-Bawerk's concept of an 'average period of production' is 'nonsensical', that the theory is static. Such criticisms of the technical apparatus of the theory have since been developed in more refined and sophisticated form (see Harris, 1978, 1981; Dobb, 1969). Moreover, certain weaknesses in Bukharin's presentation, such as an apparent confusion between marginal and total utility and misconception of the meaning of interdependent markets, can now be readily recognized. But these are matters that were not well understood at the time, even by exponents of the theory. Bukharin views them as matters of lesser importance. What is crucial for him is 'the point of departure of the . . . theory, its ignoring the social–historical character of economic phenomena' (1917, p. 73). This criticism is applied with particular force to the treatment of the problem of capital, the nature of consumer demand and the process of economic evolution. As to the sociological criticism, his central thesis is that the theory is the ideological expression of the rentier class eliminated from the process of production and interested solely in disposing of their income through consumption. This thesis can be faulted for giving too mechanical and simplistic an interpretation of the relation between economic theory and ideology where a dialectical interpretation is called for (compare, for instance, Dobb, 1973, ch. 1, and Meek, 1967). But the issue of the social-ideological roots of the marginal revolution remains a problematic one, as yet unresolved, with direct relevance to current interest in the nature of scientific revolutions in the social sciences (see Kuhn, 1970; Latsis, 1976).

Secondly, Bukharin's work clearly articulates a conception of the development of capitalism as a world system to a more advanced stage than that of industrial capitalism which Marx had earlier analysed. This new stage is characterized by the rise of monopoly or 'state trusts' within advanced capitalist states, intensified international competition among different national monopolies leading to a quest for economic, political and military control over 'spheres of influence', and breaking out into destructive wars between states. These conditions are seen as inevitable results deriving from inherent tendencies in the capitalist accumulation process, at the heart of which is a supposed falling tendency in the overall average rate of profit. Altogether they are viewed as an expression of the anarchic and contradictory character of capitalism. The formation of monopolies is supposed to take place through reorganization of production by finance capitalists as a way of finding new sources of profitable investment and of exercising centralized regulation and control of the national economy. This transformation succeeds for a time at the national level but only to raise the contradictions to the level of the world economy where they can be resolved only through revolutions breaking out at different 'weak links' of the world-capitalist system. The idea of a necessary long-term decline in the rate of profit, and also the specific role assigned to financial enterprises as such, can be disputed. A crucial ingredient of the argument is the idea of oligopolistic rivalry and international mobility of capital as essential factors governing international relations. In this respect the argument anticipates ideas that are only now being recognized and absorbed into the orthodox theory of international trade and which, in his own time, were conspicuously neglected within the entire corpus of existing economic theory. Much of the analysis as regards a necessary tendency to uneven development between an advanced *centre* and underdeveloped *periphery* of the world economy has also been absorbed into contemporary theories of underdevelopment. Underpinning the whole argument is a curious theory of 'social equilibrium' and of 'crisis' originating from a loss of equilibrium. 'To find the law of this equilibrium', he suggests ([1920] 1979, p. 149), 'is the basic problem of theoretical economics and theoretical economics as a scientific system is the result of an examination of the entire capitalist system in its state of equilibrium'.

The third component is a comprehensive conception of the process of socialist construction in a backward country. These ideas came out of the practical concerns and rich intellectual ferment associated with the early period of Soviet development but have a generality and relevance extending down to current debates both in the development literature and on problems of socialist planning. The overall framework is one that conceives of socialist development as a long-drawn-out process 'embracing a whole enormous epoch' and going through four revolutionary phases: ideological, political, economic and technical. The process is seen as occurring in the context of a kind of war economy

69

involving highly centralized state control, though there is an optimistic prediction of an ultimate 'dying off of the state power'. Room is allowed for preserving and maintaining small-scale private enterprise. The agricultural sector is seen as posing special problems, due to the assumed character of peasant production, which can only be overcome through transformation by stages to collectivized large-scale production. Even so, it is firmly held (in 1919) that 'for a long time to come small-scale peasant farming will be the predominant form of Russian agriculture'. In industry, too, small-scale industry, handicraft, and home industry are to be supported, so that the all-round strategy is one that seems quite similar to that of 'walking-on two-legs' later propounded by Mao for China. An extensive discussion is presented of almost every detail of the economic programme, from technology to public health, but little or no attention is given to issues of incentives and organizational problems of centralization/decentralization which have emerged as crucial considerations in later work.

SELECTED WORKS

1917. *Economic Theory of the Leisure Class*. New York: Monthly Review Press, 1972.
1917. *Imperialism and World Economy*. New York: Monthly Review Press, 1973.
1919. (With E. Preobrazhensky.) *The ABC of Communism*. Harmondsworth: Penguin Books, 1969.
1920. The economics of the transition period. In *The Politics and Economics of the Transition Period*, ed. K.J. Tarbuck, London: Routledge & Kegan Paul, 1979.
1921. *Historical Materialism, A System of Sociology*. Ann Arbor: University of Michigan Press, 1969.
1924. *Imperialism and the Accumulation of Capital*. New York: Monthly Review Press, 1972.

BIBLIOGRAPHY

Cohen, S.F. 1973. *Bukharin and the Bolshevik Revolution: a political biography 1888–1938*. New York: Knopf; Oxford: Oxford University Press, 1980.
Dobb, M. 1969. *Welfare Economics and the Economics of Socialism*. Cambridge: Cambridge University Press.
Dobb, M. 1973. *Theories of Value and Distribution since Adam Smith*. Cambridge and New York: Cambridge University Press.
Harris, D.J. 1978. *Capital Accumulation and Income Distribution*. Stanford: Stanford University Press.
Harris, D.J. Profits, productivity, and thrift: the neoclassical theory of capital and distribution revisited. *Journal of Post-Keynesian Economics* 3(3), Spring, 359–82.
Heitman, S. 1962. Between Lenin and Stalin: Nikolai Bukharin. In *Revisionism*, ed. Leopold Labedz, New York: Praeger.
Heitman, S. 1969. *Nikolai I. Bukharin: a Bibliography*. Stanford: Hoover Institution.
Kuhn, T. 1970. *The Structure of Scientific Revolutions*. 2nd edn, enlarged, Chicago: University of Chicago Press.
Latsis, S. (ed.) 1976. *Method and Appraisal in Economics*. Cambridge and New York: Cambridge University Press.

Lenin, V.I. 1917. *Imperialism, the Highest Stage of Capitalism*. New York: International Publishers, 1939.
Meek, R.L. 1967. *Economics and Ideology and Other Essays*. London: Chapman & Hall.
Marx, K. 1961–3. *Theories of Surplus Value*, Vols I–III. London: Lawrence & Wishart, 1969.

Capital as a Social Relation

ANWAR SHAIKH

Taken by itself, a sharp stone is simply a relic of some ancient and inexorable geological process. But appropriated as a cutting instrument, it is a tool or, in a somewhat more murderous vein, a weapon. As a stone, it is a natural object. But as a tool or weapon, it is an eminently social object whose natural form is merely the carrier of the social relations which, so to speak, happen to have seized upon it.

Even any particular social object, such as a tool, can enter into many different sets of social relations. For instance, whenever a loom is used to weave cloth, it is a part of the *means of production* of a cloth-making labour process. However, because any such labour activity is itself part of the social division of labour, its true content can only be grasped by analysing it as part of a greater whole. For instance, the cloth-making process may be part of the collective labour of a family or community, in which the cloth is intended for direct consumption. Alternatively, the very same people may end up using the same type of loom, in a capitalist factory in which the whole purpose of the labour process is to produce a profit for the owners. In the case of cloth produced for direct use, it is properties such as quality and durability which directly concern the producers. But in the case of cloth produced in a capitalist factory, the salient property of the cloth is the *profit* it can generate. All other properties are then reduced to mere vehicles for profit, and as we know only too well, the packaging of the product can easily displace its actual usefulness. This at any rate establishes that even two labour processes which are technically identical can nonetheless have subsantially different dynamics, precisely because they exist within very different social frameworks.

The above result also applies to the tools of the labour process. For instance, in both communal and capitalist production, the loom serves as means of production in a labour process. But only in the latter case does it also function as *capital*. That is to say, for its capitalist owners, the significance of the loom lies not in its character as means of production, but rather in its role as means towards profit; while for the workers labouring alongside it, the loom functions not as their own instrument but rather as a proper capitalist tool. Indeed, if we look more closely at the capitalist factory, we will see that not only the loom, but also money, yarn, and even the capacity to labour all serve at various points as particular incarnations of the owners' capital. This is because *capital is not a thing, but rather a definite set of social relations* which belong to a definite historical period in human development, and which give the things enmeshed within these relations their specific content as social objects. To understand Capital, one must therefore decipher its character as a social relation (Marx, 1894, ch. 48; Marx, 1867, Appendix, II–III).

CAPITAL AND CLASS. Human society is structured by complex networks of social relations within which people exist and reproduce. The reproduction of any given society in turn requires not only the reproduction of its people, but also of the things they need for their existence, and of the social relations which surround both people and things.

The things which people need for their daily existence form the material base of society. Although the specific character of these things, and even of the needs they satisfy, may vary according to time and circumstance, no society can exist for long without them. Moreover, in all but the most primitive of societies, the vast bulk of the necessary social objects must be produced through human labour. Production, and the social allocation of labour upon which it rests, thus emerge as absolutely fundamental aspects of social reproduction. But social labour involves acting on nature while interacting with other people, in-and-through specific social relations. Thus, the labour process ends up as crucial not only in the production of new wealth, but also in the reproduction of the social relations surrounding this production, as well as of any other social relations directly contingent upon them.

The preceding point assumes particular significance in the case of class societies. In effect, a class society is structured in such a way as to enable one set of people to live off the labour of the others. For this to be possible, the subordinate classes must not only be able to produce more than they themselves appropriate, they must also somehow be regularly induced to do so. In other words, they must be made to work longer than that required by their own needs, so that their surplus labour and corresponding surplus product can be used to support their rulers. Thus, the very existence of a ruling class is predicated on the *exploitation of labour*, and on the reproduction of the social and material conditions of this exploitation. Moreover, since any such process is a fundamentally antagonistic one, all class societies are marked by a simmering hostility between rulers and ruled, punctuated by periods of riots, rebellions and revolutions. This is why class societies always rely heavily on ideology to motivate and rationalize the fundamental social cleavage upon which they rest, and on force to provide the necessary discipline when all else fails.

Capitalism is no different in this respect. It is a class society, in which the capitalist class exists by virtue of its ownership and control of the vast bulk of the society's means of production. The working class is in turn comprised of those who have been 'freed' of this self-same burden of property in means of production, and who must therefore earn their livelihood by selling their capacity to labour (labour power) to the capitalist class. As Marx so elegantly demonstrates, the *general social condition* for the regular sale of labour power is that the working class as a whole be induced to perform surplus labour, for it is this surplus labour which forms the basis of capitalist profit, and it is this profit which in turn keeps the capitalist class willing and able to re-employ workers. And as capitalism itself makes abundantly clear, the struggle among the classes about the conditions, terms and future of these relations has always been an integral part of its history (Marx, 1867, Part II and Appendix.)

CAPITAL AS INDIVIDUAL VERSUS DOMINANT SOCIAL RELATIONS. In the preceding section we spoke about already constituted capitalist society. But no social form springs full blown into being. Instead, its constituent elements must either already exist within other societies, albeit in dissociated form, or else they must arise and be nurtured within the structure of its direct predecessor. This distinction between elements and the whole is important because it allows us to differentiate between capital as an individual social relation, and capitalism as a social formation in which capital is the *dominant* social relation.

Capital as an individual social relation is concerned most of all with the making of profit. In its most general form, this means advancing a sum of money M in order to recoup a larger sum of money M'. The general *circuit of capital* is therefore always attended by the two poles M and M', and their span is always the overall measure of its success. Note that money functions here as a means of making money (i.e. as money-capital), rather than merely as a means of purchasing commodities to be consumed (i.e. as money-revenue). Marx draws many significant and powerful implications from the above functional difference between money-capital and money-revenue.

Even within the circuit of capital, there are three distinct routes possible between its two poles. First, money capital M may be advanced as a loan, in return for a subsequent repayment M' which covers both the original advance and an additional sum over and above it. This is the circuit $M - M'$ of financial capital, in which an initial sum of money appears to directly beget a greater sum, through the apparently magical device of interest. Second, money capital M may be utilized to buy commodities C, and these very same commodities may then be resold for more money M'. This is the circuit $M - C - C - M'$ of commercial capital, in which the double appearance of C as an intermediate term signifies that it is the same set of commodities which first exists as the object of purchase of the capitalist, and then later as their object of (re)sale. Here, it is the acumen of the capitalist in 'buying cheap and selling dear' which appears to generate the circuit's profit. Finally, money capital M may be advanced to purchase commodities C comparing means of production (materials, plant and equipment) and labour power, these latter elements set into motion as a production process P, and the resultant product C' then sold for (expanded) money capital M'. This is the circuit $M - C \dots P \dots C' - M'$ of industrial capital, in which the characteristic intermediate term is that of the production process P. Now, it is the capitalist's ability to keep the productivity of labour ahead of the real wage which appears as the fount of all profit.

The most prevalent early incarnations of capital are those of usurer's capital $M - M'$ and merchant capital $M - C - C' - M'$. Both of these are virtually as old as money itself, and have existed over the millennia within many different civilizations. However, they almost always appear as parasitic relations, either within a particular host society or between two or more cultures. Often despised and occasionally feared, these individual activities were nonetheless generally tolerated as long as they conformed to the overall structure of the social formation within which they existed. It is only in feudal Europe, particularly in England, that these antediluvian forms of capital fused together with industrial capital to form the entirely new social formation that we call the capitalist mode of production. Only then, on the foundation of surplus labour extracted directly by itself and for itself, do we find capital as the dominant social relation and its individual forms as mere particular moments of the same overall process (Marx, 1858, p. 266 and 1867, Appendix).

GENERAL LAWS OF CAPITAL. The social dominance of capital gives rise to certain patterns which are characteristic of the capitalist mode of production.

We have already encountered the first of these, which is that the class relation between capital and labour is a fundamentally antagonistic one, marked by an intrinsic struggle over the conditions and terms of the extraction of surplus labour. Though ever present, this antagonism can sometimes erupt with a force and ferocity which can shake the very foundations of the system itself.

Second, capitalism as a form of social organization pits each element against the other in a generalized climate of conflict: capitalist against worker in the labour process, worker against worker in the competition for jobs, capitalist against capitalist in the battle for market position and sales, and nation against nation in the world market. Like the class struggle, these other conflicts also periodically erupt into acute and open combat between the participants, whether it be the battles of strikers against scabs, or capitalists against their rivals, or even of world wars between one set of capitalist nations and another. It is precisely this real conflict which the bourgeois notion of 'perfect competition' is designed to conceal (Shaikh, 1982).

Thirdly, the relations among people are mediated by relations among things. This stems from the very nature of capitalist production itself, in which individual labours are undertaken solely with the aim of making a profit on their product. The various individual labours are thus articulated into a social division of labour only under the 'objectified husk' of their products. It is the products which therefore step to the fore, and the producers who follow behind. From this derives the famous Fetishism of Commodity Relations, i.e. exchangeability appears to be a natural property of all objects, rather than a historically specific way of evaluating the social content of the labour which produced them.

The fourth point follows directly from the third. As noted above, under capitalist relations of production individual labour processes are undertaken in the hope of private gain, with no prior consideration of a social division of labour. But any ensemble of such labours can survive only if they happen to collectively reproduce both the material and social basis of their existence: capitalist society, like all society, requires a particular pattern of labour in order to reproduce its general structure. Thus, under capitalist production, the various individual labours end up being *forcibly articulated into a moving social division of labour*, through a process of trial-through-error, of overshooting and undershooting, of discrepancy, disruption and even occasional ruptures in the process of reproduction. This pattern of apparent anarchy regulated by inner laws of motion is the characteristic form of capitalist reproduction. Notice how different this concept is from that of general equilibrium, where the whole process is reduced to one of immediate and perfect stasis.

The fifth point stems from the fact that capitalist production is driven by profit. Each capitalist is compelled to try and widen the gap between the intial advance M and the final return M'; those who are most successful prosper and grow, those who fall behind soon face the spectre of extinction. Within the labour process, this shows up in the tendency to stretch the length and intensity of the working day to its social limits, while at the same time constantly seeking to reshape the labour process along lines which are ever more 'rational' from the point of view of capital. This compulsion is directly responsible for capitalism's historically revolutionary role in raising the productivity of labour to new heights. And it is the associated capitalist rationality which is most perfectly expressed in the routinization of production, in the reduction of human activities to repetitive and automatic operations, and in the eventual replacement of the now machine-like human labour by actual machines. As Marx notes, the so-called Industrial Revlution is merely the signal, not the cause, of the advent of capitalist relations of production. And whereas earlier the tool was an instrument of labour, now it is the worker who is an instrument of the machine (Marx, 1867, Parts III–IV).

THE CONCEPTION OF CAPITAL WITHIN ORTHODOX ECONOMICS. Within orthodox economics, the term 'capital' generally refers to the means of production. Thus capital, along with labour, is said to exist in every society. From this point of view, social forms are to be distinguished from one another by the manner in which they 'bring together' the factors of production, the capital and labour, at their respective disposals. Capitalism is then defined as a system which utilizes the market to accomplish this task, in the context of the private ownership of the means of production (Alchian and Allen, 1983, chs 1 and 8).

By treating human labouring activity as a factory of production on a par with raw materials and tools, *hence as a thing*, orthodox economics succeeds in reducing the labour process to a technical relation between so-called inputs and output (e.g. a production function). All struggles over the terms and condition of labour thereby disappear from view.

Moreover, once labour is defined as a factor of production, every (able-bodied) individual is an owner of at least one factor. Of course, some may be fortunate enough to also own large quantities of capital. But that is a mere detail of the distribution of 'initial endowments', and on such things orthodox economics remains studiously neutral. What matters instead is that under capitalism the notion that everybody owns a factor of production bespeaks of an inherent equality among individuals. Any reference to the concept of class is therefore blocked from the start.

Next, because labour is merely one of the factors of production which individuals are free to utilize in any manner they choose, this labour-as-thing cannot be said to be exploited. The exploitation of labour thus drops out of sight, to be replaced by the notion of the cooperation of Capital and Labour, each of which contributes its component to the product and receives in turn its commensurate reward (as in marginal productivity theories of distribution). With this, the sanctification of capitalism is complete.

THE HISTORICAL LIMITS OF CAPITAL AS A SOCIAL RELATION. The last general point has to do with the historical specificity of capitalist production. On the one hand, capitalism is a powerful and highly flexible social structure. It has developed its forces of production to extraordinary heights, and has proved itself capable of dissolving or destroying all previous social forms. Its inherently expansive nature has led to the creation of vast quantities of wealth, and to a dominion which extends all over the globe. But on the other hand, this very same progressive aspect feeds off a dark and enormously destructive side whose nature becomes particularly clear when viewed on a world scale. The capital–labour relation is a profoundly unequal one, and the concentration and centralization of capital which attends capitalist development only deepens the inequality. The competitive struggle of all against all creates an alienated and selfish social character, imprisons each in an atmosphere of suspicion and stress, and heaps its miseries precisely on those who are in the weakest positions. Finally, as capitalism develops, so too does its level of mechanization, so that it is progressively less able to absorb labour. In the developed capitalist countries, this manifests itself as a growing mass of unemployed people at any given 'natural' rate of unemployment. In the Third World, as the incursion of capitalist relations lays waste to earlier social forms, the mechanized processes which replace them are able to pick up only a fraction of the huge numbers previously 'set free'. Thus the rising productivity of capitalist production is accompanied by a growing pool of redundant labour all across the globe. The presence of starving masses in the Third World, as well as of floating populations of unemployed in the developed capitalist world, are bitter reminders of these inherent tendencies.

The above perspective forcibly reminds us that capitalism is only one particular historical form of social organization, subject to deep contradictions which are inherent in the very structure of its being. Precisely because these contradictions are built-in, any successful struggle against their destructive effects must move beyond reform to the rejection of the structure itself. In the 20th century such efforts have taken a variety of forms, ranging from so-called parliamentary socialism to socialist revolution. Whatever we may think of the strengths and weaknesses of these various fledgling social movements, the general tendency is itself part of an age-old human process. History teaches us that no social form lasts forever, and capital as a social relation is no exception to this rule.

BIBLIOGRAPHY

Alchian, A.A. and Allen, W.A. 1983. *Exchange and Production: Competition, Coordination, and Control*. 3rd edn, Belmont, California: Wadsworth Publishing Co.

Mandel, E. 1976. Introduction to Vol. I of *Capital* by K. Marx (1867) London: Penguin.

Marx, K. 1858. *Grundrisse*. London: Penguin, 1973.

Marx, K. 1867. *Capital*, Vol. I. London: Penguin, 1976.

Marx, K. 1894. *Capital*, Vol. III. Introduced by Ernest Mandel, New York: Vintage, 1981.

Rosdolsky, R. 1977. *The Making of Marx's Capital*. London: Pluto Press.

Shaikh, A. 1982. Neo-Ricardian economics: a wealth of algebra, a poverty of theory. *Review of Radical Political Economics* 14(2), Summer, 67–83.

Class

J. FOSTER

The word originates from the Latin 'classis', which included among its uses the subdivision of the population by wealth (most notably in the constitution of Servius Tullius). In modern usage it was adopted by Defoe (1728) to define 'classes of people' in terms of occupation and income. It was widely used by the Physiocratic School (Cantillon, 1755, and Steuart, 1767) and most centrally by Quesnay (1758) to define socio-economic functions. Quesnay's *Tableau Oeconomique* made farmers the *classe productive*, landlords the *classe distributive* and merchants the *classe sterile*.

Adam Smith, while referring to this usage by Quesnay, did not himself adopt it. His categorization of economic relationships was by direct reference to landlords, capitalists and labourers, and his analysis of social relationships was posed separately in terms of 'ranks' and 'orders'. The first use of the term in a way that specifically linked economic function to social activity was, most probably, by the Scottish lawyer and historian, John Millar (1787). He described the Dark Ages as marked by the 'separation of a whole people into two great classes', and argued that in a commercial nation the division of labour and the unequal distribution of wealth held the danger of 'the class of mechanics and labourers' being 'debarred from extensive information' and 'becoming the dupes of their superiors'.

By the beginning of the 19th century the term was in wide popular use: 'lower', 'middle' and 'upper' classes being the most frequent but with increasing reference to the 'working classes' (as in Robert Owen's *A New View of Society* in 1816).

The connotation of 'class' as a social collectivity was clearly present in 1817 when Ricardo (1817, p. 5) established the term as a central concept of political economy. The *Principles* begin:

> the product of the earth – all that is derived from its surface by the united application of labour, machinery and capital, is divided among these classes

of the community.... In different stages of society, the proportions of the whole produce of the earth which will be allotted to each of these, under the name of rent, profit and wages, will be essentially different.... To determine the laws which regulate this distribution is the principal problem in political economy.

Subsequently Ravenstone (1821) and Hodgskin (1825) argued from Ricardo's work that there existed an inherent conflict of interest between the 'classes' of labour and capital. Hodgskin additionally claimed that this could only be resolved by the collective action of labour.

It was this usage that Marx and Engels inherited and then extended radically. The individual elements within their analysis were not new. The concept of social progress, of transformation through the unfolding contradictions of thought and consciousness, was common to all young Hegelians. The idea of economically defined stages was present in Smith, Millar and Adam Ferguson. The explanation of political action in terms of economically defined classes was also widespread.

What was new in the work of Marx and Engels was the way in which they combined these elements and then embodied them in the one central concept of 'class'. Class struggle became, for them, the motive force of human history. The progressive advance of productive capacity demanded, they argued, the existence of labour surpluses. Historically, these had been achieved exploitatively within a series of social systems, each marked by different forms of property relations and distinguished by the precise way in which its 'ruling class' was able to extract the surplus from the direct producers.

> At a certain stage of their development, the material productive forces of society come into conflict with the existing relations of production.... From forms of development of the productive forces these relations turn into fetters. Then begins the epoch of social revolution.... In broad outlines Asiatic, ancient, feudal and modern bourgeois modes of production can be designated as progressive epochs in the economic formation of society (Marx, 1859, pp. 20–22).

Hence, in the words of the *Communist Manifesto*, 'the history of all hitherto existing society is the history of class struggles' (Marx and Engels [1848] 1976, p. 478). The Manifesto argued, on the basis of its analysis of previous stages of human history, that the social injustices of capitalist society could only be overcome through the collective exercise of power by a new revolutionary class. Under capitalism this revolutionary class was the working class, and its historical objective, springing from its experience of the material conditions of capitalist production, was to be the establishment of an ultimately classless society in which the surplus would be controlled collectively. Initially, this would require the working class to destroy the capitalist state and constitute its own state power.

Marx gave this working class, as a class 'in itself', a very comprehensive definition. He included within it all those who had to sell their labour power in order to subsist: Marx argued, in contrast to Adam Smith, that productive labour was not to be conceived narrowly in terms of the manual character of the task, a definition which broke what he saw as the central linkage between hand and head, consciousness and physical action. On the contrary, productive labour within capitalism was to be defined by its social relationship to capital. Moreover, as capitalism's means of production became progressively more social in character, and the division of labour more marked 'so, as a necessary consequence, does our notion of productive labour, and of its agent the productive labourer, become extended. In order to labour productively it is no longer necessary for you to do manual work yourself; enough if you are an organ of the collective labourer, and perform one of its subordinate functions' (Marx, 1867, pp. 476–7). In *Theories of Surplus Value* Marx pointed out that productive labour included artists and writers as long as they were employees whose labour assisted in the creation of surplus value (Marx, 1905, p. 157).

However, at the same time as insisting on this broad definition of productive labour, Marx also argued that the 'class consciousness' necessary for the working class to constitute itself as a class 'for itself' developed unevenly and did so first and foremost among workers within large-scale industry. The *Communist Manifesto* presents this as a historical process, with 'various stages of development' in which workers are cumulatively exposed to the material contradictions of capitalist production (Marx and Engels, 1848, p. 492). Marx first systematically enumerated these stages in *The Poverty of Philosophy* (Marx, 1847). They were the need of all workers to combine in the face of competition, the erosion of craft through the division of labour, the loss of control over labour through 'real subordination' to the machine, the exposure to capitalist crisis which brought an understanding of the system's contradictions and finally the industrial concentration which provided an awareness of collective strength. The end result was the unification of local struggles into national struggles and 'consequently into a political party'.

This classic usage of the term 'class' may, in sum, be said to possess the following characteristics. First, it defines class in terms of collective position within a series of historically definite production relations:

It is always the direct relationship of the owners of the conditions of production to the direct producers – a relation always naturally corresponding to a definite stage in the development of the methods of labour and thereby its social productivity – which reveals the innermost secret, the hidden basis of the entire social structure, and with it the political form of the relation of sovereignty and dependence, in short, the corresponding form of the state (Marx, 1894, p. 791).

Second, it understands these relations to be exploitative and hence to be sustained coercively through the exercise of state power. Third, it conceives social progress, the process by which human beings made their own history, as dialectical, driven by its own contradictions. Each successive stage is achieved through collective, conscious class struggle in which the new revolutionary class destroys the state power of the old and creates its own. The state, therefore, is entirely the product of, and based within, existing class relations – *not* 'an independent entity that possesses its own intellectual, ethical and libertarian basis' (Marx, 1891, p. 25).

Marx gave this perspective precise definition in 1852 when he described his essential discovery not as the existence of classes or class struggle but 'that the *existence of classes* is only bound up with *particular, historic phases in the development of production*; that the class struggle necessarily leads to the *dictatorship of the proletariat*; that this dictatorship itself only constitutes the transition to the *abolition of all classes* and to a *classless* society' (Marx, 1983, pp. 64–5).

Since Marx's death most re-definitions of class have attempted to untie this tight knot of argument and claim that its dialectical linkage of production relations, state power and class struggle is empirically or theoretically illegitimate.

Max Weber, while never making an explicit critique of Marx's usage of 'class', left a number of comments which have provided the basis for most counter-hypotheses.

Weber proposed three conceptually distinct dimensions for the analysis of social position. These were: 'class situation' which referred to a person's material 'life chance' (or economic advantages) within any market situation, be it as consumer, employees or landlord; 'status situation' which was determined by the social 'honour' accorded to particular social groupings and any objective 'life chance' advantages which flow from this; and 'power' which defined a group's differential access to the legitimate use of force (Weber, 1922).

These categories reasserted the separateness of economic, social and political spheres. In this way, it was claimed, it was possible to test empirically for any correspondence of position between the three dimensions rather than simply asserting it. It also made it possible to categorize societies by the degree to which status stratification or class formation (conceived as conflict within a market) was dominant.

None of these categories, however, directly corresponds to Marx's concept of class. All three refer to different forms of *distribution* – with Weber's concept of class referring to the distribution of resources which occurs 'economically' within a market situation. To this extent, it is quite distinct from the classical usage which refers to position within the social relations of *production* and categorizes social systems by the particular way in which the surplus is extracted.

Recent elaborations of the Weberian approach maintain this distinction. Parkin argues that the principal class division within modern society is that deriving from the different market opportunities of manual and non-manual occupations. This is because those in non-manual occupations are able to exploit the mechanism of 'social closure': a 'process by which collectivities seek to maximise rewards by restricting access to a limited number of eligibles'. For Parkin, therefore, the class division between the 'bourgeoisie and the proletariat' is not defined by the ownership or non-ownership of capital but occurs *within* the occupational labour market and results from the way in which 'social closure' gives non-manual occupations a significantly greater control over resources (Parkin, 1971 and 1974)

Giddens also bases his analysis on market strength but sees modern society as divided into three 'social classes': 'groupings whose class – or market – situations are sufficiently similar to justify the aggregate being termed a social class.' These are defined by the particular character of their power within the market (or 'mediate structuration'), and consist of an 'upper class' (having ownership and control of property), a 'middle class' (possessing technical and education skills) and a 'lower class' (having only labour to sell) (Giddens, 1973).

A somewhat similar re-definition of class was provided by Poulantzas. He also argues that modern capitalist society contains three 'social classes'. These are the bourgeoisie defined by its possession and real economic control of capital, the working class whose labour is employed manually in material production of use values and the 'new petty bourgeoisie' which includes all other wage workers. Unlike Marx, therefore, Poulantzas uses a narrow definition of productive labour. Additionally, and following Althusser, he see the 'structural determination of class' as taking place at a 'political' and 'ideological' as well as 'economic' level. Accordingly, he places non-manual wage workers in the petty bourgeoisie on the grounds that politically they supervise manual workers and that ideologically, as mental workers, they participate in 'secret knowledge' (Poulantzas, 1973).

Olin Wright, taking a position somewhat closer to that of classical Marxism, contests the validity of Poulantzas's 'new petty bourgeoisie'. He argues that Poulantzas's rationale for excluding non-manual employees from the working class elevates the 'political' and 'ideological' spheres above the economic, and reduces the economic to a market opposition similar to that used by Weber. Instead Olin Wright argues that there exists between the working class and the bourgeoisie a number of 'contradictory class locations' (Wright, 1978).

The most succinct 20th-century restatement of Marx's original linkage of class to state coercion and systems of production remains Lenin's *State and Revolution* (1917) and *A Great Beginning* (1919).

BIBLIOGRAPHY

Cantillon, R. 1755. *Essai sur la nature du commerce en générale*. Ed. H. Higgs, London: Macmillan, 1931.

Defoe, D. 1827. *Extracts from the Plan of the English Commerce*. In *A Select Collection of Scarce and Valuable Tracts on Commerce*, ed. J. McCulloch, London, 1859.

Giddens, A. 1973. *The Class Structure of the Advanced Societies*. London: Hutchinson; New York: Harper & Row.

Hodgskin, T. 1825. *Labour Defended against the Claims of Capital*. London.

Lenin, V.I. 1917. State and Revolution. *Collected Works*, XXV, Moscow, 1964.

Lenin, V.I. 1919. A Great Beginning. *Collected Works*, XXIX, Moscow, 1965.

Marx, K. 1847. Poverty of Philosophy. *Collected Works*, VI, Moscow, 1976.

Marx, K. 1859. *A Contribution to the Critique of Political Economy*. Moscow, 1970.

Marx, K. 1867. *Capital*, Vol. I. Moscow, 1953.

Marx, K. 1891. *Critique of the Gotha Programme*. Moscow, 1966.

Marx, K. 1894. *Capital*, Vol. III. Moscow, 1959.

Marx, K. 1905. *Theories of Surplus Value*, Part I. Moscow, 1971.

Marx, K. 1983. *Collected Works*, XXXIX. Moscow.

Marx, K. and Engels, F. 1848. The Manifesto of the Communist Party. *Collected Works*, VI. Moscow, 1976.

Millar, J. 1787. *An Historical View of English Government*, Vol. IV. London, 1803.

Owen, R. 1816. *A New View of Society*. London.

Parkin, F. 1971. *Class Inequality and Political Order*. London: MacGibbon; New York: Praeger.

Parkin, F. 1974. Strategies of social closure in class formation. In *The Social Analysis of Class Structure*, ed. F. Parkin, London: Tavistock; New York; Harper.

Poulantzas, N. 1973. *Political Power and Social Classes*. London: New Left Books. Distributed in U.S.A. by Humanities Press.

Quesnay, F. 1758. *Tableau Oeconomique*. Paris.

Ravenstone, P. 1821. *The Source and Remedy of the National Difficulties*. London.

Ricardo, D. 1817. *The Principles of Political Economy*. In *Works and Correspondence of David Ricardo*, ed. P. Sraffa, Vol. I, Cambridge: Cambridge University Press, 1951; New York: Cambridge University Press, 1973.

Steuart, J. 1767. *Inquiry into the Principles of Political Economy*. Ed. A. Skinner, Edinburgh: Oliver & Boyd, 1966; Chicago: University of Chicago Press, 1966.

Weber, M. 1922. *Wirtschaft und Gesellschaft; grundriss der verstehenden Soziologie*, Parts II and III. Tübingen, 1922.

Wright, E.O. 1978. *Class, Crisis and the State*. London: New Left Books. Distributed in U.S.A. by Schucken Books.

Commodity Fetishism

A. HUSSAIN

This term is used by Marx to characterize the perception of social relations under the sway of commodity exchange. It is under capitalism that fetishism of commodities assumes its most comprehensive form. In *Capital*, the notion is developed initially with reference to commodity exchange between atomistic self-employed producers. The principal characteristic of such an economy is that each economic agent produces goods which he himself does not consume, and, in turn, consumes goods which he has not produced. For Marx, the important feature is that the mutual interdependence of economic agents is established *ex post* when they come to exchange their products rather than *ex ante* when they embark on production. Marx draws attention to the contrast between the coordination of production decisons through the 'invisible hand' of the market, and that through a production plan.

The notion of fetishism of commodities is premised on the contention that the coordination mechanism is not neutral but has an effect on the way in which economic agents perceive their mutual interdependence and the terms in which they are characterized. Under commodity production in general, and capitalism in particular, economic agents are characterized first and foremost as potential buyers and sellers of commodities, and commodity exchange serves as a paradigm of relations between them. It may be argued that the 'rational economic man' of economic theory is not a fiction but an effect of coordination through the invisible hand of the market. The fact which singles out capitalism is that under it labour-time (labour power, in Marx's terminology) too becomes a commodity appearing on a par with other commodities. This appearance masks the special character of the labour market. For the participants in the labour market are on the one hand the labourers who have nothing to sell but their labour-time, and on the other, the capitalists who own means of production. On the surface, the relations between capitalists and labourers appear as no more than those of sellers and purchasers, masking the fact that the value-added by the employed labourers exceeds their wages, thus giving give to profit or 'surplus value'.

What has been the effect of the notion of fetishism of commodities on Marxist analyses? First of all, it has furnished the foundation for the analyses of ideology under capitalism, an exemplar of which is Althusser's essay on ideology. Further, Pašukanis, a Soviet jurisprudential theorist of the 1920s, used the notion of fetishism of commodities to sketch a Marxist theory of law. In economic analyses it has led to a denigration of exchange relations and the emphasis on production relation as the vantage point for the analysis of economic systems. As a result, the formation of prices and the systems of market exchange have remained a neglected area in Marxist economic analyses. Furthermore it has instituted an unquestioned distinction between ideological and scientific categories. The former is to be avoided in favour of the latter. It has led Marxist economists to spurn marginal calculus, including linear programming, as ideological. In all, the notion of fetishism of commodities, while fecund in the formation of theories of ideology and law, has been an obstacle in the development of Marxist economic analyses.

BIBLIOGRAPHY

Althusser, L. 1971. Ideology and ideological state apparatus. In L. Althusser, *Lenin and Philosophy and Other Essays*, London: New Left Books; New York: Monthly Review Press, 1972.
Marx, K. 1867. *Capital*, Vol. I. Moscow: Progress Publishers, 1965.
Pašukanis, E.B. 1970. *La théorie générale du droit et le Marxisme*. Paris: EDI.

Communism

ERNEST MANDEL

The term 'communism' was first used in modern times to designate a specific economic doctrine (or regime), and a political creed intending to introduce such a regime, by the French lawyer Etiénne Cabet in the late 1830s; his works, especially the utopia *L'Icarie*, were influential among the Paris working class before the revolution of 1848. In 1840, the first 'communist banquet' was held in Paris – banquets and banquet speeches were a common form of political protest under the July monarchy. The term spread rapidly, so that Karl Marx could entitle one of his first political articles of 16 October 1842 'Der Kommunismus und die Augsburger *Allgemeine Zeitung*'. He noted that 'communism' was already an international movement, manifesting itself in Britain and Germany besides France, and traced its origin to Plato. He could have mentioned ancient Jewish sects and early Christian monasteries too.

In fact, some of the so-called 'Utopian socialists', in the first place the German Weitling, called themselves communists and spread the influence of the new doctrine among German itinerant handicraftsmen all over Europe, as well as among the more settled industrial workers of the Rhineland. Under the influence of Marx and Engels, the League of the Just (Bund des Gerechten) they had created, changed is name to the Communist League in 1846. The League requested the two young German authors to draft a declaration of principle for their organization. This declaration would appear in February 1848 under the title *Communist Manifesto*, which would make the words 'communism' and 'communists' famous the world over.

Communism, from then on, would designate both a classes society without property, without ownership – either private or nationalized – of the means of production, without commodity production, money or a state apparatus separate and apart from the members of the community, and the social-political movement to arrive at that society. After the victory of the Russian October revolution in 1917, that movement would tend to be identified by and large with Communist parties and a Communist International (or at least an 'international communist movement'), though there exists a tiny minority of communists, inspired by the Dutch astronomer Pannekoek, who are hostile to a party organization of any kind (the so-called 'council communists', *Rätekommunisten*).

The first attempts to arrive at a communist society (leaving aside early, medieval and more modern christian communities) were made in the United States in the 19th century, through the establishment of small agrarian settlements baed upon collective property, communally organized labour and the total absence of money inside their boundaries. From that point of view, they differed radically from the production cooperatives promoted for example by the English industrialist and philanthropist Robert Owen. Weitling himself created such a community, significantly called Communia. Although they were generally established by a selected group of followers who shared common convictions and interests, these agrarian communities did not survive long in a hostile environment. The nearest contemporary extension of these early communist settlements are the *kibbutzim* in Israel.

Rather rapidly, and certainly after the appearance of the *Communist Manifesto*, communism came to be associated less with small communities set up by morally or intellectually selected elites, but with the general movement of emancipation of the modern working class, if not in its totality at least in its majority, encompassing furthermore the main countries (wealth-wise and population-wise) of the world. In the major theoretical treatise of their younger years, *The German Ideology*, Marx and Engels stated emphatically:

> Empirically, communism is only possible as the act of dominant peoples 'all at once' and simultaneously, which presupposes the universal development of productive forces and the world intercourse bound up with them.... The proletariat can thus only exist world-historically, just as communism, its activity, can only have a 'world-historical' existence.

And, earlier in the same passage,

> ... This development of productive forces (which at the same time implies the actual empirical existence of men in their *world-historical*, instead of local, being) is an absolutely necessary practical premise, because without it privation is merely made general, and with *want* the struggle for necessities would begin again, and all the old filthy business would necessarily be restored ... ([1845–6] 1976, p. 49).

That line of argument is to-day repeated by most orthodox marxists (communists), who find in it an explanation of what 'went wrong' in Soviet Russia, once it was isolated in a capital environment as a result of the defeat of revolution in other European countries in the 1918–23 period. But many 'official' Communist Parties still stick to Stalin's particular version of communism, according to which it is possible to successfully complete the building of socialism and communism in a single country, or in a small number of countries.

The radical and international definition of a communist society given by Marx and Engels inevitably leads to the perspective of a *transition* (transition period) between capitalism and communism. Marx and Engels first, notably in their writings about the Paris Commune – *The Civil War in France* – and in their *Critique of the Gotha Programme* [of the German social-democratic party], Lenin later – especially in his book *State and Revolution* – tried to give at least a general sketch of what that transition would be like. It centres around the following ideas:

The proletariat, as the only social class radicaly opposed to private ownership of the means of production, and likewise as the only class which has potentially the power to paralyse and overthrow bourgeois society, as well as the inclination to collective cooperation and solidarity which are the motive forces of the building of communism, conquers political (state) power. It uses that power ('the dictatorship of the proletariat') to make more and more 'despotic inroads' into the realm of private property and private production, substituting for them collectively and consciously (planned) organized output, increasingly turned towards direct satisfaction of needs. This implies a gradual withering away of market economy.

The dictatorship of the proletariat, however, being the instrument of the majority to hold down a minority, does not need a heavy apparatus of full-time functionaries, and certainly no heavy apparatus of repression. It is a state *sui generis*, a state which starts to wither away from its inception, i.e. it starts to devolve more and more of the traditional state functions to self-administrating bodies of citizens, to society in its totality. This withering away of the state goes hand in hand with the indicated withering away of commodity production and of money, accompanying a general withering away of social classes and social stratification, i.e. of the division of society between administrators and administrated, between 'bosses' and 'bossed over' people.

That vision of transition towards communism as an essentially evolutionary process obviously has preconditions: that the countries engaged on that road already enjoy a relatively high level of development (industrialization, modernization, material wealth, stock of infrastructure, level of skill and culture of the people, etc.), created by capitalism itself; that the building of the new society is supported by the majority of the population (i.e. that the wage-earners already represent the great majority of the producers and that they have passed the threshhold of a necessary level of socialist political class consciousness); that the process encompasses the major countries of the world.

Marx, Engels, Lenin and their main disciples and co-thinkers like Rosa Luxemburg, Trotsky, Gramsci, Otto Bauer, Rudolf Hilferding, Bukharin et al. – incidentally also Stalin until 1928 – distinguished successive stages of the communist society: the lower stage, generally called 'socialism', in which there would be neither commodity production nor classes, but in which the individual's access to the consumption fund would still be strictly measured by his quantitative labour input, evaluated in hours of labour; and a higher stage, generally called 'communism', in which the principle of *satisfaction of needs* for everyone would apply, independently of any exact measurement of work performed. Marx established that basic difference between the two stages of communism in his

Critique of the Gotha Programme, together with so much else. It was also elaborated at length in Lenin's *State and Revolution*.

In the light of these principles, it is clear that no socialist or communist society exists anywhere in the world today. It is only possible to speak about 'really existing socialism' at present, if one introduces a new, 'reductionist' definition of a socialist society, as being only identical with predominantly nationalized property of the means of production and central economic planning. This is obviously different from the definition of socialism in the classical marxist scriptures. Whether such a new definition is legitimate or not in the light of historical experience is a matter of political and philosphical judgement. It is in any case another matter altogether than ascertaining whether the radical emancipatory goals projected by the founders of contemporary communism have been realized in these really existing societies or not. This is obviously not the case.

BIBLIOGRAPHY

Marx, K. and Engels, F. 1845–6. *The German Ideology*. As in Karl Marx and Frederick Engels, *Collected Works*, Vol. 5, London: Lawrence & Wishart, 1976.

Constant and Variable Capital

N. OKISHIO

1 DEFINITION

In *Das Kapital* Marx defined Constant Capital as that part of capital advanced in the means of production; he defined Variable Capital as the part of capital advanced in wages (Marx, 1867, Vol. I, ch. 6). These definitions come from his concept of Value: he defined the value of commodities as the amount of labour directly and indirectly necessary to produce commodities (Vol. I, ch. 1). In other words, the value of commodities is the sum of C and N, where C is the value of the means of production necessary to produce them and N is the amount of labour used that is directly necessary to produce them. The value of the capital advanced in the means of production is equal to C.

However, the value of the capital advanced in wages is obviously not equal to N, because it is the value of the commodities which labourers can buy with their wages, and has no direct relationship with the amount of labour which they actually expend. Therefore, while the value of the part of capital that is advanced in the means of production is transferred to the value of the products without quantitative change, the value of the capital advanced in wages undergoes quantitative change in the process of transfer to the value of the products. This is the reason why Marx proposed the definitions of constant capital C and variable capital V.

The definition of constant capital and variable capital must not be confused with the definition of fixed capital and liquid capital. Fixed capital is a part of constant capital which is totally used in production process but transfers its value to products only partially. Liquid capital is a part of constant capital which is totally used up and transfers its whole value within one production process. So constant capital is composed of both fixed capital and liquid capital, and on the other hand liquid capital belongs partly to constant capital and partly to variable capital.

Marx introduced the concept 'value-composition of capital', μ, which is defined as the ratio of constant capital C to variable capital V:

$$\mu \equiv \frac{C}{V}. \qquad (1.1)$$

Marx knew well that the value composition of capital reflects not only material characteristics of the process of production but also the social relationship between capitalists and labourers. In fact definition (1.1) can be rewritten as

$$\mu = \frac{C}{N} \cdot \frac{N}{V} \qquad (1.2)$$

C/N reflects the character of the process of production and N/V reflects the class relationship between capitalists and labourers. C/N is the ratio of the amount of labour necessary to produce the means of production to the amount of labour directly bestowed, which is completely determined by the material condition in the process of production, while N/V is the ratio of the amount of labour which labourers actually expend to the amount of labour that is necessary in order to produce commodities which labourers can purchase with their wages. If labourers are forced to work longer with less wages, this ratio must rise.

Marx proposed to call the value-composition of capital, insofar as it is determined by the material condition of the process of production, 'the organic composition of capital'. More explicitly, 'The value-composition of capital, inasmuch as it is determined by, and reflects, its technical composition, is called the *organic* composition of capital' (*Capital*, Vol. III, ch. 8). However, as shown above, the value composition of capital is not deterined by the material condition of the process of production alone. So it is better to introduce the ratio C/N in the place of the organic composition of capital, which is determined only by the material condition in the process of production. In order to avoid confusion, I call this ratio the 'organic composition of production'. This is the ratio of dead labour to living labour, which Marx himself frequently used in *Das Kapital*.

2 VARIABLE CAPITAL AND SOURCE OF PROFIT

In contrast to Smith, Ricardo and others, Marx attached great importance to analysis to find the source of profit. He found that source in surplus labour, which is the excess of labour expended by labourers over the value of commodities which labourers can obtain with their wages (*Capital*, vol. I, ch. 5). Using the notation introduced above, $N > V$ is the necessary condition for profit to exist. In order to illuminate this fact, he called capital advanced in wages *Variable Capital*. So the validity of this name depends on his analysis of the source of profit. How is it justified?

For simplicity we set up the simplest model which can reflect the fundamental characteristics of a capitalistic economy; these characteristics are the prevalence of commodity production, and the existence of class relations between labourers and capitalists. There are only two kinds of commodities: the means of production (commodity 1) and consumption goods (commodity 2). In order to produce one unit of the ith commodity an amount of a_i units of means of production and an amount of labour τ_i are necessary as input. Labourers are forced to work for T hours per day and earn the money wage rate w.

In order for profit to exist in both industries the following inequalities are necessary

$$p_1 > a_1 p_1 + \tau_1 w \tag{2.1}$$

$$p_2 > a_2 p_1 + \tau_2 w \tag{2.2}$$

where p_1 and p_2 denote the price of the means of production and consumption goods respectively. As labourers work for T hours a day at money wage w per hour, they can purchase an amount B of consumption goods.

$$B = \frac{wT}{p_2}, \qquad B/T = R \tag{2.3}$$

where R is the real wage rate.

In the first volume of *Das Kapital*, Marx assumed that all commodities are exchanged at prices exactly proportionate to their unit value (equivalent exchange). Unit values of commodities are determined by the following equations

$$t_1 = a_1 t_1 + \tau_1 \tag{2.4}$$

$$t_2 = a_2 t_1 + \tau_2 \tag{2.5}$$

which assure unique and positive values, provided $a_1 < 1$ (Dmitriev, 1898; May, 1949–50; Okishio, 1955a, 1955b).

Under the assumption of equivalent exchange, we have

$$p_i = \lambda t_i \tag{2.6}$$

where λ is a constant which converts the dimension from hours to, say, dollars. Substituting (2.3) and (2.6) into (2.1) and (2.2), respectively, we get

$$t_1 > a_1 t_1 + \tau_1 \frac{B}{T} t_2 \tag{2.7}$$

$$t_2 > a_2 t_1 + \tau_2 \frac{B}{T} t_2. \tag{2.8}$$

By equation (2.4) and (2.5) and the above inequalities, we have

$$\tau_1 \left(1 - \frac{B}{T} t_2 \right) > 0 \tag{2.9}$$

$$\tau_2 \left(1 - \frac{B}{T} t_2 \right) > 0. \tag{2.10}$$

Consequently we arrive at the conclusion

$$T > Bt_2. \tag{2.11}$$

This inequality implies the existence of surplus value, because surplus value is the excess of working hours T over the amount of labour necessary to produce commodities which labourers can receive with wages B. If the number of workers employed is n, then total expended labour is nT and variable capital measured in terms of value is Bt_2n. So the inequality (2.11) can be rewritten as

$$N > V. \tag{2.12}$$

This is the reason Marx called capital advanced in wages variable capital.

As shown above, Marx proved the theorem of the source of profit under the assumption of equivalent exchange. Though this is a clear-cut way to show the results, it has induced various critiques. Many critics have said that Marx's theorem would be right if all exchanges were equivalent exchange, but that in reality exchanges are seldom equivalent so his theorem cannot be valid. In order to refute such a criticism we must prove the theorem without the assumption of equivalent exchange (see Okishio 1955a, 1955b, 1963, 1972, 1978; Morishima, 1973). Mathematically, our task is to find necessary and sufficient conditions for inequalities (2.1), (2.2) and (2.3) to have non-negative solutions for p_1, p_2. From (2.1) we know easily that the condition

$$1 - a_1 > 0 \tag{2.13}$$

is necessary for p_1 to be positive. This condition ensures that the society will obtain net output.

Next, substitute (2.3) into (2.1), and from (2.13) we have

$$\frac{p_1}{p_2} > \frac{\tau_1 B}{T(1 - a_1)}. \tag{2.14}$$

On the other hand, from (2.2) and (2.3) we get

$$\frac{p_1}{p_2} > \frac{T - \tau_2 B}{Ta_2}. \tag{2.15}$$

We can easily get from (2.14) and (2.15)

$$\frac{a_2 \tau_1 B}{(1 - a_1)} < T - \tau_2 B. \tag{2.16}$$

Inequality (2.16) is rewritten as

$$T > B\left(\frac{a_2 \tau_1}{1 - a_1} + \tau_2\right). \tag{2.17}$$

By (2.17), (2.4) and (2.5) the above becomes

$$T > Bt_2. \tag{2.18}$$

Thus we can arrive at Marx's result.

For later convenience we show another expression for the existence of surplus value.

Dividing (2.1) and (2.2) by w, we get

$$\frac{p_1}{w} > a_1 \frac{p_1}{w} + \tau_1 \tag{2.19}$$

$$\frac{p_2}{w} > a_2 \frac{p_1}{w} + \tau_2 \tag{2.20}$$

By comparing (2.19) and (2.20), and (2.4) and (2.5), we get

$$\frac{p_i}{w} > t_i. \quad (i = 1, 2) \tag{2.21}$$

Equation (2.21) implies that if positive profit exists, then the price–wage ratio (the amount of commanded labour) is greater than the amount of value (necessary labour). In the famous controversy with Ricardo, Malthus pointed out this difference between labour commanded and labour embodied. Though he wrongly thought that this difference injured the validity of the labour theory of value, he had come near to the Marxian theory of the source of profit (see Malthus, 1820, pp. 61–3, 120).

Condition (2.21) is rewritten as

$$1/t_i > w/p_i.$$

This condition shows that if positive profit exists, then the productivity of labour $(1/t_i)$ must be greater than the rate of real wages (w/p_i).

3 ORGANIC COMPOSITION AND PRODUCTION PRICE

The concept of organic composition of capital plays an important role in Marx's analysis of prices.

The price of production (Ricardo's 'natural price') that gives every industry the equal rate of profit is determined by the following equations:

$$p_1 = (1 + r)(a_1 p_1 + \tau_1 w) \tag{3.1}$$

$$p_2 = (1 + r)(a_2 p_1 + \tau_2 w) \tag{3.2}$$

$$w = R p_2 \tag{3.3}$$

where r is the general (equal) rate of profit.

The first problem is to examine the relationship between

$$\frac{t_1}{t_2} \sim \frac{p_1}{p_2}.$$

If they are equal then we have equivalent exchange, if not we have non-equivalent exchange from the point of view of the labour theory of value. The values of the commodities are determined by (2.4) and (2.5). The ratio of the value of production-goods to consumption-goods t_1/t_2 is given as

$$\frac{t_1}{t_2} = \frac{\tau_1\left(\dfrac{a_1 t_1}{\tau_1} + 1\right)}{\tau_2\left(\dfrac{a_2 t_1}{\tau_2} + 1\right)}. \tag{3.4}$$

The relative price of production-goods to consumption-goods determined by (3.1) and (3.2) is given as

$$\frac{p_1}{p_2} = \frac{\tau_1\left(\dfrac{a_1 p_1}{\tau_1} + w\right)}{\tau_2\left(\dfrac{a_2 p_1}{\tau_2} + w\right)}. \tag{3.5}$$

Comparing (3.4) with (3.5), we obtain

$$\frac{t_1}{t_2} - \frac{p_1}{p_2} = \frac{\tau_1}{\tau_2}\left[\frac{\dfrac{a_1 t_1}{\tau_1} + 1}{\dfrac{a_2 t_1}{\tau_2} + 1} - \frac{\dfrac{a_1 p_1}{\tau_1} + w}{\dfrac{a_2 p_1}{\tau_2} + w}\right]. \tag{3.6}$$

The expression in brackets on the RHS of (3.6) is given by

$$[\ ] = (t_1 w - p_1)\left(\frac{a_1}{\tau_1} - \frac{a_2}{\tau_2}\right)A, \qquad A > 0. \tag{3.7}$$

If profit is positive, from (2.21) $t_1 w - p_1$ is negative. So we can conclude

$$\frac{t_1}{t_2} \gtreqless \frac{p_1}{p_2} \Leftrightarrow \frac{a_1}{\tau_1} \lesseqgtr \frac{a_2}{\tau_2}. \tag{3.8}$$

The RHS of the above means the comparison of the organic composition of production and also the organic composition of capital, because as shown above the organic composition of production is $a_i t_1/\tau_i$ and the organic composition of capital is $a_i t_1/\tau_i R t_2$.

The second problem is to examine the influence of the change in real wage rate on the relative prices determined by (3.1), (3.2) and (3.3):

$$\mathrm{d}\left(\frac{p_1}{p_2}\right)\bigg/\mathrm{d}R.$$

Denoting the relative price of production-goods to consumption-goods as p, from (3.1), (3.2) and (3.3) we obtain

$$f(p) \equiv a_2 p^2 + (\tau_2 R - a_1)p - \tau_1 R = 0. \tag{3.9}$$

Differentiating (3.9) with respect to R, we have

$$\frac{dp}{dR} = \frac{\tau_1 - \tau_2 p}{2a_2 p + \tau_2 R - a_1}. \tag{3.10}$$

The denominator above is positive, because from (3.9)

$$\text{denominator} \times p = a_2 p^2 + \tau_1 R > 0.$$

We shall show that the sign of the numerator depends on the comparison between the organic composition of capital in both sectors.

The function $f(p)$ in (3.9) is drawn in Figure 1. The meaningful solution of the equation (3.9) is given at p^*. Substituting τ_1/τ_2 into $f(p)$, we get

$$f\left(\frac{\tau_1}{\tau_2}\right) = \tau_1(a_2\tau_1 - a_1\tau_2).$$

Therefore if $a_2\tau_1 - a_1\tau_2 > 0$ then $f(\tau_1/\tau_2) > 0$, so considering the graph of $f(p)$ we know that $\tau_1/\tau_2 > p^*$. In the same way we can conclude that if $a_2\tau_1 - a_1\tau_2 \gtreqqless 0$, then $\tau_1/\tau_2 \gtreqqless p$. Consequently, from (3.10) we can conclude

$$d\left(\frac{p_1}{p_2}\right) \Big/ dR \gtreqqless 0 \Leftrightarrow \frac{a_1}{\tau_1} \lesseqqgtr \frac{a_2}{\tau_2}.$$

This proposition is first established in Ricardo's *Principles* (1821, p. 43).

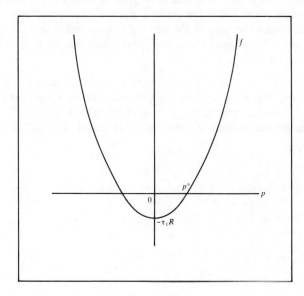

Figure 1

97

4 ORGANIC COMPOSITION AND THE RATE OF PROFIT

The concept of organic composition of capital plays an important role in Marx's analysis of the movement of the rate of profit.

Marx defined the rate of profit as

$$r = \frac{S}{C+V}.\qquad(4.1)$$

By (1.1), equation (4.1) is rewritten as

$$r = \frac{e}{\mu+1}, \qquad e = S/V \qquad(4.2)$$

where e is the rate of exploitation.

He asserted that if the organic composition of capital μ increases sufficiently then the rate of profit r must inevitably decrease. This is the faous 'law of the tendency for the rate of profit to fall' (*Capital*, vol. III, ch. 13).

Many people have criticized this theorem. They have said that if the rate of exploitation e increases sufficiently, r may increase in spite of the increase of μ. So r does not necessarily decrease, even if μ increases sufficiently (Robinson, 1942; Sweezy, 1942). Such a critique overlooks the logic of Marx's argument. Marx stated:

> Since the mass of the employed living labour is continually on the decline as compared to the mass of materialized labour set in motion by it, i.e., to the productively consumed means of production, it follows that the portion of living labour, unpaid and congealed in surplus-value, must also be continually on the decrease compared to the amount of value represented by the invested total capital. Since the ratio of the mass of surplus-value to the value of the invested total capital forms the rate of profit, this rate must constantly fall (*Capital*, vol. III, ch. 13, p. 213).

Therefore Marx's true intention is to insist that if the organic composition of production $v = C/N$ (the ratio of the mass of materialized labour to the mass of living labour) increases sufficiently, the rate of profit must fall.

This can be proved as follows (Okishio, 1972). From (4.1) and (4.2), and

$$v = C/N \qquad(4.3)$$

we have

$$r_{t+1} - r_t = \frac{S_{t+1}}{C_{t+1} + V_{t+1}} - r_t$$

$$= \frac{e_{t+1}}{v_{t+1}(1 + e_{t+1}) + 1} - r_t$$

$$= \frac{1}{v_{t+1}(1/e_{t+1} + 1) + 1/e_{t+1}} - r_t \qquad(4.4)$$

where suffixes t, $t+1$ denote periods.

The RHS of (4.4) is an increasing function of e. If we take the limiting value as e tends to infinity, we have

$$r_{t+1} - r_t < \frac{1}{v_{t+1}} - r_t.$$

Therefore we conclude, if $v_{t+1} > 1/r_t$, then $r_{t+1} - r_t < 0$.

The above reasoning can be restated. The reciprocal of the organic composition of production sets an upper limit to the rate of profit, because

$$r = \frac{S}{C+V} < \frac{S+N}{C} = \frac{N}{C}. \tag{4.5}$$

If this upper limit decreases sufficiently, the rate of profit must eventually decrease, as shown in Figure 2.

In response to criticisms of this view we must say that as far as we accept Marx's assumption that the inverse of the organic composition (N/C) tends toward zero, Marx's conclusion inevitably follows.

So far we have defined the rate of profit as (4.1) and C, V, S are all measured in terms of labour value. However, the general rate of profit r must be determined by (3.1), 3.2) and (3.3). Can we derive the same conclusions for such a redefined r?

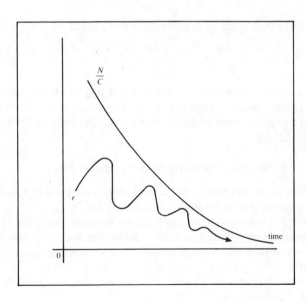

Figure 2

Eliminating p_1, p_2, w from (3.1), (3.2) and (3.3) we have

$$f(r, R) \equiv (1 + r)^2 R(a_1\tau_2 - a_2\tau_1) - (1 + r)(a_1 + \tau_2 R) + 1 = 0. \qquad (4.6)$$

Differentiating $f(r, R)$ we have

$$f_r \, dr + f_R \, dR = 0 \qquad (4.7)$$

where

$$f_r = 2(1 + r)R(a_1\tau_2 - a_2\tau_1) - (a_1 + \tau_2 R)$$
$$f_R = (1 + r)^2(a_1\tau_2 - a_2\tau_1) - (1 + r)\tau_2.$$

Considering (4.6)

$$(1 + r)f_r = (a_1 + \tau_2 R)(1 + r) - 2. \qquad (4.8)$$

From (3.1), (3.2), (3.3), we know

$$1 - (1 + r)a_1 > 0 \qquad 1 - (1 + r)\tau_2 R > 0. \qquad (4.9)$$

From (4.8), $f_r < 0$. f_R is rewritten as

$$f_R = (1 + r)\{[(1 + r)a_1 - 1]\tau_2 - (1 + r)a_2\tau_1\}.$$

So by (4.9), $f_R < 0$, from which $dr/dR < 0$. As R goes to zero r tends to its upper limit, which is obtained from (4.6)

$$r_{max} = \frac{1 - a_1}{a_1}. \qquad (4.10)$$

Since the value of the means of production is determined by (2.4), we have

$$\frac{1 - a_1}{a_1} = \frac{(1 - a_1)t_1}{a_1 t_1} = \frac{\tau_1}{a_1 t_1} = \frac{N_1}{C_1}. \qquad (4.11)$$

Thus the upper limit of the general rate of profit is given by the reciprocal of the organic composition of production in the means of production sector. Therefore if the organic composition in that sector rises sufficiently, the general rate of profit must fall.

5 ORGANIC COMPOSITION AND UNEMPLOYMENT

The concept of organic composition of capital plays an important role in Marx's analysis of the movement of employment (*Capital*, vol. I, ch. 23).

Marx assumed a rise in labour productivity to accompany the rise in the organic composition of production C/N. If C/N rises then from the definition of organic composition the amount of employment must decrease relative to constant capital.

However, how does the increase in the organic composition influence the absolute level of employment?

Many people thought that even if C/N rises sufficiently, if constant capital C

still increases then the absolute level of employment can also increase, though less than proportionately to constant capital (Oppenheimer, 1903). But by reasoning similar to that used for 'the tendency of the rate of profit to fall', we can prove that if organic composition rises sufficiently, then the absolute level of employment must actually decrease.

The organic composition of production in the tth period v_t is defined as

$$v_t = \frac{C_t}{N_t}. \tag{5.1}$$

The accumulation of constant capital $\Delta C = C_{t+1} - C_t$ is financed from surplus value S:

$$C_{t+1} - C_t < S_t. \tag{5.2}$$

The surplus value S is a part of the amount of living labour which labourers expend

$$S_t < N_t. \tag{5.3}$$

By (5.1), we obtain,

$$N_{t+1} - N_t = \frac{1}{v_{t+1}} C_{t+1} - \frac{1}{v_t} C_t$$

$$= \frac{1}{v_{t+1}} (C_{t+1} - C_t) + C_t \left(\frac{1}{v_{t+1}} - \frac{1}{v_t} \right).$$

From (5.2) and (5.3) we get

$$N_{t+1} - N_t < \frac{1}{v_{t+1}} S_t + C_t \left(\frac{1}{v_{t+1}} - \frac{1}{v_t} \right) < \frac{N_t}{v_{t+1}} + C_t \left(\frac{1}{v_{t+1}} - \frac{1}{v_t} \right)$$

$$= \frac{C}{v_{t+1} v_t} (1 + v_t - v_{t+1}).$$

We can say, if $(1 + v_t - v_{t+1}) < 0$, then $N_{t+1} - N_t < 0$. Therefore, if the organic composition of production in the $t + 1$th period, v_{t+1}, increases sufficiently so as to exceed $1 + v_t$, then the amount of employed labour, N_{t+1}, must inevitably become less than N_t, however high the rate of accumulation of capital may be (Okishio, 1972). The rate of accumulation of capital $\Delta C/C$ itself is bounded by the reciprocal of the organic composition. From (5.2) and (5.3)

$$\frac{\Delta C}{C} < \frac{N}{C} = \frac{1}{v}$$

so that, because it is reasonable to assume that the growth rate of labour supply is non-negative, we can say that if the organic composition rises sufficiently the rate of unemployment inevitably rises. Though Marx did not state this explicitly, we think that this is what he wanted to say.

In analysing Marx's theorem on the movement of the rate of profit and employment, we have accepted his central assumption that the organic composition of production rises sufficiently over time. However, there arises the problem: under what conditions do capitalists choose techniques that have sufficiently high organic compositions of production?

Marx seemed to think that the rise in labour productivity and the rise in the organic composition are two aspects of the same thing. But these two do not always go together. Marx himself knew that if labour productivity in the means of production sector rises very high then even if technical composition rises, still the value composition may remain constant or decrease.

As to the capitalists' introduction of new techniques we have the following propositions (see Okishio, 1987):

(1) if the real wage rate remains constant and capitalists introduce new techniques which raise the rate of profit (calculated at the current prevailing prices and wage) then the new general rate of profit does not decrease, whatever the organic composition may be.

(2) if the real wage rate rises and capitalists adapt to this situation with the introduction of new techniques, then the new general rate of profit is higher than the one which would be expected if such a new technique were not introduced.

For the proofs of these propositions, see Okishio (1987).

BIBLIOGRAPHY

Dmitriev, V.K. 1898. The theory of value of David Ricardo. In V.K. Dmitriev, *Economic Essays on Value, Competition and Utility*, ed. D.M. Nuti, Cambridge: Cambridge University Press, 1974.

Malthus, R. 1820. *Principles of Political Economy considered with a View to their Practical Application*. 1st edn, London; 2nd edn, New York, A.M. Kelley, 1951.

Marx, K. 1867–94. *Capital*. Translated from the third German edition by Samuel Moore and Edward Aveling, ed. Frederick Engels. New York: International Publishers, 1967.

May, K. 1949. The structure of classical theories. *Review of Economic Studies* 17(1), 60–69.

Morishima, M. 1973. *Marx's Economics: A Dual Theory of Value and Growth*. Cambridge and New York: Cambridge University Press.

Okishio, N. 1955a. Kachi to Kakaku (Value and production price). *Keizaigaku Kenkyu Nempo* (The Annals of Economic Studies), Kobe University, No. 19.

Okishio, N. 1955b. Monopoly and the rate of profit. *Kobe University Economic Review* 1, 71–88.

Okishio, N. 1963. A mathematical note on Marxian theorems. *Weltwirtschaftliches Archiv* 91, pt. 2, 287–98.

Okishio, N. 1972. A formal proof of Marx's two theorems. *Kobe University Economic Review* 18, 1–6.

Okishio, N., et al. 1978. Three topics on Marxian fundamental theorems. *Kobe University Economic Review* 24, 1–18.

Okishio, N. 1987. Choice of technique and the rate of profit. In *The New Palgrave: A Dictionary of Economics* I, 418–21.

Oppenheimer, T. 1903. *Das Grundgesetz der Marxschen Gesellschaftslehre*. Book II, ch. 25. Berlin: Reimer.

Ricardo, D. 1821. *On the Principles of Political Economy and Taxation.* Vol. 1 in *Works and Correspondence of David Ricardo*, ed. P. Sraffa, Cambridge: Cambridge University Press, 1951–73; New York: Cambridge University Press, 1973.

Robinson, J. 1942. *An Essay on Marxian Economics.* London: Macmillan 2nd edn, New York: St. Martin's Press, 1961.

Sweezy, P.M. 1942. *The Theory of Capitalist Development: Principles of Marxian Political Economy.* New York: Oxford University Press.

Contradictions of Capitalism

ANDREW GLYN

Writers in the Marxist tradition frequently make use of the term 'contradiction of capitalism'. It is sometimes used, in a very loose sense, to describe virtually any malfunction or indeed objectionable feature of the capitalist system. But in Marx's theory of historical materialism the notion of contradiction played a more fundamental role. One of the central tenets of the theory is that there can be a contradiction between a society's system of economic organization and its capacity to develop its productive potential. Indeed it is precisely such a contradiction between the relations of production (relations of ownership, control, etc.) and the forces of production (productive potential), which necessitates, through some mechanism or other, a transformation of the economic system. Thus, argued Marx, at a certain stage the rigidities of the feudal system hampered economic growth, which required for its promotion the full and unfettered development of production for the market. The development of productive potential under capitalism formed the basis on which socialism *could* be constructed. The contradictions of capitalism, its inability in turn to take society forward beyond a certain stage, ensured that it *would* be superseded by socialism (see Elster, 1985, especially chapter 5).

LABOUR POWER AND THE LABOUR PROCESS. For Marx the defining feature of capitalism is that *labour power*, workers' capacity to work, becomes a commodity, which has to be sold by workers who do not have the means of production necessary to work on their own account. The capitalist class pays for this labour power at its value, that is, at a wage determined by social and historical circumstances. But labour power has the capacity to create more value than is contained in it – more precisely, the working class is forced to work longer than is required to produce the goods required to sustain it, leaving a surplus value to be appropriated by the capitalist.

This analysis of the source and nature of profit focuses attention on the factory floor as the locus of the exploitative relation between capital and labour. Labour power is a special commodity in that it cannot be detached from the worker. They do not literally leave their labour power at the factory gate each morning and pick it up in the evening in order to reconstitute it with food and sleep. While this is obvious, it has to be emphasized, since the conventional treatment of production as a matter of technically combining 'labour services' and 'capital services' pays no attention to the active participation of workers in the process of production (see Rowthorn, 1980). In fact, discipline, supervision, *control* over work are integral to the capitalist system. In turn this means that conflict between workers and employers over all aspects of the labour process is endemic.

Control over labour, and the conflict involved, is clearly a problem for the functioning of capitalism ignored by theories which describe it in terms of the harmonious cooperation between the classes (or owners of factors of production). But does it constitute a contradiction in the sense that it is unresolvable on the basis of private ownership of the means of production, and will lead to increasing malfunctioning of the system as a whole?

It is quite possible to conceive of situations in which inability to control labour in the labour process would become chronic. If it were the case that the development of capitalist production necessarily crowded workers into larger and larger factories, with deteriorating working conditions, but increasing opportunities for organization and resistance, then the question of control over labour could become critical. In fact trends have been more complex. In the advanced capitalist countries, firms have grown enormously in terms of numbers employed, but average plant size has grown much less. Whilst Ford-type production lines may have represented the ultimate in the imposition of capitalist control over the labour process by mechanical means, the continued requirement for skilled work, demanding judgement, has prevented such systems of work organization being instituted in all industries. Indeed in some industries, worker opposition, or a trend towards more sophisticated products, has led to a reversion to smaller-scale, more integrated methods of production where work is more varied, skilled and responsible.

What is striking, however, is that such trends have in part derived precisely from the resistance engendered by large-scale production. To take the case only of the motor industry, the development of worker resistance in US car plants in the 1960s led to widespread attempts to 'humanize' work by introducing team methods of production and payment. In Italy, conflict in Fiat car factories led to a deliberate policy of decentralizing the less skilled processes of production in order to overcome the problem of controlling 'mass work' in the factories. The production system of Japanese car companies is widely admired, whereby the most important and technically sophisticated stages of production are carried out in large factories, by trained workers, with high wages, paternalistic welfare provisions, tight labour discipline and a modicum of consultation, leaving many components to be produced in much smaller plants by subcontractors, paying lower wages and with less security of employment.

The most important point is a more general one. The shape of development of the capitalist system is determined by the problems and difficulties it encounters.

It does not evolve out of some inexorable pattern of technical development; indeed, technology is consciously shaped to overcome social problems (like control over workers) as well as technical ones. A contradiction does not have to spell increasing malfunctioning, let alone capitalism's destruction, to heavily influence the way the system develops.

LABOUR SHORTAGE. If the first special characteristic of the commodity labour power is that its 'consumption' in the labour process involves the seller (the worker), the second is that its 'production' does not involve the capitalists. For workers are of course 'reproduced' in the home, not produced in factories. The supply of labour power, therefore, cannot like other commodities be increased by a simple redistribution of resources to the sector producing it. The supply of labour, while by no means independent of economic conditions, is not regulated by them as simply as other commodities. Availability of consumer goods does not spell availability of workers. This feature of labour power, together with the issue of control of work already discussed, explains why in analysing production, workers cannot be represented by the consumer goods they live on.

The supply of labour is not entirely fixed, of course. Higher wages may increase population growth (as child mortality declines for example), but the social development which accompanies increased living standards may lead to smaller families. This in turn may permit greater participation by women in the labour force. But increased educational standards may delay entry into the labour force, welfare provisions may enable earlier retirement, and part of increased living standards may be taken in reduced hours of work. As pre-capitalist forms of production decline, the possibility for recruiting wage labour from their ranks is diminished; immigration from countries with a labour surplus may meet social and political barriers.

While the supply of labour depends on a host of these factors, not very amenable to short-term manipulation, the demand for labour depends on the rate at which capital is accumulated and its form. Rapid capital accumulation leads to increased demand for labour as workers are required for the new factories. But the new investment may be of a labour-saving variety, requiring fewer workers per machine as compared to earlier vintages. The rise in labour demand depends on the balance between these two forces. If accumulation is sufficiently rapid (as in the advanced capitalist countries in the 1950s and 1960s for example), so that demand for labour rises faster than the supply, then the reserve army of labour (the unemployed and underemployed) shrinks. This improves workers' bargaining position, with consequent difficulties for the employers in controlling work and wages. A crisis of 'overaccumulation' results.

Increased wages and difficulties in keeping up productivity levels both tend to reduce profits. This leads to reduce investment, insufficient demand for commodities and labour, and stagnation. The 'law of value' does not apply to labour power, so that shortage of supply does not lead to increased profitability in its production and thus increased supply. This can be seen as a fundamental 'contradiction' of capitalism, in the sense that the functioning of capitalism requires labour power to be fully a commodity, and yet this is impossible (see Itoh, 1980). Of course this does not establish that the contradiction is irresolvable. If the unemployment which results has the expected effect of reducing workers' bargaining power, then wages can be forced down and productivity up, profits and investment recover and a cyclical upturn results.

INDIVIDUAL AND CLASS INTERESTS. The development of such a crisis of 'over-accumulation' is an example of a more general category of problems. Each individual capitalist is attempting to maximize his profits through securing more labour; yet this leads to lower profits for the capitalist class as a whole as they bid up wages and find increasing problems in work organization. So the rationality of the individual economic agents conflicts with what is rational for the system as a whole. It seems very reasonable to describe this as a 'contradiction' in the functioning of capitalism (Elster, 1985). It would require a degree of coordination, which is actually impossible under normal circumstances in a competitive decentralized economy, for the individual employers to hold back from accumulating at a rate which in aggregate is unsustainable. There is no mechanism to tailor the rate of accumulation to what, given the pattern of technical progress, is compatible with the growth of the labour supply, or adjust the pattern of technical progress to what is compatible with the other two variables. What has to 'give' is the rate of profit, and there is no guarantee that the response to a profit squeeze will be a smooth reduction in accumulation to the appropriate level.

There are other examples of 'contradictions' between the interests of individual capitalists and their class interest. Suppose an economic crisis has developed with unused capacity and unemployed labour. Each capitalist may try to improve his competitive position by cutting his employees' wages. But in aggregate the effect of such a strategy would be to reduce consumer demand, which could make the crisis worse. Exactly the same argument applies to the policies of individual capitalist countries trying to solve their problems by increasing their competitiveness. For the context may be a 'negative sum game', whereby cutting wages actually worsens the overall situation. Attempting to cut workers' wages, whilst exhorting other capitalists' workers through advertisements to consume more, is a profoundly contradictory situation.

The famous example of this type of contradicton, described by Marx was his Law of the Tendency of the Rate of Profit to Fall (LTRPF). He argued that the individual attempts of capitalists to maximize their profits led them to introduce techniques of production which reduces the profit rate for the class as a whole. As described elsewhere (*see* MARXIST ECONOMICS), Marx's argument is not satisfactory. But this weakness may not seem of great importance, since we have seen in the discussion of overaccumulation that it is perfectly possible to describe a situation where capitalists do act in such a way as to lead to lower profits for them all. The LTRPF leads to a prediction of a continuous decline in the profit rate, and a declining rate of accumulation, leading, if the process developed that

107

far, to absolute stagnation. The actions of capitalists would, in the long run, destroy the very motor of the system, capital accumulation. Crises of over-accumulation, however, are less fundamental in the sense they they are contingent on a particular pattern of accumulation, technical progress and labour supply. Moreover, while they might be repeated, there is no basis for asserting an inevitable tendency that they should become deeper and deeper. They can hardly be said therefore to amount to an absolute contradiction in the capitalist process of accumulation, which is the way Marx himself interpreted the LTRPF.

COMPETITION AND CONCENTRATION. The driving force of capitalism, according to Marx, is competition. This forces the individual capitalist to accumulate capital in the form of new factories, embodying the latest technology. If he fails to do this he will be defeated by his rivals in the battle for markets since his costs will be greater. In modern conditions, where investment is so necessary to generate new products, and where economies of scale in marketing are important alongside those in production, this pressure is stronger than ever. According to Marx the advantages of large-scale production lead to its concentration (he uses the term centralization) in the hands of fewer and fewer firms. As the most dynamic firms knock out, or take over, those that invest less effectively the degree of competition is reduced. At a certain stage this could weaken the pressure to accumulate and generate stagnation in the economy.

Such a contradiction was particularly emphasized by writers basing their ideas on the postwar dominance of giant US firms (see Baran and Sweezy, 1966). The development of Japanese and European industry, however, challenged this dominance and, during the 1960s, ushered in a great increase in competition on world markets. While monopolization has increased within each country, there has been a tremendous rise in competition through trade and foreign investment. Some of the Newly Industrialized Countries of South East Asia have begun to break into world markets as well.

The process of competition is, therefore, a complex one. The notion that increased concentration would both reduce the pressure to invest and increase the resources for investment (through higher prices and profits) does not stand as a convincing general trend. That is not to say however that, should a new era of protectionism develop, the high degree of industrial concentration within countries would not exacerbate a tendency to stagnation.

WASTED RESOURCES AND UNUSED POTENTIAL. Capitalist production is guided by profit, not social need, or to put it more abstractly, by exchange value rather than use value. The existence of unemployment is the most obvious example of such a contradiction. Unemployed workers could produce the very commodities which they, and the rest of society, need. But since production is for profit, they will only be taken on if the employers foresee a profit. In a situation of unemployment and unused capacity, capital accumulation and thus the intro-duction of new technology will be held back. The development of technology itself will be reduced if lower profits lead to cuts in research and development

108

spending. For these reasons, society's capacity to produce will be reduced below what is feasible, as well as actual production being reduced below capacity.

These then are some of the senses in which capitalism has been deemed by Marxists to be a 'contradictory' system. The idea, prevalent in the 1950s and 1960s, that these contradictions had been overcome by the expansion of state activities or the advent of the managerial corporation, has disappeared with the collapse of the great postwar boom. Whether capitalism will find a way out of its problems, and lay the basis for rapid growth and full employment, depends of course on how fundamental these contradictions actually are. Even if less binding than some in the Marxist tradition have tended to assert, the idea that such contradictions generate powerful pressures for changes in the economic system remains a powerful and important one.

BIBLIOGRAPHY

Baran, P. and Sweezy, P. 1966. *Monopoly Capital*. New York: Monthly Review Press; London: Penguin.

Elster, J. 1985. *Making Sense of Marx*. Cambridge: Cambridge University Press.

Itoh, M. 1980. *Value and Crisis*. London: Pluto.

Rowthorn, R.E. 1980. *Capitalism, Conflict and Inflation*. London: Lawrence & Wishart. Distributed in U.S.A. by Humanities Press.

Crises

P. KENWAY

The term 'crisis' as used in economics is principally associated with Marx. While other writers use the term, Marx attempted rigorously to theorize crises as they occur in capitalism. It is therefore his work which will be discussed here.

In one sense, what Marx meant by an economic crisis accords perfectly well with the common use of the term: for example, it would be quite approriate to use it to describe the liquidation of a company due to bankruptcy or a major financial disruption, involving the collapse of a number of banks. Marx however used the term 'crisis' rather more precisely, applying it to any situation where the process of renewal and expansion of capital was interrupted. Thus, for example, overproduction by one sector of the economy would cause a crisis, whether restricted to that one sector alone, or not. The term also includes the most general crisis, affecting all branches of the economy and many national economies simultaneously.

For Marx, long periods of economic decline or stagnation were not 'crises'. Neither should it by thought that by *the* crisis is meant solely the final demise of capitalism. For crises were (and are) a normal and frequent feature of capitalism, and they represent not only a breakdown in the process of capital accumulation, but also the means through which capital reorganizes itself for a fresh burst of accumulation.

Two important points must be made about Marx's theory of crises. The first is that Marx identified the forces which give rise to the possibility of crisis within the process of capitalist production itself. While not disputing that economic crises could also arise as a result of disturbances from outside the economic sphere (such as natural disasters), there were not Marx's concern. Marx attempted to show that crises could be generated 'internally' by capitalism. The second point is to emphasize that there is a distinction within the theory between the analysis of the features of capitalism which give rise to the possibility of crisis, and the analysis of those conditions which turn this latent possibility into reality. Although the 'theory of the possibility of crisis' grows over into the consideration of crises proper, it inevitably precedes it and lays the foundation for this analysis.

Most analyses of the actual content of crises begin with the circuit of capital, M–C–M. The purpose of the theory of the possibility of crisis is to show why that form, M–C–M, contains the *potential* for crisis. It is that theory which will be discussed here.

Capitalist production is the production of commodities. To show that crises were intrinsic to capitalism, Marx had therefore to develop the theory of the possibility of crisis from his analysis of the commodity.

A commodity, Marx observed, is a product produced for exchange. It is not produced to meet the needs of the person who produces it. The commodity has two sides to it, its use-value (or usefulness) which is entirely dependent on its physical properties, and its value, the magnitude of which is measured by the amount of socially necessary labour time required for its production. As it is produced for exchange, it has to pass through a series of distinct forms: firstly as 'commodity' then as money and then again as 'commodity'. This commodity circuit is usually depicted as C–M–C.

It is worth explaining this in a little more detail to avoid any ambiguity. Suppose that I manufacture an item for sale. At this stage, my commodity is in its natural or 'commodity' form. Suppose now that I succeed in selling it. My commodity now takes the form of money. It is still a commodity (money is a commodity) but it now takes the form of money where previously it took a physical form. If I now use this money to make a purchase, my commodity has now once more reverted to a natural, 'commodity' form. C–M–C refers to the phases through which the one commodity has to pass, though its circuit is of course intertwined with the circuits of other commodities. In accordance with common sense, the first phase (C–M) is the sale and the second (M–C), the purchase.

A number of observations may now be made. Since the commodity is produced for sale, it must undergo the metamorphosis from 'commodity' to money. Whether it succeeds in this depends on conditions which are external to the commodity, conditions which may or may not prevail. The fact that it must attempt this transformation, the success of which depends upon conditions external to the commodity, is what creates 'the germ of the possibility of crisis' (Marx, 1861, p. 507). The possibility of crisis arises from the fact that the commodity may fail to complete this metamorphosis: it may fail to be sold.

It may seem that Marx was doing no more than state the obvious: a commodity must be sold. Such an assessment would be wrong for two reasons. It should be remembered that it is a result derived from his analysis of the commodity, not merely an assertion. Secondly, it is significant that those who deny that crises are an inevitable feature of capitalist production, do so essentially by ignoring or assuming away the very characteristics which Marx's analysis uncovered.

To illustrate this, it is worth looking at how Marx challenged Ricardo's denial of the possibility of general overproduction. Ricardo's position was that: 'Productions are always bought by productions, or by services; money is only the medium by which the exchange is effected' (Ricardo, 1821, pp. 291–2). To this, Marx replied:

> Here...the exchange of commodities is transformed into mere barter of products, of simple use-values. This is a return not only to the time before capitalist production, but even to the time before there was simple commodity production: and the most complicated phenomenon of capitalist production – the world market crisis – is flatly denied by denying the first condition of capitalist production, namely that the product must be a commodity and therefore express itself as money and undergo the process of metamorphosis (Marx, 1861, p. 501).

But if the possiblity of crisis lies firstly in the simple metamorphosis of the commodity, in the commodity circuit C–M–C, it is far from fully developed. 'For the development of this possibility into reality', Marx observed, 'a whole series of conditions is required which do not even exist from the standpoint of the simple circulation of commodities' (Marx, 1867, p. 209). Thus the theory of the possibility of crisis must be extended to take account of the implications of the circuit of capital.

Although the circulation of commodities is the starting point of capital, the circuit is a dramatic transformation of that followed by the commodity. Instead of C–M–C, the capital circuit is M–C–M (Money–'Commodity'–Money). In the capital circuit, capital, as money, is firstly used to buy commodities (means of production, raw materials and labour-power). These are then put to use to produce items for sale which are then sold, if possible, at a profit. With this sale, capital has once more returned to the money form.

It is worth noting that money plays a quite different role in C–M–C, compared with M–C–M. In the circulation of the commodity, money acts merely as money, as medium of circulation, whereas 'money which describes the latter course in its movement is transformed into capital, becomes capital, and from the point of view of is function, is capital' (Marx, 1867, p. 248).

Two more points of contrast between M–C–M and C–M–C should be mentioned. Firstly, the goal of the simple circulation of the commodity is the acquisition of further commodities for their use-value: the goal is consumption. In contrast, the driving force of the circulation of capital, its determining purpose, is exchange value (Marx, 1867, p. 240). Secondly, although both C–M–C and M–C–M contain a sale phase and a purchase phase, the order of the two phases is inverted. In C–M–C, it is selling in order to buy. In M–C–M, it is buying in order to sell.

This inversion has a direct bearing on the development of the possibility of crisis. For obviously, if the circuit is broken, it will be during the sale phase. This creates a problem even under the simple circulation of commodities but its impact is likely to be limited. Once the circuit becomes a capital circuit, a failure to sell has more far-reaching consequences, because it means that the very purpose of production has been thwarted.

Marx illustrated this in his discussion on money as a means of payment.

Essentially, a chain of mutual financial obligations develops: should the cloth fail to be sold, then many capitalists will be affected, not just the cloth merchant. The weaver will not be paid; he in turn will be unable to pay the spinner; neither will be able to pay the machine manufacturer and he in turn will be unable to pay the suppliers of iron, timber and coal. 'This is nothing other than the possibility of crisis described when dealing with money as a means of payment; but here – in capitalist production – we can already see the connection between the mutual claims and obligations, the sales and purchases, through which the possibility can develop into actuality' (Marx, 1861, p. 512).

Ricardo's denial of the possibility of general overproduction is now worth another look. His main argument was this:

No man produces, but with a view to consume or sell, and he never sells but with an intention to purchase some other commodity, which may be immediately useful to him, or which may contribute to future production. By producing, then, he necessarily becomes either the consumer of his own goods, or the purchaser and consumer of the goods of some other person. It is not to be supposed that he should, for any length of time be ill-informed of the commodities which he can most advantageously produce, to attain the object which he has in view, namely, the possession of other goods; and therefore, it is not probable that he will continuously produce a commodity for which there is no demand (Ricardo, 1821, p. 290).

Marx found fault with this on three counts. Firstly, in saying that a man must produce in order to consume. Ricardo was again overlooking the fact that commodities are produced to be sold, and not to meet the needs of the producer. It is true that where production is for the direct satisfaction of the producer, there are no crises. But such a situation is not even simple commodity production, let alone capitalist production (Marx, 1861, p. 502).

Marx's second criticism goes to the very heart of the matter:

A man who has produced does not have the choice of selling or not selling. He must sell. In the crisis there arises the very situation in which he cannot sell or can only sell below the cost price or must even sell at a positive loss. What difference does it make to him or us that he has produced in order to sell? The very question we want to solve is what has thwarted that good intention of his? (Marx, 1861, p. 503).

Finally, 'no man sells but with an intention to purchase'? Not so, said Marx, who added that a capitalist may sell in order to pay, especially during a crisis. And:

During the crisis, a man may be very pleased if he has sold his commodities without immediately thinking of a purchase.... The immediate purpose of capitalist production is not 'possession of other goods' but the appropriation of money, of abstract wealth (Marx, 1861, p. 503).

In the circulation of capital, M–C–M, the possibility of crisis is developed to its fullest extent. Firstly, it is a development of the 'simple' circulation of commodities, C–M–C, and therefore contains the 'simple' possibility of crisis, namely that commodities must (yet may not be able to) undergo a sequence of transformations. Secondly, under capitalist production, money as means of payment introduces a far-reaching set of connections between capitals. Thirdly, the fact that the goal of capitalist production is the acquisition of abstract wealth, rather than other use-values, means that the presence of use-values for sale is no longer sufficient to ensure that sales will take place, let alone at prices which will give the desired return.

Marx's criticism of Ricardo has a wider significance. Ricardo was criticized here not for erring in his deductions, but rather because the starting point for those deductions, his 'model', was inappropriate. Leaving aside those unfortunate moments when he was using arguments relevant only to a barter economy, Ricardo's model was one of simple commodity production, characterized by the circuit C–M–C. This was inappropriate, said Marx, because the circulation of capital, M–C–M, contains new possibilities for crises, not contained in the simple circulation C–M–C.

If Marx was right about this, then any model of production and exchange where the objective is consumption (that is, the acquisition of use-values rather than value in general) by its very nature excludes those specifically *capitalist* causes by the possibility of crisis.

The converse of this is that a proper consideration of capitalist crisis must consider not only use-values but value too: 'value, abstract wealth, money'. In this respect, Keynes's introduction of effective demand into the orthodox theory of his time can be seen as an attempt to remedy the same one-sidedness of that theory which Marx criticized in Ricardo. Indeed, the theory of the possibility of crisis can help show why 'effective demand' – a monetary quantity – is important in its own right and why Keynes was justified in elevating it to a place of considerable importance (Kenway, 1980).

Ricardo denied that crises could arise out of the production process itself. In his defence, Marx commented that Ricardo himself did not actually experience any such crises (Marx, 1861, p. 497). All the crises between 1800 and 1815 could be attributed to external conditions: poor harvest; interference with the currency by the authorities; the wars. After 1815, the crises could be explained quite readily by reference to the strains of the change from war to peace. Yet as Marx observed, these interpretations were not available to Ricardo's followers. And neither, of course, are they available today.

BIBLIOGRAPHY

Kenway, P.M. 1980. Marx, Keynes and the possibility of crisis. *Cambridge Journal of Economics* 4(1) March, 23–36.

Marx, K. 1861. *Theories of Surplus Value*, Part 2. London: Lawrence & Wishart, 1969; New York: A.M. Kelley, 1966.

Marx, K. 1867. *Capital*, Vol. I. Harmondsworth: Penguin, 1976.

Ricardo, D. 1821. *Collected Works and Correspondence*, Vol. I. Ed. P. Sraffa, Cambridge: Cambridge University Press, 1951; New York: Cambridge University Press, 1973.

Dialectical Materialism

ROY EDGLEY

Dialectical materialism is what Engels in the Preface to the second edition of the *Anti-Dühring* calls 'the communist world outlook'. The term 'dialectical materialism' was probably first used by 'the father of Russian Marxism', Plekhanov, in 1891. It was unknown to Marx himself. Engels came close to coining it, and it was in fact Engels who was chiefly responsible for founding dialectical materialism: the relevant books are his *Anti-Dühring* (published 1877–8), *Dialectics of Nature* (written 1878–82, first published 1927) and *Ludwig Feuerbach and the End of Classical German Philosophy* (published 1886–8).

Marx's distinctive intellectual work was a theory of society, specifically of economics as the basis of society, and in particular, in his *Capital*, of the economics of capitalism. This social theory is known as 'historical materialism'. Dialectical materialism is distinguished from and related to historical materialism in various ways. For a start, it is a theory not simply about society but about reality as a whole, nature as well as society. The presupposition of dialectical materialism, in the words of the Preface to the second edition of the *Anti-Dühring*, is that 'in nature ... the same laws ... force their way through as those which in history govern ... events'. Thus the basic theories of dialectical materialism are formulated as laws of a completely universal application, governing 'nature, society, and thought' (*Anti-Dühring*, pt. I, ch. xiii). Second, in accordance with this claim of complete universality, dialectical materialism is generally regarded as philosophy, whereas historical materialism claims to be not philosophy but science, social science. Third, and further to its status as philosophy rather than science, it yields a very general account of the structural relations of the special sciences.

What we have here is a traditional rather than distinctively modern conception of philosophy and its relation to science. A philosophy is a 'world outlook', a synoptic view of the totality of things achieved in this case by revealing in the special sciences a common content, an underlying general conception of reality that they all share and express. This philosophy is therefore itself regarded as scientific, a kind of 'natural philosophy' exemplified in and supported by the findings of the special sciences as they investigate their own limited domains of reality.

Engels' case for dialectical materialism has a special political point for Marxism: namely to argue it scientifically. The case is that historical materialism shares with the natural sciences not, or not only, a method of inquiry but the same 'world outlook'. Historical materialism's claim to scientific status is of crucial importance to it. Marxism rejects as more or less unscientific both other (bourgeois) social theories and other forms of socialism such as ethical or utopian socialism. It seeks to recruit to its support the cognitive authority of science, distinguishing itself within the socialist movement as what Engels called 'scientific socialism'.

With the rise of the bourgeoisie, the Scientific Revolution and Enlightenment had seen the establishment of the natural sciences of astronomy, physics and chemistry. But it was not until the late 18th and early 19th centuries that the social sciences began to develop, in a process in which social theory sought to transform itself from philosophy into science. When in the 1840s Marx and Engels embarked on their construction of a unified and comprehensive social science they rejected as models not only the existing (bourgeois) forms of social theory, such as classical political economy, but also the earlier forms of the modern natural sciences. In their view each major social revolution, basically in the dominant mode of production, involves also an ideological revolution, a revolution in world outlook. Thus in the transition from feudalism to capitalism the religion-dominated ideology of the Middle Ages had given way to a general conception of reality shaped decisively by natural science. A central element in this 'natural philosophy' of the bourgeois era was the so-called 'mechanical philosophy'. According to this, the objective reality investigated by science is a mechanism of matter in motion, a kind of cosmic clockwork, and understanding this reality is knowing the laws governing the mechanism. Between this and the new world outlook of the rising working class there would be both continuities and breaks, but even the breaks would be prepared in bourgeois society. Thus for Marx and Engels the natural sciences in the later part of the 18th century had already begun to change in a significant way, developing one of the most basic and characteristic aspects of the new communist point of view.

Newton has said that in the beginning God threw the planets round the sun, creating processes ruled by the laws of motion and gravity, processes of repetitive or cyclical movement in a system that itself remained essentially unchanged and unchanging. But the Kant–Laplace nebular hypothesis rejected this static conception and replaced it with a theory representing the present solar system as the latest stage in a long and continuing evolution. For Marx and Engels, what this showed was that 'Nature has a history' and that the natural sciences were themselves evolving from a static conception of nature towards a recognition of its historicity. Lyle's geology and Darwin's biology seemed to confirm this tendency.

The key to understand this mode of non-cyclical (progressive) change, according to Marx and Engels, had already been prepared within philosophy, by Hegel. This key was the dialectic. They believed, however, that in Hegel the dialectic suffers a deformation characteristic of philosophy, especially bourgeois philosophy. Its form is idealist, not materialist. For Hegel, in other words, reality is ideal, the activity and product of spirit or mind, so that its dialectical nature is its nature as an essentially non-material process.

Dialectical materialism, then, results from the crossing of two bourgeois philosophies, Hegel's dialectical idealism and the mechanistic materialism of the Scientific Revolution and Enlightenment. Hegel's idealism is incompatible with materialism, and the mechanicism of traditional materialism is incompatible with dialectic. They are therefore rejected, leaving a conception of reality that is both dialectical and materialist.

In this unification of dialectic and materialism both doctrines are transformed. Traditional materialism, being non-dialectical, is reductive, a 'nothing-but' theory: it holds that reality is nothing but matter in motion, and thus that processes that appear to be otherwise are really not otherwise because they are 'reducible' to matter in motion. Ideas, for example, are reducible to and ultimately identical with material processes. On this view change itself, that is the development of difference and novelty, is really nothing but the continuation of the same basic processes and laws. The dialectical point of view, on the contrary, claims that concrete reality is a unity, but a differentiated unity in which the elements are all essentially interrelated and integrated but not reducible to one another. Indeed, differentiation means opposition and contradiction. Thus the material and ideal themselves are really different and opposed, but they exist and are related within a unity in which the material is basic: matter can exist without mind but not mind without matter. Epistemologically, then, physics yields, contrary to idealism, knowledge of an objective mind-independent reality, and forms the base of a unified system of the special sciences that, contrary to traditional materialism, are nevertheless not reducible to physics. Moreover, differentiation is not a static condition but an active process. Reality is a unity that is specifically contradictory, and it is the conflict of opposites within unity that drives reality onwards in a historical process of progressive change. This change is both evolutionary and revolutionary, both quantitative and qualitative: its revolutionary or discontinuous moments yield genuine novelty, change of a qualitative kind. Mind itself on this view is such an emergent novelty.

This dialectical world outlook is standardly summarized in the form of three fundamental laws: (1) the law of the unity of opposites, according to which concrete reality is a unity in conflict, a unity that is contradictory; (2) the law of the negation of the negation, which says that in the conflict of opposites one term negates the other, but preserves something of the negated term and is then itself negated in a historical process that in this way rises to ever higher levels; (3) the law of the transformation of quantity into quality, which says that in the evolutionary process of gradual quantitative change contradictions intensify to the point at which a revolutionary qualitative change occurs. The popularized version of these laws represents dialectic as a triadic process of thesis, antithesis and synthesis.

Dialectic claims to revolutionize our thinking at all levels, including – even most particularly – the intellectually fundamental level of logic. Among its most controversial elements is its use of the logical category of contradiction. Dialectic presupposes the doctrine that there are contradictions in reality, and is thought to imply that therefore traditional formal logic, with its central principle of non-contradiction, must be superseded by a logic that permits contradictory propositions as true of this contradictory reality. The orthodox rejoinder has argued that two *ideas* can be contradictory but that such ideas cannot both be true, i.e. that reality itself cannot be contradictory. Hegel rejects this distinction between ideas and reality, but may be seen as ultimately accepting, through his idealism, the orthodox view that contradiction is a relation between ideas. What is distinctive, even outrageous, about dialectical materialism is that it takes the logical category of contradiction to be applicable to material reality.

What are the implications of dialectical materialism for economics? Economic theory, on this view, takes the form of laws in which major contradictions are identified within the processes of production, exchange and distribution, and are used to explain historical change in society. In particular, these laws reveal how the gradual intensification of contradictions leads to crisis and ultimately to a revolution in which a qualitatively new economic system establishes itself.

But dialectical materialism has implications not only for the form of economic theory but also for the relation in which economics stands to the other social sciences, such as political science. First, the totalizing perspective of dialectic, according to which all things are so closely integrated that they can be understood only in their interrelation, rejects the conception of economics as a specialist social science capable of understanding its own domain of social phenomena independently of other domains and other social sciences. For the dialectic, economics is less a social science than an integral part or aspect of social science, of a comprehensive and unified theory about a unified, if contradictory, social totality. Second, however, materialism asserts that within the social totality economic processes have overriding importance. The general philosophical materialism associated with the rise of natural science contrasts matter with mind and ideas, and holds that matter is the most fundamental, or even the only ultimate, component of reality. In application to society, in distinction from nature, materialism contrasts ideas and theory with practice and claims that the most fundamental aspect of any social system is its most material practice, its economic practice, and in particular its mode of (material) production. Thus for dialectical materialism, social structure and social change in general are explained ultimately in terms of economic structure and economic change. Economics is the most basic part of social science.

Indeed, under the sway of dialectical materialism Marxism has tended to exaggerate this doctrine to the point of vulgarization. In representing the scientificity of historical materialism as consisting in its sharing a world outlook with the natural sciences, dialectical materialism conceives historical materialism as a natural science of society. This attempt to combine dialectic and materialism within the general perspective of natural science has been a standing temptation to leave within 'the communist world outlook' unreconstructed residues from the bourgeois world outlook. The result has been a variety of intellectual pressures converging on an influential distortion, namely the vulgar version of Marxism that Lenin labelled 'economism'.

On the side of dialectic, the orthodox view that contradiction, as a logical relation, is a relation between ideas seems incompatible with its application to material reality. In consequence, the category of contradiction has tended to be identified with that of conflict (conflict of forces) and its specifically logical and critical content evacuated. What this has helped to undermine is the possibility of conceiving the social science of historical materialism as social *critique*.

On the side of materialism, classical scientific materialism is reductive and determinist, and conceives of 'matter' as an inert substance subject to 'iron laws' of nature. For a Marxism under the influence of this tendency, the political and theoretical superstructure are epiphenomena of society's material base. Only that material base, the economy, and perhaps only its most material aspect, technology, has real causal agency. The effect of this on socialist strategy is anti-Marxist: concentration on working-class action within the economic base rather than it extension to politics and the state. In fact, even this limited activity is threatened as either impossible or unnecessary by the conception of the science of economics encouraged by a materialism of the natural science sort. Though it was Engels who was chiefly responsible for dialectical materialism, Marx himself sometimes lends support to this version of economics. In the Preface to the first German edition of *Capital* he refers to 'the natural laws of capitalist production' as 'tendencies working with iron necessity towards inevitable results'; and in the Afterword to the second German edition he speaks favourably of the reviewer who says that 'Marx treats the social movement as a process of natural history, governed by laws not only independent of human will, consciousness and intelligence, but rather, on the contrary, determining that will, consciousness and intelligence...'. Whatever space this leaves for socialist action, if any, it seems inadequate for anything as large in scale and conscious in purpose as revolutionary class war. Lenin, though a committed believer in dialectical materialism, found it necessary to argue persistently against the anti-revolutionary tendencies of economism.

Marx once declared that he was not a Marxist. It was among the first generation of his followers after Marx's death that Marxism took shape, in the period that culminated in the Russian Revolution. Those followers learned their Marxism chiefly from the two most famous books of the founders, Marx's *Capital* and Engels' *Anti-Dühring*, the former regarded as constituting the basic economic science of historical materialism, the latter the philosophy of Marxism, specifically dialectical materialism. Dialectical materialism was an essential component of that first-generation Marxism, the generation of the Second International. It became, and remained, equally central to Soviet communism and to the Communist Party orthodoxy established under Soviet leadership. Between the two world wars, as Soviet communism slid into the tyranny of Stalinist dictatorship and party bureaucracy, this first Marxist philosophy of dialectical materialism came under attack from within that part of the Marxist movement outside the USSR and began to give way to a second form of Marxist philosophy. This was Marxist humanism, since then the characteristic form of 'Western Marxism'. Its chief theorists were Lukacs, Korsch and Gramsci, followed by the thinkers of the Frankfurt School and by Sartre's attempt to fuse Marxism and Existentialism. They attacked the materialism of the natural sciences, and in emphasizing Marx's debt to Hegel and dialectic insisted on the necessary roles in social change of politics and ideology. Their revisions of Marxism found some confirmation in the rediscovery, in the 1920s and 1930s, of Marx's early writings, especially his *Economic and Philosophical Manuscripts* of 1844. In their turn, since the 1960s these Hegelianizing tendencies have themselves come under attack, chiefly from Althusser and his followers. But 'diamat' (to use the abbreviated name of dialectical materialism common in the USSR) has remained characteristic mainly of Soviet communism and of the Communist Parties dominated by Russia.

BIBLIOGRAPHY

Colletti, L. 1969. *Marxism and Hegel*. London: New Left Books, 1973.

Colletti, L. 1975. Marxism and the dialectic. *New Left Review* 93.

Engels, F. 1877–8. *Anti-Dühring*. Moscow: Foreign Languages Publishing House, 1954.

Engels, F. 1886–8. *Ludwig Feuerbach and the End of Classical German Philosophy*. In K. Marx and F. Engels *Selected Works*, Vol. 2, Moscow: Foreign Languages Publishing House, 1962.

Engels, F. 1927, written 1878–82. *Dialectics of Nature*. Moscow: Progress Publishers, 1974.

Graham, L.R. 1973. *Science and Philosophy in the Soviet Union*. London: Allen Lane.

Jordan, Z.A. 1967. *The Evolution of Dialectical Materialism*. London: Macmillan; New York; St. Martin's Press.

Lefebvre, H. 1939. *Dialectical Materialism*. London: Jonathan Cape, 1968.

Lenin, V.I. 1895–1916. *Philosophical Notebooks*. Vol. 38 of the *Collected Works*, Moscow: Foreign Languages Publishing House, 1963.

Lenin, V.I. 1902. *What is to be Done?* Moscow: Progress Publishers, 1969.

Lenin, V.I. 1908. *Materialism and Empirico-Criticism*. Moscow: Foreign Language Publishing House, 1952.

Mao Tse-tung. 1937. On Contradiction. In *Selected Works*, Vol. 2, London: Lawrence and Wishart, 1954.

Marx, K. 1888, written 1845. *Theses on Feuerbach*. In K. Marx and F. Engels, *The German Idelogy* (written 1845–6), London: Lawrence & Wishart, 1970.

Norman, R. and Sayers, S. 1980. *Hegel, Marx and Dialectic*. Brighton: Harvester.

Plekhanov, G.V. 1908. *Fundamental Problems of Marxism*. London: Lawrence & Wishart, 1969; New York: International Publishers.

Sartre, J.-P. 1960. *Critique of Dialectical Reason*. London: New Left Books, 1976.

Stalin, J.V. 1924. *Problems of Leninism*. Moscow: Foreign Languages Publishing House, 1945.

Wetter, G.A. 1952. *Dialectical Materialism*. London: Routledge and Kegan Paul, 1958; New York: F.A. Praeger, 1959.

Dialectical Reasoning

GARETH STEDMAN JONES

This notoriously elusive and multifaceted notion assumed importance in the history of political economy because Marx's 'critique of political economy', *Capital*, and particularly its first draft, the *Grundrisse* of 1857–8, was presented in a dialectical form. Part of the difficulty of encapsulating the dialectic within any concise definition derives from the fact that it may be conceived as a method of thought, a set of laws governing the world, the immanent movement of history or any combination of the three. The dialectic originated in ancient Greek philosophy. The original meaning of '*dialogos*' was to reason by splitting in two. In one form of its development, dialectic was associated with reason. Starting with Zeno's paradoxes, dialectical forms of reasoning were found in most of the philosophies of the ancient world and continued into medieval forms of disputation. It was this form of reasoning that Kant attacked in his distinction between the logic of understanding which, applied to the data of sensation, yielded knowledge of the phenomenal world, and dialectic or the logic of reasoning, which proceeded independently of experience and purported to give knowledge of the transcendant order of things in themselves. In another form of dialectic, the focus was primarily upon processes: either an ascending dialectic in which the existence of a higher reality is demonstrated, or in a descending form in which this higher reality is shown to manifest itself in the phenomenal world. Such conceptions were particularly associated with Christian eschatology, neo-platonism and illuminism, and typically patterned themselves into conceptions of original unity, division or loss, and ultimate reunification.

For practical purposes, however, the form in which the dialectic was inherited and modified by Marx was that in which it had been elaborated by Hegel. 'Hegel's dialectics is the basic form of all dialectics, but only *after* it has been stripped of its mystified form, and it is precisely this which distinguishes my method' (Marx, letter to Kugelmann, 6 March 1868).

In Hegel, the dialectic is a self-generating and self-differentiating process of reason (reason being understood both to be the process of cognition and the

121

process of the world). The Hegelian Absolute actualizes itself by alienating itself from itself and then by restoring its self-unity. This corresponds to the three basic divisions of the Hegelian system: the *Logic*, the *Philosophy of Nature* and the *Philosophy of Mind*. It is free because self-determined. Its freedom consists in recognizing that its alienation into its other (nature) is but a free expression of itself. The truth is the whole and it unfolds through a dialectical progression of categories, concepts and forms of consciousness from the most simple and empty to the most complex and concrete. Each category reveals itself to the observer to be incomplete, lacking and contradictory; it thus passes over into a more adequate category capable of resolving the one-sided and contradictory aspects of its predecessor, though throwing up new contradictions in its turn. Against Kant, this process of dialectical reason is not concerned with the transcendent, but is immanent in reality itself. Reflective understanding is not false, but partial. It abstracts from reality and decomposes objects into their elements. Analytic understanding represents a localized standpoint which sets up an unsurpassable barrier between subject and object and thus cannot grasp the systematic interconnection between things or the total process of which is a part. The absolute subject contains both itself and its other (both being and thought) which is revealed to be identical with itself. Human history, human thought are vehicles through which the absolute achieves self-consciousness, but humanity as such is not the subject of the process. Thus the absolute spirit dwells in human activity without being reducible to it, just as the categories of the *Logic* precede their embodiment in nature and history.

The character of the marxian dialectic is yet harder to pin down than that of Hegel. In some well-known lines in the Post-Face to the Second Edition of *Capital* in 1873, Marx stated,

> I criticised the mystificatory side of the Hegelian dialectic nearly thirty years ago ... [but] the mystification which the dialectic suffers in Hegel's hands by no means prevents him from being the first to present its general form of motion in a comprehensive and conscious manner. With him it is standing on its head. It must be inverted in order to discover the rational kernel within the mystical shell (Marx [1873], 1976, pp. 102–3).

This statement has satisfied practically no one. How can a dialectic be inverted? How can a rational kernel be extracted from a mystical shell? To critics from empiricist, positivist or structuralist traditions, anxious to free Marx from the clutches of Hegelianism, the dialectic is intrinsically unworkable and must either be dropped or stated in quite other terms (e.g. Bernstein, 1899; Della Volpe, 1950; Althusser, 1965; Cohen, 1978; Elster, 1985). To a second group, the dialectical understanding of capitalism is only a particular instance of more general dialectical laws which govern reality as a whole, both natural and social (Engels, dialectical materialism). To a third group, the Hegelian roots of Marx's thought are not sufficiently emphasized in this statement; Marxism is only Hegelianism taken to its logical revolutionary conclusions in the discovery of the proletariat as the subject-order of history and the 'totality' as the distinguishing feature of its world-outlook (Lukács, 1923 and much of 20th-century Western Marxism). This *Methodenstreit* cannot be discussed here. All that can be attempted is to give some sense to Marx's statement and in particular to indicate how it informed his critique of political economy.

Marx specifically criticized 'the mystificatory side of the Hegelian dialectic' in his 1843 *Critique of Hegel's Philosophy of Right* and in the concluding section of the *1844 Manuscripts* (both of which were only published in the 20th century). In these texts. Marx followed Feuerbach in considering Hegelian philosophy to be the conceptual equivalent of Christian theology; both were forms of alienation of man's species attributes; Christianity transposed human emotion into a religious Godhead, while Hegel projected human thinking into a fictive subject, the Absolute Idea, which in turn supposedly generated the empirical world. Employing Feuerbach's 'transformative method' (the origin of the inversion metaphor) subject and predicate were reversed and hence the correct starting point of philosophy was the finite, man. Nature similarly was not the alienated expression of Absolute Spirit, it was irreducibly distinct. Thus there could be no speculative identity of being and thought. Man, however, as a natural being, could interact harmoniously with nature, his inorganic body. Once the absolute spirit had been dismantled and the identity of being and thought eliminated, it could be argued that the barrier against the harmonious interpenetration of man and nature and the free expression of human nature, was not 'objectification', the division between subject and object constitutive of the finite human condition, but rather the inhuman alienation of man's species life activity in property, religion and the state. True Communism, humanism, meant the reappropriation of man's essential powers, the generic use of his conscious life activity. In contrast to the predominant Young Hegelian position, therefore, which counterposed Hegel's revolutionary 'method' (the dialectic) to his 'conservative system', Marx argued that there was no incompatibility between the two. For while Hegel's dialectic ostensibly negated the empirical world, it covertly depended upon it. Not only was the moment of contradiction a prelude to the higher moment of reconciliation and the restoration of identity, but the ideas themselves were tacitly drawn from untheorized experience. The effect of the dialectical chain which embodied the world was not to subvert the existing state of affairs, but to sanctify it.

In the crucial period that followed, that of the *German Ideology* and the *Poverty of Philosophy*, in which the basic architecture of the 'materialist conception of history' was elaborated, the attack upon speculative idealism was made more radical. The generic notion of 'conscious life activity', 'praxis', was replaced by the more specific notion of production. Hegel and the Idealist tradition were given credit for emphasizing the active transformative side of human history, but castigated for recognizing this activity only in the form of thought. Thought itself was now made a wholly derivative activity. The fundamental activity was labour and what developed in history were the productive powers men employed in their interaction with nature, 'the productive forces'. Stages in the development of these productive forces were accompanied by successive 'forms of human intercourse', what became 'the relations of production'. Finally, 'man' as a generic being was dispersed into the struggle between different classes of men, between those who produced and those who owned and controlled the means of production.

In this new theorization of history, explicit references to Hegel were few and the dialectic scarcely mentioned. But Hegel re-entered the story as soon as Marx attempted to write up a systematic theory of the capitalist mode of production in 1857–8. To see why, we must briefly survey his economic writings up to that date.

Marx's 1843 critique of Hegel has led him to the conclusion that civil society was the foundation of the state and that the anatomy of civil society was to be found in political economy. However, if his preoccupation with political economy dated from this point, it was not that of an economist. In the 1844 Manuscripts what is to be found is a humanist critique of both political economy and civil society; not an alternative theory of the economy, but rather a juxtaposition between the 'economic' and the 'human', the former being judged in terms of the latter. No distinction is made between political economy and the economic reality it purports to address, the one is simply seen as the mirror of the other.

The first attempt to define capitalism as an economic phenomenon occurred in the *Poverty of Philosophy* (1847). However, whatever the significance of that work in other respects, it did not outline any specifically marxian portrayal of the capitalist economy. As in 1844 there was no internal critique of classical political economy. The main difference was that whereas in 1844 Marx saw that economy through the eyes of Adam Smith, he now saw it through the eyes of Ricardo. In particular, he adopted what he took to be Ricardo's theory of value and belaboured Proudhon for positing as an ideal – the equivalence of value and price – what he considered to be the actual situation under capitalism. The only critique of Ricardo to be found there was a purely external historicist one: that Ricardo was the scientific expression of the epoch of capitalist triumph, but that that epoch had already passed away, that its gravediggers had already appeared and that its collapse was already at hand.

When Marx resumed his economic studies after the 1848 revolutions, Proudhonism was still the main object of attack. It occupied a major part of his unfinished economic manuscripts of 1850–51 and the attack on the Proudhonist banking schemes of Darimon took up the first part of the written-up notebooks of 1857–8, the *Grundrisse*. Proudhonism was the main object of attack because it could be taken for the predominant form of socialist or radical reasoning about the economy. Ricardo could again be utilized to attack such reasoning in order to argue that it represented a nostalgia for petty commodity production under conditions of equal exchange, a situation supposedly preceding modern capitalism rather than representing an emancipation from it. However, if the capitalist mode of production and its historical limits were to be grasped in theory, this would have to involve a critique of Ricardo himself.

The form this critique took involved problematizing Ricardo's theory of value (or rather Marx's reading of it; Steedman (1979) has argued strongly that Marx misconstrued Ricardo's theory, though Ricardo's shifting of position between the three editions of the *Principles*, and the fact that Marx only used the third edition, makes his mistake an understandable one). On the one hand, it raised a question never posed by Ricardo: the source of profit in a system of equal exchange. On the other hand, it involved juxtaposing wealth in the form of productive forces, i.e. as a collection of use values, against the translation of all wealth into exchange values within capitalism. Ricardo, it was argued, possessed no criterion for distinguishing between the content – or the material elements – and the form of the economy, such as Marx possessed in the distinction between forces and relations of production. Ricardo never problematized the 'value form'; he linked the object of measurement with the measurement itself. For this reason, Ricardo was considered to possess no conception of the historicity of capitalism. Once the material could be distinguished from the social, the content from the form, the capitalist mode of production could be conceived as a dynamic system whose principle of movement could be located in the contradictory relationship between matter and form.

It is here that Hegel came in. We know that during the writing of the *Grundrisse* at the beginning of 1858, Marx re-read Hegel, in particular the *Science of Logic*. He wrote to Engels, 'I am getting some nice developments, e.g. I have overthrown the entire doctrine of profit as previously conceived. In the method of working, it was of great service to me that by mere accident I leafed through Hegel's *Logic* again' (Marx to Engels, 16 January 1858).

It is not really mysterious what Marx found so useful in his reading of Hegel's *Logik* at this time. It suggested a way of elaborating the contradictory elements that Marx had discerned in the value form into a theoretization of the trajectory of the capitalist mode of production as a whole. The point is emphasised by Marx in his Post-Face to Capital: the dialectic 'includes in its positive understanding of what exists a simultaneous recognition of its negation, its inevitable destruction; because it regards every historically developed form as being in a fluid state, in motion, and therefore grasps its transient aspect as well' ([1873] 1976, p. 103). The dialectic offered a means of grasping a structure in movement, a process – the subtitle of *Capital*, Volume I was 'the process of capitalist production'. If capitalism could be represented as a process and not just a structure, then concomitantly its building blocks were not factors, but, as in Hegel, 'moments'. As Marx put it in the *Grundrisse*:

When we consider bourgeois society in the long view and as a whole, then the final result of the process of social production always appears as the society itself i.e. the human being itself in its social relations. Everything that has a fixed form, such as the product etc., appears as merely a moment, a vanishing moment in this movement. The conditions and objectifications of the process are themselves equally moments of it, and its only subjects are the individuals, but individuals in mutual relationships, which they equally reproduce and produce anew ... in which they renew themselves even as they renew the world of wealth they create (Marx [1857–8], 1973, p. 712).

Marx's attempt to utilize the *Logic* can be seen most clearly in the *Grundrisse*. There one can see the genesis of particular concepts which in *Capital* appear in more polished form. What is clear, is that the *Logic* is used as a first means of setting terms in relation to each other. The text is littered with Hegelian expressions and turns of phrase; indeed sometimes it appears as if lumps of Hegelian ratiocination have simply been transposed, undigested, to sketch the more intractable links in the chain. Here, for instance, is money striving to become capital: '... already for that reason, value which insists on itself as value preserves itself through increase; and it preserves itself precisely only by constantly driving beyond its quantitative barrier, which contradicts its character as form, its inner generality' (ibid., p. 270). But at the same time we can see Marx remind himself to correct the 'idealist manner of presentation, which makes it seem as if it were merely a matter of conceptual determination and of the dialectic of these concepts' (ibid., p. 151).

But the interest of dialectical logic for Marx was not simply that it offered him a way of outlining a structure in movement; more fundamentally it enabled him to depict contradiction as the motor of this movement. This was why the dialectic was 'in its very essence critical and revolutionary' (Marx [1873], 1976, p. 103), in that both in Hegel and in ancient Greek usage, movement was contradiction. This appears closely in the dramatic relationship that Marx sets up between the circulation system and the production system in *Capital*. The system of exchange, of the market is the public face of capitalism. It is 'in fact a very Eden of the innate rights of Man' (ibid., p. 280). Exchanges are equal. To look for the source of inequality in the exchange system, like the Proudhonists, is to look in the wrong place. Yet, if exchanges are equal how does capital accumulation take place? Equal exchange implies the principle of identity, of non-contradiction. It is, in Hegel's sense, the sphere of 'simple immediacy', the world as it first appears to the senses. It cannot move or develop, because it apparently contains no contradictory relations.

But this surface of things is not self-sufficient. It is 'the phenomenon of a process taking place behind it'. As a surface it is not nothing, but rather a boundary or limit. Contradiction and therefore movement is located in production. Here there is non-identity, the extraction of surplus labour disguised by the surface value form and its tendency to limitless expansion.

Thus, there are two processes, on the one hand that of the surface, that of immediate identity lacking the motive power of its own regeneration; on the other hand, that beneath the surface, a process of contradiction. Thus in Hegelian terms, the whole could then be defined as 'the identity of identity and non-identity'. In this whole, contradiction is the overriding moment, but the surface places increasingly formidable obstacles to its development, for instance, so-called 'realization' crises. Values can only be realized in an act of exchange and the medium of this exchange is money. But there is no guarantee that these exchanges must take place. The 'anarchy' of the market place is such that overproduction or disportionality between sectors of production can only be seen after the event. Hence trade crises and slumps (see M. Nicolaus, Introduction to Marx [1857–8]).

This is only one example of how Marx employed dialectical principles in his attempt to conceptualize the process or movement of a contradictory whole. Another would be the six books Marx originally planned to write in 1857–8, the original blueprint of *Capital*. Their order would have been: Capital, Wage Labour, Landed Property, State, World Market, Crises. This plan is reminiscent of Hegel's *Encyclopaedia*. It describes a circle in a Hegelian sense. The point of departure is not capital *per se*, but commercial exchange as appearance, then proceeding through the contradictory world of production and eventually returning to commercial exchange again as the world market, but this time enriched by the whole of the preceding analysis.

There has been much controversy about the proximity or distance between the Hegelian and Marxian dialectics. Those who like Althusser (1965) argue for their radical dissimilarity, are on their strongest ground when arguing that in Marx the terms of the dialectic have been radically transformed. The contradiction between forces and relations of production cannot be reduced to the ultimate simplicity of that between Hegel's master and slave or of that between proletariat and bourgeoisie in the hegelianized marxist account of Lukács. But it is far more difficult to establish as unambiguously the difference in the relationship between the terms in their respective dialectics. On the one hand, the relation between matter and form in Hegel is only one of apparent exteriority. Matter relates to form as other only because form is not yet posited within it. Once the terms are related, they are declared to be identical. Marx, on the other hand, insists upon the irreducible difference between matter and form, between the material and the social (even if he is not wholly successful in keeping them apart). Not only are matter and form different, but the one determines the other: value is determined in relation to the material production of use value; the opposite is not true. Relations of determination would seem to exclude identity, and this is confirmed by Marx's avoidance of the Hegelian notion of 'sublation' (*Aufhebung*), the higher moment of synthesis. The dialectical clash between forces and relations of production in the capitalist mode of production does not of itself produce a higher unity (socialism); rather what crises do, is to make manifest the otherwise hidden determination of value by use value, of form by matter. Against this, however, must be set one or two passages, including a famous peroration in *Capital* Volume I, where Marx does conceive the end of capitalism as a return to a higher but differentiated unity and does employ the notion of the negation of the negation (Marx [1873], 1976, p. 929), and, despite the best efforts of some modern commentators, it is difficult honestly to deny the strongly technical imagination which underpins the whole enterprise of *Capital*.

Finally, in two important respects, Hegelian dialectic, however surreal, is less vulnerable than that of Marx. Firstly, Hegel's *Science of Logic* takes place outside spatio-temporal constraints. It is a purely logical progression of concepts, even if the principles on which one ontological category is derived from another 'have resisted analysis to this day' (Elster, 1985, p. 37). Marx's effort to avoid giving any impression of the 'self-determination' of the concept, took the form of attempting to demonstrate the 'the ideal is nothing but the material world reflected in the mind of man and translated into forms of thought' (Marx [1873], 1976, p. 102). In practical terms this implied that there was some systematic relationship between the logical sequence of concepts in the exposition of the argument and the chronological order of their appearance in historical time. But this turned out to impose insurmountable difficulties in terms of presentation (and it is significant that having begun with the product in the *Grundrisse*, he began with the commodity in *Capital*). Thus Marx both stated his position and violated it, bequeathing insoluble ambiguities surrounding his interpretation of value, of the meaning of 'reflection' and of the relationship between history and logic which have plagued even his closest followers ever since. Secondly, when it came to applying his dialectic to history, Hegel was categorical in refusing to project his theory into the future. The philosophy could explain the rationality of what had happened; it was only then that it could be grasped in thought. Marx, despite all his strictures against the voluntarism of other Young Hegelians and some of his fellow revolutionaries, was unable by the very nature of his project fully to abide by the Hegelian restriction. Thus, while Hegel's owl of Minerva flew at dusk, the marxian owl, unfortunately, took flight at high noon.

BIBLIOGRAPHY

Althusser, L. 1965. *For Marx*. London: Allen Lane, 1969; New York: Vintage Books, 1970.

Bernstein, E. 1899. *Evolutionary Socialism*. Stuttgart. English trans. by Edith C. Harvey, London: Independent Labour Party, 1909.

Bhaskar, R. 1983. *Dialectic, Materialism and Human Emancipation*. London: New Left Books.

Cohen, G. 1978. *Karl Marx's Theory of History: A Defence*. London: Oxford University Press; Princeton, N.J.: Princeton University Press, 1979.

Elster, J. 1985. *Making Sense of Marx*. Cambridge: Cambridge University Press.

Hegel, G.W.F. 1812–16. *The Science of Logic*. London: Allen & Unwin, 1961; New York: Macmillan.

Kolakowski, L. 1978. *Main Currents of Marxism*. Vol. I: *The Founders*, Oxford and New York: Oxford University Press.

Lukács, G. 1923. *History and Class Consciousness*. London: Merlin, 1971.

Marx, K. 1844. *Economic and Philosophical Manuscripts of 1844*. In K. Marx and F. Engels, *Collected Works*, Vol. 3, London: Lawrence & Wishart, 1975.

Marx, K. 1847. *The Poverty of Philosophy*. In *Collected Works*, Vol. 6, London: Lawrence & Wishart, 1976.

Marx, K. [1857–8]. *Grundrisse*. Harmondsworth: Penguin 1973.

Marx, K. 1873. *Capital*, Vol. I. 2nd edn, Harmondsworth: Penguin, 1976.

Rosdolsky, R. 1968. *The Making of Marx's Capital*. Trans. by Peter Burgess, London: Pluto Pres, 1977.

Steedman, I. 1979. Marx on Ricardo. University of Manchester, Department of Economics, Discussion Paper 10.

Volpe, G. della. 1950. *Logica come scienza positiva*. Messina: G. d'Anna.

Distribution Theories

DAVID M. GORDON

It is hard to imagine a more important topic within Marxian economics than the distribution of income and the means of production among the principal classes in capitalist economies. For example: (1) The share of profits (or, inversely, the share of wages) constitutes one important component of the rate of profit. (2) The rate of profit operates as a fundamental determinant of the pace of investment and, therefore, of accumulation. (3) The rate of accumulation serves as a kind of life-force invigorating capitalist economies over time – regulating their growth and development, and the wealth of their participants. (4) Distribution, production and accumulation are thus fundamentally interconnected, forming the foundation of lives and livelihoods in capitalist societies.

In this respect, indeed, Marx himself regarded 'distribution relations' as part of the core of the capitalist economy. Criticizing those who ventured an 'initial, but still handicapped, criticism of bourgeois economy' by seeking to distinguish between the level of priority of production and distribution, Marx affirmed that both production relations and distribution relations are part of the 'material foundations and social forms' of any given historical epoch. Distribution relations and production relations are 'essentially coincident', he argued, since 'both share the same historically transitory character'. (Marx, 1894, pp. 883, 878).

And yet, despite these reasonably self-evident theoretical connections, the analysis of distribution has remained substantially underdeveloped in the historical evolution of Marxian economics. While such classic issues as crisis theory, the transformation problem and the usefulness of the labour theory of value have been intensively and vigorously reviewed, the determination of distribution patterns over time and cross-sectionally has been elided in synthetic treatments of Marxian analytics and largely ignored in more focused scholarly investigations.

More recent developments in Marxian economics, fortunately, have finally begun to overcome this traditional reticence. This essay provides a brief review of traditional attention – or, more accurately, *in*attention – to the problem of distribution and then surveys some promising recent cultivations of this historically fallow terrain.

Before beginning that review, however, it will be useful to clarify the defining boundaries of this topic.

It is probably most useful to begin with the role of distribution in the determination of profitability, that central fulcrum of economic behaviour. A familiar accounting identity reminds us that the rate of profit of the individual firm, r, can be expressed as the product of the share of profits in firm value-added, s_r, the ratio of output to utilized capital stock, y_u, and the ratio of utilized to owned capital stock, k^*, or

$$r \equiv s_r \cdot y_u \cdot k^*, \tag{1}$$

where

$$r \equiv \Pi/K_0; \qquad s_r \equiv \Pi/Y; \qquad y_u = Y/K_u; \qquad k^* \equiv K_u/K_0; \tag{2}$$

and Π is firm profits, K_0 is the value of the firm's owned capital stock, Y is firm value-added, and K_u is the portion of the owned capital stock which is currently utilized. In the aggregate, abstracting from variation among firms for such purposes, the same accounting identity applies.

In this accounting identity, distribution relations primarily affect the level of and changes in s_r, the share of profits in firm revenue. Factors affecting the rate of capital accumulation and the productivity of the means of production primarily affect y_u. Secular trends in the robustness of aggregate demand and its fluctuations over the business cycle have their most direct impact on k^*.

At this first level of approximation, then, analysis of distribution relations among the principal classes of a capitalist economy can begin with a focus on the determinants of s_r. Such analyses would immediately concern themselves with the wage share, s_w, as well, since $s_w \equiv (1 - s_r)$.

This is, of course, only a first level of approximation. At a second level of investigation, we must deal with three further refinements of focus.

1. Accounting equation (1) is formulated in revenue terms, not in value terms, so it does not yet encompass the Marxian concern with the value-theoretic determinations of economic relations. But this additional consideration requires simply that we add an analysis of the *rate of exploitation* (or the rate of surplus value), ε, to the definition of our task, since conventional Marxian value analytics establish a straightforward transformation between the profit share and the rate of exploitation. In one simple formulation, for example, the rate of exploitation is equal to the ratio of profits (Π) to wages (W) weighted by the capital–labour ratio (k_L), or $\varepsilon \equiv k_L \cdot (\Pi/W)$. (See Marglin, 1984, pp. 57–60 and 191–2, for a useful elaboration of these relations of equivalence.)

2. The first levels of approximation, represented by equations (1) and (2), also allows for the existence of only two classes in capitalist groupings or subsidiary

classes. At a second level of approximation, therefore, we must also consider the existence and determination of the shares of any other category of economic agents beyond our starting groups of capitalists and workers, which may seem relevant or necessary for our analyses.

3. A share of revenue need not necessarily translate into an exactly equivalent share of real income, since the prices confronting workers and capitalists may not exactly parallel each other over time. The relative purchasing power of their revenues received, and therefore the distribution of income, may consequently vary as a result of changes in the relative prices of capital goods and wage goods as well. It is conceivably useful, therefore, to decompose the profit share in equation (1) into two terms, one involving a ratio of 'real' profits to real income and the other a ratio of capital-goods prices to an index of (weighted) output prices. (See Weisskopf, 1979, for useful elaboration of this kind of decomposition.)

A final consideration seems critical for defining the scope of our analysis. It is taken for granted within the Marxian tradition that a given class's share of revenues is conditioned, at the most basic level, by the extent of its power over the means of production. And yet, over time, a given class's relative control of the means of production will be responsive to systematic changes in its share of revenues. It is not at all inappropriate, therefore, to treat the class distribution of revenues and the class distribution of control over the means of production as interdependent and mutually-determining over the long term. We may therefore define our task most broadly, in this respect, as *the analysis of the determination of class (and group) shares of revenue (and therefore of income) and of the class distribution of relative control over the means of production.*

Marx was himself clear on the importance of defining the analysis of distribution in both of these two senses. 'It may be said ...', he wrote at the end of Volume III of *Capital*, 'that capital itself ... already presupposes a distribution: the expropriation of the labourer from the conditions of labour [and] the concentration of these conditions in the hands of a minority of individuals ...' This underlying dimension of distribution 'differs altogether', he continued 'from what is understood by distribution relations ... [as] the various titles to that portion of the product which goes into individual consumption'. This does not in any way suggest, he insisted, that distribution in this former sense does not involve 'distribution relations' or should somehow remain peripheral to our analysis:

> The aforementioned distribution relations, on the contrary, are the basis of special social functions performed within the production relations by certain of their agents .... They imbue the conditions of production themselves and their representatives with a specific social quality. They determine the entire character and the entire movement of production (Marx, 1894, p. 879).

TRADITIONAL ANALYSIS

Inherited approaches to the problem of distribution are most easily viewed through three somewhat separable lenses: the growth-theoretic perspective, crisis-theoretic hypotheses of a rising profit share and antipodal crisis theories based on a falling profit share.

Long-term trajectories. Marxian economics has not always found it congenial to reflect upon the long-term growth paths of capitalist economies, since such perspectives are tainted in some minds by associations with concepts like 'stability' and 'equilibrium'. It is nonetheless possible to extract from traditional Marxian analses a clear approach to the logic of determination of 'steady-state' tendencies – provided this exercise is understood, in Marglin's words (1984, p. 52), 'as a subset of Marxian theory and not as an attempt to represent the whole'.

It seems reasonably clear, in that context, that distribution relations are exogeneously given to the traditional model, determined *outside* the set of basic interactions which jointly establish 'equilibrium' rates of growth and rates of profit. Historical conditions, not directly subject to internal economic analysis, establish a 'customary' wage. Existing levels of productiveness, also exogenous to the system, determine the level of output per hour and therefore, given the wage, the profit share as a residual. The behavioural hypothesis that capitalists save all profits combines with the determination of consumption by customary wage levels to create the conditions for a feasible and warranted steady-state combination of profit rates and growth rates. Marglin concludes (1984, p. 62): 'In contrast with the inherited neoclassical approach, in which resource allocation determines income distribution, causality here runs from [exogenously-determined] distribution to growth.'

There is, of course, nothing intrinsically wrong with these assumptions about directions of causality. Treating distribution as exogenous to the internal operations of the capitalist economy has simply meant that Marxian economists have tended to elide the factors determining distribution, setting them aside as consequences of 'historical and moral elements' and the 'technical' conditions of production.

Hypotheses of a rising profit share. Distribution has played a somewhat more explicit role in analyses of tendencies toward economic crisis. One group of theories has built upon hypotheses of a secular tendency toward an increasing profit share.

Perhaps the first systematic example of this hypothesis emerges in Lenin's account of imperialism and monopoly capitalism (1917). In its essence, Lenin's argument begins with the relatively simple hypothesis of increasing oligopoly and therefore, 'since monopoly prices are established' (p. 241), of relatively reduced competitive pressures. With the help of financial oligarchies, corporations are able to achieve a continuously rising profit share and therefore to amass 'an enormous "surplus of capital"' (p. 212). With this surplus of capital, capitalists are prompted to export capital overseas and, eventually, to reduce efforts at technical improvements. Over time, 'the *tendency* to stagnation and decay, which is characteristic of monopoly, continues to operates ...' (p. 241; emphasis in the original).

The model begins therefore, with a strong hypothesis about distribution – presuming a strong initial tendency under monopoly capitalism towards a rising profit share. And yet, the conditions which would be necessary to derive this as a prevailing long-term tendency are unexplored. There is no real analysis of wages, although prevailing assumptions about competitive labour markets are implicitly incorporated into the model. There is equal taciturnity about the initial determination of real productivity, even though the rate of growth of real productivity must exceed the growth of real wages for the initial condition of a rising profit share and an ultimate 'surplus of capital' to hold. And, despite the international orientation of the analysis, there is no real incorporation of a model of international pricing and exchange which would support the hypothesis of rising profit shares in all the the advanced countries.

These elisions are subsequently reproduced in most 20th-century analyses of underconsumption and monopoly capital. The models begin with a premise of growing capitalist power, most frequently from increasing monopoly control over product markets. This power leads to a rising 'surplus' and therefore to a rising profit share. From that set of initial premises, the problems of effective demand and urgent efforts to absorb the surplus follow naturally (Bleaney, 1976; Baran and Sweezy, 1966). As with Lenin, however, there is remarkably little attention to the conditions which permit this initial increase in the profit share. What about wages? Or labour productivity? Or conditions of international pricing? There is, in general, the simple presumption that conditions have evolved in such a way as to permit consistent increases in the profit share, but little reflection on the relations which make those conditions possible. Baran and Sweezy admit some of this inattention, particularly to the social relations which would allow real productivity growth to outstrip real wage growth (1966, pp. 8–9):

> We do not claim that directing attention to the generation and absorption of surplus gives a complete picture of this or any other society. And we are particularly conscious of the fact that this approach, as we have used it, has resulted in almost total neglect of a subject which occupies a central place in Marx's study of capitalism: the labour process.

Hypothesis of a falling profit share. For completeness, it is useful to consider the alternative hypothesis of a falling profit share, although attention to this possibility has only emerged within Marxian analysis more recently, primarily in the post-World War II era.

This hypothesis has relatively simple analytic foundations. For whatever reasons, working-class power may increase sufficiently to allow wages to rise more rapidly than labour productivity and therefore to result in a persistent increase in the wage share of revenues.

The hypothesis follows most naturally in a cyclical context and bears close connections to Marx's own analysis of cyclical dynamics in Chapter XXV of Vol. I of *Capital* (1867). In the short run, rapid expansion may lead to tight labour markets, increasing workers' bargaining power and resulting in a rising wage share. (Boddy and Crotty (1975) provide a useful development of this cyclical model in relatively traditional terms.)

The hypothesis needs further grounding in order to serve as the basis for a theory of economic crisis, however. The forces which lead to tight labour markets in short-term expansions could plausibly result in comparably slack labour markets during short-term contractions and therefore to a recovery of the profit share. In order properly to ground a theory of secular crisis upon this hypothesis of a falling profit share – and therefore fully to develop a 'profit squeeze' theory of economic crisis – one must show why cyclical contractions do not restore the profit share and, other things equal, the rate of profit. This requires analyses of conditions which permit rising worker power – even in the age of oligopolistic competition – from one business cycle to the next. Until the mid-1970s, Glyn and Sutcliffe (1972) were the principal Marxian economists to have formally developed such an analysis, and in their case primarily for the case of England.

Even in their case, however, the analytic requirements for the secular version of the 'profit squeeze' theory of crisis are not fully developed. What are the explicit conditions of labour market competition which explain particular patterns of wage growth? Under what conditions in the organization of production and the promotion of technical change would real productivity growth fail to keep pace with real wage growth? What are the conditions of international economic linkages which would or would not support tendencies towards a falling profit share? A further problem involves the closeness of the relationship between profits and surplus value; Shaikh (1978) reviews some of the problems with causal assumptions about this connection.

Kalecki and Mandel as connecting writers. We can find in the work of Michal Kalecki and Ernest Mandel some early instances of the kinds of concerns which have fuelled more recent explorations.

Particularly in his later essays, Kalecki identifies but does not yet develop some of the lines of inquiry which would be necessary for a more advanced analysis of distribution. In 'Class Struggle and Distribution of National Income' (1971), Kalecki refines the analysis of the relationship between wages and the profit share, noting that analyses of the conditions of product market competition are necessary 'to arrive at any reasonable conclusion on the impact of bargaining for wages on the distribution of income' (p. 159); that trade union power is likely, *ceteris paribus*, to reduce the level of the mark-up; and that, in general,

> class struggle as reflected in trade-union bargaining may affect the distribution of national income but in a much more sophisticated fashion than expressed by the crude doctrine: when wages are raised, profits fall *pro tanto* (p. 163).

In 'Trend and Business Cycle' (1968), Kalecki develops what he regards as a more satisfactory analysis of the relationship between short- and longer-term determinants of investment and therefore, *a fortiori*, the conditions which are likely to affect movements in the profit share over time.

Both of these analyses are entirely preliminary, however, since they constitute more of a programme for further work than a report on completed analyses. In particular, Kalecki notes that most of his analysis hangs on a handful of coefficients which he takes as given for his purposes, including the level of labour productivity, the share of gross profits flowing into capitalist consumption, capitalists' propensities to invest, and the rate of embodied technical progress. 'To my mind', he concluded, 'future inquiry ... should be directed ... towards treating ... the coefficients used in our equations ... as slowly changing variables rooted in past development of the system' (p. 183). The real problem, in short, is not to assume the central parameters of the determination of profits and investment but rather to derive them from determinant structural and historical analysis.

Mandel serves as a transitional figure in a different way. Although much of Mandel's analysis is hard to pin down precisely, he has nonetheless helped highlight the importance of an integration between formal Marxian analytics and structural/historical analysis. In *Late Capitalism* (1972), in particular, he suggests the rich possiblities for analysis of the particular conditions which might or might not give rise to variations in the rate of surplus value. There is much to learn, he urged (p. 183):

> Late capitalism is a great school for the proletariat, teaching it to concern itself not only with the immediate apportionment of newly created value between wages and profits, but with all questions of economic policy and development, and particularly with all questions revolving on the organization of labour, the process of production and the exercise of political power.

RECENT EXPLORATIONS

As this review is being written, a rich range of Marxian work on distribution in advanced capitalist societies has recently been completed or is currently under way. Since much of it is still in progress and unpublished, full references are difficult and probably inappropriate for an enduring encyclopedia. This final section will therefore concentrate on a synthetic review of the kinds of explorations which have recently been undertaken and the promising possibilities which have begun to emerge.

Changing power relations. One central problem in traditional Marxian analysis, which the examples of Kalecki and Mandel as connecting figures help to highlight, was the reluctance to forge determinate linkages between formal analytic categories, on one side, and the structure of and changes in power relations, on the other. Many appear to have felt either that these two loci of investigation operated at different levels of logical abstraction or that power relations, with all the social complexity of phenomena like the class struggle, could not be rendered analytically or studied empirically in any kind of formal or rigorous fashion. One is left with analyses, to quote Harris (1978, p. 166), which remain 'essentially ad hoc and tentative'.

Recent work has begun to overcome these hesitations. It has pursued careful and analytically determinate investigations of the relationship between power relations and, among other variables, the profit share. Attention has been focused primarily on three different dimensions of power relations: capital–labour relations, global linkages, and contests over state policy and practice.

Capital–labour relations. It has been recognized since Marx that class struggle over wages could conceivably affect distribution. But the formal linkage of conditions of class struggle to the determination of wage and profit shares has been hampered by the impression that levels and rates of change of productivity are determined orthogonally – by technical conditions and the pace of investment – and therefore that the two kinds of concerns could not somehow be combined into a single, inclusive, determinate analysis of changes in the profit share itself.

This problem appears to have been overcome. In recent work, particularly by Weisskopf, Bowles and Gordon (1983), a 'social model of productivity growth' has formally linked factors affecting capital–labour relations with the more traditional analyses. Several hypotheses about factors affecting the level of labour intensity in production have been both elaborated mathematically and tested empirically. This 'social model' appears to provide a robust explanation of variations in rates of productivity in the United States in the decades following World War II.

One crucial insight in that work is also beginning to invigorate Marxian wage analysis. Traditional perspectives on wage determination, building upon the 'reserve army' effect, focused on the relationship between wage bargaining and the threat of unemployment. As capitalist societies have developed, however, the threat of unemployment has been tempered by the availability of various components of what is typically called the 'social wage' – such as unemployment insurance and income maintenance expenditures. This has prompted the development of a more inclusive measure of the threat to workers of job dismissal: an index of 'the cost of job loss'. It calculates the expected income loss resulting from job termination, usually calculated as a percentage of the expected annual income if still employed, and incorporates estimates of the average wage in employment, expected unemployment duration, available income-replacing benefits and available non-income-replacing benefits (which workers receive whether employed or not). (For provisional definition and measurement, see Weisskopf, Bowles and Gordon, 1983.) Building upon these insights, it is likely that we will soon see much more fully developed and sophisticated analyses both of the determinants of wage growth and of the relationship between wage growth and labour demand.

Taken together, these new hypotheses about wage change and productivity growth themselves combine to provide the possibility of much more advanced hypotheses about determinants of changes in the profit share. Given that it is formally true that the rate of change of the real profit share is equal to the rate of change of real productivity minus the rate of change of real wages, analytic determinations of changes in the class distribution of revenues can now properly reflect both 'social' and 'technical' determinations.

Global power. As noted above, another elision in traditional Marxian analyses of distribution has involved international connections. Traditional analyses have either assumed perfect competition, an awkward first approximation, or have tended, following models of monopoly capitalism, to assume a constant or rising price mark-up. But in an open economy, neither assumption seems useful, even as a first approximation, because of the likelihood of secular changes in a given economy's relations with other suppliers and buyers in global markets. And these changes are quite likely to affect the distribution of revenues, since they are bound to affect either relative input prices or the mark-up and through either path potentially to influence the real profit share.

Analyses of interational linkages have lagged behind studies of capital–labour relations, but some promising initial explorations are under way. Two principal avenues of approach seem to be emerging. One seeks explicitly to model the effects of changes in the level and variability of the terms of trade on domestic productivity and profitability. The other aims at understanding and eventually modelling the effects of changing conditions of international power and, in particular, the effects of the internationalization of capital and growing multinational corporate leverage over domestic labour. (Bluestone and Harrison (1982) provide a useful early account of some of these latter effects for the US.) This kind of work is still in its early stages but seems increasingly essential in a more and more interdependent economy.

State policy and practice. The state can obviously have important effects on the private distribution of income among classes, both through tax policies and through the effects of expenditures on the costs of production and the relative bargaining power of the respective classes. Work on these connections has not yet moved beyond is early stages. Gough (1979) reviews the paths of likely effect on both the tax and expenditure side. Bowles and Gintis (1982) provide one provisional study of the effects of state policies on the profit share in the United States. And some of the studies of capital–labour relations discussed above are beginning to shed important light on the effects of 'social wage' expenditures on private-sector wage and productivity determination.

Combined effects. These three dimensions of power relations need not be quarantined in separate cells of analytic isolation. It is possible to derive an inclusive model of their combined effects which retains a focus on the power relationships incumbent in each. Bowles, Gordon and Weisskopf (1986) provide one such model of the determination of the profit rate; it includes factors affecting labour intensity, relative international power and relationships with the state. Applied econometrically, the model appears to provide the most robust account available of variations in the rate of profit in the US in the postwar era. Although the study focuses on the rate of profit as a dependent variable, its approach could also permit more focused analysis of the profit share as a potentially separable component of profitability.

137

Comparative analysis. It seems equally important, finally, to advance our understanding of the factors which explain cross-sectional variations in the levels and time patterns of the class distribution of revenues and income. This task must inevitably come rather late in the game, since it largely presupposes the availability of existing models of distribution which work for at least one country or groups of countries on their own terms. At the time of writing, some promising initial studies of cross-national variations in the determination of profit rates and shares are just under way. The best existing review of the political economic history upon which such studies must build is the excellent comparative analysis provided by Armstrong, Glyn and Harrison (1984).

One, two ... many classes? One final analytic task remains. Almost all recent studies of distribution have accepted the traditional preoccupation with a two-class model of capitalist economies – focusing almost exclusively on the single pair of opposing magnitudes, the profit share and the wage share. It is important at least to consider the possibility that a more variegated categorization of individuals would be fruitful, even for traditional Marxian problematics. What about managers? The petty bourgeoisie? Financiers? Different strata of the working class?

Empirical analyses aimed in this direction have lagged in large part because of continuing uncertainty and conflict over the appropriate definition of group boundaries and their interrelationships. Two main approaches appear to have emerged as the principal lines of inquiry within the Marxian perspective.

One approach seeks to derive a more complex mapping of primary and 'intermediate' or 'subsumed' classes from the method and essential categories of traditional Marxian analysis. Sharp debates nearly overwhelmed these efforts in the mid- to late-1970s, but it is conceivable that a relatively widespread agreement on the terms of analysis may be emerging in the mid- to late-1980s. Almost all of these analyses presuppose the usefulness of a single category of 'productive workers' and seek to distinguish, as carefully as possible, among various groups of intermediate agents and non-productive workers whose incomes largely draw upon realized surplus value. Wright (1978) offers one useful early review of the possibilities and problems in this approach, while Resnick and Wolff (1985) present an interesting recent treatment.

A second approach, usually encompassed under the general heading of 'segmentation theory', has paid primary attention to the importance of various divisions within the working class. Different analyses of labour segmentation have emerged in studies of various countries, and it is not at all clear that a single uniform model of labour segmentation in advanced capitalist formations can or should emerge. These studies nonetheless suggest the promise and importance of studying (a) the effects of different structures of production and labour on the opportunities and realized incomes of individual members of the working class; and (b) the potential impact of systematically structured divisions within the working class on the wage share of the class as a whole. Gordon, Edwards and Reich (1982) provide one important analysis of segmentation for the United States; Wilkinson (1981) offers one useful early compilation of comparative studies; while Bowles and Gintis (1977) provide a formal analytic integration of segmentation analysis within the value-theoretic context of more traditional Marxian theory.

These two approaches are potentially complementary, not conflicting, since the former concentrates largely on the group distribution of realized surplus value while the latter primarily explores the group distribution of variable capital. They have not yet been properly vetted, compared and integrated, however, so we still await a complete and satisfactory theoretical and empirical account of the distribution of revenues among all the relevant categories of individuals in capitalist economies.

BIBLIOGRAPHY

Armstrong, P., Glyn, A. and Harrison, J. 1984. *Capitalism since World War II*. London: Fontana.

Baran, P.A. and Sweezy, P.M. 1966. *Monopoly Capital: An Essay on the American Economic and Social Order*. New York: Monthly Review Press.

Bleaney, M. 1976. *Underconsumption Theories*. New York: International Publishers.

Bluestone, B. and Harrison, B. 1982. *The Deindustrialization of America*. New York: Basic Books.

Boddy, R. and Crotty, J. 1975. Class conflict and macro policy: the political business cycle. *Review of Radical Political Economics*, Spring.

Bowles, S. and Gintis, H. 1977. The Marxian theory of value and heterogeneous labour: a critique and reformulation. *Cambridge Journal of Economics*, 1(2), June 173–92.

Bowles, S. and Gintis, H. 1982. The crisis of liberal democratic capitalism: the case of the U.S. *Politics and Society*, Winter.

Bowles, S., Gordon, D.M. and Weisskopf, T.E. 1986. Power and profits: The social structure of accumulation and the profitability of the postwar U.S. economy. *Review of Radical Political Economics*, Spring-Summer.

Glyn, A. and Sutcliffe, B. 1972. *British Capitalism, Workers and the Profits Squeeze*. Harmondsworth: Penguin.

Gordon, D.M., Edwards, R. and Reich, M. 1982. *Segmented Work, Divided Workers*. New York: Cambridge University Press.

Gough, I. 1979. *The Political Economy of the Welfare State*. London: Macmillan. Distributed in U.S.A. by Humanities Press.

Harris, D.J. 1978. *Capital Accumulation and Income Distribution*. Stanford: Stanford University Press.

Kalecki, M. 1968. Trend and business cycle. In M. Kalecki, *Selected Essays on the Dynamics of the Capitalist Economy, 1933–1970,* Cambridge: Cambridge University Press, 1971.

Kalecki, M. 1971. Class struggle and distribution of national income. In M. Kalecki, *Selected Essays on the Dynamics of the Capitalist Economy, 1933–1970*. Cambridge and New York: Cambridge University Press.

Lenin, V.I. 1917. Imperialism, the highest stage of capitalism. In *Selected Works*, one-volume edition, New York: International Publishers, 1971.

Mandel, E. 1972. *Late Capitalism*. English edition, trans. Joris De Bres, London: New Left Books, 1975.

139

Marglin, S. 1984. *Growth, Distribution, and Prices.* Cambridge, Mass.: Harvard University Press.

Marx, K. 1867. *Capital,* Vol. I. New York: International Publishers, 1967.

Marx, K. 1894. *Capital,* Vol. III. New York: International Publshers, 1967.

Resnick, S.A. and Wolff, R.D. 1985. A Marxian reconceptualization of income and its distribution. In *Rethinking Marxism,* ed. S.A. Resnick and R.D. Wolff, Brooklyn, NY: Autonomedia.

Shaikh, A. 1978. An introduction to the history of crisis theories. In *U.S. Capitalism in Crisis.* New York: Union for Radical Political Economics.

Weisskopf, T.E. 1979. Marxian crisis theory and the rate of profit in the postwar U.S. economy. *Cambridge Journal of Economics* 3(4), December, 341–78.

Weisskopf, T.E., Bowles, S. and Gordon, D.M. 1983. Hearts and minds: a social model of U.S. productivity growth. *Brookings Papers on Economic Activity,* No. 2.

Wilkinson, F. (ed.) 1981. *The Dynamics of Labour Market Segmentation.* London: Academic Press.

Wright, E.O. 1978. *Class, Crisis, and the State.* London: New Left Books. Distributed in U.S.A. by Schocken Books.

Maurice Herbert Dobb

AMARTYA SEN

Maurice Dobb (1900–1976) was undoubtedly one of the outstanding political economists of this century. He was a Marxist, and was one of the most creative contributors to Marxian economics. As Ronald Meek put it, in his obituary of Dobb for the British Academy, 'over a period of fifty years [Dobb] established and maintained his position as one of the most eminent Marxist economists in the world'. Dobb's *Political Economy and Capitalism* (1937) and *Studies in the Development of Capitalism* (1946) stand out as his two most outstanding contributions to Marxian economics. The former is primarily concerned with economic theory (including such subjects as value theory, economic crises, imperialism, socialist economies), and the latter with economic history (particularly the emergence of capitalism from feudalism). These two fields – economic theory and economic history – were intimately connected in Dobb's approach to economics. He also wrote an influential book on Soviet economic development. This was first published under the title *Russian Economic Development since the Revolution* (1928), and later in a revised edition as *Soviet Economic Development since 1917* (1948).

Maurice Dobb was born on 24 July 1900 in London. His father Walter Herbert Dobb had a draper's retail business and his mother Elsie Annie Moire came from a Scottish merchant's family. He was educated at Charterhouse, and then at Pembroke College, Cambridge, where he studied economics. This was followed by two postgraduate years at the London School of Economics, where he did his PhD on 'The Entrepreneur'. The thesis formed the basis of his book *Capitalist Enterprise and Social Progress* (1925). Dobb returned to Cambridge at the end of 1924 on being appointed as a Lecturer in Economics and taught there until his retirement in 1967. He was a Fellow of Trinity College, and was elected to a University Readership in 1959. He received honorary degrees from the Charles University of Prague, the University of Budapest and Leicester University, and was elected a Fellow of the British Academy. After retirement he and his wife, Barbara, stayed on in the neighbouring village of Fulborn. He died on 17 August 1976.

Dobb was a theorist of great originality and reach. He was also, throughout his life, deeply concerned with economic policy and planning. His foundational critique of 'market socialism' as developed by Oscar Lange and Abba Lerner, appeared in the *Economic Journal* of 1933, later reproduced along with a number of related contributions in his *On Economic Theory and Socialism* (1955). His relatively elementary book *Wages* (1928) presented not merely a simple introduction to labour economics, but also an alternative outlook on these questions, including their policy implications, leading to interesting disputations with John Hicks, among others. In later years Dobb was much concerned with planning for economic development. In three lectures delivered at the Delhi School of Economics, later published as *Some Aspects of Economic Development* (1951), Dobb discussed some of the central issues of development planning for an economy with unemployed or underutilized labour, and his ideas were more extensively developed in his later book, *An Essay on Economic Growth and Planning* (1960).

Maurice Dobb also published a number of papers on more traditional fields in economic theory, including welfare economics, and some of these papers were collected together in his *Welfare Economics and the Economics of Socialism* (1969). In his *Theories of Value and Distribution since Adam Smith: Ideology and Economic Theory* (1973), he responded *inter alia* to the new developments in Cambridge political economy, including the influential *Prelude to a Critique of Economic Theory* by Piero Sraffa (1960). Maurice Dobb's association with Piero Sraffa extended over a long period, both as a colleague at Trinity College, and also as a collaborator in editing *Works and Correspondence of David Ricardo*, published in eleven volumes between 1951 and 1973 (on the latter, see Pollitt, 1985).

In addition to academic writings, Maurice Dobb also did a good deal of popular writing, both for workers' education and for general public discussion. He wrote a number of pamphlets, including *The Development of Modern Capitalism* (1922), *Money and Prices* (1924), *An Outline of European History* (1926), *Modern Capitalism* (1927), *On Marxism Today* (1932), *Planning and Capitalism* (1937), *Soviet Planning and Labour in Peace and War* (1942), *Marx as an Economist, An Essay* (1943), *Capitalism Yesterday and Today* (1958), and *Economic Growth and Underdeveloped Countries* (1963) and many others. Dobb was a superb communicator, and the nature of his own research was much influenced by policy debates and public discussions. Dobb the economist was not only close to Dobb the historian, but also in constant company of Dobb the member of the public. It would be difficult to find another economist who could match Dobb in his extraordinary combination of genuinely 'high-brow' theory, on the one hand, and popular writing on the other. The author of *Political Economy and Capitalism* (from the appearance of which – as Ronald Meek (1978) rightly notes – 'future historians of economic thought will probably date the emergence of Marxist economics as a really serious economic discipline') was also spending a good deal of effort writing pamphlets and material for labour education, and doing straightforward journalism. It is not possible to appreciate fully Maurice Dobb's contributions to economics without taking note of his views of the role of economics in public discussions and debates.

Another interesting issue in understanding Dobb's approach to economics concerns his adherence to the labour theory of value. The labour theory has been under attack not only from neoclassical economists, but also from such anti-neoclassical political economists as Joan Robinson and, indirectly, even Piero Sraffa. In his last major work, *Theories of Value and Distribution since Adam Smith* (1973), Maurice Dobb speaks much in support of the relevance of Sraffa's (1960) major contribution, which eschews the use of labour values (on this see Steedman, 1977), but without abandoning his insistence on the importance of the labour theory of value. It is easy to think that there is some inconsistency here, and it is tempting to trace the origin of this alleged inconsistency to Dobb's earlier writings, which made Abram Bergson remark that 'in Dobb's analysis the labour theory is not so much an analytic tool as excess baggage' (Bergson, 1949, p. 445).

The key to understanding Dobb's attitude to the labour theory of value is to recognize that he did not see it just as an intermediate product in explaining relative prices and distributions. He took 'the labour-principle' as 'making an important qualitative statement about the nature of the economic problem' (Dobb, 1937, p. 21). He rejected seeing the labour theory of value as simply a 'first approximation' containing 'nothing essential that cannot be expressed equally well and easily in other terms' (Dobb, 1973, pp. 148–9). The description of the production process in terms of labour involvement has an interest that extends far beyond the role of the labour value magnitudes in providing a 'first approximation' for relative prices. As Dobb (1973) put it,

> there is something in the first approximation that is lacking in later approximations or cannot be expressed so easily in those terms (e.g., the first approximation may be a device for emphasising and throwing into relief something of greater generality and less particularity) (pp. 148–9).

Any description of reality involves some selection of facts to emphasize certain features and to underplay others, and the labour theory of value was seen by Dobb as emphasizing the role of those who are involved in 'personal participation in the process of production *per se*' in contrast with those who do not have such personal involvement.

> As such 'exploitation' is neither something 'metaphysical' nor simply an ethical judgement (still less 'just a noise') as has sometimes been depicted: it is a factual description of a socio-economic relationship, as much as is Marc Bloch's apt characterisation of Feudalism as a system where feudal Lords 'lived on the labour of other men' (Dobb, 1973, p. 145).

The possibility of calculating prices without going through value magnitudes, and the greater efficiency of doing that (on this see Steedman, 1977), does not affect this descriptive relevance of the labour theory of value in any way. Maurice Dobb also outlined the relationship of this primarily descriptive interpretation of the labour theory of value with evaluative questions, e.g., assessing the 'right of ownership' (see especially Dobb, 1937).

The importance for Dobb of descriptive relevance is brought out also by his complex attitude to the utility theory of value. While he rejected the view that the utility picture is the best way of seeing relative values ('by taking as its foundation a fact of individual consciousness'), he lamented the descriptive impoverishment that is brought about by replacing the subjective utility theory by the 'revealed preference' approach.

> If all that is postulated is simply that men *choose*, without anything being stated even as to how they choose or what governs their choice, it would seem impossible for economics to provide us with any more than a sort of algebra of human choice (Dobb, 1937, p. 171).

Indeed as early as 1929, a long time before the 'revealed preference theory' was formally inaugurated by Paul Samuelson, Dobb had warned:

> Actually the whole tendency of modern theory is to abandon such psychological conceptions: to make utility and disutility coincident with observed offers in the market; to abandon a 'theory of value' in pursuit of a 'theory of price'. But this is to surrender, not to solve the problem (Dobb, 1929, p. 32).

Maurice Dobb's open-minded attitude to non-Marxian traditions in economics added strength and reach to his own Marxist theorizing. He could combine Marxist reasoning and methodology with other traditions, and he was eager to be able to communicate with economists belonging to other schools. Dobb's honesty and lack of dogmatism were important for the development of the Marxist economic tradition in the English-speaking world, because he occupied a unique position in Marxist thinking in Britain. As Eric Hobsbawm has noted,

> for several generations (as these are measured in the brief lives of students) he was not just the only Marxist economist in a British university of whom most people had heard, but virtually the only don known as a communist to the wider world (Hobsbawm, 1967, p. 1).

The Marxist economic tradition was well served by Maurice Dobb's willingness to engage in spirited but courteous debates with economists of other schools. Dobb achieved this without compromising the integrity of his position. The distinctly Marxist quality of his economic writings was as important as his willingness to listen and dispassionately analyse the claims of other schools of thought with which he engaged in systematic disputation. The gentleness of Dobb's style of disputation arose from strength rather than from weakness.

Dobb's willingness to appreciate positive elements in other economic traditions while retaining the distinctive qualities of his own approach is brought out very clearly also in his truly far-reaching critique of the theory of socialist pricing as presented by Lange, Lerner, Dickinson and others in the 1930s. Dobb noted the efficiency advantages of a price mechanism, especially in a static context. He was, however, one of the first economists to analyse clearly the conflict between the demands of efficiency expressed in the equilibrium conditions of the Langer–Lerner price mechanism (and also of course in a perfectly competitive market equilibrium), and the demands that would be imposed by the requirements of equality, given the initial conditions. In his paper called 'Economic Theory and the Problems of a Socialist Economy' published in 1933, Maurice Dobb argued thus:

> If carpenters are scarcer or more costly to train than scavengers, the market will place a higher value upon their services, and carpenters will derive a higher income and have greater 'voting power' as consumers. On the side of supply the extra 'costliness' of carpenters will receive expression, but only at the expense of giving carpenters a differential 'pull' as consumers, and hence vitiating the index of demand. On the other hand, if carpenters and scavengers are to be given equal weight as consumers by assuring them equal incomes, then the extra costliness of carpenters will find no expression in costs of production. Here is the central dilemma. Precisely because consumers are also producers, both costs and needs are precluded from receiving simultaneous expression in the same system of market valuations. Precisely to the extent that market valuations are rendered adequate in one direction they lose significance in the other (Dobb, 1933, p. 37).

The fact that given an initial distribution of resources the demands of efficiency and those of equity may – and typically will – conflict is, of course, one of the major issues in the theory of resource allocation, with implications for market socialism as well as for competitive markets in a private ownership economy. As a matter of fact, Marx had *inter alia* noted this conflict in his *Critique of the Gotha Programme*, but in the discussion centring around Langer–Lerner systems, this deep conflict had attracted relatively little attention, except in the arguments presented by Maurice Dobb. The fact that even a socialist economy has to cope with inequalities of initial resource distribution (arising from, among other things, differences in inherited talents and acquired skills) makes it a relevant question for a socialist economy as well as for competitive economies, and Dobb's was one of the first clear analyses of this central question of resource allocation.

The second respect in which Maurice Dobb found the literature on market socialism inadequate concerns allocation over time. In discussing the achievements and failures of the market mechanism, Maurice Dobb argued that the planning of investment decisions

> may contribute much more to human welfare than could the most perfect micro-economic adjustment, of which the market (if it worked like the textbooks, at least, and there were no income-inequalities) is admittedly more fitted in most cases to take care (Dobb, 1960, p. 76).

In his book *An Essay on Economic Growth and Planning* (1960), Dobb provided a major investigation of the basis of planned investment decisions, covering overall investment rates, sectorial divisions, choice of techniques, and pricing policies related to allocation (including that over time).

This contribution of Dobb relates closely to his analysis of the problems of economic development. In his earlier book *Some Aspects of Economic Development* (1951), Dobb had already presented a pioneering analysis of the problem of economic development in a surplus-labour economy, with shortage of capital and of many skills. While, on the one hand, he anticipated W.A. Lewis's more well-known investigation of economic growth with 'unlimited supplies of labour', he also went on to demonstrate the far-reaching implications of the over-all savings rates being socially sub-optimal and inadequate. Briefly, he showed that this requires not only policies directly aimed at raising the rates of saving and investment, but it also has implications for the choice of techniques, sectoral balances and price fixation.

In such a brief note, it is not possible to do justice to the enormous range of Maurice Dobb's contributions to economic theory, applied economics and economic history. Different authors influenced by Maurice Dobb have emphasized different aspects of his many-sided works (see, for example, Feinstein (ed.), 1967, and the Maurice Dobb Memorial Issue, 1978). He has also had influence even outside professional economics, particularly in history, especially through his analysis of the development of capitalism.

Dobb (1946) argued that the decline of feudalism was caused primarily by 'the inefficiency of Feudalism as a system of production, coupled with the growing needs of the ruling class for revenue' (p. 42). This view of feudal decline, with its emphasis on *internal* pressures, became the subject of a lively debate in the early 1950s. An alternative position, forcefully presented by Paul Sweezy in particular, emphasized some *external* developments, especially the growth of trade, operating through the relations between the feudal countryside and the towns that developed on its periphery. No matter what view is taken as to 'who won' the debates on the transition from feudalism to capitalism, Dobb's creative role in opening up a central question in economic history as well as a major issue in Marxist political economy can scarcely be disputed. Indeed, *Studies in the Development of Capitalism* (1946) has been a prime mover in the emergence of the powerful Marxian tradition of economic history in the English-speaking world, which has produced scholars of the eminence of Christopher Hill, Rodney Hilton, Eric Hobsbawm, Edward Thompson and others.

It is worth emphasizing that aside from the explicit contributions made by Maurice Dobb to economic history, he also did use a historical approach to economic analysis in general. Maurice Dobb's deep involvement in descriptive richness (as exemplified by his analysis of 'the requirements of a theory of value'), his insistence on not neglecting the long-run features of resource allocation (influencing his work on planning as well as development), his concern with observed phenomena in slumps and depressions in examining theories of 'crises', and so on, all relate to the historian's perspective. Dobb's works in the apparently divergent areas of economic theory, applied economics and economic history are, in fact, quite closely related to each other.

Maurice Dobb was not only a major bridge-builder between Marxist and non-Marxist economic traditions (aside from pioneering the development of

Marxist economics in Britain and to some extent in the entire English-speaking world), he also built many bridges beween the different pursuits of economic theorists, applied economists and economic historians. Dobb's political economy involved the rejection of the narrowly economic as well as the narrowly doctrinaire. He was a great economist in the best of the broad tradition of classical political economy.

SELECTED WORKS

1925. *Capitalist Enterprise and Social Progress*. London: Routledge.

1928. *Russian Economic Development since the Revolution*. London: Routledge.

1928. *Wages*. London: Nisbet; Cambridge: Cambridge University Press.

1929. A sceptical view of the theory of wages. *Economic Journal* 39, December, 506–19.

1933. Economic theory and the problems of a socialist economy. *Economic Journal* 43, December, 588–98.

1937. *Political Economy and Capitalism: Some Essays in Economic Tradition*. London: Routledge.

1946. *Studies in the Development of Capitalism*. London: Routledge; New York: International Publishers, 1947.

1948. *Soviet Economic Development since 1917*. London: Routledge.

1950. Reply (to Paul Sweezy's article on the transition from feudalism to capitalism). *Science and Society* 14(2), *Spring*, 157–67.

1951. *Some Aspects of Economic Development: Three Lectures*. Delhi: Ranjit Publishers, for the Delhi School of Economics.

1955. *On Economic Theory and Socialism*. London: Routledge; New York: International Publishers.

1960. *An Essay on Economic Growth and Planning*. London: Routledge; New York: Monthly Review Press.

1969. *Welfare Economics and the Economics of Socialism*. Cambridge: Cambridge University Press.

1973. *Theories of Value and Distribution since Adam Smith: Ideology and Economic Theory*. Cambridge and New York: Cambridge University Press.

BIBLIOGRAPHY

Bergson, A. 1949. Socialist economics. In *A Survey of Contemporary Economics*, ed. H.S. Ellis, Philadelphia: Blakiston.

Feinstein, C. (ed.) 1967. *Socialism, Capitalism and Economic Growth: Essays Presented to Maurice Dobb*. Cambridge: Cambridge University Press.

Hobsbawm, E.J. 1967. Maurice Dobb. In Feinstein (1967).

Maurice Dobb Memorial Issue. 1978. *Cambridge Journal of Economics* 2(2), June.

Meeks, R. 1978. Obituary of Maurice Herbert Dobb. *Proceedings of the British Academy 1977* 53, 333–44.

Pollitt, B.H. 1985. Clearing the path for 'Production of Commodities by Means of Commodities': Notes on the Collaboration of Maurice Dobb in Piero Sraffa's edition of 'The Works and Correspondence of David Ricardo'. Mimeographed.

Sraffa, P. 1960. *Production of Commodities by Means of Commodities: Prelude to a Critique of Economic Theory*. Cambridge: Cambridge University Press.

Sraffa, P., with the collaboration of M.H. Dobb. 1951–73. *Works and Correspondence of David Ricardo*. 11 vols, Cambridge: Cambridge University Press.

Steedman, I. 1977. *Marx after Sraffa*. London: New Left Books.

Economic Interpretation of History

ERNEST GELLNER

Marxism does not possess a monopoly of the economic interpretation of history. Other theories of this kind can be formulated – for instance that which can be found in the very distinguished work of Karl Polanyi, dividing the history of mankind into three stages, each defined by a different type of economy. If Polanyi is right in suggesting that reciprocity, redistribution and the market each defined a different kind of society, this is, in a way, tantamount to saying that the economy is primary, and thus his work constitutes a species of the economic interpretation of history. Nevertheless, despite the importance of Polanyi's work and the possibility of other rival economic interpretations, Marxism remains the most influential, the most important and perhaps the best elaborated of all theories, and we shall concentrate on it.

One often approaches a theory by seeing what it denies and what it repudiates. This approach is quite frequently adopted in the case of Marxism, where it is both fitting and misleading. We shall begin by adopting this approach, and turn to its dangers subsequently.

Marxism began as the reaction to the romantic idealism of Hegel, in the ambience of whose thought the young Karl Marx reached maturity. This no doubt is the best advertised fact about the origin of Marxism. The central point about Hegelianism was that it was acutely concerned with history and social change, placing these at the centre of philosophical attention (instead of treating them as mere distractions from the contemplation of timeless objects, which had been a more frequent philosophical attitude); and secondly, it taught that history was basically determined by intellectual, spiritual, conceptual or religious forces. As Marx and Engels put it in *The German Ideology*, 'The Young Hegelians are in agreement with the Old Hegelians in their belief in the rule of religion, of concepts, of an abstract general principle in the existing world' (Marx and Engels, 1845–6, p. 5).

Now the question is – why did Hegel and followers believe this? If it is interpreted in a concrete sense, as a doctrine claiming that the ideas of men determined their other activities, it does not have a great deal of plausibility, especially when put forward as an unrestricted generalization. If it is formulated – as it was by Hegel – as the view that some kind of abstract principle or entity dominates history, the question may well be asked: what evidence do we have for the very existence of this mysterious poltergeist allegedly manipulating historical events? Given the fact that the doctrine is either implausible or obscure, or indeed both, why were intelligent men so strongly drawn to it?

The answer to this may be complex, but the main elements in it can perhaps be formulated simply and briefly. Hegelianism enters the scene when the notion of what we now call *culture* enters public debate. The point is this: men are not machines. When they are they do not simply respond to some kind of push. When they do something, they generally have an idea, a concept, of the action which they are performing. The idea or conception in turn is part of a whole system. A man who goes through the ceremony of marriage has an *idea* of what the institution means in the soceity of which he is part, and his understanding of the institution is an integral part of his action. A man who commits an act of violence as part of a family feud has an idea of what family and honour *mean*, and is committed to those ideas. And each of these ideas is not something which the individual had excogitated for himself. He took it over from a corpus of ideas which differ from community to community, and which *change* over time, and which are now known as *culture*.

Put in this way, the 'conceptual' determination of human conduct no longer seems fanciful, but on the contrary is liable to seem obvious and trite. In various terminologies ('hermeneutics', 'structuralism', and others) it is rather fashionable nowadays. The idea that conduct is concept-saturated and that concepts come not singly but as *systems*, and are carried not by individuals but by on-going historic communities, has great plausibility and force. Admittedly, those who propose it, in Hegel's day and in ours, do not always define their position with precision. They do not always make clear whether they are merely saying that culture in this sense is important (which is hardly disputable), or claiming that it is the prime determinant of other things and the ultimate source of change, which is a much stronger and much more contentious claim. Nonetheless, the idea that culture is important and pervasive is very plausible and suggestive, and Hegelianism can be credited with being one of the philosophies which, in its own peculiar language, had introduced this idea. It is important to add that Hegelianism often speaks of 'Spirit' in the singular; our suggestion is that this can be interpreted as *culture*, as the spirit of the age. This made it easy for Hegelianism to operate as a kind of surrogate Christianity: those no longer able to believe in a personal god could tell themselves that this had been a parable of a kind of guiding historical spirit. For those who wanted to use it in that way, Hegelianism was the continuation of religion by other means.

But Hegelianism is not exhausted by its sense of culture, expressed in somewhat strange language. It is also pervaded by another idea, fused with the first one, and one which it shares with many thinkers of its period: a sense of *historical plan*. The turn of the 18th and 19th centuries was a time when men became imbued with the sense of cumulative historical change, pointing in an upward direction – in other words, the idea of Progress.

The basic fact about Marxism is that it retains this second idea, the 'plan' of history, but aims at inverting the first idea, the romantic idealism, the attribution of agency to culture. As the two founders of Marxism put it themselves in *The German Ideology* (pp. 14–15),

> In direct contrast to German philosophy which descends from heaven to earth, here we ascend from earth to heaven ... We set out from real active men, and on the basis of their real life-process we demonstrate the development of the ideological reflexes and echoes of this life-process ... Morality, religion, metaphysics, all the rest of ideology and their corresponding forms of consciousness, thus no longer retain the semblance of independence. They have no history, no development; but men, developing their material production and their material intercourse, alter, along with their real existence, their thinking and the products of their thinking. Life is not determined by consciousness, but consciousness by life.

Later on in the same work, the two founders of Marxism specify the recipe which, according to them, was followed by those who produced the idealistic mystification. First of all, ideas were separated from empirical context and the interests of the rulers who put them forward. Secondly, a set of logical connections was found linking successive ruling ideas, and their logic is then meant to explain the pattern of history. (This links the concept-saturation of history to the notion of historic *design*. Historic pattern is the reflection of the internal logical connection of successive ideas.) Thirdly, to diminish the mystical appearance of all this, the free-floating, self-transforming concept was once again credited to a person or group of persons.

If this kind of theory is false, what then is true? In the same work a little later, the authors tell us:

> This sum of productive forces, forms of capital and social forms of intercourse, which every individual and generation finds in existence as something given, is the real basis of ... the ... 'essence of man'... These conditions of life, which different generations find in existence, decide also whether or not the periodically recurring revolutionary convulsion will be strong enough to over-throw the basis of all existing forms. And if these material elements of a complete revolution are not present ... then, as far as practical developments are concerned, it is absolutely immaterial whether the 'idea' of this revolution has been expressed a hundred times already ... (p. 30).

The passage seems unambiguous: what is retained is the idea of a plan, and also the idea of primarily internal, endogenous propulsion. What has changed is the identification of the propulsion, of the driving force of the trans-formation. Change continues to be the law of all things, and it is governed by a plan, it is not random; but the mechanism which controls it is now identified in a new manner.

From then on, the criticisms of the position can really be divided into two major species: some challenge the identification of the ruling mechanism, and others the idea of historic *plan*. As the most dramatic presentation of Marxist development, Robert Tucker's *Philosophy and Myth in Karl Marx* (1961, p. 123) puts it:

> Marx founded Marxism in an outburst of Hegelizing. He considered himself to be engaged in ... [an] ... act of translation of the already discovered truth ... from the language of idealism into that of materialism .... Hegelianism itself was latently or esoterically an economic interpretation of history. It treated history as 'a history of production' ... in which spirit externalizes itself in thought-objects. But this was simply a mystified presentation of *man* externalizing himself in *material* objects.

This highlights both the origin *and* the validity or otherwise of the economic interpretation of history. Some obvious but important points can be made at this stage. The Hegel/Marx confrontation owes much of its drama and appeal to the extreme and unqualified manner in which the opposition is presented. This unqualified, unrestricted interpretation can certainly be found in the basic texts of Marxism. Whether it is the 'correct' interpretation is an inherently undecidable question: it simply depends on which texts one treats as final – those which affirm the position without restriction and without qualification, or those which contain modifications, qualifications and restrictions.

The same dilemma no doubt arises on the Hegelian side, where it is further accompanied by the question as to whether the motive force, the spirit of history, is to be seen as some kind of abstract principle (in which case the idea seems absurd to most of us), or whether this is merely to be treated as a way of referring to what we now term culture (in which case it is interesting and contentious).

One must point out that these two positions, the Hegelian and the Marxist, are contraries, but not contradictories. They cannot both be true, but they can perfectly well both be false. A world is easily conceivable where neither of them is true: a world in which social changes sometimes occur as a consequence of changes in economic activities, and sometimes as a consequence of strains and stresses in the culture. Not only is such a world conceivable, but it does really rather look as if that is the kind of world we do actually live in. (Part of the appeal of Marxism in its early days always hinged on presenting Hegel-type idealism and Marxism as two contradictories, and 'demonstrating' the validity of Marxism as a simple corollary of the manifest absurdity of strong versions of Hegelianism.) In this connection, it is worth noticing that by far the most influential (and not unsympathetic) sociological critic of Marx is Max Weber, who upholds precisely this kind of position. Strangely enough, despite explicit and categorical denials on his own part, he is often misrepresented as offering a return to some kind of idealism (without perhaps the mystical idea of the agency of abstract concepts which was present in Hegel). For instance, Michio

Morishima, in *Why has Japan 'Succeeded'?* (1982), p. 1), observes: 'Whereas Karl Marx contended that ideology and ethics were no more than reflections ... Max Weber ... made the case for the existence of quite the reverse relationship.' Weber was sensitive to both kinds of constraint; he merely insisted that on occasion, a 'cultural' or 'religious' element might make a crucial difference.

Connected with this, there is another important theoretical difference to be found in Weber and many contemporary sociologists. The idea of the inherent historical plan, which had united Hegel and Marx, is abandoned. If the crucial moving power of history comes from one source only, though this does not strictly speaking entail that there should be a plan, an unfolding of design, it nevertheless does make it at least very plausible. If that crucial moving power had been *consciousness*, and its aim the arrival at self-consciousness, then it was natural to conclude that with the passage of time, there would indeed be more and more of such consciousness. So the historical plan could be seen as the manifestation of the striving of the Absolute Spirit or humanity, towards ever greater awareness. Alternatively, if the motive force was the growth of the forces of production, then, once again, it was not unreasonable to suppose that history might be a series of organizational adjustments to expanding productive powers, culminating in a full adjustment to the final great flowering of our productive capacity. (Something like that is the essence of the Marxist vision of history.)

If on the other hand the motive forces and the triggers come from a *number* of sources, which moreover are inherently diverse, there is no clear reason why history should have a pattern in the sense of coming ever closer to satisfying some single criterion (consciousness, productivity, congruence between productivity and social ethos, or whatever). So in the Weberian and more modern vision, the dramatic and unique developments of the modern industrial world are no longer seen as the inevitable fulfilment and culmination of a potential that had always been there, but rather as a development which only occurred because a certain set of factors happened to operate at a given time simultaneously, and which would otherwise not have occurred, and which was in no way *bound* to occur. Contingency replaces fatality.

So much for the central problem connected with the economic interpretation of history. The question concerning the relative importance of conceptual (cultural) and productive factors is the best known, most conspicuous and best advertised issue in this problem area. But in fact, it is very far from obvious that it is really the most important issue, the most critical testing ground for the economic theory of history. There is another problem, less immediately obvious, less well known, but probably of greater importance, theoretically and practically. That is the relative importance of productive and *coercive* activities.

The normal associations which are likely to be evoked by the phrase 'historical materialism' do indeed imply the downgrading of purely conceptual, intellectual and cultural elements as explanatory factors in history. But it does not naturally suggest the downgrading of force, violence, coercion. On the contrary, for most people the idea of coercion by threat or violence, or death and pain, seems just as 'realistic', just as 'materialistic' as the imperatives imposed by material need for sustenance and shelter. Normally one assumes that the difference between coercion by violence or the threat of violence, and coercion by fear of destitution, is simply that the former is more immediate and works more quickly. One might even argue that *all* coercion is ultimately coercion by violence: a man or a group in society which coerces other members by controlling the food supply, for instance, can only do it if they control and defend the store of food or some other vital necessity by force, even if that force is kept in reserve. Economic constraint, it could be argued (as Marxists themselves argue in other contexts), only operates because a certain set of rules is enforced by the state, which may well remain in the background. But economic constraint is in this way parasitic on the ultimate presence of enforcement, based on the monopoly of control of the tools of violence.

The logic of this argument may seem persuasive, but it is contradicted by a very central tenet of the Marxist variant of the economic theory of history. Violence, according to the theory, is not fundamental or primary, it does not intiate fundamental social change, nor is it a fundamental basis of any social order. This is the central contention of Marxism, and at this point, real Marxism diverges from what might be called the vulgar image possessed of it by non-specialists. Marxism stresses economic factors, and downgrades not merely the importance of conceptual, 'superstructural' ones, but equally, and very significantly, the role of coercive factors.

A place where this is vigorously expressed is Engels's 'Anti-Dühring' (1878):

> ... historically, private property by no means makes its appearance as the result of robbery or violence.... Everywhere where private property developed, this took place as the result of altered relations of production and exchange, in the interests of increased production and in furtherance of intercourse – that is to say, as a result of economic causes. Force plays no part in this at all. Indeed, it is clear that the institution of private property must be already in existence before the robber can *appropriate* another person's property... Nor can we use either force or property founded on force to explain the 'enslavement of man for menial labour' in its most modern form – wage labour .... The whole process is explained by purely economic causes; robbery, force, and the state of political interference of any kind are unnecessary at any point whatever (Burns, 1935, pp. 267–9).

Engles goes on to argue the same specifically in connection with the institutions of slavery:

> Thus force, instead of controlling the economic order, was on the contrary pressed into the service of the economic order. *Slavery* was invented. It soon became the predominant form of production among all peoples who were developing beyond the primitive community, but in the end was also one of the chief causes of the decay of that system (ibid., p. 274).

Engels a little earlier in the same work was on slightly more favourable ground when he discussed the replacement of the nobility by the bourgeoisie as the most powerful estate in the land. If physical force were crucial, how should the peaceful merchants and producers have prevailed over the professional warriors? As Engels puts it: 'During the whole of this struggle, political forces were on the side of the nobility ...' (ibid., p. 270).

One can of course think of explanations for this paradox: the nobility might have slaughtered each other, or there might be an alliance between the monarchy and the middle class (Engels himself mentioned this possibility, but does not think it constitutes a real explanation) and so forth. In any case, valid or not, this particular victory of producers over warriors would seem to constitute a prima facie example of the non-dominance of force in history. The difficulty for the theory arises when the point is generalized to cover all social orders and all major transitions, which is precisely what Marxism does.

Engels tries to argue this point in connection with a social formation which one might normally consider to be the very paradigm of the domination by force: 'oriental despotism'. (In fact, it is for this very reason that some later Marxists have maintained that this social formation is incompatible with Marxist theory, and hence may not exist.) Engels does it, interestingly enough, by means of a kind of functionalist theory of society and government: the essential function, the essential role and duty, of despotic governments in hydraulic societies is to keep production going by looking after the irrigation system. As he puts it:

> However great the number of despotic governments which rose and fell in India and Persia, each was fully aware that its first duty was the general maintenance of irrigation throughout the valleys, without which no agriculture was possible (Burns, 1935, p. 273).

It is a curious argument. He cannot seriously maintain that these oriental despots were always motivated by a sense of duty towards the people they governed. What he must mean is something like this: unless they did their 'duty', the society in question could not survive, and they themselves, as its political parasites, would not survive either. So the real foundation of 'oriental despotism' was not the force of the despot, but the functional imperatives of despotically imposed irrigation systems. Economic need, as in the case of slavery, makes use of violence for its own ends, but violence itself initiates or maintains nothing. The interpretation is related to what Engels says a little further on. Those who use force can either aid economic development or accelerate it, or go against it, which they do rarely (though he admits that it occasionally occurs), and they they themselves usually go under: 'Where ... the internal public force of the country stands in opposition to economic development ... the context has always ended with the downfall of the political power' (Burns, 1935, p. 277).

We have seen that Engels's materialism is curiously functional, indeed teleological: the economic potential of a society or of its productive base somehow seeks out available force, and enlists it on its own behalf. Coercion is and ought to be the slave of production, he might well have said. This teleological element is found again in what is perhaps the most famous and most concise formulation of Marxist theory, namely certain passages in Marx's preface to *A Contribution to 'The Critique of Political Economy'* (1859):

> A social system never perishes before all the productive forces have developed for which it is wide enough; and new, higher productive relationships never come into being before the material conditions for their existence have been brought to maturity within the womb of the old society itself. Therefore, mankind always sets itself only such problems as it can solve; for when we look closer we will always find that the problem itself only arises when the material conditions for its solution are already present, or at least in the process of coming into being. In broad outline, the Asiatic, the ancient, the feudal, and the modern bourgeois mode of production can be indicated as progressive epochs in the economic system of society (Burns, 1935, p. 372).

The claim that a new order does not come into being before the conditions for it are available, is virtually a tautology: nothing comes into being unless the conditions for it exist. That is what 'conditions' mean. But the idea that a social system never perishes before it has used up all its potential is both strangely teleological and disputable. Why should it not be replaced even before it plays itself out to the full? Why should not some of its potential be wasted?

It is obvious from this passage that the purposive, upward surge of successive modes of production cannot be hindered by force, nor even aided by it. Engels, in 'Anti-Dühring', sneers at rulers such as Friedrich Wilhelm IV, or the then Tsar of Russia, who despite the power and size of their armies are unable to defy the economic logic of the situation. Engels also treats ironically Herr Dühring's fear of force as the 'absolute evil', the belief that the 'first act of force is the original sin', and so forth. In his view, on the contrary, force simply does not have the capacity to initiate evil. It does however have another 'role in history, a revolutionary role'; this role, in Marxist words, is midwifery:

> ... it is the midwife of every old society which is pregnant with the new, ... the instrument by the aid of which social movement forces its way through and shatters the dead, fossilized, political forms ... (Burns, 1935, p. 278).

The midwifery simile is excellent and conveys the basic idea extremely well. A midwife cannot create babies, she can only aid and slightly speed up their birth, and once the infant is born the midwife cannot do much harm either. The most one can say for her capacity is that she may be necessary for a successful birth. Engels seems to have no fear that this sinister midwife might linger after the birth and refuse to go away. He makes this plain by his comment on the possibility of a 'violent collision' in Germany which 'would at least have the advantage of wiping out the servility which has permeated the national consciousness as a result of the humiliation of the Thirty Years War'.

There is perhaps an element of truth in the theory that coercion is and ought to be the slave of production. The element of truth is this: in pre-agrarian hunting and gathering societies, surrounding by a relative abundance of sustenance but lacking means of storing it, there is no persistent, social, economic motive for coercion, no *sustained* employment for a slave. By contrast, once wealth is systematically produced and stored, coercion and violence or the threat thereof acquire an inescapable function and became endemic. The surplus needs to be guarded, its socially 'legitimate' distribution enforced. There is some evidence to support the view that hunting and gathering societies were more peaceful than the agrarian societies which succeeded them.

One may put it like this: in societies devoid of a stored surplus, no surplus needs to be guarded and the principles governing its distribution do not need to be enforced. By contrast, societies endowed with a surplus face the problem of protecting it against internal and external aggression, and enforcing the principles of its distribution. Hence they are doomed to the deployment, overt or indirect, of violence or the threat thereof. But all of this, true though it is, does not mean that surplus-less societies are necessarily free of violence: it only means that they are not positively obliged to experience it. Still less does it mean that within the class of societies endowed with a surplus, violence on its own may not occasionally or frequently engender changes, or inhibit them. The argument does not preclude coercion either from initiating social change, or from thwarting change which would otherwise have occurred. The founding fathers of Marxism directed their invective at those who raised this possibility, but they never succeeded in establishing that this possibility is not genuine. All historical evidence would seem to suggest that this possibility does indeed often correspond to reality.

Why is the totally unsubstantiated and indeed incorrect doctrine of the social unimportance of violence so central to Marxism?

The essence of Marxism lies in the retention of the notion of an historical plan, but a re-specification of its driving force. But the idea of a purposive historical plan is not upheld merely out of an intellectual desire for an elegant conceptual unification of historical events There is also a deeper motive. Marxism is a salvation religion, guaranteeing not indeed individual salvation, but the collective salvation of all mankind. Ironically, its conception of the blessed condition is profoundly bourgeois. Indeed, it constitutes the ultimate apotheosis of the bourgeois vision of life. The bourgeois preference for peaceful production over violent predation is elevated into the universal principle of historical change. The wish is father of the faith. The work ethic is transformed into the essence, the very species-definition of man. Work is our fulfilment, but work patterns are also the crucial determinants of historical change. Spontaneous, unconstrained work, creativity, is our purpose and our destiny. Work patterns also determine the course of history and engender patterns of coercion, and *not* vice versa. Domination and the mastery of techniques of violence is neither a valid ideal, nor ever decisive in history. All this is no doubt gratifying to those imbued with the producer ethic and hostile to the ethic of domination and violence: but is it true?

Note that, were it true, Marxism is free to commend spontaneously cooperative production, devoid of ownership and without any agency of enforcement, as against production by competition, with centrally enforced ground rules. It is free to do it, without needing to consider the argument that only competition keeps away centralized coercion, and that the attempt to bring about propertyless and total cooperation only engenders a new form of centralized tyranny. *If* tyranny *only* emerges as a protector of basically pathological forms or organization of work, then a sound work-pattern will on its own free us for ever from the need for either authority or checks on authority. Man is held to be alienated from his true essence as long as he works for extraneous ends: he finds his true being only when he indulges in work for the sake of creativity, and choses his own form of creativity. This is of course precisely the way in which the middle class likes to see its own life. It takes pride in productive activity, and chooses its own form of creativity, and it understands what it does. Work is not an unintelligible extraneous imposition for it, but the deepest fulfilment.

On the Marxist economic interpretation of history, mankind as a whole is being propelled towards this very goal, this bourgeois-style fulfilment in work without coercion. But the guarantee that this fulfilment will be reached is only possible if the driving force of history is such as to ensure this happy outcome. If a whole multitude of factors, economic, cultural, coercive, could all interact unpredictably, there could hardly be any historic plan. But if on the other hand only one factor is fundamental, and that factor is something which has a kind of vectorial quality, something which increases over time and inevitably points in one direction only (namely the augmentation of the productive force of man), then the necessary historical plan does after all have a firm, unprecarious base. This is what the theory requires, and this is what is indeed asserted.

The general problem of the requirement, ultimately, of a *single-factor theory*, with its well-directed and persistent factor, is of course related to the problems which arise from the plan that Marxists discern in history. According to the above quotation from Marx, subsequent to primitive communism, four class-endowed stages arise, namely the Asiatic, the ancient, the feudal and the modern bourgeois, which is said to be the last 'antagonistic' stage (peaceful fulfilment follows thereafter). Marxism has notoriously had trouble with the 'Asiatic' stage because, notwithstanding what Engels claimed, it *does* seem to exemplify and highlight the autonomy of coercion in history, and the suspension of progress by a stagnant, self-maintaining social system.

But leaving that aside, in order to be loyal to its basic underlying intuition of a guaranteed progression and a final happy outcome, Marxism is not committed to any particular number or even any particular sequence of stages. The factual difficulties which Marxist historiography has had in finding all the stages and all the historical sequences, and in the right order, are not by themselves necessarily disastrous. A rigid unification is not absolutely essential to the system. What it *does* require (apart from the exclusiveness, in the last analysis, of that single driving force) is the denial of the possibility of stagnation, whether in the form of absolute stagnation and immobility, or in the form of circular, repetitive developments. If this possibility is to be excluded, a number of things need to be true: all exploitative social forms must be inherently unstable; the number of such forms must be finite; and circular social developments must not be possible.

If all this is so, then the alienation of man from his true essence – free fulfilment in unconstrained work – *must* eventually be attained. But if the system can get stuck, or move in circles, the promise of salvation goes by the board. This would be so even if the system came to be stuck for purely economic reasons. It would be doubly disastrous for it if other factors, such as coercion, were capable of freezing it. The denial of any autonomous role for violence in history is the most important, and most contentious, element in the Marxian economic theory of history.

So what the Marxist economic interpretation of history really requires is that no non-economic factor can ever freeze the development of society, that the development of society itself be pushed forward by the continuous (even if on occasion slow) growth of productive forces, that the social forms accompanying various stages of the development of productive forces should be finite in number, and that the last one be wholly compatible with the fullest possible development of productive forces and of human potentialities.

The profound irony is that a social system marked by the prominence and pervasiveness of centralized coercion, should be justified and brought about by a system of ideas which denies autonomous historical agency both to coercion and to ideas. The independent effectiveness both of coercion and of ideas can best be shown by considering a society built on a *theory*, and one which denies the effectiveness of either.

BIBLIOGRAPHY
Burns, E. (ed.) 1935. *A Handbook of Marxism*. London: Victor Gollanz.
Engels, F. 1878. 'Anti-Dühring'. In Burns (1935).
Marx, K. 1859. A Contribution to 'The Critique of Political Economy'. In Burns (1935).
Marx, K. and Engels, F. 1845–6. *The German Ideology*. London: Lawrence & Wishart, 1940.
Morishima, M. 1982. *Why has Japan 'Succeeded'? Western Technology and the Japanese Ethos*. Cambridge: Cambridge University Press.
Tucker, R.C. 1961. *Philosophy and Myth in Karl Marx*. Cambridge: Cambridge University Press.

Friedrich Engels

GARETH STEDMAN JONES

Born in Barmen, the eldest son of a textile manufacturer in Westphalia, Engels (1820–1895) was trained for a merchant's profession. From school onwards however, he developed radical literary ambitions which eventually brought him into contact with the Young Hegelian circle in Berlin in 1841. In 1842, Engels left for England to work in his father's Manchester firm. Already converted by Moses Hess to a belief in 'communism' and the imminence of an English social revolution, he used his two-year stay to study the conditions which would bring it about. From this visit, came two works which were to make an important contribution to the formation of Marxian socialism: 'Outlines of a Critique of Political Economy' (generally called the 'Umrisse') published in 1844 and *The Condition of the Working Class in England*, published in Leipzig in 1845.

Returning home via Paris in 1844, Engels had his first serious meeting with Marx. Their life-long collaboration dated from this point with an agreement to produce a joint work (*The Holy Family*), setting out their positions against other tendencies within Young Hegelianism. This was followed by a second unfinished joint enterprise, (*The German Ideology*, 1845–7), where their materialist conception of history was expounded systematically for the first time.

Between 1845 and 1848, Engels was engaged in political work among German communist groups in Paris and Brussels. In the 1848 revolution itself, he took a full part, first as a collaborator with Marx on the *Neue Rheinische Zeitung* and subsequently in the last phase of armed resistance to counter-revolution in the summer of 1849.

In 1850, Engels returned once more to Manchester to work for his father's firm and remained there until he retired in 1870. During this period, in addition to numerous journalistic contributions, including attempts to publicize Marx's *Critique of Political Economy* (1859) and *Capital*, Volume One (1867), he first developed his interest in the relationship between historical materialism and the natural sciences. These writings were posthumously published as *The Dialectics of Nature* (1925). In 1870 Engels moved to London.

As Marx's health declined, Engels took over most of his political work in the last years of the First International (1864–72) and took increasing responsibility for corresponding with the newly founded German Social Democratic Party and other infant socialist parties. Engels's most important work during this period was his polemic against the positivist German socialist, Eugen Dühring. The *Anti-Dühring* (1877) was the first comprehensive exposition of a marxian socialism in the realms of philosophy, history and political economy. The success of this work, and in particular of extracts from it like *Socialism, Utopian and Scientific*, represented the decisive turning point in the international diffusion of Marxism and shaped its understanding as a theory in the period before 1914.

In his last years after Marx's death in 1883, Engels devoted most of his time to the editing and publishing of the remaining volumes of *Capital* from Marx's manuscripts. Volume Two appeared in 1885, Volume Three in 1894, a year before his death. Engels had also hoped to prepare the final volume dealing with the history of political economy. But the difficulty of deciphering Marx's handwriting, his own failing eyesight and the formidable editorial problems encountered in constructing Volumes Two and Three, induced him to hand over this task to Karl Kautsky, who subsequently published it under the title *Theories of Surplus Value*.

Engels's work was of importance, both in the construction and interpretation of Marxian economic theory and in the laying down of important guidelines in the subsequent development of marxist economic policy.

In the realm of theory, his contribution is of particular significance in three respects.

First, and of real importance in the formation of a distinctively marxian stance towards political economy was Engels's 'Outlines of a Critique of Political Economy' (the 'Umrisse'), published in 1844. In 1859 in his own *Critique of Political Economy*, Marx acknowledged this sketch as 'brilliant' (Marx, 1859) and its impact is discernible in Marx's 1844 writings. The *Umrisse* represented the first systematic confrontation between the 'communist' stand of Young Hegelianism and political economy. The communist aspiration was expressed in Feuerbachian language, while the mode of analysis was Hegelian. But, as has recently been demonstrated (Claeys, 1984), the content of Engels's critique was first and foremost a product of his early stay in Manchester. For, apart from some indebtedness to Proudhon's *What is Property?* (1841), the main source of Engels's essay was John Watts, *The Facts and Fictions of Political Economy* (1842), a resumé of the Owenite case against the propositions of political economy. At this stage, Engels's own acquaintance with the work of political economists seems to have been mainly at second hand.

The *Umrisse* was an attempt to demonstrate that all the categories of political economy presupposed competition which in turn presupposed private property. He began with an analysis of value, which juxtaposed a 'subjective' conception of value as utility ascribed to Say with an 'objective' conception of value as cost of production attributed to Ricardo and McCulloch. Reconciling these two definitions in Hegelian fashion, Engels defined value as the relation of production costs to utility. This was the equitable basis of exchange, but one impossible to implement on the basis of competition which was responsive to market demand rather than social need. (Engels still adhered to this definition of value thirty years later in the *Anti-Dühring*. Discussing the disappearance of the 'law of value' with the end of commodity production, he wrote:

> As long ago as 1844, I stated that the above mentioned balancing of useful effects and expenditure of labour would be all that would be left, in a communist society, of the concept of value as it appears in political economy.... The scientific justification for this statement, however,... was only made possible by Marx's *Capital* (Engels, 1877, pp. 367–8).

This shows how much greater continuity of thought there was between the young and the old Engels than is normally imagined.)

He next analysed rent, counterposing a Ricardian notion of differential productivity to one attributed to Smith and T.P. Thompson based upon competition. Interestingly, in this analysis Engels differed both from Watts and Proudhon, in denying the radical form of the labour theory – the right to the whole product of labour – both by citing the case of the need to support children and in querying the possibility of calculating the share of labour in the product.

Finally, after an attack on the Malthusian population theory, which closely followed Alison and Watts, Engels attacked competition itself, both because it provided no mechanism of reconciling general and individual interest, and because it was argued to be self-contradictory. Competition based on self-interest bred monopoly. Competition as an immanent law of private property led to polarization and the centralization of property. Thus private property under competition is self-consuming.

What particularly impressed Marx was the argument that all the categories of political economy were tied to the assumption of competition based on private property. This, for him, represented an important advance over Proudhon whose notion of equal wage would lead to a society conceived as 'abstract capitalist' and whose conception of labour right presupposed private property. Proudhon had not seen that labour was the essence of private property. His critique was of 'political economy from the standpoint of political economy'. He had not 'considered the further creations of private property, e.g. wages, trade, value, price, money etc. as forms of private property in themselves' (Marx, 1844, p. 312). The Umrisse suggested a new means of underpinning the marxian ambition to transcend the categorical world of political economy and private property altogether. Moreover, by representing competition as a law which would produce its opposite, monopoly, the elimination of private property and revolution, Engels preceded Marx in positing the 'free trade system' as a process moving towards self-destruction through the operation of laws immanent within it.

These conclusions were amplified in Engels's other major work of this period, *The Condition of the Working Class in England*. Here, the law of competition by engendering 'the industrial revolution' had created a revolutionary new force, the working class. The single thread underlying the development of the working class movement had been the attempt to overcome competition. Such an analysis prefigured the famous statement in the *Communist Manifesto* that the capitalists were begetting their own gravediggers (Stedman Jones, 1977).

Between the mid-1840s and the mid-1870s, Engels played no discernible part in the elaboration of *Capital* beyond supplying Marx with practical business information. His vital contributions to the pre-history of the theory were forgotten and it was only in his better-known role as interpreter and publicist of Marx's work that his writings received widespread attention. During the Second International period, these writings attained almost canonical status, but in the 20th century they have generally provided a polemical target for all those attempting to retheorize Marx in the light of the publication of his early writings.

In the realm of political economy more narrowly conceived, Engels helped to set up the 'transformation' debate by his dramatization of Marx's switch from value to production price in his introductions to Volumes Two and Three of *Capital*. Engels's own contribution to this debate in his last published article in *Neue Zeit* in 1895 (now published as 'Supplement and Addendum' to Volume Three of *Capital*) was to argue that the shift from value to production price was not merely a logical development entailed by the enlargement of the scope of investigation to include circulation and the 'process of capitalist production as a whole', but also reflected a real historical transition from the stage of simple commodity production to that of capitalism proper. 'The Marxian law of value has a universal economic validity for an era lasting from the beginning of the exchange that transforms products into commodities down to the fifteenth century of our epoch' (Marx, 1894, p. 1037).

Leaving aside the empirical question whether during the pre-capitalist era commodities were exchanged in accordance with the amount of labour embodied in them, commentators as diverse as Bernstein and Rubin, have objected that this makes no sense in terms of Marx's theory, since during this epoch, there exists 'no mechanism of the general equalisation of different individual labour expenditures in separate economic units on the market' and that consequently it was not appropriate to speak of 'abstract and socially necessary labour which is the basis of the theory of value' (Rubin, 1928, p. 254). They have further objected, appealing to Marx's 1857 'Introduction to the Critique of Political Economy', that there is no necessary connection between the logical and historical sequence of concepts, and that the order of appearance of concepts in *Capital* is determined simply by the logical place they occupy in an exposition of the theory of the capitalist mode of production.

Engels could certainly claim explicit textual support from Volume Three for his historical interpretation of value ('It is also quite apposite to view the value of commodities not only as theoretically prior to the prices of production, but also as historically prior to them. This applies to those conditions in which the means of production belong to the worker...': Marx 1894, p. 277.) It should also be stressed that there was nothing new in Engels's representation of the character of Marx's theory. Back in 1859, in a review of Marx's *Critique of*

Political Economy, Engels stated,'Marx was, and is, the only one who could undertake the work of extracting from the Hegelian Logic the kernel which comprised Hegel's real discoveries ... and to construct the dialectical method divested of its idealistic trappings' (Engels 1859, pp. 474–5); and in characterizing that method as a form of identity between logical and historical progression, he continued, 'the chain of thought must begin with the same thing that this history begins with, and its further course will be nothing but the mirror image of the historical course in abstract and theoretically consistent form ...' (ibid., p. 475). It is implausible to suppose that Marx at this time should have sanctioned a fundamental distortion of his method and it is suggestive that he himself, describing his relationship to Hegel should have endorsed the metaphor of discovering 'the rational kernel in the mystical shell' in his 1873 Postface to the Second Edition of *Capital* (Marx, 1873, p. 103). Perhaps the real difficulty lies not in Engels, but in Marx himself. It may be, as Louis Althusser has claimed, that Marx did not find a suitable language in which to characterize the distinctiveness of his approach, or it may be more simply that Marx remained ambivalent about how to characterize the theory. In any event, it is not difficult to establish disjunctions between the way he proceeds and the descriptions he gives of his procedures. Engels stuck fairly closely to Marx's descriptions of his procedures and can hardly be reproached for taking Marx at his word.

The problem of Engels's role as an interpreter of Marx's theory debouches onto a third and potentially yet more contentious aspect of Engels's legacy, his role as editor of *Capital*, Volumes Two and Three. Engels's work was not confined to the transcription of Marx's illegible handwriting. He had to make active editorial choices. The published versions of these volumes contain over 1300 pages, but the original manuscripts amount to almost twice as many. For Volume Two for instance, Marx had composed eight versions of his treatment of the process of circulation, from which Engels made a collation. In the absence of an independent transcription and publication of the manuscripts, from which Engels worked, it is impossible to assess whether the emphasis and meaning of the published Volumes differ in any significant way from the original. What seems clear, is that in his cautious desire to reproduce as much of the original material as possible, Engels produced a much bulkier and more repetitive version than Marx originally intended. Marx, it seems, always hoped that *Capital* should consist of two volumes and a further volume on the history of political economy (Rubel 1968, Levine, 1984). From a detailed comparison of Volume Two, Part 1, with the original manuscripts, it appears that Engels also occasionally committed inaccuracies in the citation of the manuscripts he had used (Levine, 1984). Much more doubtful, given all we know of Engels's caution as an editor, is the further suggestion that Engels's editing procedures may have shifted the meaning of the text in ways that lent support to a 'collapse theory' of capitalism (*Zusammenbruchstheorie*) (Levine, 1984). Apart from the smallness of the sample and Engels's own reservations about such a theory, the fact is that proponents of such a position already had sufficient ammunition from *Capital*, Volume One.

Moreover, it simply begs the question whether Marx's attitude to the collapse of capitalism was any more or less apocalyptic than that of Engels.

This discussion by no means exhausts Engels's importance in the history of economic theory or policy. A fuller treatment would have to discuss his analysis of the 'peasant question' which included the important prescription that collectivisation must be by example rather than force, his definition of political economy in the *Anti-Dühring*, his interpolations in *Capital*, Volume Three, on banks, the stock exchange and cartels which set the agenda for the early 20th-century discussion of finance capital, his various writings on the relationship between the state and economic forces and his later surveys of English developments since 1844 which prepared the way for later marxist theories of labour aristocracy. These are only some of the more salient examples.

Finally, at a time when it seems that the technical debate on value seems to have reached a moment of exhaustion, it is perhaps worth going back to Engels if only to remind us of the anti-economic purpose underlying Marx's attempt to construct a theory of value in the first place.

SELECTED WORKS

1843. *Outlines of a Critique of Political Economy.* In Karl Marx and Frederick Engels, *Collected Works* [MECW], Vol. III, London: Lawrence & Wishart, 1975.

1845. *The Condition of the Working Class in England.* MECW, Vol. IV, London: Lawrence & Wishart, 1975.

1859. Karl Marx, *A Contribution to the Critique of Political Economy.* MECW, Vol. XVI, London: Lawrence & Wishart, 1976.

1877. *Anti-Dühring.* Moscow: Foreign Languages Publishing House, 1954.

1894. *The Peasant Question in France and Germany.* In Karl Marx and Frederick Engels, *Selected Works*, Vol. 3, Moscow: Progress Publishers, 1970.

n.d. *Engels on Capital.* London: Lawrence & Wishart.

BIBLIOGRAPHY

Claeys, G. 1984. Engels' *Outlines of a critique of political economy* (1843) and the origins of the Marxist critique of capitalism. *History of Political Economy* 16(2), Summer, 207–32.

Levine, N. 1984. *Dialogue within Dialectics.* London: Allen & Unwin.

Marx, K. and Engels, F. 1844. *The Holy Family.* In *Collected Works*, Vol. IV.

Marx, K. 1859. *Contribution to a Critique of Political Economy: preface.* In Marx–Engels, *Collected Works* (MECW), vol. XV.

Marx, K. 1873. *Capital*, Vol. I, 2nd edn. Harmondsworth: Penguin, 1976.

Marx, K. 1894. *Capital*, Vol. III. Harmondsworth: Penguin, 1981.

Rubel, M. (ed.) 1968. *Karl Marx, Oeuvres*, Vol. II. Paris: Gallimard.

Rubin, I. 1928. *Essays on Marx's Theory of Value.* Detroit: Black & Red, 1972.

Stedman Jones, G. 1977. Engels and the history of Marxism. In *The History of Marxism*, ed. E.J. Hobsbawm, Hassocks: Harvester, 1983.

Exploitation

ANWAR SHAIKH

In the most general sense, to exploit something means to make use of it for some particular end, as in the exploitation of natural resources for social benefit or for private profit. Insofar as this use takes advantage of other people, exploitation also implies something unscrupulous. If the other people are endemically powerless, as in the case of the poor in relation to their landlords, creditors and the like, then the term exploitation takes on the connotation of oppression.

Marx uses the word exploitation in all the above senses. But he also defines a new concept, the *exploitation of labour*, which refers specifically to the extraction of the surplus plus upon which class society is founded. In this latter sense, exploitation becomes one of the basic concepts of the Marxist theory of social formations.

EXPLOITATION AND CLASS. Society consists of people living within-and-through complex networks of social relations which shape their very existence. Marx argues that the relations which structure the social division of labour lie at the base of social reproduction, because the division of labour simultaneously accomplishes two distinct social goals: first, the production of the many different objects which people use in their myriad activities of daily life; and second, the reproduction of the basic social framework under which this production takes place, and hence of the social structures which rest on this foundation. Social reproduction is always the reproduction of individuals as *social individuals*.

Class societies are those in which the ruler of one set of people over another is founded upon a particular kind of social division of labour. This particularity arises from the fact that the dominant class maintains itself by controlling a process through which the subordinate classes are required to devote a portion of their working time to the production of things needed by the ruling class. The social division of labour within a class society must therefore be structured around the extraction of *surplus labour*, i.e. of labour time over and above that required to produce for the needs of the labouring classes themselves. In effect,

165

it is the subordinate classes which do the work for the reproduction of the ruling class, and which therefore end up *working to reproduce the very conditions of their own subordination.* This is why Marx refers to the extraction of surplus labour in class societies as the exploitation of labour (Marx, 1867, Part 3 and Appendix). It should be clear from this, incidentally, that the mere performance of labour beyond that needed to satisfy immediate needs does not in itself constitute exploitation. Robinson Crusoe, labouring away in his solitude in order to plant crops for future consumption or to create fortification against possible attacks, is merely performing some of the labour necessary for his own needs. He is neither exploiter nor exploited. But all this changes once he manages to subordinate the man Friday, to 'educate' him through the promise of religion and the threat of force to his new place in life, and to set him to work building a proper microcosm of English society. Now it is Robinson who is the exploiter, and Friday the exploited whose surplus labour only serves to bind him ever more tightly to his new conditions of exploitation (Hymer, 1971).

Although the exploitation of labour is inherent in all class societies, the form it takes varies considerably from one mode of production to another. Under slavery, for instance, the slave belongs to the owner, so that the whole of his or her labour and corresponding net product (i.e. product after replacement of the means of production used up) is ostensibly appropriated by the slave owner. But in fact the slave too must be maintained out of this very same net product. Thus it is the surplus product (the portion of the net product over that needed to maintain the slaves), and hence the surplus labour of the slaves, which in the end sustains the slave-owning class. In a similar vein, under feudalism the surplus labour of the serf and tenant supports the ruling apparatus. But here, the forms of its extraction are many and varied: sometimes direct, as in the case of the quantities of annual labour and/or product which the serf or tenant is required to hand over to Lord, Church and State; and sometimes indirect, as in the payment of money rents, tithes and taxes which in effect require the serf or tenant to produce a surplus product and sell it for cash in order to meet those imposed obligations.

The material wealth of the dominant class is directly linked to the size of the surplus product. And this surplus product is in turn greater the smaller the standard of living of the subordinate classes, and the longer, more intense or more productive their working day. Both of these propositions translate directly into a higher ratio of surplus labour time to the labour time necessary to reproduce the labourers themselves, that is, into a higher *rate of exploitation* of labour: given the productivity of labour and the length and intensity of the working day, the smaller the portion of the product consumed by the producing class, the greater the portion of their working day which is in effect devoted to surplus labour; similarly, given the consumption level of the average peasant or worker, the longer, more intense and/or more productive their labour, the smaller the portion of their working day which has to be devoted to their own consumption needs, and hence the greater the portion which corresponds to surplus labour.

Because the magnitude of the surplus product can be raised in the above ways,

166

it is always in the direct interest of the ruling class to try and push the rate of exploitation towards its social and historical limits. By the same token, it is in the interest of the subordinate classes not only to resist such efforts but also to fight against the social conditions which make this struggle necessary in the first place. The exploitative base of class society makes it a fundamentally antagonistic mode of human existence, marked by a simmering hostility between rulers and ruled, and punctuated by periods of riots, rebellions and revolutions. This is why class societies must always rely heavily on ideology to motivate and rationalize the fundamental social cleavage upon which they rest, and on force to provide the necessary discipline when all else fails.

CAPITALISM AND EXPLOITATION. Capitalism shares the above general attributes. It is a class society, in which the domination of the capitalist class is founded upon its ownership and control of the vast bulk of the society's means of production. The working class, on the other hand, is made up of those who have been 'freed' of this self-same burden of property in means of production, and who must therefore earn their livelihood by working for the capitalist class. As Marx so elegantly demonstrates, the *general social condition* for the reproduction of these relations is that the working class as a whole be induced to perform surplus labour, because it is this surplus labour which forms the basis of capitalist profit, and it is this profit which in turn keeps the capitalist class willing and able to reemploy workers. And as the history of capitalism makes perfectly clear, the whole process is permeated by the struggle between the classes about the conditions, terms and occasionally even about the future, of these relations.

The historical specificity of capitalism arises from the fact that its relations of exploitation are almost completely hidden behind the surface of its relations of exchange. At first glance, the transaction between the worker and capitalist is a perfectly fair one. The former offers labour power for sale, the latter offers a wage rate, and the bargain is struck when both sides come to terms. But once this phase is completed, we leave the sphere of freedom and apparent equality and enter into 'the hidden abode of production' within which lurks the familiar domain of surplus labour (Marx, 1867, ch. 6). We find here a world of hierarchy and inequality, of orders and obedience, of bosses and subordinates, in which the working class is set to work to produce a certain amount of product for its employers. Of this total product, a portion which corresponds to the materials and depreciation costs of the total product is purchased by the capitalists themselves, in order to replace the means of production previously used up. A second portion is purchased by the workers with the wages previously paid to them by their employers. But if these two portions happen to exhaust the total product, then the capitalists will have succeeded in producing only enough to cover their own (materials, depreciation and wage) costs of production. *There would be no aggregate profit.* It follows, therefore, that for capitalist production to be successful, i.e. for it to create its own profit, workers must be induced to work longer than the time required to produce their own means of consumption.

167

They must, in other words, perform surplus labour time in order to produce the surplus product upon which profit is founded.

The above propositions can be derived analytically (Morishima, 1973, ch. 7). More importantly, they are demonstrated *in practice* whenever working time is lost through labour strikes or slowdowns. Then, as surplus labour time is eroded, the normally hidden connection between surplus labour and profit manifests itself as a corresponding fall in profitability. Every practising capitalist must learn this lesson sooner or later.

Orthodox economics, encapsulated within its magic kingdom of production functions, perfect competition and general equilibrium, usually manages to avoid such issues. Indeed, it concerns itself principally with the construction and refinement of an idealized image of capitalism, whose properties it then investigates with a concentration so ferocious that it is often able to entirely ignore the reality which surrounds it. Within this construct, production is a disembodied process undertaken by an intangible entity called the firm. This firm hires 'factors of production' called capital and labour in order to produce an output, paying for each factor according to its estimated incremental contribution to the total output (i.e. according to the value of its marginal product). If all goes well, the sum of these payments turn out to exhaust exactly the net revenues actually received by the firm, and the ground is set for yet another round.

Notice that this conception puts a thing (capital) and a human capacity (labour power) on equal footing, both as so-called factors of production. This enables the theory to deny any class difference between capitalists and workers by treating all individuals as essentially equal because they are all owners of at least one factor of production. The fact that 'factor endowments' may vary considerably across individuals is then merely a second-order detail whose explanation is said to lie outside of economic theory. Next, by treating production as some disembodied process, the human labour process is reduced to a mere technical relation, to a production function which 'maps' things called inputs (which include labour power) into a thing called output. All struggle over the labour process thus disappears from view. Finally, since capital and labour are mere things, they cannot be said to be exploited. However, to the extent that the payment for some factors falls short of equality with its particular marginal product, the *owner* of this factor may be said to be exploited. In this sense, exploitation is defined as a discrepancy between an actual and an ideal 'factor payment' (it can be established that a very similar construction underlies notions of unequal exchange such as those in Emmanuel, 1969). More importantly, exploitation as defined above can in principle apply just as well to profits as to wages. Capitalism thus emerges as a system in which capitalists are just as liable to be exploited by workers as vice versa (Hodgson, 1980, section 2). With this last step, the very notion of exploitation is reduced to utter triviality.

EXPLOITATION, GENDER AND RACE. We have focused on the notion of exploitaton as the extraction of surplus labour because this relation is the foundation upon which class society is built, in the sense that the other legal, political and personal relations within the society are structured and limited by this central one. This does not mean that these other relations lack a history and logic of their own. It only means that within any given mode of production, they are bound to the system by the force field of this central relation, and characteristically shaped by its ever present gravitational pull.

In the same vein, the notion that class society is marked by oppression along class lines obviously does not exclude other equally egregious forms of subjugation. It is evident, for instance, that the oppression of women by men is common to all known societies, and to all classes within them. Thus any proper understanding of the oppression of workers by capitalists must also encompass the oppression of working-class women by men of all classes, as well as the oppression of ruling-class women by men of their own class.

But even this is not enough. It is not sufficient to say that class and patriarchy are coexistent forms of oppression. We need to know also how they relate to one another. And it is here that Marxists generally give preeminence to class, not because class oppression is more grievous, but because of the sense that it is the nature of the class relation which modulates and shapes the corresponding form of patriarchy. That is to say, Marxists argue that capitalist patriarchy is distinct from feudal patriarchy precisely because capitalist relations of production are characteristically different from feudal ones.

Needless to say, there is still considerable controversy about the exact relationship between patriarchy and class (Barrett, 1980), as there is about the relation of race to either of them (Davis, 1981). These are issues of great theoretical significance. Most importantly, a united struggle against these various forms of oppression has truly revolutionary potential.

BIBLIOGRAPHY

Barrett, M. 1980. *Women's Oppression Today*: *Problems in Marxist Feminist Analysis*. London: Verso.

Davis, A.Y. 1981. *Women, Race and Class*. New York: Vintage, 1983.

Emmanuel, A. 1969. *Unequal Exchange*: *A Study of the Imperialism of Trade*. New York: Monthly Review Press.

Hodgson, G. 1980. A theory of exploitation without the labor theory of value. *Science and Society* 44(3), Fall, 257–73.

Hymer, S. 1971. Robinson Crusoe and the secret of primitive accumulation. *Monthly Review* 23 (4), September, 11–36.

Marx, K. 1867. *Capital*, Vol. I. London: Penguin Books, 1976.

Morishima, M. 1973. *Marx's Economics*. Cambridge: Cambridge University Press.

Feudalism

ROBERT BRENNER

Modern discussions of feudalism have been bedevilled by disagreement over the definition of that term. There are three main competing conceptualizations. (1) Feudalism refers strictly to those social institutions which create and regulate a quite specific form of legal relationships between men. It constitutes a relationship in which a freeman (vassal) assumes an obligation to obey and to provide, primarily military, services to an overload, who, in turn, assumes a reciprocal obligation to provide protection and maintenance, typically in the form of a fief, a landed estate to be held by the vassal on condition of fulfilment of obligations (Bloch, 1939–40). (2) Feudalism refers, more broadly, to a form of government or political domination. It is a form of rule in which political power is profoundly fragmented geographically; in which, even within the smallest political units, no single ruler has a monopoly of political authority; and in which political power is privately held, and can thus be inherited, divided among heirs, given as a marriage portion, mortgaged, and bought and sold. Finally, the armed forces involve, as a key element, a heavy armed cavalry which is secured through private contracts, whereby military service is exchanged for benefits of some kind (Strayer, 1965; Ganshof, 1947). (3) Feudalism refers to a type of socio-economic organization of society as a whole, a mode of production and of the reproduction of social classes. It is defined in terms of the social relationships by which its two fundamental social classes constitute and maintain themselves. Specifically, the peasants, who constitute the overwhelming majority of the producing population, maintain themselves by virtue of their possession of their full means of subsistence, land and tools, so require no productive contribution by the lords to survive. This possession is secured by means of the peasants' collective political organization into self-governing communities, which stand as the ultimate guardian of the individual peasant's land. As a result of the peasants' possession and their consequent economic independence, mere ownership of property cannot be assumed to yield an economic rent; in consequence, the lords are obliged to maintain themselves by appropriating a feudal levy by the exercise of *extra-economic* coercion. The lords are able to extract a rent by extra-economic coercion only in consequence of their political self-organization into lordly groups or communities, by means of which they exert a degree of domination over the peasants, varying in degree from enserfment to mere tribute taking (Marx, 1894; Dobb, 1946).

Though often thought to be in conflict, these conceptions are not only complementary but in fact integrally related to one another. While the lords' very existence as lords was based, as Marxists correctly insist, upon their appropriating a rent from the peasantry by extra-economic coercion, their capacity actually to exert such force in the rent relationship depended upon their ability to construct and maintain the classically political ties of interdependence which joined overlord to knightly follower and thereby constituted the feudal groups which were the ultimate source of the lords' power. Conversely, while feudal bonds of interdependence were constructed, as the Weberians emphasize, to build highly localized governments capable at once of waging warfare, dispensing justice and keeping the peace, the *raison d'être* of the mini-states thus created was to constitute the dominant class of feudal society by establishing the instruments for extracting, redistributing and consuming the wealth upon which this class depended for their maintenance and reproduction. State and ruling class were thus two sides of the same coin. The distinctive ties which bound man to man in feudal society (not only the relations of vassalage strictly speaking, but also the more loosely defined associations structured by patronage, clientage and family) constituted the building blocks, at one and the same time, for the peculiarly fragmented locally based and politically competitive character of the feudal ruling class and for the peculiarly particularized nature of the feudal state. It was the lords' feudal levies which provided the material base for the feudal policy. It was the parcellized character of the feudal state, itself the obverse side of the decentralized structure of lordship through which rent was appropriated from the peasantry, which thus created the basic opportunities, set the ultimate limits and posed the fundamental problems for the lords' reproduction as a ruling class.

THE ORIGINS OF FEUDALISM. The rise of feudalism was conditioned by an extended process of political fragmentation within the old Carolingian Empire. This is understandable, in part, in terms of a tendency to decentralization inherent in patrimonial rule. The patrimonial lord, to maintain his following, had, paradoxically, to provide his followers with the means to establish their independence from him. He could counteract their tendency to assert their autonomy through successful warfare and conquest, in which the followers found it worth their while to continue to submit to his authority. But in the absence of such profitable aggression, the followers had every incentive to assert their independence. It was in this way that the devolution and dissolution of more centralized forms of authority took place within the Carolingian Empire during the 9th and 10th centuries, as the Franks and their followers ceased to be conquerors, following a long period in which the empire had expanded.

Fragmentaton was hastened by the contemporaneous invasions of the Northmen, Saracens and Magyars. Effective authority fell, successively, from the king to his princes, to the counts and, ultimately, to local castleholders and even manorial lords, as the newly-emerging, highly localized rulers turned their pillaging from foreign enemies to the local population (Weber, 1956; Duby, 1978, pp. 147ff).

Feudalism originally took shape in the early part of the 11th century in many parts of Western Europe, including much of France, northern Italy and western Germany. Feudal rule was first constituted through the formation of lordly political groups, initially organized around a castle and led by the castellan. The castellan's power was derived from his knightly followers. The knights possessed military training, fought on horseback wearing (increasingly elaborate) coats of armour, often lived in the castle, and, from around the mid 11th century, tended to be bound to the castellan through ties of vassalage. The castellan's hegemony was manifested in his capacity to exert the right of the ban over his district – whose outer limits were usually no more than half a day's ride from the central fortress. The right of the ban, traditionally in the hands of the early medieval kings and the direct expression of their authority, allowed the castellan, above all, to extract dues from the peasant households within his jurisdiction, as well as to dispense justice and keep the peace. Although the surrounding lesser lords were usually tied to a castellan, in some cases they retained their full independence, not only collecting feudal rents derived from their authority over their tenants, but imposing taxes and exerting justice within their manorial mini-jurisdictions. In any case, all these lords confirmed their membership of the dominant class by claiming exemption from fiscal exactions: freedom under feudalism thus took the form of privilege. The peasants' unfreedom in some cases originated from their ancestors' having formally commended themselves to their lord; that is, their having subjected themselves to his domination in exchange for his assuring their safety. But, with the crystallization of feudal domination, it simply expressed the lords' having appropriated the right to extort protection money from them. The peasants' unfreedom was thus defined and constituted precisely by their subjection to arbitrary levies (Duby, 1973, 1978).

The feudal economy was thus structured, on the one hand, by a form of precapitalist property relations in which the individual peasant families, as members of a village community, *individually possessed* their means of reproduction. This contrasted with other precapitalist property forms in which the village community itself was the possessor (or more of one). On the other hand, under feudalism, the individual lords reproduced themselves by *individually appropriating* part of the peasants' product, backed up by localized communities of lords connected by various sorts of political bond, classically vassalage. This contrasted with other precapitalist property systems, in which the community, or communities, of lords appropriated the peasants' product collectively (as a tax) and shared out the proceeds among the community's, or communities', members.

FEUDAL PROPERTY RELATIONS AND THE FORMS OF INDIVIDUAL ECONOMIC RATIONALITY. The fundamental feudal property relationships of peasant possession and of lordly surplus extraction by extra-economic compulsion shaped the long-term evolution of the feudal economy. This was because these relationships were systematically maintained by the conscious actions of communities of peasants and of lords and thus constituted relatively inalterable constraints under which individual peasants and lords were obliged to choose the pattern of economic activity most sensible for them to adopt in order to maintain and improve their condition. The potential for economic development under feudalism was thus sharply restricted because both lords and peasants found it in their rational self-interest to pursue individual economic strategies which were largely incompatible with, if not positively antithetical to, specialization, productive investment and innovation in agriculture.

First, and perhaps most fundamental, because both lords and peasants were in full possession of what they needed to maintain themselves as lords and peasants, they were free from the *necessity* to buy on the market what they needed to reproduce, thus freed from dependence on the market and the necessity to produce for exchange, and thus exempt from the requirement to sell their output competitively on the market. In consequence, both lords and peasants were free from the necessity to produce at the socially necessary rate so as to maximize their rate of return and, in consequence, relieved of the requirement to cut cost so as to maintain themselves, and so of the necessity constantly to improve production through specialization and/or accumulation and/or innovation. Feudal property relations, in themselves, thus failed to *impose* on the direct producers that relentless drive to improve efficiency so as to survive, which is the *differentia specifica* of modern economic growth, and required of the economic actors under capitalist property relations in consequence of their subjection to production for exchange and economic competition.

Absent the necessity to produce so as to maximize exchange values and, in view of the underdeveloped state of the economy as a whole, the peasants tended to find it most sensible actually to deploy their resources so to ensure their maintenance by producing directly the full range of their necessities; that is, *to produce for subsistence*. Given the low level of agricultural productivity which perforce prevailed, harvests and therefore food supplies were highly uncertain. Since food constituted so large a part of total consumption, the uncertainty of the food market brought with it highly uncertain markets for other commercial crops. It was therefore rational for peasants to avoid the risks attached to dependence upon the market, and to do so, they had to diversify rather than specialize, marketing only physical surpluses. In fact, beyond their concern to minimize the risk of losing their livelihood, the peasants appear to have found it desirable to carry out diversified production simply because they wished to maintain their established mode of life – and, specifically, to avoid the subjection to the market which production for exchange entails, and the total transformation of their existence which that would have meant.

To make possible ongoing production for subsistence, the peasants naturally aimed to maintain their plots as the basis for their existence. To ensure the continuation of their families into the future, they also sought to ensure their children's inheritance of their holdings. Meanwhile, they tended to find it rational to have as many children as possible, so as to ensure themselves adequate support in their old age. The upshot was relatively large families and the subdivision of plots on inheritance.

Like the peasants, the lords occupied a 'patriarchal' position, possessing all that they needed to survive and thus freed of any necessity to increase their productive capacities. Moreover, even to the extent they wished, for whatever reason, to increase the output of their estates, the lords faced nearly insuperable difficulties in accomplishing this by means of increasing the productive powers of their labour and their land. Thus, if the lords wished to organize production themselves, they had no choice but to depend for labour on their peasants, who possessed their means of subsistence. But precisely because the peasants were possessors, the lords could get them to work only by directly coercing them (by taking their feudal rent in the form of labour) and could *not* credibly threaten to 'fire' them. The lords were thereby deprived of perhaps the most effective means yet discovered to impose labour discipline in class-divided societies. Because the peasant labourers had no *economic* incentive to work diligently or efficiently for the lords, the lords found it extremely difficult to get them to use advanced means of production in an effective manner. They could force them to do so only by making costly unproductive investments in supervision.

In view of both the lords' and the peasants' restricted ability effectively to allocate investment funds to improved means of production to increase agricultural efficiency, both lords and peasants found that the only really effective way to raise their income via productive investment was by opening up new lands. Colonization, which resulted in the multiplication of units of production on already existing lines, was thus the preferred form of productive investment for both lords and peasants under feudalism.

Beyond colonization and the purchaser of land, feudal economic actors, above all feudal lords, found that the best way to improve their income was by forcefully *redistributing* wealth away from the peasants or from other lords. This meant that they had to deploy their resources (surpluses) towards building up their *means of coercion* by means of investment in military men and equipment, in particular to improve their ability to fight wars. A drive to *political accumulation*, or state building, was the feudal analogue to the capitalist drive to accumulate capital.

THE LONG-TERM PATTERNS OF FEUDAL ECONOMIC DEVELOPMENT. Feudal property relations, once established, thus obliged lords and peasants to adopt quite specific patterns of individual economic behaviour. Peasants sought to produce for subsistence, to hold on to their plots, to produce large families and to provide for their families' future generations by bequeathing their plots. Both lords and peasants sought to use available surpluses funds to open new lands. Lords directed their resources to the amassing of greater and better means of coercion.

Generalized on a society-wide basis, these patterns of individual economic action determined the following developmental patterns, or laws of motion, for the feudal economy as a whole:

(i) *Declining productivity in agriculture* (Bois, 1976; Hilton, 1966; Postan, 1966). The generalized tendency to adopt production for subsistence on the part of the peasantry naturally constituted a powerful obstacle to commercial specialization in agriculture and to the emergence of those competitive pressures which drive a modern economy forward. In so doing, it also posed a major barrier to agricultural improvement by the peasantry, since a significant degree of specialization was required to adopt almost all those technical improvements which would come to constitute 'the new husbandry' or the agricultural revolution (fodder crops, up-and-down farming, etc.). In addition, production aimed at subsistence and the maintenance of the plot as the basis for the family's existence posed a major barrier to those rural accumulators, richer peasants and lords, who wished to amass land or to hire wage labour, since the peasants would not readily part with their plots, which were the immediate bases for their existence, unless compelled to do so; nor could they be expected to work for a wage unless they actually needed to.

Further counteracting any drive to the accumulation of land and labour was the tendency on the part of the possessing peasants to produce large families and subdivide their holdings among their children. The peasants' parcellization of plots under population growth tended to overwhelm any tendency towards the build-up of large holdings in the agricultural economy as a whole, further reducing the potential for agriculture improvement.

Finally, individual peasant plots were, most often, integrated within a village agriculture which was, in critical ways, controlled by the community of cultivators. The peasant village regulated the use of the pasture and waste on which animals were raised, and the rotation of crops in the common fields. Individual peasants thus tended to face significant limitations on their ability to decide how to farm their plots and thus, very often, on their capacity to specialize, build up larger consolidated holdings, and so forth.

To the extent that the lords succeeded in increasing their wealth by means of improving their ability coercively to redistribute income away from the peasantry, they further limited the agricultural economy's capacity to improve. Increased rents in whatever form reduced the peasants' ability to make investments in the means of production. Meanwhile, the lords' allocation of their income to military followers and equipment and to luxury consumption, ensured that the social surplus was used unproductively, indeed wasted. To the extent – more or less – that the lords increased their income, the agricultural economy was undermined.

(ii) *Population growth* (Postan, 1966). The long-term tendency to the decline of agricultural productivity thus conditioned by the feudal structure of property was realized in practice as a consequence of rising population. The peasants' possession of land allowed children to accede to plots and, on that basis, to form families at a relatively early age. Married couples, as noted, had an incentive to have many children, both to provide insurance for their old age and to assure that the line would be continued. The result was that all across the European feudal economy, we witness a powerful tendency to population growth from around the beginning of the 12th century, which led, almost everywhere, to a doubling of population over the following two centuries.

(iii) *Colonization* (Postan, 1966; Duby, 1968). The only significant method by which the feudal economy achieved real growth and counteracted the tendency to declining agricultural productivity, was by way of opening up new land for cultivation. Indeed, economic development in feudal Europe may be understood, at one level, in terms of the familiar race between the growth of the area of settlement and the growth of population. During the 12th and 13th centuries, feudal Europe was the scene of great movements of colonization, as settlers pushed eastward across the Elbe and southward into Spain, while reclaiming portions of the North Sea in what became the Netherlands. The opening of new land did, for a time, counteract and delay the decline of agricultural productivity. Nevertheless, in the long run – as expansion continued, as less fertile land was brought into cultivation, and as the man/land ratio rose – rents rose, food prices increased, and the terms of trade increasingly favoured agricultural as opposed to industrial goods. At various points during the 13th and early 14th centuries, all across Europe, population and production appear to have reached their upper limits, and there began to ensue a process of demographic adjustment along Malthusian lines.

(iv) *Political accumulation or state building* (Dobb, 1946; Anderson, 1974; Brenner, 1982). Give the limited potential for developing the agricultural productive forces and the limited supply of cultivable land, the lordly class, as noted, tended to find the build-up of the means of force for the purpose of redistributing income to be the best route for amassing wealth. Indeed, the lords found themselves more or less *obliged* to try to increase their income in order to finance the build-up of their capacity to exert politico-military power. This was, first of all, because they could not easily escape the politico-military conflict or competition that was the inevitable consequence of the individual lords' direct possession of the means of force (the indispensable requirement for their maintenance as members of the ruling class over and against the peasants) and thus of the wide dispersal of the means of coercion throughout the society. It was, secondly, because they had to confront increasingly well-organized peasant communities and, as feudal society expanded geographically, to counteract the effects of increasing peasant mobility.

In the first instance, of course, politico-military efficacy required the collecting and organizing of followers. But to gain and retain the loyalty of their followers the overlords had to feed and equip them and, in the long run, competitively reward them. Minimally, the overlord's household had to become a focus of lavish display, conspicuous consumption and gift-giving, on par with that of other overlords. But beyond this, it was generally necessary to provide followers with the means to maintain their status as members of the dominant class – that is, a permanent source of income, requiring a grant of land with associated lordly prerogatives (classically the fief). But naturally such grants tended to increase the followers' independence from the overlords, leading to renewed potential for disorganization, fragmentation and anarchy. This was the perennial problem of all forms of patrimonial rule and at the centre of feudal concerns from the beginning. The tendency to fragmentation was, moreover, exacerbated as a result of the pressure to divide lordships and lands among children. To an important degree, then, feudal evolution may be understood as a product of lordly efforts to counteract political fragmentation and to construct firmer intra-lordly bonds with the purpose of withstanding intra-lordly politico-military competition and indeed of carrying on the successful warfare that provided the best means to amass the wealth ultimately required to maintain feudal solidarity. This meant not only the development of better weapons and improved military organization, but also the creation of larger and more sophisticated political institutions, and naturally entailed increased military and luxury consumption.

Actually to achieve more effective political organization of lordly groups required political innovation. Speaking broadly, the constitution of military bands around a leading warlord for external warfare, especially conquest, most often provided the initial basis for intra-lordly cohesion. This served as the foundation for developing more effective collaboration within the group of lords for the protection of one another's property and for controlling the peasantry. As a further step in this direction, the overlord would establish his pre-eminence in settling disputes among his vassals (as in Norman England). Next, the leading lord might extend feudal centralization by establishing immediate relations with the undertenants of his vassals. One way this took place was through constructing direct ties of dependence with these rear vassals (as in 11th century England). More generally, it was accomplished by the extension of central justice to ever broader layers of the lordly class, indeed the free population as a whole. Sometimes the growth of central justice was achieved through the more or less conscious collaboration of the aristocracy as a whole (as in 12th-century England). On other occasions it had to be accomplished through more conflicted processes whereby the leading lord (monarch, prince) would accept appeals over the heads of his vassals from their courts (as in medieval France). Ultimately, the feudal state could be further strengthened only by the levying of taxes, and this almost always required the constitution of representative assemblies of the lordly class.

This is not to say that a high-level of lordly organization was always required. Nor is it to argue that state building took place as an automatic or universal process. At the frontiers of European feudal society, to the south and east, colonization long remained an easy option, and there was relatively little (internally generated) pressure upon the lordly class to improve its self-organization. At the same time, just because stronger feudal states might become necessary did not always determine that they could be successfully constructed. Witness the failure of the German kings to strengthen their feudal state in the

12th century, and the long-term strengthening of the German principalities which ensued. The point is that to the degree that disorganization and competition prevailed within and between groups of feudal lords, they would tend to be that much more vulnerable not only to depredations from the outside, but to the erosion of their very dominance over the peasants. The French feudal aristocracy thus paid a heavy price for their early, highly decentralized feudal organization, suffering not only significant losses of territory to the Anglo-Normans, but a serious reduction in their control over peasant communities and a consequent decline in dues. The French aristocracy's later recovery and successes may be attributed, at least in large part, to their evolution of a new, more centralized, more tightly-knit form of political organization – the tax/office state, where property in office (rather than lordship/land) gave the aristocracy rights to a share in centralized taxation (rather than feudal rent) from the peasants. In sum, the economic success of individual lords, or groups of them, does seem to have depended upon successful feudal state building, and the long-term trend throughout Europe, from the 11th through to the 17th century, appears to have been towards ever more powerful and sophisticated feudal states.

TRADE, TOWNS AND FEUDAL CRISIS. The growing requirements of the lordly class for the weaponry and luxury goods (especially, fine textiles) needed to carry on intra-feudal politico-military competition were at the source of the expansion of commerce in feudal Europe. The growth of trade made possible the rise of a circuit of interdependent productions in which the artisan-produced manufactures of the towns were exchanged for peasant-produced necessities (food) and raw materials, appropriated by the lords and sold to merchant middlemen. Great towns thus emerged in Flanders and north Italy in the 11th and 12th centuries on the basis of their industries' ability to capture a preponderance of the demand for textiles and armaments of the European lordly class as a whole.

In the first instance, the growth of this social division of labour within feudal society benefited the lords, for it reduced costs through increasing specialization, thus making luxury goods relatively cheaper. Nevertheless, in the long run it meant a growing disproportion between productive and unproductive labour in the economy as a whole, for little of the output of the growing urban centres went back into production to augment the means of production or the means of subsistence of the direct peasant producers; it went instead to military destruction and conspicuous waste. Over time, increasingly sophisticated political structures and technically more advanced weaponry meant growing costs and thus increased unproductive expenditures. At the very time, then, that the agricultural economy was reaching its limits, the weight of urban society upon it grew significantly, inviting serious disruption.

Because the growth of lordly consumption proceeded in response to the requirements of intra-feudal competition in an era of increasingly well-constructed feudal states, the lords could not take into account its effect on the underlying agricultural productive structure. All else being equal, the growth of population beyond the resources to feed it could have been expected to call forth a Malthusian adjustment, and most of Europe did witness the onset of famine and the beginning of demographic downturn in the early 14th century. Nevertheless, while the decline of population meant fewer mouths to feed with the available resources, it also meant fewer rent-paying tenants and so, in general, lower returns to the lords. The decline in seigneurial incomes induced the lords to seek to increase their demands on the peasantry, as well as to initiate military attacks upon one another. The peasants were thus subjected to increasing rents and the ravages of warfare at the very moment that their capacity to respond was at its weakest, and their ability to produce and to feed themselves was further undermined. Further population decline brought further reductions in revenue leading to further lordly demands – resulting in a downward spiral which was not reversed in many places for more than a century. The lordly revenue crisis and the ensuing seigneurial reaction thus prevented the normal Malthusian return to equilibrium. A general socio-economic crisis, the product of the overall feudal class/political system, rather than a mere Malthusian downturn, gripped the European agrarian economy until the middle of the 15th century (Dobb, 1946; Hilton, 1969; Bois, 1976; Brenner, 1982).

In the long run, feudal crisis brought its own solution. With the decline of population, peasant cultivation drew back onto the better land, making for the potential of increased output per capita and growing peasant surpluses. Meanwhile, civil and external warfare seem to have abated, a reflection perhaps of the exhaustion of the lordly class, and the weight of ruling class exactions on the peasantry declined correspondingly, especially as the peasants were now in a far better position to pay. The upshot was a new period of population increase and expansion of the area under cultivation, of the growth of European commerce, industry and towns, and, ultimately, of the familiar outrunning of production by population. Meanwhile, lordly political organization continued to improve, feudal states continued to grow, intra-feudal competition continued to intensify, and, over the long run, lordly demands on the peasants continued to increase even as the capacity of the peasantry began, once again, to decline. By the end of the 16th century one witnesses, through most of Europe, a descent into the 'general crisis of the 17th century' which took a form very similar to that of the 'general crisis of the 14th and 15th centuries'. Clearly, through most of Europe, the old feudal property relations persisted, undergirding the repetition of established patterns of feudal economic non-development.

APPROACHES TO TRANSITION. It is an implication of the foregoing analysis that so long as feudal property relations persisted, the repetition of the same long-term economic patterns could be expected. So long as feudal property relations obtained, lords and peasants could be expected to find it rational to adopt the same patterns of individual economic behaviour; in consequence, one could expect the same long-term cyclical tendencies to declining agricultural productivity, population growth and the opening of new land, issuing in a tendency to Malthusian adjustment but overlaid by a continuation of the secular tendency to lordly state building and growing unproductive expenditures. Generally speaking, so long as feudal property relations obtained, no inauguration of a long-term pattern of modern economic growth could be expected. From these premises, it is logical to conclude that the onset of economic development depended on the transformation of feudal property relations into capitalist property relations, and that indeed is the point of departure of a long line of theorists and historians (Marx, 1894; Dobb, 1946; Hilton, 1969; Bois, 1976).

Nevertheless, beginning with Adam Smith himself, a whole school of historically-sensitive theorists have found it quite possible to ignore, or sharply to downplay, the problem of the transformation of property relations and of social relationships more generally in seeking to explain economic development. These theorists naturally refuse to go along with the Adam Smith of *Wealth of Nations* Book I in contending that the mere application of individual economic rationality will, directly and automatically, bring economic development. They nevertheless follow the Adam Smith of *Wealth of Nations* Book III in arguing that, given the appearance of certain specific, *quite-reasonable-to-expect* exogenous economic stimuli, rational self-interested individuals can indeed be expected to take economic actions which will detonate a pattern of modern economic growth. Specifically, it is their hypothesis that the growth of commerce, an enormously widespread if not universal phenomenon of human societies, systematically has led precapitalist economic actors to assume capitalist motivations or goals, to adopt capitalist norms of economic behaviour, and, eventually, to bring about the transformation of precapitalist to capitalist property relations. It is undoubtedly because Adam Smith and his followers have believed that the growth of exchange will *in itself* sooner or later create the necessary conditions for modern economic growth that they have not greatly concerned themselves with these conditions or viewed their emergence as a problem which needs addressing.

Thus, Smith and a long line of followers, prominently including the economic historian of medieval Europe Henri Pirenne and the Marxist economist Paul Sweezy, have all produced analyses which follow essentially the same progression. First, merchants, emanating from outside feudal society, offer previously unobtainable products to lords and peasants who hitherto had produced only for subsistence. This is understood as a more or less epoch-making historical event, an original rise of trade. Next, the very opportunity to purchase these new commodities induces the individual economic actors to adopt businesslike attitude and capitalist motivations, specifically to relinquish their norm of production for subsistence and to adopt the economic strategy of capitalists-in-embryo – viz., production for exchange so as to maximize returns by way of cost cutting. Third, since precapitalist property relations, marked by the producers' possession of the means of subsistence and by the lord's extraction of a surplus by means of extra-economic coercion, prevent the individual economic actors from most effectively deploying their resources to maximize exchange values, both lords and peasants move, on a unit-by-unit basis, to transform these property relations in the direction of capitalist property relations. In particular, the lords dispense with their (unproductive) military followers and military luxury expenditures; they free their hitherto-dominated peasant producers; they expropriate these peasants from the land; then, finally, they enter into contractual relations with these free, expropriated peasants. This gives rise, within each unit to the installation of free, necessarily commercialized (market dependent) tenants on economic leases, who, ultimately, hire wage labourers. The end result is the establishment of capitalist property relations and capitalist economic norms in the society as a whole, and the onset of economic development (Smith, 1776; Pirenne, 1937; Sweezy, 1950).

The foregoing argument of what might be called the Smithian school is designed, implicitly or explicitly, to show how the rise of exchange in a feudal setting in itself creates the conditions under which rational economic actors will pursue self-interested action which leads, on an economy wide basis, to modern economic growth. Nevertheless, the validity of each step in the Smithian argument can be, and has been, challenged by those who take as their point of departure the historically-established property relations. It is the essence of their position that the Smithians can sustain their argument only by failing sufficiently to understand what patterns of economic activity individual lords and peasants will find it rational to adopt in response to the rise of trade, *given* the prevalence of feudal property relations (Marx, 1894; Dobb, 1946; Bois, 1976).

In the first place, although long-distance merchants may bring to feudal lords and peasants commodities they could not previously obtain, the merchants' mere offer of these commodities cannot ensure that the lords and peasants will, in turn, put their own products on the market in order to buy them. Given the existence of feudal property relations, both lords and peasants may be assumed to have everything they need to maintain themselves. The opportunity to buy new goods may very well make it possible for the precapitalist economic actors to increase or enrich their consumption, but this does not mean that they will take advantage of this opportunity. The increased potential for exchange cannot simply determine that exchange will increase (Luxemburg, 1913).

Secondly, even where the appearance of new goods brought by merchants does induce the lords to try to increase their consumption by raising their output and increasing the degree to which they orient their production towards exchange, this will hardly lead them to find it in their rational self-interest to dismantle, in piecemeal fashion, the existing feudal property relations by freeing and expropriating their peasants. Given the reproduction of feudal property relations by communities of feudal lords and peasants, the individual lords can hardly find it in their rational self-interest to free their peasants, for they could lose thereby their very ability to exploit them, and thus their ability to make an income. The point is that, once freed from the lord's extra-economic domination, his *possessing* peasants would have no need to pay *any* levy to him, let alone increase the quality and quantity of their work for him. Moreover, even if the lord could, at one and the same time, free *and* expropriate his peasants, he would still lose by the resulting transformation of his unfree peasant possessors into free landless tenants and wage labourers, for the newly-landless tenants or wage labourers would have no reason to stay and work for their former lord or to take up a lease from him.

To the degree, then, that lords sought to increase their output in response to trade, they appear to have found it in their rational self-interest not to transform but to intensify the precapitalist property relations. Because they found it, on the one hand, difficult to get their possessing peasants effectively to use more productive techniques on their estates, and, on the other hand, irrational to install capitalist property relations within their units, they seem to have had little choice but to try to do so within the constraints imposed by feudal property relations – by increasing their levies on the direct producers in money, kind or labour. To make this possible, they had no choice but to try to strengthen their institutionalized relationship of domination over their peasants, by investing in improved means of coercion and by improving the politico-military organization of their lordly groups. It needs to be emphasized that the lords could not be sure they could succeed in this, for the peasants would likely resist, and perhaps successfully. But in so far as the lords could dictate terms, this was the route they found most promising. Witness the growth of demesne farming in response to the growth of the London market in 13th-century England or, more spectacularly, the rise of a neo-serfdom throughout later medieval and early modern Eastern Europe in response to the growth of trade with the West (Dobb, 1946).

Finally, it needs to be noted that the sort of products on the market which were most likely to stimulate the exploiters to try to increase their income for the purpose of trade were goods which 'fit' their specific reproductive needs. These were not producer goods but, on the contrary, means of consumption – specifially, materials useful for building up the exploiters' political and military strength. They were certainly not luxury goods in the ordinary sense of superfluities, for they were, in fact, necessities for the exploiters. But they were luxuries in that their production involved a subtraction from the means available to the economy to expand its fundamental productive base.

Paradoxically, then, to the extent that the rise of trading opportunities, *in itself*, can be expected to affect precapitalist economies, it is likely to bring about not the loosening but the tightening of precapitalist property forms, the growth of unproductive expenditure, and the quickening not of economic growth but of stagnation and decline.

FROM FEUDALISM TO CAPITALISM. The onset of modern economic growth thus appears to have required the break-up of precapitalist property relations characterized by the peasants' possession of their means of subsistence and the lords' surplus extraction by extra-economic compulsion. Nevertheless, neither the regular recurrence of system-wide socio-economic crisis nor the widespread growth of exchange could, in themselves, accomplish this. The problem which thus emerges is how feudal property relations could ever have been transformed?

To begin to confront this question, one can advance two basic hypotheses which follow more or less directly from the central themes of this article:

1. In so far as lords and peasants, acting either individually or as organized into communities, were able to realize their conscious goals, they succeeded, in one way or another, in maintaining precapitalist property forms. This is to say, once again, that the patterns of economic activity that individual lords and peasants found it reasonable to pursue could not aim at transforming the feudal property structure. It is also to emphasize that, because peasants and lords organized themselves into communities for the very purpose of maintaining and strengthening, respectively, peasant possession and the institutionalized relationships required for taking a feudal rent by extra-economic coercion, lords and peasants acting as communities were unlikely to aim at undermining feudal property forms. Peasants might, through collective action, conceivably have reduced to zero the lords' levies and eliminated the lords' domination; but, even in this extreme case, they would have ended up constituting a community of peasants fully in possession of their means of subsistence, with all of the barriers to economic development entailed by that set of property relations. Were the lords, on the other hand, to have succeeded to the greatest extent conceivable in overcoming peasant resistance, they would only to that degree have strengthened their controls over the peasants and increased their rate of rent, thus tightening feudal property relations.

2. Where breakthroughs took place to modern economic growth in later medieval and early modern Europe, these must be understood as *unintended consequences* of the actions by individual lords and peasants and by lordly communities and peasant communities in seeking to maintain themselves as lords and peasants in feudal ways. In other words, the initial transitions from feudal to capitalist property relations resulted from the attempts by feudal economic actors, as individuals and collectivities, to follow feudal economic norms or to reproduce feudal property relations under conditions where, doing so, actually had the effect – for various reasons – of undermining those relations.

To give substance to these hypotheses would require a lengthy discussion. It is here possible only to note a broad contrast in the historical evolutions of the different European regions during the late medieval and early modern periods. Through most of pre-industrial Europe, East and West, varying processes of class formation brought, in one form or another, the reproduction of feudal property relations and, in turn, the repetition of long-term developmental patterns familiar from the medieval period. However, in a few European regions, feudal property relations dissolved themselves, giving rise, for the first time, to essentially modern processes of economic development.

Thus through much of later medieval and early modern Western Europe (France and parts of Western Germany), although peasants succeeded in very much strengthening peasant possession, winning their freedom and destroying all forms of surplus extraction by extra-economic coercion by individual lords, the lords succeeded, in response, in maintaining themselves by means of constituting a new, more potent form of now-collective surplus extraction by extra-economic compulsion, the tax/office state. At the same time, throughout late medieval and early modern Eastern Europe, despite the peasants' initially very powerful rights in the land and the lords' initially very weak feudal controls, the lords ended up erecting an extremely tight form of individual lordly domination and surplus extraction by extra-economic compulsion – serf-operated demesne production. The consequence of these reconsolidations of essentially feudal property relations throughout most of Europe, East and West, was the reappearance throughout most of Europe during the early modern period of the same trends toward demographically powered expansion, toward the continued build-up of larger and more sophisticated states and, ultimately, toward socio-economic crisis as had characterized the medieval period.

The evolution of property relations in late medieval and early modern England was in some contrast to that of both Eastern and (most of) Western Europe, with epochal consequences for the long-term pattern of economic development. During this period, English lords, unlike those in Eastern Europe, failed, as did those throughout almost all of Western Europe, in their attempts to maintain, let alone intensify, their extra-economic controls over their peasantry. On the other hand, the English lords, unlike those throughout much of Western Europe, did ultimately succeed in maintaining their positions by means of preventing their customary tenants from achieving full property in their plots. They were able, in consequence, to consign these tenants to leasehold status, and thus to assert their own full property in the land.

The unintended consequences of the actions of English peasants and lords aiming to maintain themselves as peasants and lords in feudal ways was thus to introduce a new system of now-capitalist property relations in which the direct producers were free from the lords' extra-economic domination but also separated from their full means of reproduction (subsistence). In the upshot, tenants without direct access to their means of reproduction, had no choice but to produce competitively for exchange and thus, so far as possible, to specialize, accumulate and innovate. At the same time, the landlords found themselves obliged to create larger, consolidated and well-equipped farms if they wished to attract the most productive tenants. The long-run results were epoch making. Under the pressures of competition, processes of differentiation led to the emergence of an entrepreneurial class of capitalist tenant farmers who were ultimately able to employ wage labourers. Meanwhile, the drive to cut costs in agricultural production ultimately brought about an agricultural revolution, as market-dependent farmers were obliged to adopt techniques which long had been available, but long eschewed by possessing peasants who would not intentionally take the risks of specialization, let alone make the necessary capital investments. The secular decline in food costs and the secular rise in living standards which resulted underpinned the movement of population off the land and into industry and made possible the rise of the home market. Industry and agriculture, for the first time, proved mutually supporting, rather than mutually competitive, and population increase served to stimulate economic growth rather than to undermine it. England experienced unbroken industrial and demographic growth right through the 17th and 18th centuries, which ultimately issued in the Industrial Revolution.

BIBLIOGRAPHY

Anderson, P. 1974. *Passages from Antiquity to Feudalism*. London: New Left Books. Distributed in U.S.A. by Humanities Press.

Bois, G. 1976. *La crise du féodalisme*. Paris: Editions EHESS.

Bloch, M. 1939–40. *Feudal Society*. L.A. Manyon, Chicago: University of Chicago Press, 1961, 2 vols.

Brenner, R. 1982. The agrarian roots of European feudalism. In *The Brenner Debate: Agrarian Class Structure and Economic Development in Preindustrial Europe*, ed. T.H. Aston, Cambridge: Cambridge University Press, 1985.

Dobb, M. 1946. *Studies in the Development of Capitalism*. London: Routledge & Kegan Paul; New York: International Publishers, 1947.

Duby, G. 1968. *Rural Economy and Country Life in the Medieval West*. Trans C. Postan, Columbia: University of South Carolina Press.

Duby, G. 1973. *The Early Growth of the European Economy*. Trans. H.B. Clarke, Ithaca, Cornell University Press, 1974.

Duby, G. 1978. *The Three Orders of Society*. Trans. T.N. Bisson, Chicago: University of Chicago Press, 1980.

Ganshof, F.L. 1947. *Feudalism*. Trans. P. Grierson, New York: Harper & Row, 1961.

Hilton, R.H. 1966. *A Medieval Society*. New York: Wiley.

Hilton, R.H. 1969. *The Decline of Serfdom*. London: Macmillan; New York: St. Martin's Press.

Luxemburg, R. 1913. *The Accumulation of Capital*. Trans. A. Schwarzschild, New York: Monthly Review Press, 1968.

Marx, K. 1895. *Capital*, Vol. III. New York: International Publishers, 1967.

Pirenne, H. 1937. *Economic and Social History of Medieval Europe*. New York: Harcourt Brace & Co.

Postan, M.M. 1966. Medieval agrarian society in its prime: England. In *The Cambridge Economic History of Europe*, Vol. 1: *The Agrarian Life of the Middle Ages*, 2nd edn, ed. M.M. Postan and H.J. Habakkuk, Cambridge: Cambridge University Press.

Smith, A. 1776. *An Inquiry into the Nature and Causes of the Wealth of Nations*. Oxford: Oxford University Press, 1976; New York: Random House, 1965.

Strayer, J.R. 1965. *Feudalism*. New York: Van Nostrand Reinhold.

Sweezy, P. 1950. The transition from feudalism to capitalism. *Science and Society* 14(2), Spring, 134–57.

Weber, M. 1956. Patriarchalism and patrimonialism. Feudalism, Standestaat, and patrimonialism. In *Economy and Society*, 2 vols, ed. G. Roth and C. Wittich, Berkeley: University of California Press, 1978.

Fictitious Capital

S. DE BRUNHOFF

The concept of 'fictitious capital' is rarely used by economists today. According to the rather small, though diverse, group of authors who have used the notion, it refers to the finance of productive activity by means of credit. Whatever their differences, all authors contrast 'fictitious capital' with 'real capital', where the latter usually refers to produced means of production, but may also include what Marxists call 'money-capital'. One group of authors contrasts finance by means of fictitious capital with voluntary (i.e. not forced) saving of the means of production. Hayek (1939) is a member of this group and refers to Viner's (1937) brief discussion of the use of the concept by English economists (e.g. by Lauderdale and Ricardo). On the other hand, Marx (1894), and Hilferding (1910), analyse the concept of 'fictitious capital' with respect to different forms of 'borrowed capital' and to the significance of the market value of financial titles and their relation to the value produced by labour.

Hayek (1939) argues that fictitious capital is the product of an increase in bank credit which distorts the capital market. When the plans of consumers and entrepreneurs coincide, the credit offered by the former to the latter corresponds to the placement of savings, and the stability of the capital market is assured. However, an increase in bank credit which encourages entrepreneurs to invest without a corresponding increase in saving results in what Hayek calls a crisis of 'over consumption', with, at the same time, a scarcity of capital and an excess supply of unused capital goods. Here the notion of 'fictitious capital' has a pejorative character as if it referred to counterfeit money or a *traite de cavalerie*. It is no longer solely the source of an illusory stimulus but a source of distortion and crisis.

Fictitious capital violates the necessary neutrality of money by establishing a direct relationship between banks and enterprises, in place of the banks' intermediary role. The interpretation of this relationship as illusory or harmful is related to a quantitative conception of the supply of money.

186

Marx (1894) discusses his quite different notion of 'fictitious capital' in the context of his theory of money and credit. According to him, productive capital, the value of which is created by labour, appears in diverse forms – first, that of money-capital, which is necessary for the payment of wages and the purchase of capital-goods. This money-capital, which is owned by a capitalist, may be loaned by a financier to an entrepreneur. Interest is payable, but this is solely a financial revenue derived from gross profit and has no 'natural' character. According to his $A-A'$ formula (expressing the cycle of loaned capital), 'capital seems to produce money like a pear-tree produces pears', divorced from the process of production and the exploitation of labour. This is why, according to Marx, interest-bearing capital is the most fetishized form of capital.

The notion of 'fictitious capital' derives from that of loaned money-capital. It suggests a principle of evaluation which is opposed to that which is based on labour-value: 'The formation of fictitious capital is called capitalization. Capitalization takes place by calculating the sum of capital which, at the average rate of interest, would regularly yield given receipts of all kinds.' According to Marx, financial revenues regulate the evaluation of all other receipts. It is 'totally absurd' to capitalize wages as if they were a return to 'human capital', and an 'illusion' to do the same with interest on the public debt to which there corresponds no productive investment.

Nevertheless, the issue of bonds provides the right to a part of the surplus which will be created by future work. Hilferding remains faithful to Marx when he states that 'on the stock exchange, capitalist property appears in its pure form… outside the process of production'. Although doubly fetished, in the circuit $A-A'$ and on the financial markets, this fictitious capital has some real roots – the necessity of there being money-capital, credit and the means of financial circulation as an expression of the functioning of the capitalist mode of production.

Used in these different ways the notion of 'fictitious capital' has often, for various reasons, a pejorative character. Although little used, it is at the centre of major economic problems: the relation between circulation and production, banks and enterprises and, fundamentally, the distribution of income.

BIBLIOGRAPHY
Hayek, F.A. 1939. Price expectations, monetary disturbances and malinvestments. In Hayek, *Profits, Interest and Investment*, London: Routledge.
Hilferding, R. 1910. *Finance Capital*. London: Routledge & Kegan Paul, 1981, Pt 2.
Marx, K. 1894. *Capital*, Vol. 3, Part V. Moscow: International Publishers, 1967.
Viner, J. 1937. *Studies in the Theory of International Trade*. London: Harper.

Finance Capital

J. TOMLINSON

The concept of finance capital encapsulates the most theoretically significant attempt by the orthodox Marxism of the pre-1914 period to come to terms with the developments of capitalism in the late 19th century. After the Bolshevik Revolution the concept was much less frequently employed. In part this demise reflected the breakdown of orthodox Marxism as a relatively unified but developing body of doctrine, but it also reflected the inherent problems of the concept.

The term itself is not to be found in Marx's work. But subsequent formulations relied heavily on the schematic outline by Marx in Part V of Volume III of *Capital*, especially chapter 27 on 'The Role of Credit in Capitalist Production'. Marx's arguments, penned in the 1860s, but not published until 1894, focus on the two processes of the multiplication of forms of credit available to industrial capital, and the formation of joint stock companies. The two processes together he saw as heralding 'the abolition of capital as private property within the framework of capitalist production itself' (1894, p. 436).

On the basis of Marx's brief outline, Hilferding in his *Finanzkapital* (1908), built a systematic argument, conceiving finance capital as the highest stage of capitalism. Hilferding's book presents a theoretical history of the evolution of relations between money and productive (industrial) capital. This relationship is seen as having gone through a series of historical transformations, particularly on the basis of changes in the form of credit and credit-giving institutions. Trade credit (or 'circulation credit') is seen as the initial form of credit, emerging from interruptions to the cycle of capital, and tying credit creation directly to the production and sale of commodities. This form of credit facilitated an extension of the scale of production by using funds otherwise idle.

Subsequently there developed banks which not only recycled capitalists' own idle funds but put money from other sources at the disposal of industrial capitalists. When this process of credit expansion encompassed the financing of fixed capital the relationship of the banks to industrial capital began to change, as banks came to have an enduring rather than a monetary interest in the fortunes of the industrial enterprise they lent to. So emerged the characteristically 'German' interlinking of banks and industry, with banks controlling large blocks of industrial equity and sharing large numbers of directors with industry.

The changing relationship encouraged the growth of larger banks, which could afford to tie up funds in this way, but also were enabled by expansion in size to finance lots of firms in order to spread their risks. This growing concentration of banks was seen as interacting with the growth of concentration amongst industrial firms, and is thereby closely linked with the development of the joint stock company. The growth of shares, which Hilferding stresses should be seen as another form of (irredeemable) credit, is a pre-condition of the growth of the joint stock company, which in turn is a pre-condition of a full utilization of the possibilities of technological advance (pp. 122–3).

These joint stock companies become more and more concentrated and tend to the elimination of free competition. This is paralleled by the growth of 'an ever more intimate relationship' between banks and industrial capital: 'Through this relationship ... capital assumes the form of finance capital, its supreme and most abstract expression' (p. 21).

But for Hilferding finance capital is not just a concept but a real social and political force (as indeed it was in Germany). It has its own economic policies, which are both protective of the home market and promote expansion abroad. This latter impetus leads to an intimate relationship between finance capital and the state, which is used to pursue policies of territorial aggrandizement, built partly on the desire to export commodities, but above all to facilitate the export of capital. Hence the characteristic ideology of fianance capital (unlike competitive industrial capital) is aggressively expansionist and aspires to political as well as economic domination. 'Thus the ideology of imperialism arises on the ruins of the old liberal ideals, whose naivety it derides' (p. 334).

Hilferding's analysis of the structure of finance capital can be read as largely a Marxist version of the well known story of the 'divorce of ownership and control' via the development of the joint stock company. Such a parallel would not be entirely misplaced, but it would obscure some of the most important elements of Hilferding's theories.

Least surprisingly, Hilferding's analysis deploys Marx's theory of value, and this, for example, leads him to picture finance capital seizing profits originally produced by industrial capital. Such analysis simply reflects the Marxist concept of industrial capital as productive of surplus value, with other capitals obtaining their profits by redistribution from this original source. But the conceptual background of Marx's theory of value has more specific implications for Hilferding's work.

The argument that values and profits arise originally only in the industrial sector leads to the characterization of share capital as 'fictitious' capital (a term also deployed by Marx), compared with 'genuinely functioning industrial capital' (p. 111). This essentially moralistic approach cuts across the useful discussion by Hilferding of the role of share capital in making possible the joint stock

189

company form of organization, with the progressiveness of this form for the development of production. Similarly, this allegiance to the primacy of industrial capital leads him to assert that 'the techniques of banking itself generate tendencies which affect the concentration of the banks and industry alike, but the concentration of industry is the ultimate cause of concentration in the banking system' (p. 98). Yet his analysis elsewhere makes clear that the development of the banking system, and credit system more generally, were more commonly pre-conditions of the development of forms of industrial capital than vice versa.

A problem of a rather different order is Hilferding's treatment of the relationship between banks and industry as the defining characteristic of finance capital. This leads to the view that countries such as England, where these close relations never existed, are deviants from the norm of development: '... the English system is an outmoded one and is everywhere on the decline because it makes control of the loaned-out bank capital more difficult, and hence obstructs the expansion of bank capital itself' (p. 293). But Hilferding's own arguments on the stock exchange, as the basis of a particular form of credit creation, undercuts this identification of finance capital with one particular financial institution – banks. For what is clearly at stake in Hilferding's general arguments is the development of different types of *credit*, which then impinges on forms of industrial organization, but where these types are not tied to any particular institutional form. (This is quite clear in most of his discussion of the stock exchange.)

Hilferding thus imparts a strong evolutionary element into his argument, where the normal path of development is towards the 'German' model of the relationship between banks and industry. This evolutionism is also more broadly present in Hilferding when he follows Marx in seeing the growth of finance capital and the joint stock company as a socialization of production, that is, a step towards socialist organization of the economy. This socialization is theorized as consisting of a development of a complex division of labour organized by a very few sites of decision-making. Hence the struggle for socialism in this framework is reduced to a struggle to dispossess the oligarchy who currently control production, but who have unwittingly created the 'final organizational prerequisites for socialism' (p. 368). This extraordinary line of argument implies that there is nothing specifically capitalist about the organization of large-scale capitalist industry, except who controls it – surely a *reductio ad absurdum* of the notion of the productive forces developing independently of the relations of production.

The concept of finance capital was most famously deployed by Lenin in his work on Imperialism. Lenin's aim was quite clearly to engage in a political polemic not a theoretical analysis, and he adds nothing new to the discussion of the concept. His main difference with Hilferding was to take further the stress on the aggressive tendencies of finance capital, and to argue the inescapability of imperialist war in such conditions, a conclusion not drawn by Hilferding. Whatever the merits or otherwise of Lenin's political polemic, the association of Hilferding's work with it tended to obscure the theoretical significance of *Finanz-kapital*.

190

After Lenin, the concept of Finance Capital has played a much lesser role in Marxist discussions. Instead, Bolshevized Marxism has tended to place more emphasis on the monopoly characteristics of modern capitalism, rather than the finance aspect; hence the common deployment of concepts of Monopoly Capitalism, and State Monopoly Capitalism. But even within the conceptual approaches of this post-1917 orthodox Marxism this emphasis appears misplaced. As Hussain (1976) has convincingly argued, in terms of standard Marxist categories the concept of finance capital provides a basis for the periodization of capitalism which monopoly capital cannot. It is the relationship of finance to industrial capital which largely determines the structure and size of firms, and hence finance determines the level of 'monopoly'. Starting with the total social capital, as Marx does, it is the relation of finance to industrial capital which determines the distribution of capital into firms. Within an orthodox Marxist framework, finance could in this way provide a basis for periodizing capitalism, that is, on the basis of changes in the relationship of finance to industrial capital and their implications.

Hilferding's work shares some of the defects of Marx's *Capital* in which it was so clearly grounded. Its evolutionism and its adherence to Marx's theory of value, in particular, tend to obscure what is most valuable in the analysis. Nevertheless, with the growing prominence of financial institutions and financial calculation in advanced capitalist countries, any work which provides a detailed theoretical study of the workings of finance under capitalism needs to be taken seriously. This is especially so when the study, at its best, provides analyses which avoid both the speculative character of discussion of the 'total social capital', and the empiricism of institutional description. Rather, the concept of finance capital provides an entry into analysing the nexus of relationships between financial and industrial institutions, but where these institutions are seen neither as simply representations of broader social forces, nor as complex entities knowable only through description.

More specifically, the concept of finance capital leads us to treat the industrial structure as an effect of the changes in the relationship between industrial and financial capital. Thus, for example, the well-known growth of industrial concentration in the UK and other countries in the 1950s and 1960s would be analysed primarily as an effect of the operations of the stock market, and of the credit-creating criteria deployed in that market. Equally, prediction of future trends in the industrial structure would depend upon views about the future evolution of the financial system. The development of the industrial structure, seen in this light, would neither be technologically determined, as commonly suggested, nor, as in some Marxist treatments, would it be seen as tied to the idea of the appropriation by a new class of capitalist of power over the means of production. Rather, the focus would be on the conditions of existence of the credit-giving criteria employed by financial institutions, and how these structured the forms of calculation used by firms in their deployment of means of production. In this way, forms of calculation would be seen as central to the analysis of capitalist firms, but where these forms were themselves seen as dependent upon the mechanisms of allocation of credit in the economy.

It would be an impossible project to 'revive' the orthodox Marxism of the pre-1914 period. Its theoretical presuppositions are in crucial respects no longer tenable, and its specific analyses often tied to circumstances which have changed out of all recognition. Nevertheless, this was a period when Marxism was a relatively open programme of research, and the results of that are not to be simply discarded. The concept of finance capital, shorn of some of its theoretical baggage, could be seen as a potentially fruitful legacy from that period.

BIBLIOGRAPHY

Hilferding, R. 1908. *Finanzkapital.* Translated into English as *Finance Capital*, with an introduction by T.B. Bottomore, London: Routledge & Kegan Paul, 1981.

Hussain, A. 1976. Hilferding's *Finance Capital. Bulletin of the Conference of Socialist Economists.*

Marx, K. 1894. *Capital*, Vol. III. Ed. F. Engels, London: Lawrence & Wishart, 1968.

Full Communism

P.J.D. WILES

In Marx and Marxism, Full Communism is that final state of humanity in which productivity is higher than wants and everyone can help himself in the warehouses (not shops!). Since productivity cannot be unlimited, this entails that wants are limited: a direct contradiction to one of the basic propositions of Western economics. This is only possible because *wants have been reduced to needs*. Originally a governmental concept, needs are accepted as valid by each consumer, and internalized to become the new wants.

If wants are to fall below productivity, people must work seriously but voluntarily, that is *work too must become a need and so again a want*. The link between labour and reward is cut, so that everyone gets a 'dividend' and no one gets a wage, however much or little, well or ill, he or she works – and never mind at what job. Moreover that dividend must in total quantity correspond to the individual's consumption needs, so it is *nearly equal* for all people.

Since people would be 'well brought up', they would not help themselves to more than their 'need dividend' should they have the opportunity – for example, in the common mess hall or at the clothing warehouse. In more moderate versions large durables and housing are not offered in profusion without control, but *rationed*. However, the basic principle is not to ration, but to issue on demand, to a body of consumers too idealistic to 'break the bank'. Either way, *no money* is used inside the community. Moreover in the extreme version *nothing is scarce*. The lack of scrutiny *removes the optimal allocation problem*, and causes the end of economics (if we accept that definition of it) as an intellectual subject.

Though allocations need no longer be optimal they must still be made, both of goods and of labour. The *state*, however, meaning the coercive organs of the governing class, in this case the proletariat, *has withered away*, so there is a big question-mark over the nature of this allocating authority. At least, since economic scarcity has ceased, its yoke is light. On the other hand this authority must be conducting the propaganda that persuades everyone to internalize the new value system. Short on police power, the authority is long

193

on spiritual power. It might, for instance, well be a Communist party without a security police.

In particular, however, unpopular labour, and labour threatening to convey political power to its performers (notably within the allocating authority), must both be *rotated*. Indeed, in extreme versions, all jobs are rotated, to relieve boredom and broaden human development. This is the (utterly impossible and now very embarrassing to Soviet scholars) abolition of the division of labour. This foolishness stems from Marx and Lenin's notion that advanced technology simplifies all labour.

We have only used the words 'utterly impossible' once, and we have presented the whole concept in ordinary Western language. This is partly because the kibbutz does embody Full Communism in practice, as indeed do most monasteries and nunneries. Elements of it are also included by other organizations such as cities under siege, countries immediately after Communist revolutions and military forces. Perhaps above all the nuclear family, even the extended family, brings this utopia down to earth.

The kibbutz and the family, the former hardly Marxist, the latter originally scheduled to disappear under Full Communism, both illuminate the Marxist neglect of the *spiritual diseconomies of scale*. The altruism that we feel in not 'breaking the bank' with our consumption need not be very warm, but it must be there, if only as a sense of duty. The larger our community, the less warmth and eventually the less duty we feel. *Homo economicus* simply becomes an empirically more probable mode. But for Full Communism he must be altogether negated, at least on the consumption side. However, generous a view we take of needs, only a very 'well-brought-up' population can reduce its wants to that, or indeed to any other than an infiitely high, level. In particular, while we can always want very little more than what we now have, it is almost impossible to want nothing more. So wants always grow, and are fed by *envy* and exceed needs by more and more.

It is a commonplace that the modern kibbutz cannot stop people consuming, but it can make people work. Work, after all, is in part natural. Up to a (very variable) point it is thought of as a duty and a pleasure. Deprivation of it is felt as painful, even when income is constant. *Homo economicus* explains work very badly, however large or smaller, rich or poor, capitalist or socialist, our community: he is already negated, in all systems.

PLANNING UNDER FULL COMMUNISM. The kibbutz has a labour committee, which has the fairly simple task of drawing up a labour plan each week; and a consumption committee which, in the avowed presence of economic scarcity, adopts a mix of the following allocation instruments:

(i) Free supply; one just takes what one wants. This rule reigns, in respect of quantity but not quality, in the mess hall. Note that if there had been prices, demand here would have been inelastic in respect to both price and income. Similarly when Russia went through its Full Communism post-revolutionary fit (June 1918–April 1921) local transport and postage were made uncompromisingly moneyless.

(ii) Rationed supply: housing and all durables, even clothing.

(iii) Pocket-money and actual prices: 'imported' luxuries such as cigarettes and sweets; coin-boxes such as telephones (also 'imported').

The pocket-money is of course divided equally, but the intrusion of money into utopia is viewed with grave misgiving. Not only is it bad in itself, but it leads to 'heterogeneous but equal' consumption. People receive unequal quantities of each thing, and this is supposed to give rise to envy, despite the overall equality of consumption volume. Another intrusion of 'money' is the use of shadow-prices by the labour committee. This is less bad in itself, but leads to narrow rationalistic calculations, whereas Full Communism requires the broad sweep of 'policy' irrespective of mere economics.

Mutatis mutandis Communist governments take the same attitudes as kibbutzim. Of course, after their post-revolutionary fit they recognize that they are only in the 'socialist' transitional phase, in which only the enterprise and not the worker/consumer figures in the command plan; the latter is guided by prices and wage-rates. But they feel they should at least be tending the sprouts of the higher phase to come. To the shadow-price problem described above is added the fact that passive inter-enterprise wholesale prices exist in reality. These must, for accounting and bonus-formation purposes, be actually paid, but have no allocative function (the far smaller kibbutz needs no such thing). It would be convenient and rational to bring the passive prices into line with the shadow-price (which has an allocative function but is never paid). Perhaps such a society, in which there were at least no retail prices and instruments (i) and (ii) of consumption planning were used, could be called Full Communism.

The *official Marxist name* for Full Communism is 'Communism'; we have used the longer phrase for clarity. The first post-revolutionary phase is 'Socialism'. Marx describes this in his Critique of the Gotha Programme in very brief terms that correspond respectably to what the Soviet economy has become. Thus it is false that Marx left no post-revolutionary blueprint, but he certainly had a very foreshortened time path. He called the intermediate phase the 'Dictatorship of the Proletariat', and Full Communism, 'Socialism' or 'Communism' indifferently.

FULL COMMUNISM AND INTERNATIONAL RELATIONS. A kibbutz is, in theoretical economics, a country. Hence our use above of the term 'imports'. People who leave it are 'emigrants', and so on. Like a communist country it uses 'foreign' money for its 'foreign' trade. But it is and is meant to be, even in high ideology, subject to the Israeli state, which is not about to wither away. However the Communist state is supposed to wither away, so who will guard its borders and administer migration and foreign trade? Some of these organs are by definition coercive. They can only wither away in a single world state – an irrefragable conclusion only lightly touched upon in Marxist writings.

Antonio Gramsci

MASSIMO L. SALVADORI

Italian communist and Marxist theorist, Gramsci was born in 1891 in Ales (Sardinia), and died in Rome in 1937.

Gramsci's work acquired national importance in Italy when in 1919, together with A. Tasca, U. Terracini and P. Togliatti, he founded the weekly magazine *Ordine nuovo*. The aim of this publication, under the influence of the Russian revolution, was to disseminate the idea of a proletarian dictatorship based on workers' 'councils' and on the alliance between the workers of northern Italy and the poor peasants of the south. Gramsci was elected member of Parliament (1924–6) and became secretary of the Italian Communist Party (PCI) in 1924. In spite of the fact that he had opposed the left in the CPSU in 1926, Gramsci, in bitter opposition to Togliatti, warned of the danger that Bukharin and Stalin's aim was to crush their opponents and subject the International to Russian national interests. Gramsci was arrested in November 1926 and condemned by the special fascist Tribunal to twenty years' imprisonment. During his time in prison he made notes and kept records which were collected in *Quaderni del carcere* (first published between 1948 and 1951). In 1930 he rejected the theory of 'social fascism' supported by the third International. He later became seriously ill and died in a clinic in Rome in 1937.

While in jail Gramsci was aided in many ways by his friend the eminent economist Piero Sraffa, who had moved to Cambridge, England, in 1927.

Gramsci's Marxist beliefs developed into an anti-positivistic attitude. He was affected by the idealism of Gentile and Croce, and also by the thought of Sorel and Bergson. It seemed to him that Lenin and the Bolshevik Party were the ideological incarnation of the new Marxism, organized into an active political force, in direct contrast to the old deterministic Marxism of the social democratic parties of the Second International.

In 1919–20 Gramsci had believed in the supremacy of the revolutionary initiative of the 'Workers' Councils'. After 1921, as a result of a deeper understanding of Leninism, he changed his perspective and underlined instead the primacy of the party as interpreter of the revolutionary process.

During the time that he was in prison, he reflected on the causes of the defeat of the Revolution in the West. He wrote in the *Quaderni* that the social, political and cultural differences between the East and West were such that the Russian Revolution could not be adopted as a model to be copied automatically. In the West the accession to power would have to be preceded by a period of intense political struggle ('war of position') during which the Communist Party (the 'Modern Prince') and the proletariat would have to form a broad front of social alliances and win a wide political and cultural 'consensus' (the theory of 'hegemony').

Gramsci believed that Italy had missed out on the opportunity of producing a national bourgeoisie capable of ensuring the development of a modern society. Italy's inability to solve the problems of the South ('the southern question') bore witness to this. Gramsci believed that it was up to the PCI to change Italian society and, by creating a new socialist order, to accomplish the difficult task of 'national' unification.

Gramsci's beliefs exerted a wide influence on the left, first in Italy, and then in Western Europe. The PCI, which had at the beginning judged him to be a great 'orthodox Leninist', later used Gramsci's 'theory of hegemony' as its main theoretical inspiration for 'Eurocommunism', thus forming a political strategy aimed at surmounting the limits of Leninism.

Gramsci never paid any systematic attention to economic theory. Nevertheless he wrote on it, especially in the *Quaderni* which includes many methodological notes. He was against using the concepts of 'laws' according a deterministic pattern both in economics and sociology. In his opinion, only Marxism was able to establish a 'critical' conception of economics. The 'value' – he stated – is the very core of Marxist economic theory, as far as it explains the 'relationship between the worker and the industrial forces of production'. And whereas the bourgeois idea of 'market' is an 'abstract' one, the Marxist idea is related to 'historicism', that is, it is based on the consciousness of the social and historical conditions of the market itself, which have to be changed in consequence of the revolutionary process.

SELECTED WORKS
1947. *Lettere dal carcere*. Turin: Einaudi. Trans. by Lynne Lawner as *Letters from Prison*, New York: Harper & Row, 1973.
1948–51. *Quaderni del carcere*. 6 vols, Turin: Einaudi. New edn, 4 vols, Turin: Einaudi, 1975. Selections trans. by Quintin Hoare and Geoffrey Nowell Smith as *Selections from the Prison Notebooks*, London: Lawrence & Wishart, 1971.
1954. *L'ordine nuovo*. Turin: Einaudi. Another edn, 1975.
1957. *The modern prince, and other writings*. New York: International Publishers.
1971. *La costruzione del Partito Comunista*. Turin: Einaudi.

BIBLIOGRAPHY
Adamson, W.L. 1980. *Hegemony and Revolution. A study of Antonio Gramsci's political and cultural theory*. Berkeley: University of California Press.
Buci-Glucksmann, C. 1975. *Gramsci et l'état*. Paris: Fayard.

Clark, M. 1977. *Antonio Gramsci and the Revolution that Failed*. New Haven: Yale University Press.

Fiori, G. 1966. *Vita di Antonio Gramsci*. Bari: Laterza.

Romeo, R. *Risorgimento e capitalismo*. Bari: Laterza.

Salvadori, M.L. 1970. *Gramsci e il problema storico della democrazia*. Turin: Einaudi.

Spriano, P. 1967. *Storia del Partito Comunista italiano*, Vol. 1. Turin: Einaudi.

Spriano, P. 1977. *Gramsci in carcere e il Partito*. Rome: Editori Riuniti. Trans. by John Fraser as *Antonio Gramsci and the Party: the Prison Years*, London: Lawrence & Wishart, 1979.

Togliatti, P. 1967. *Gramsci*. Rome: Editori Riunti.

Henryk Grossmann

JOSEF STEINDL

Grossmann was born on 14 April 1881 in Cracow and died on 24 November 1950 in Leipzig. He studied in Cracow and lived from 1908 to 1918 in Vienna (collaborating with Carl Grünberg) and 1918 to 1925 in Warsaw (at the Central Statistical office and the Free University). From 1925 to 1933 he was a political refugee in Germany (University of Frankfurt/Main) and later in France, England and USA. Grossman spent his last years in the German Democratic Republic, at the University of Leipzig.

His main work (1929), based on Marx, deals with the inevitability of the breakdown of capitalism. The method of Marx, in his view, is a step-wise approximation to reality which starts from a simplified abstract model of the accumulation process (based on the reproduction schema and assuming a closed system, two classes only, no credit, commodities sold at their values, constant value of money) and proceeds by gradually adding realistic details of secondary importance ('surface phenomena') among which he counts monopoly, money and credit, capital exports and the struggle for raw materials. In following this method Grossmann demonstrates the inevitability of breakdown and then deals with the factors which counteract and therefore delay the breakdown.

The starting point of his theory is an arithmetic example of Otto Bauer based on the reproduction schema of Marx which was intended by Bauer (in a polemic against Rosa Luxemburg) to demonstrate that realization under extended reproduction was perfectly possible. Bauer worked out his example only for four years but Grossmann extended it to 35 years in order to demonstrate that the accumulation process could not proceed without limit. Following Bauer, he made the following assumptions: 5 per cent growth of variable capital (determined exogenously by the growth of population) while the constant capital was to grow by 10 per cent; surplus value was to be constant at 100 per cent.

Since the organic composition of capital was continuously increasing, the Marxian conclusion of a declining rate of profit held good, as also shown in Bauer's example. This implied, with constant growth of capital, that the share

199

of consumption in surplus value had to decrease. Grossmann sees no difficulty in this so long as the absolute amounts of profit and consumption increase (owing to the increase in capital). For this reason he considers Marx's theory as incomplete. His own contribution is to show that the *absolute* amounts also have to decrease. The step taken from Marx seems to be fairly simple: if the declining rate of profit is combined with an exogenously given constant rate of growth of capital, then the share of consumption in surplus must ultimately go down to zero and below. This marks the point of breakdown.

Grossmann deals extensively with counteracting tendencies such as new colonial markets and real wage cuts. These can only delay and not avoid the breakdown. Their effect will appear in the form of cyclical crises which Grossmann expected would become more and more serious.

Grossmann strongly criticizes all Marxist writers before him (in particular, Hilferding and Luxemburg) for having distorted the content of Marx's teaching. His aim is to restore the orthodoxy of the true Marx which in his view is embodied in the breakdown thesis based on the increase in the organic composition of capital. Other aspects of Marx he plays down (historical materialism) or ignores (the realization problem). Since his book largely takes the form of a polemic it may be used as a source of information on Marxist and other literature, but he does scant justice to the ideas of some of these writers.

Grossmann was, however, a man of culture and learning, with considerable knowledge of the economic doctrines of 18th and early 19th centuries, and a highly esteemed historian who wrote a pioneering study on the Principality of Warsaw (a short-lived state created by Napoleon) based on census material. His surviving papers are in the archives of the Polish Academy of Sciences.

BIBLIOGRAPHY
1914. *Österreichs Handelspolitik mit Bezug auf Galizien in der Reformperiode 1772–1790.* Vienna: Konegen.
1924. *Simonde de Sismondi et ses théories économiques.* Warsaw: Bibliothèque Universitaire Libre Polonaise.
1925. Struktura społeczna i gospodarcza Księstwa Warszawskiego na podstawie spisów ludności 1808–1810 (Social and economic structure of the Warsaw Principality on the basis of the census of population 1808 to 1810). *Kwartalnik Statystyczny, Warsaw.*
1929. *Des Akkumulations- und Zusammenbruchsgesetz des kapitalistischen Systems.* Leipzig: C.L. Hirschfeld.
1975. *Marx, l'économie politique classique et le problème de la dynamique.* Preface by Paul Mattick. Paris: Editions Champ Libre.

Rudolf Hilferding

ROY GREEN

Hilferding (1877–1941) blended Marxist economics and Social Democratic politics in a career cut tragically short by the rise of fascism in Germany. He studied medicine at the University of Vienna, but soon showed more interest in organizing the student socialist society. After graduating in 1901, he helped Max Adler to found the *Marx-Studien* (1904–23), a series which was to become the theoretical flagship of 'Austro-Marxism'. The first volume contained a vigorous defence of the labour theory of value by Hilferding himself against Böhm-Bawerk's marginalist critique, *Zum Abschluss des Marxschen Systems* (1896). It earned him his intellectual spurs in the German-speaking socialist movement.

At the same time, Hilferding was already contributing to debate within the German Social Democratic Party (SPD) through is journal, *Die Neue Zeit*. There, on the controversial 'mass strike' issue, he steered a course for the party leadership between Eduard Bernstein's 'revisionist' abandonment of the socialist goal and Rosa Luxemburg's revolutionary commitment to it (1903/4, 1904/5). He was rewarded with an appointment in 1906 as economics lecturer at the party school in Berlin, and then as foreign editor of the party newspaper, *Vorwärts*. From 1907, he also wrote regularly for the newly established journal of the Austrian Social Democrats, *Der Kampf*.

Hilferding published his major work, *Das Finanzkapital*, in 1910; it was immediately hailed by such diverse figures as Kautsky (1911), Lenin (1916) and Bukharin (1917), as a path-breaking development of Marxist economic analysis. Essentially, Hilferding argued that the concentration and centralization of capital had led to the domination of industry and commerce by the large banks, which were transformed into 'finance capital' (1910, p. 225). The socialization of production effected by finance capital required a correspondingly increased economic role for the state. Society could therefore plan production by using the state to control the banking system:

> The socializing function of finance capital facilitates enormously the task of overcoming capitalism. Once finance capital has brought the most important

201

branches of production under its control, it is enough for society, through its conscious executive organ – the state conquered by the working class – to seize finance capital in order to gain immediate control of these branches of production . . . . Even today, taking possession of six large Berlin banks would mean taking possession of the most important spheres of large-scale industry . . . (ibid., pp. 367–8).

This chain of reasoning, however, tended to exaggerate not only the leverage of the banks over industry, but also the role of the state in the organization of production. While it convinced Hilferding that socialism could be introduced by a determined majority in parliament, it demonstrated to Lenin that socialism would not be possible unless the state was 'overthrown' by a determined minority outside parliament. Their common point of reference was the centrality of the state – rather than society – in the 'latest phase of capitalist development'. It forced socialists to make a choice between parliamentarism and insurrection, the very nature of which contributed to the defeat of the labour movement in Germany and the rise of party dictatorship in Russia (Neumann, 1942, pp. 13–38). Although theory cannot be held responsible for the course of history, it may influence political judgements which tip the balance at decisive moments. Hilferding's generation lived through many such moments.

When war broke out in 1914, Hilferding associated himself with the SPD minority which voted against war credits and which later formed the Independent Social Democrats (USPD). He spent most of the war on the Italian front, having been drafted into the Austrian army as a doctor, and returned to Berlin as editor of the USPD journal, *Freiheit*. Hilferding successfully opposed USPD affiliation to the Third International; his speech against Zinoviev, at the Halle conference of 1920 – published under the title, 'Revolutionäre Politik oder Machtillusionen?' – was a decisive turning point. Once the embryonic Communist Party (KPD) forced a split on the issue, however, he saw no alternative to reunification with the remnants of the SPD.

During the 1920s, Hilferding turned his attention almost entirely to the political and economic problems facing the new German republic. He was a leading member of the Reich Economic Council, twice Minister of Finance and an active participant in the discussions on 'workers' councils' and the government's 'socialization' programme. Hilferding's first stint as Minister of Finance lasted only seven weeks in the Stresemann government of 1923. Although he had no opportunity to implement his proposals, he devised a plan for currency reform involving the introduction of a *Rentenmark* backed by gold as part of an anti-inflation package. By the time Hilferding returned to the same post in the Müller government of 1928/9, economic conditions had worsened; his predicament was appreciated by Schumpeter who wrote, 'we now have a socialist minister who faces the exceptionally difficult task of curing or improving a situation bequeathed by non-socialist financial policies' (quoted in Gottschlacht, 1962, p. 24). A less sympathetic observer, however, portrayed Hilferding at this time as 'the theorist of coalition politics in the period of capitalist stabilisation' (see Gottschlacht, 1962, p. 204), blinded by theory to the imminent fascist danger.

Pursuing the logic of *Das Finanzkapital*, Hilferding had developed a theory of 'organized capitalism', a term he first used in 1915 in *Der Kampf*, and then explained more fully in 1924 in *Die Gesellschaft*. He summarized the approach at the SPD's Kiel conference in 1927: 'Organized capitalism means replacing free competition by the social principle of planned production. The task of the present Social Democratic generation is to invoke state aid in translating this economy, organized and directed by the capitalists, into an economy directed by the democratic state' (see Neumann, 1942, p. 23). Ironically, this was the very position of an earlier Social Democratic leadership which Marx had singled out for criticism. Commenting on the demand for a 'free state' in the 1875 Gotha programme, Marx wrote:

> It is by no means the goal of workers who have discarded the mentality of humble subjects to make the state 'free'. In the German Reich the 'state' has almost as much 'freedom' as in Russia. Freedom consists in converting the state from an organ superimposed on society into one thoroughly subordinate to it; and even today state forms are more or less free depending on the degree to which they restrict the 'freedom of the state' (Marx, 1891, p. 354).

While Hilferding understood that in capitalist society power lay with capital and was exercised by the representatives of capital in the management structure of the great corporations, he failed to see that democratic control over the productive forces would require a change in the relationship of power *within* the corporation itself. Organized labour could use the state to accelerate this process of social transformation and to create the centralized institutional machinery necessary for the 'associated producers' to plan directly the whole economy; but the notion that the state itself could perform this task rested upon an illusion. In attempting to replace the domination of capitalist employers with the domination of a 'democratic state', Hilferding and the party leadership achieved only one practical result: 'Unwittingly, they strengthened the monopolistic trends in German industry' (Neumann, 1942, p. 21). The state domination which followed was far from democratic.

Hilferding, a Jew, was forced into exile after 1933, first in Switzerland via Denmark and then in France. In an unfinished manuscript, *Das historische Problem*, he set about revising his whole conception of the state. The problem was now said to consist 'in the change in the relation of the state to society, brought about by the *subordination of the economy* to the coercive power of the state ...' (quoted by Bottomore, Introduction to Hilferding, 1981, p. 16, emphasis in original). Hilferding briefly presented his new approach in the New York *Socialist Courier* in 1940; there, like Marx, he drew a rueful comparison between Germany and Russia. The state had not 'withered away' under Soviet communism:

> History, that 'best of all Marxists', has taught us another lesson. It has taught us that, in spite of Engels' expectations, the 'administration of things' may

become an unlimited 'domination over men', and thus lead not only to the emancipation of the state from the economy but even to the subjection of the economy by the holders of state power (Hilferding, 1981, p. 376 fn.)

It was too late for Hilferding's brave reassessment to influence the course of events. In 1941, he died in the hands of the Gestapo.

SELECTED WORKS

1904. *Böhm-Bawerk's Criticism of Marx.* Ed. P. Sweezy, London: Merlin Press, 1975.

1902/3. Der Funktionswechsel des Schutzzolles. Tendenz der modernen Handelspolitik. *Die Neue Zeit* XXI, 2.

1903/4. Zur Frage des Generalstreik. *Cie Neue Zeit* XXII, 1.

1904/5. Parliamentarismus und Massenstreik. *Die Neue Zeit* XXIII, 2.

1910. *Finanzkapital.* Trans. as *Finance Capital: A Study of the Latest Phase of Capitalist Development.* London: Routledge & Kegan Paul, 1981.

1915. Historische Notwendigkeit und notwendige Politik. *Der Kampf* VIII.

1915. Arbeitsgemeinschaft der Klassen? *Der Kampf* VIII.

1924. Probleme der Zeit. *Die Gesellschaft* I, 1.

1924. Realistischer Pazifismus. *Die Gesellschaft* Im 2.

1933. Zwischen den Entscheidungen. *Die Gesellschaft* X.

1933/4. Revolutionärer Sozialismus. *Zeitschrift für Sozialismus* I.

1934/5. Macht ohne Diplomatie – Diplomatie ohne Macht. *Zeitschrift fur Sozialismus* II.

1940. State capitalism or totalitarian state economy. *Socialist Courier*, New York; reprinted in *Modern Review* I, (1947). *Publishes Speeches.*

1919. Zur Sozialisierungsfrage. 10th Congress of the German trade unions, Nuremberg, 30 June–5 July 1919. Berlin.

1920. Revolutionäre Politik oder Machtillusionen? Speech against Zinoviev at the annual conference of the USPD in Halle, 1920. Berlin.

1920. Die Sozialisierung und die Machtverhältnisse der Klassen. 1st Congress of Works Councils, 5 October 1920. Berlin.

1927. Die Aufgaben der Sozialdemokratie in der Repuklik. Annual conference of the SPD in Kiel, 1927. Berlin.

1931. Gesellschaftsmacht oder Privatmacht über die Wirtschaft. 4th AFA (Allgemeiner freier Angestelltenbund) trade union congress in Leipzig, 1931. Berlin.

BIBLIOGRAPHY

Böhm-Bawerk, E. von 1886. *Karl Marx and the Close of his System.* Ed. P. Sweezy, London: Merlin Press, 1975.

Bukharin, N. 1917. *Imperialism and World Economy.* London: Merlin Press, 1972.

Gottschlacht, W. 1962. *Struktur Veränderung der Gesellschaft und politisches Handeln in der Lehre von Rudolf Hilferding.* Berlin: Duncker & Humblot.

Kautsky, K. 1911. Finanzkapital und Krisen. *Die Neue Zeit* 29, 764–72, 797–803, 838–46, 864–83.

Lenin, V.I. 1916. *Imperialism, the Highest Stage of Capitalism.* Moscow: Foreign Languages Publishing House, 1947.

Marx, K. 1891. Critique of the Gotha Programme. In *The First International and After*, ed. D. Fernbach, Harmondsworth: Penguin Books, 1974.

Neumann, F. 1942. *Behemoth.* London: Victor Gollancz.

Imperialism

ALICE H. AMSDEN

Few subjects of such conspicuous historical importance have so consistently escaped lucid theoretical exposition as imperialism. The neoclassical economists have made no theoretical gains whatsoever in the field, having chosen to ignore the subject altogether. Their starting and ending point is a short essay borrowed from Schumpeter in which imperialism in the 19th and 20th centuries is attributed to the atavism of states, acting on feudal and absolutist impulses from an earlier precapitalist era. The field, therefore, has been dominated by Marxists. 'To write about theories of imperialism is already to have a theory,' states Barratt Brown (1972). In modern times, just to use the word is to label what is said as Marxist. The word – like capitalism itself – also implies a theory of broadly construed economic systems and long historical epochs. The sweep of the subject matter is reflected in the breadth of the two major propositions that Marxists have posed: that imperialism and monopoly capitalism are synonymous; and that capitalism underdevelops the third world. The sweep of the subject matter has lent itself to meaningless generalizations and reductionist arguments. But to ignore imperialism altogether on the ground that it is a political phenomenon is to abrogate a responsibility to study a major dimension of economic life, in particular the relationship between the operations of the market and coercive mechanisms.

Part of the problem lies in the ambiguity of the term. Since there is no agreement on the referent of imperialism, there is none on the meaning of the word itself. Marx and Engels did not discuss imperialism as such so they bequeathed no definition. To one of their followers, Rosa Luxemburg (1913), it was the political expression of the accumulation of capital in its competitive struggle for what is still left of the non-capitalist regions of the world. To another, Nikolai Bukharin (1917), it was a policy of conquest by finance capital that is characteristic of one stage of capitalist development. To a follower of a later generation, Samir Amin (1976), it was the perpetuation and expansion of capitalist relations abroad by force or without the willing consent of the affected people. Schumpeter (1919)

205

defined it as the objectless disposition on the part of a state to unlimited forcible expansion.

While no consensus exists, most definitions share an idea that interactions between two social formations are in some sense imperialist if they depend upon force. And the use of force is all the more likely if the two entities are of unequal strength. This is not to say that only military domination qualifies as imperialism. Or that any exchange, commercial or financial, between two parties of unequal strength is imperialism. Rather, even if the use of force is only implicit, perpetrated by the fountain pen, it qualifies as imperialist if the weaker collectivity is subjected to some sort of control by the stronger. So defined, and such is the definition followed below, imperialism is ultimately a political phenomenon, whatever its underlying tap-root.

There appear to be as many explanations for the motivations underlying imperialism as there have been wars. Yet the economic explanations are qualitatively distinct from the rest – geopolitical, psychological – because they reflect the fact that different economic systems reproduce themselves differently. In societies where reproduction was constrained by the availability of land, territorial expansion was the impetus. In societies dependent upon slavery, there was warring for slaves. To buy cheap and sell dear in the age of mercantilism, there was resort to plunder. Come the capitalist system, imperialism evolved into something more complex than theft. It was embodied in exchange relationships. And since exchange could occur peacefully, without the use of force, some, like Schumpeter, presumed that capitalism and imperialism were antithetical. Yet force has been used to accelerate the onset of exchange relationships, to preserve them, and to improve the terms of exchange. Imperialism under centralized planning involves still another dynamic, since the driving imperative for markets (for economic surplus) is absent. It has been attributed by Ota Sik, the Czechoslovak planner, to the requirement of reducing uncertainty through the control of inputs and outputs (Owen and Sutcliffe, 1972). A complex of causes, however, is evident even for an imperialism defined sensibly for a specific historical period. The so-called 'new imperialism', which is the concern here and which dates from the 1870s–80s and onwards, is attributed to economic factors by, say, Hobson (1902) and Hilferding (1910); to European diplomatic rivalries by Fieldhouse (1966) and Langer (1935); and to extreme nationalism by Hayes (1941) and Mommsen (1980).

Precisely where to draw the dividing line between imperialist episodes, however, is contentious; and more than a mere theoretical quibble in the case of the 'new imperialism'. Robinson and Gallagher (1953) argue that there is little that distinguishes the allegedly 'indifferent' mid-Victorian imperialism, when free-trade beliefs were at their height, from the 'enthusiastic' late-Victorian imperialism, when such beliefs were in decline, along with British competitiveness. According to the authors, the indifference–enthusiasm polarization leaves out too many of the facts. There were numerous additions to empire, both formal and informal, in the indifferent decades. Between 1841 and 1851 Great Britain occupied or annexed New Zealand, the Gold Coast, Natal, the Punjab,

Sind, Labuan and Hong Kong. In the next twenty years British control was asserted over Berar, Oudh, Lower Burma and Kowloon, over Lagos and the neighbourhood of Sierra Leone, over Basutoland, Griqualand and the Transvaal; and new colonies were established in Queensland and British Colmbia. What is more, in the supposedly laissez-faire period, before the 1870s, the economy of India was managed along the best mercantilist lines. Such continuity in 19th century imperialism contradicts 'those who have seen imperialism as the high stage of capitalism and the inevitable result of foreign investment ... [in] ... the period after the 1880s', Lenin included.

Lenin's towering influence on Marxist theorists derives from his pamphlet, *Imperialism, the Highest Stage of Capitalism*, written in 1916 in response to the outbreak of war. The academic establishment in Europe attributed the First World War mostly to the official mind. Lenin ascribed it to monopoly capitalism, the economic mainspring of imperialist rivalry:

> Railways are a summation of the basic capitalist industries: coal, iron and steel; ... The uneven distribution of the railways, their uneven development – sums up, as it were, modern monopolist capitalism on a world-wide scale. And this summary proves that imperialist wars are absolutely inevitable under such an economic system ... (Preface, pp. 4–5).

The economic system of monopoly capitalism is first portrayed by Lenin as being highly productive. According to a US Commission that he cites, the trusts expand their market share on the basis of scale economies and superior technology: 'Their superiority over competitors is due to the magnitude of ... [their] ... enterprises and their excellent technical equipment.' This leads Lenin to state: 'Competition becomes transformed into monopoly. The result is immense progress .... In particular, the process of technical invention and improvement becomes socialized' (p. 24). He goes on to argue, however, that industrial capital falls prey to finance capital. He also embraces the prevailing academic view of monopoly, that it is unproductive, although he is far more cautious about this than his followers were to be:

> Certainly, the possibility of reducing cost of production and increasing profits by introducing technical improvements operates in the direction of change. But the *tendency* to stagnation and decay, which is characteristic of monopoly, continues to operate, and in certain branches of industry, in certain countries, for certain periods of time, it gains the upper hand (p. 119).

Stagnation, in turn, leads to the export of capital, but Lenin is vague in his explanation for why this should be so:

> The necessity for exporting capital arises from the fact that in a few countries capitalism has became 'overripe' and (owing to the backward stage of agriculture and the impoverished state of the masses) capital cannot find a field for 'profitable' investment (p. 74).

207

The direction of capital exports is to the backward countries:

> ... surplus capital will be utilized ... for the purpose of increasing profits by exporting capital abroad to the backward countries. In these backward countries profits are usually high, for capital is scarce, the price of land is relatively low, wages are low, raw materials are cheap (p. 73).

For Lenin, therefore, imperialism becomes organically inseparable from monopoly capitalism. Whereas in common usage imperialism means forced economic gain on a global scale, to Lenin it means much more. The most concise definition he gives is 'imperialism is the monopoly stage of capitalism', uniquely characterized, it should be added, by capital export.

Capital exports rose dramatically after the turn of the twentieth century. Yet neither underconsumption, as expounded by Hobson, nor a superabundance of capital, as Lenin suggested, nor a declining profit rate, a conceivable consequence of rising capital investments at home, provide particularly good explanations. Instead, Magdoff (1972) argues that in addition to the immediate causes of the sudden upsurge of capital exports (more competitors, more exporters; more tariff walls, more foreign investment to jump them), '[t]he desire and need to operate on a world scale is built into the economics of capitalism' (p. 148). Competition creates pressures for the expansion of markets. The emergence of a significant degree of concentration does not mean the end of competition. 'It does mean that competition has been raised to a new level .... Since capital operates on a world scale, ... the competitive struggle among the giants for markets stretches over large sections of the globe' (p. 157). Although the scramble for colonies preceded rather than followed the rise of monopoly and capital exports, annexation was not what Lenin meant by imperialism. On the contrary, Sutcliffe states, in response to Robinson and Gallagher, 'it was a prelude to imperialism .... The system changed its character at the end of the century because from then on both expansion and rivalry between the major capitalist powers would have to take new forms since the chances of territorial expansion had been exhausted' (Sutcliffe, 1972, p. 314).

Lenin based his analysis of imperialism on the stranglehold of finance capital, by which he meant the leading role that banks came to play in economic decision making. The financiers were perceived to have the biggest stake in imperialism and their hunger for quick returns led to economic chaos. Yet in fact after World War I finance capital decidedly took a back seat as the multinational firm grew in the US, Europe and, belatedly, England. As evidence for this, there was a shift over time away from indirect foreign investment, that is, portfolio or debt capital, to direct foreign investment, or equity capital. Roughly two-thirds of foreign investment took the form of debt capital before World War I. Thereafter, direct foreign investment became predominant, although a new type of portfolio investment rose again sharply in the late 1970s–early 1980s.

Chandler (1980) writes about the *form* that the growth of large-scale firms assumed:

... modern industrial enterprise ... grew by adding new units of production and distribution, by adding sales and purchasing offices, by adding facilities for producing raw and semi-finished materials, by obtaining ... transportation units, and even by building research laboratories ... (p. 397).

These new specializations of large business enterprises are the crux of Hymer's (1976) explanation for why capital exports were increasingly direct rather than indirect. According to him, the specializations that Chandler mentions – management expertise, capability in manufacturing, technology, distribution – constituted firm-specific monopolistic assets. To take full monetary advantage of them, firms exerted direct control over overaseas operations, through equity ownership.

Yet foreign investment, whether direct or indirect, did not flow preponderantly to backward regions. In the interwar period and even before 1914, the main destination for overseas funds was Europe and North America. British colonies, including India, accounted for only about 20 per cent, and South America for another 20 per cent (Barratt Brown, 1972). After 1929, the share of the advanced countries in the inflow of direct foreign investment rose even further, reaching around 75 per cent of the total in the mid-1970s. The share was higher still for direct foreign investment in the manufacturing sector (USDC, various years). Thus, while the locus of socialist revolutions was backward regions, not advanced ones, capital exports flowed increasingly to advanced regions, not backward ones. The direction of foreign investment is significant because it suggests an altogether different centre of gravity in economic activity under monopoly capitalism from the one Lenin's followers entertained.

Beginning at the turn of the century, the principal orientation of the economic activity of advanced countries was, in general, toward each other, not the backward regions. Like foreign investment, foreign trade in manufactures largely engaged the advanced countries. Their competitive struggle involved mainly invasions of each other's markets. The major contest in economic strength after World War II, between the US and Japan, barely stretched to third world shores.

Explanations other than international differences in gross profit rates must be sought for the geographical distribution of foreign investment. No definitive data exist to compare profit rates across countries. Yet profit rates are likely to have been relatively higher in backward countries, as Lenin suggests, because rates of surplus value, in the Marxist accounting sense, were higher there, at least in the 1970s in the manufacturing sector (Amsden, 1981). One reason why foreign investment and trade primarily occupied the richer countries is that their per capita incomes were growing faster than the poorer regions, the newly industrializing countries excluded. The higher *level* of income in advanced countries also made them better markets. In turn, high income markets complemented the type of competition that became characteristic of monopoly capitalism. The monopolistic assets of large business enterprises were the competitive weapons. The coming of age of industrial capital witnessed an intensification of competition on the technology front. New products, new processes, new production systems constituted the razor's edge of the competitive battle, moderating the demand for protection and price-fixing cartels. Such technology was not designed with third world domination in mind. The location of industry in the course of a product cycle from the 1950s at least through the 1980s progressed from the innovating country, to other advanced countries and only belatedly to backward regions (Vernon, 1966); and then only if new discoveries did not short circuit the cycle such that production returned to the innovator's country of origin.

The monopolistic assets of large business enterprises did not all work productively, and Marxists pointed to the wasteful effects of advertising and to the ruinous effects of financial manipulation in the form of takeover waves at home and periodic, aggressive bouts of lending to the backward regions. But technological competition was the stuff out of which monopoly capitalism was made after World War II. So to equate monopoly capitalism and imperialism robs both terms of much of their meaning. The two cannot be reduced to one another.

Even if, following Stokes (1969), one attributes to Lenin what has come to be a non-'Leninist' view, that the contestation of imperialist rivalries occurs not in the third world but in the monopolized countries themselves, then the conflation of monopoly capitalism and imperialism is still obfuscating. Whereas such rivalries engaged Europe in war at the time Lenin was writing, they were mediated peacefully there for at least forty years after World War II.

Nor is Lenin especially illuminating on why capital exports are the *specifica differentia* of monopoly capitalism. Was foreign investment more likely to precipitate the use of force than foreign trade? No, because trade in raw materials in the 19th century presupposed foreign investment. And what is the significance of the shift from indirect to direct foreign investment? Marxists have not systematically explored the answer. History teaches us that finance capital increasingly falls under the control of a few large banks, but it comprises much less differentiable products than industrial capital and, therefore, is more at the mercy of the laws of supply and demand. To prevent interest rates from falling, the banks look overseas for profitable investment outlets, and when they compete on the basis of price, they look in particular to the backward regions. The upsurge of portfolio investment in the late 1970s–early 1980s was accounted for overwhelmingly by the third world. Presumably the backward regions will become a more important locale for industrial capital as technological competition among advanced countries grows more even and product differentiation converges. Then manufacturers may be expected to locate their production facilities in lower wage, higher profit countries in order to compete better on the basis of price. That they did not do so to any significant extent before the 1980s suggests not a shortage of profitable investment outlets in advanced countries, supposedly a hallmark of monopoly, but a surplus of such outlets. Even though profit rates in the manufacturing sector were lower in the advanced countries, assuming the numbers are correct, marginal profit rates are likely to have been equal or higher, due to an outpouring of innovations.

The backward regions, however, were hardly inconsequential, to either industrial or finance capital. Certain third world raw materials, not least of all petroleum, remained critical business cost factors. The third world's debt crises undermined global monetary stability. The 'defection' of third world countries to socialism precipitated armed intervention. And, while the capital that flowed from the advanced countries to the third world through most of the tenure of the 'new imperialism' amounted to a mere trickle, there was a massive net transfer of surplus from the third world to the advanced countries (Bagchi, 1982). Capitalism, after all, had become a world system. The relationship between imperialism and the economic development of the backward regions was the subject of as much literature as the relationship between imperialism and monopoly capitalism. Indeed, more was written on the former, because the neoclassical economists contributed; discretely, the term imperialism never being mentioned.

Imperialism before and after World War II was quite distinct, as formal colonialism ended and large portions of Asia and Africa gained independence. One would expect economic growth in the backward regions to be quite distinct in each period as well, as a consequence of such political change. Yet, curiously, both Marxist and neoclassical economists saw continuity. In the neoclassical view, the backward regions had as good a chance to develop under colonialism as under independent rule so long as they organized their economies in the pursuit of comparative advantage. For the Marxists, underdevelopment was the expected outcome whatever the political regime, so long as the economic mechanisms of imperialism were fundamentally unaltered.

But how did these mechanisms operate? And did they remain unaltered amidst shifts in political circumstance? Schumpeter's argument, that imperialism under capitalism was a throwback to precapitalist impulses, was based on the premise that peaceful exchange was preferable to the use of force for all self-interested parties, and that ultimately reason would prevail over atavism. Yet, at minimum, force might be rational for one party to hasten another's *entry* into capitalist exchange relationships or to prevent another's *exit* into an altogether different economic system. The latter appears to have driven a good deal of US imperialism after World War II, notwithstanding the fact that the US had no precapitalist history. In the war's aftermath, American aid to Greece and Turkey limited leftist activity and the US government helped opponents of socialist and communist candidates for office in France and Italy. Vietnam apart, the US intervened either directly through the military or covertly through the Central Intelligence Agency to halt what was perceived as socialist aggression in Greece, Iran, Guatemala, Indonesia, Lebanon, Laos, Cuba, the Congo, British Guiana, the Dominican Republic, Chile and possibly Brazil.

The onset of capitalist relations in the third world was also replete with the use of force. In many colonies where foreign enclaves were established in the 19th century for the purpose of producing primary products for export, population was scarce, so in retrospect 'overpopulation' cannot be held responsible for the underdevelopment that ensued. Indeed, one would have expected not underdevelopment but the onset of a 'high wage economy', given a scarcity of labour and a growing demand for labour's services in the mines and on the plantations. But wages did not rise (Myint, 1964). For the neoclassical paradigm of peaceful market exchange, this constitutes a paradox. For more institutionally oriented economists, this seeming paradox was resolved with the artifice of the 'backward bending labor supply curve'. It was imagined that self-sufficient peasants who migrated to the mines and plantations offered their services with the limited purpose of obtaining only a 'target' income. If higher wages were paid, their objective would be met all the faster, with the consequence of a smaller, not larger labour supply. In fact, foreign firms in the mining and plantation sectors were faced with a decision – of whether to pay in excess of labour productivity in the short run or to coerce an adequate labour supply at a low wage rate equal to (or below) the prevailing level of productivity – and they opted for force. Colonial authorities passed legislation that indirectly compelled natives to work: but taxes were imposed that had to be paid in cash, not kind, and alternative income-earning opportunities were limited through encroachments on land and restrictions on the cultivation of cash crops. The result was the onset of a 'low wage economy', that effectively channeled the 'secondary multiplier effects' of enclave production to the advanced countries and doomed the backward regions to a 'vicious circle' of poverty (Myrdal, 1957; Nurkse, 1953; Singer, 1950).

Outright appropriation of land and labour was more blatant in the earlier than the later phases of imperialism and in some backward regions (Indonesia, the Congo) than in others (India, Latin America). But it was often possible to extract more surplus through indirect taxation and through purchase of commodities and sale of manufacturers from and to the peasants. 'The British', writes Bagchi, 'may indeed be regarded as the real founders of modern neocolonialism, for both in Latin America and in India in the late nineteenth century they depended more on economic power and political influence than on direct use of political power at every stage for obtaining the lion's share of the surplus of the dominated economies' (1982, p. 78). Land taxes, payable in cash, either reduced the peasants to landless proletarians or required them to produce export crops, with little surplus to diversify in the event of unfavourable terms of trade. Free trade itself destroyed domestic manufactures, made it unprofitable to invest in anything other than export crops and impeded the growth of capitalist classes that could have challenged foreign domination. Even in the bottom of the barrel, backward regions characterized by peasant export economies with little to offer foreigners in the way of raw materials or markets (say, West Africa, Burma, Thailand and Vietnam), the functioning of the market mechanism was not devoid of coercive elements. Peasants who entered the money economy became vulnerable to international commodity price fluctuations. Foreigners, acting as monopolistic middlemen, gained the upper hand and reinvested the surplus elsewhere. Local moneylenders, who controlled credit, foreclosed on indebted peasants where land had become alienable. Railways and other infrastructure supported external rather than internal exchange, thereby discouraging domestic manufactures.

In reality, therefore, no ideal, pure market exchange between rich and poor countries existed that could be delinked neatly from imperialism. Mechanisms of coercion and mechanisms of exchange operated hand-in-hand. From the Marxist perspective it followed that imperialism was neither atavistic nor limited merely to entry and exit to and from capitalist exchange. Rather, force was pervasive and imperialism was business as usual.

If, to varying degrees, force was pervasive in market relationships, then as force changed its colours in tandem with political change, one would expect some change in market relationships as well. Imperialism, after all, is a political phenomenon. Yet in the post-World War II period, no attempt was made by Marxists to distinguish the intrinsic from the historical elements of different economic practices and their effect on growth prospects. Instead, all intercourse with advanced countries was condemned as leading to underdevelopment, in sharp contradistinction to Marx, Engels and even Lenin. The economic practices singled out for special opprobrium were those in which intercourse between the advanced countries and backward regions was most direct – foreign trade, foreign investment and even foreign aid. As Brenner (1977) put it, Adam Smith was turned on his head.

Yet the effect of any given economic practice on economic development clearly depended on the political setting. Aid helped Europe after World War II but seemingly hurt Bangladesh. Whereas export-led growth based on a primary product or 'staple' led to underdevelopment in the backward regions, it led to prosperity in the regions of recent settlement (Canada, Australia, New Zealand, white South Africa, white Rhodesia, etc.). Evidently there was nothing inherent in exporting that led irrevocably to either development or underdevelopment. Rather, what happened depended on local conditions. Unlike the backward regions, the regions of recent settlement retained the surplus by dint of their 'high wage economies' and reared a manufacturing sector by erecting protective tariffs. In the case of direct foreign investment, the expected gains to the 'host' country were *a priori* indeterminate. On the one hand, direct foreign investment promised a transfer of modern management techniques to backward regions. On the other hand, motivated by a wish to make use of monopolistic assets, there was nothing to insure that the multinationals would share their know-how with local managers. In fact, the outcome depended on the political conditions imposed on foreign capital; so Canada benefited far more than say, Chile, from overseas investment.

If Marxists saw foreign trade and foreign investment as dooming the third world to underdevelopment, neoclassical economists followed the same logic but arrived at an opposite conclusion: that foreign trade and foreign investment were the key to third world prosperity (Little, 1982). Now this flew in the face of reality. The economies of the backward regions had long been oriented to foreign trade and foreign investment but were hardly prosperous. Two different tacks were taken to reconcile any seeming inconsistency between theory and practice. One, it was argued that the backward regions had not been sufficiently singleminded in their pursuit of free trade. They had broken faith after World War II in particular, by embracing the 'dogma of dirigisme' (whereupon, it may be added, they grew the fastest ever; Lal, 1984). Two, it was argued that, in fact, the backward regions had long been growing at a fairly rapid clip, although to be sure, there were exceptions to the rule. According to Reynolds (1985): '... against the view that "life began in 1950" ... the third world has a rich record of prior growth, beginning for most countries in the 1850–1914 era' (p. 4). In anticipation of the obvious objection, that developing countries are still desperately poor, Reynolds writes:

> Certainly people in Western Europe and the United States are much better off than people in Sri Lanka [the example he uses], though not as much better off as the World Bank tables suggests ... conversion from local currencies to U.S. dollars at official exchange rates exaggerates the actual difference in consumption levels (p. 40).

Both Marxist and neoclassical analysis suffered from a failure to look beyond either the historical specificities of 'export-led exploitation' (the term is Bagchi's) or the formalism of export-led growth, as the case may be, to the underlying power structures in the backward regions. Beginning with Baran (1957), Marxists portrayed political and social life in the third world simplistically. The state and whatever local capitalists existed were seen as corrupt puppets of advanced country powers. No scope was given to the possibility of local initiatives to mediate foreign trade, foreign investment and foreign aid to advantage. It is fair to say the neoclassical economists largely ignored local conditions in developing countries, even economic ones. When Jacob Viner (1953) delivered a lecture series in Brazil in 1950, he expressed confidence in a growth strategy based on agricultural exports. As evidence, he pointed to the correlation between high per capita incomes and agricultural exports in the regions of recent settlement, overlooking any other factors in these regions that may also have contributed to growth. The result was an inability to grasp what came to constitute a serious challenge to both theories: the economic development along capitalist lines after World War II of a handful of nations (or nation states) in East Asia, South Korea and Taiwan in particular.

The development of these countries posed a challenge to neoclassical theory because, while all the countries in question were highly oriented to trade, they were by no means committed to laissez-faire (Amsden, 1985). They exerted strong centralized control over their economies. They flouted static comparative advantage and were protectionist. Their large private or public conglomerates were a mirror image of concentrations of economic power under monopoly capitalism in advanced countries. They fought force with force, as it were, in dealing with foreign capital. To say that these countries could have grown even faster had they adopted laissez-faire policies is beside the point. The development of these countries posed a challenge to Marxist theory because it wasn't supposed to happen. Such development, therefore, was preemptively dismissed. It was attributed either to a fluke – geopolitics and a superabundance of foreign aid [sic] – or repression of workers, although Engels (1878) cautions against the view that it is possible to industrialize by the gun.

214

The one dissenting voice among Marxists against the notion that capitalism underdevelops the third world missed the point. For Warren (1980), the problem of underdevelopment was not too much foreign capital but too little. Yet, however great the flow of foreign capital to South Korea and Taiwan (mostly, it may be noted, in the form of finance rather than industrial capital), much more accounted for development in these countries than capital per se.

The intellectual antecedents of Warren's view are traceable directly to Marx, so to suggest that Warren missed the point about economic development is also to suggest that Marx himself missed the point. Marx's point is that colonies like India were destined to develop because the capitalist system was compelled to replicate itself around the globe. With the destruction of the Asiatic mode of production, with the imposition of market relationships and with the arrival of the railroad, India would become another England (Marx and Engels, 1960). Yet markets and technology alone do not make for economic development. What appears to be critical are the power relationships and institutions that unfold on their own terms to guide the accumulation process. But Marx is silent about these.

The dirigiste state stands at the opposite extreme of Marx's liberal view of the market as the engine of growth. But neither is a dirigiste regime a sufficient condition for economic development. Dirigisme and underdevelopment are both rampant in the third world. Instead, what Japan and a few South Koreans suggest is that economic development in the 20th century hinges on a delicate relationship between the operations of the market and coercive mechanisms.

Marxists have focused on this relationship in the general case, which is the starting point for any theory of imperialism, and presuppose that markets and force are impenetrable. Yet their equation of imperialism and monopoly capitalism led them to misjudge the relationship after World War II, because imperialism was not the key to the rapid growth of the advanced countries. And their second *idée fixe*, that capitalism underdevelops the third world, led again to the relationship's misjudgement, because proof of economic development in even a handful of third world countries deprived their theory of analytical clarity. Nonetheless, to operate with the world view of the neoclassicists – of a separation between markets and power – is to deny the very existence of imperialism and to forego the conceptual tools to analyse it.

BIBLIOGRAPHY

Amin, S. 1976. *Unequal Development*. New York: Monthly Review Press.

Amsden, A.H. 1981. An international comparison of the rate of surplus value in manufacturing industries. *Cambridge Journal of Economics* 5(3), September, 229–49.

Amsden, A.H. 1985. The state and Taiwan's economic development. In *Bringing the State Back In*, ed. P. Evans et al., Cambridge: Cambridge University Press.

Bagchi, A. 1982. *The Political Economy of Underdevelopment*. Cambridge and New York: Cambridge University Press.

Baran, P.A. 1957. *The Political Economy of Growth*. New York: Monthly Review Press.

Barratt Brown, M. 1963. *After Imperialism*. London: Merlin Press, 1970; New York: Humanities Press.

Barratt Brown, M. 1972. A critique of Marxist theories of imperialism. In Owen and Sutcliffe (1972).

Brenner, R. 1977. The origins of capitalist development: a critique of neo-Smithian Marxism. *New Left Review* No. 194, July–August, 25–92.

Bukharin, N. 1914. *Imperialism and World Economy*. New York: Monthly Review Press, 1972.

Chandler, A. 1980. The growth of the transnational industrial firm in the United States and the United Kingdom: a comparative analysis. *Economic History Review* 33, August, 396–410.

Engels, F. 1878. *Anti-Dühring*. New York: International Publishers.

Fieldhouse, K.D. 1966. *The Colonial Empires: A Comparative Study from the Eighteenth Century*. London: Weidenfeld & Nicolson.

Hayes, C.J.H. 1941. *A Generation of Materialism 1871–1900*. New York: Harper.

Hilferding, R. 1910. *Finance Capital: A Study of the Latest Phase of Capitalist Development*. London: Routledge & Kegan Paul, 1981.

Hobson, J.A. 1902. *Imperialism: A Study*. London: Allen & Unwin, 1938.

Hymer, S. 1976. *The International Operations of National Firms: A Study of Direct Foreign Investment*. Cambridge, Mass.: MIT Press.

Lal, D. 1984. *The Poverty of 'Development Economics'*. London: Institute of Economic Affairs.

Langer, W.L. 1935. *The Diplomacy of Imperialism 1890–1902*. 2nd edn, New York: Knopf.

Lenin, V.I. 1973. *Imperialism, The Highest Stage of Capitalism*. Peking: Foreign Language Press.

Little, I. 1982. *Economic Development: Theory, Policy, and International Relations*. New York: Basic Books.

Luxemburg, R. 1913. *The Accumulation of Capital*. Trans. Agnes Schwarzschild, London: Routledge & Kegan Paul, 1951; New Haven: Yale University Press.

Magdoff, H. 1972. Imperialism without colonies. In Owen and Sutcliffe (1972).

Marx, K. and Engels, F. 1960. *On Colonialism*. London: Lawrence & Wishart.

Mommsen, W. 1980. *Theories of Imperialism*. Trans. P.S. Falla, New York: Random House.

Myint, H. 1964. *The Economics of the Developing Countries*. New York: Praeger.

Myrdal, G. 1957. *Rich Lands and Poor: The Road to World Prosperity*. New York: Harper.

Nurkse, R. 1953. *Problems of Capital Formation in Underdeveloped Countries*. New York: Oxford University Press.

Owen, R. and Sutcliffe, B. (eds) 1972. *Studies in the Theory of Imperialism*. New York: Longmans.

Reynolds, L.G. 1985. *Economic Growth in the Third World, 1850–1980*. New Haven: Yale University Press.

Robinson, R. and Gallagher, R. 1953. The imperialism of free trade. *Economic History Review*, 2nd Series 6(1), 1–15.

Schumpeter, J. 1919. *Imperialism and Social Classes*. Trans., New York: Augustus M. Kelley.

Singer, H.W. 1950. The distribution of gains between investing and borrowing countries. *American Economic Review, Papers and Proceedings* 40, May, 473–85.

Sutcliffe, B. 1972. Conclusion. In Owen and Sutcliffe (1972).

Stokes, E. 1969. Late nineteenth-century colonial expansion and the attack on the theory of economic imperialism: a case of mistaken identity? *Historical Journal* 12, 285–301.

United States Department of Commerce (USDC). (Various years.) *Survey of Current Business*.

Vernon, R. 1966. International investment and international trade in the product cycle. *Quarterly Journal of Economics* 80, May, 190–207.

Viner, J. 1953. *International Trade and Economic Development*, Oxford: Clarendon Press.

Warren, B. 1980. *Imperialism: Pioneer of Capitalism*. London: Verso.

Karl Kautsky

TADEUSZ KOWALIK

Kautsky was born in Prague on 16 October 1854 and died in Amsterdam on 17 October 1938. Marxist thinker and writer, leading theoretician of the German Social Democratic Party (SPD) and the Second International, he studied law and arts in Vienna. Fascinated by the theories of Marx and Engels (both of whom he met and befriended in London in 1881), Kautsky must be credited with the spread and development of their ideas in all his embodiments – as a prodigal and versatile columnist; as founder and editor (1883–1917) of the SPD theoretical journal *Die Neue Zeit* which soon became the chief Marxist forum in Europe; as editor of Marx's books and unfinished manuscripts (Kautsky edited them in three volumes called *Theorien über den Mehrwert*, which appeared in 1905–10); and also as socialist thinker. Kautsky presented his ideas systematically in *Die materialistische Geschichtsauffassung* (1927), expounding a theory of social development which combined Marx's and Engels's historical materialism with Darwin's naturalism.

Kautsky's first major popular book designed to spread Marxian theories was *Karl Marx's ökonomische Lehren* (1897), which expounds the substance of the first volume of *Das Kapital*. It went into numerous editions in German and other languages, and in some countries (as in Russia) its effect on the spread of Marxism was significant.

His original contribution to Marxian theory was his *Agrarfrage* (1899), described by Lenin as the most outstanding work since the third volume of *Das Kapital* had appeared in print. In it, Kautsky analyses trends of development in agricultural production against the backdrop of Marx's theory of capitalism, of capitalist development's own specific features and, in particular, of the then much-discussed question of persistence of small peasant holdings. Kautsky studied the causes of small private farms' relative viability, a phenomenon which at that time was often cited as evidence that Marx's concentration theory was wrong. He attributed the survival of small peasant holdings to the undernourishment and excessive toil of peasant families, to the demand for seasonal labour

218

by large landed estates and to their interest in preserving local labour reserves. Kautsky also pointed out that, in agriculture, concentration of production does not necessarily go along with increases of crop area but may result from more intensive cultivation. Generally, though, he believed that the conquest of agriculture by capitalism was just a question of time.

Kautsky's motive for studying the agrarian question was pragmatic; he wanted to answer the question of whether or not the SPD needed an agricultural policy of its own. In particular, it was unclear whether the SPD ought to defend peasants on their own holdings against the adverse effects of capitalism. Kautsky came to believe that such a move would only hamper what was an inexorable social process, namely the emergence of large capitalist farms relying on hired labour, and hence would hamper the ascent of socialism. Without compromising its own tenets and aspirations, Kautsky said, the SPD could demand the abolition of all vestiges of feudalism in the countryside and defend peasants as working people, as semi-proletarians. But he thought the idea of defending peasants as smallholders a reactionary utopia. He used the same logic to interpret the role of the capitalist metropolitan countries in subjugating colonies.

Kautsky wrote the *Agrarfrage*, as well as his studies concerning crises, as polemics against 'revisionists', who argued that the spread of cartels and trusts, along with the expansion of bank activities, eliminated the anarchy in capitalist production and hence was likely to allay or forestall crises in the future. Kautsky opposed these theories in a series of articles (1901–2) in *Die Neue Zeit* which he wrote in reaction to a German translation of Mikhail Tugan-Baranovsky's *Studien zur Theorie und Geschichte der Handelskrisen in England* (1901). Tugan-Baranovsky reinterpreted Marx's reproduction models in terms of Say's Law and attributed the causes of crises to the disproportions of capitalist development. The spread of cartels, Tugan-Baranovsky argued, eliminated those disproportions and hence also forestalled crises.

Kautsky defended the theory of underconsumption as the basis of business cycles and argued that cartels and other similar organizations of capitalists, keen as they were on maximizing profits, were unable to keep control of production and demand on a national scale, to say nothing of the world economy. He countered the optimistic picture presented by the 'revisionists' with his own hypothesis of capitalism's inexorable drift toward 'a chronic depression'. That was one of the first-ever theories of stagnation. Later (1910), Kautsky was inclined to attribute the principal cause of 'recent' crises to the circumstance that agricultural growth was slower than and lagging behind industrial growth. He also cited this particular disproportion in his concept of imperialism as the expansion of advanced industrial countries into agrarian markets. During World War I Kautsky formulated his well-known hypothesis portraying ultra-imperialism as an alliance of previously rival imperialist powers for a joint exploitation of world resources.

In many studies Kautsky returned to the political and economic problems of the transition to socialism and to the organization and operation of the socialist economy. At first, those problems were overshadowed by the dominant question of political revolution to seize power and of proletarian dictatorship, and Kautsky's causal remarks indicate he regarded a socialist economy simply as the negative of a market-dominated capitalist economy. But from the war onwards, especially in the 1920s, he interpreted socialism and the socialist economy as a continuation and further development of capitalist accomplishments not only in economics but also in terms of social advancement and political progress. His writings are pervaded by a concern for freedom and democracy. Accordingly, he views the transition period as a long process of socialization of production during which those accomplishments would be preserved and economic efficiency would be maintained.

Kautsky was one of the first socialist writers to dispute the idea of a natural, that is money-free, socialist economy. Already at the turn of the century (1902) he argued that money and market were indispensable if freedom of choice in consumption and jobs was to be preserved. Two decades later, when the wave of revolution in Germany, but especially in the Soviet Union, made the construction of socialism a topical question. Kautsky considered the question in a systematic manner (1922). Apart from reaffirming the advantages of money and prices, Kautsky acknowledged the importance of money as a measure of value which permitted the quantitative assessment of production by means of accounting techniques and as a device for identifying benefits that may be gained from trade transactions. However, he failed to furnish a clear picture of how he interpreted economic choice in the allocation of resources. He was probably not quite consistent on this point. On the one hand, he wrote in the spirit of 'market socialism' that socialist society would be governed by the law of value. On the other hand, he overrated the benefits of economies of scale, that is, the supremacy of large-scale over small-scale production, and he was adamant in his faith in vertical and horizontal integration. If his beliefs came true, the integration was bound to lead to ubiquitous monopolistic practices on the part of socialist industrial giants.

He also believed that full socialization of production and of the bank credit system would render the latter superfluous. He accepted that interest rates might be charged by the socialized banks, but solely in order not to deprive them of their competitive edge in relations with capitalist banks and only in the transition period. His idea of economic planning also seems incompatible with 'market socialism'. In his view, economic planning would amount to the entire community of consumers negotiating output volumes and prices with the branch producers. Since this implied that a lot of time would be needed to build an efficient system of statistical· records, Kautsky believed full economic planning was a remote prospect. But what would a fulfilment of those plans actually guarantee? Kautsky failed to realize how complex a question that was, although some of his remarks, such as his comments about the important part that talented production organizers, who are as rare as talented artists, might play in socialism, sound quite up-to-date.

Opposed as he was to total state control, Kautsky was an advocate of a plurality of ownership forms in socialism. Apart from a certain scope for state ownership of production (which would not be managed by state-employed functionaries), he saw in socialism room for production cooperatives, for municipal enterprises, and for union-sponsored autonomous enterprises similar in character to those advanced by Guild Socialists. He regarded the general idea of Guild Socialism as excellent and inspiring, but he thought that this school focused its attention too much on producers to the detriment of consumers, and he resisted in particular attempts to present Guild Socialism as the only feasible production organization model for socialism.

SELECTED WORKS

1887. *Karl Marx's Okonomische Lehren.* Stuttgart.
1899. *Agrarfrage, Eine Ubersicht über die Tendenzen der modernen Landwirtschaft und die Agrarpolitik der Sozialdemokratie.* Stuttgart.
1901–2. Kriesentheorien. *Neue Zeit,* Nos. 2, 3, 4 and 5.
1902. *Die soziale Revolution.* Berlin. Trans. by J.B. Askew as *The Social Revolution and On the Morrow of the Revolution,* London: Twentieth Century Press, 1903.
1905–10. (ed.) K. Marx, *Theorien über den Mehrserf.*
1910. *Vermehrung und Entwicklung in Natur und Gesellschaft.* Stuttgart.
1922. *Die proletarische Revolution und ihr Programm.* Trans. by H.J. Stenning as *The Labour Revolution,* New York: Dial Press, 1925.

Labour Power

G. DE VIVO

The introduction of this notion has generally been regarded by Marxists as a crucial difference between their own and bourgeois economic theory. They have claimed that it allowed Marx to overcome a basic difficulty in Ricardo's (and, more generally, in classical) theory.

The most authoritative interpretation in the Marxist tradition, of the importance of the distinction between labour and labour-power, is the one given by Engels in his 1891 introduction to *Wage Labour and Capital*, where he argues that it could avoid the 'contradiction' into which 'economists' fell, when they 'applied the determination of value by labour to the commodity "labour"'. The contradiction would have been that

> for twelve hours' labour the worker receives as an equivalent value the product of six hours' labour. Either, therefore, labour has two values, ... or twelve equals six! In both cases we get pure nonsense (Engels, 1891, pp. 199–200).

But this nonsensical conclusion merely derives from a confusion between the value of labour (i.e. the wage) and the value of its product. No such confusion is to be found in Ricardo, or in those works of Marx of the 1840s (e.g. *The Poverty of Philosophy*, or the articles later republished as *Wage Labour and Capital*), where he had not made the distinction between labour and labour-power, and had simply treated labour as a commodity like anyone else.

Marxists have generally followed Engels' argument (see, e.g. Mandel, 1967, p. 81 f.) and have accordingly failed to give a satisfactory explanation of the problem that the distinction was intended to solve.

The contradiction in Ricardo's theory, which he, according to Marx, had not even seen, can be formulated as follows. From the point of view of production of surplus value, materialized labour and living labour have different values. Indeed, surplus value ... arises ... from the fact that commodities or money (i.e., materialized labour) are exchanged for *more* living labour than is embodied ... in them (Marx, 1862–3, III, pp. 15–16).

But Marx also notices that in Ricardo's theory

the value of a commodity is equally determined by the quantity of *materialized* (*past*) labour and by the quantity of *living* (*immediate*) labour required for its production.

He therefore asks:

If this difference [between *materialized* and *living* labour] is of no significance in the determination of the value of commodities, why does it assume such decisive importance when past labour (capital) is exchanged against living labour? Why should it, in this case, invalidate the law of value, since the difference *in itself*, as shown in the case of commodities, has no effect on the determination of value? Ricardo does not answer this question, he does not even raise it (Marx, 1862–3, II, pp. 398–9).

Thus the problem is that 'labour has two values', as Engels had written, but in a sense wholly different from the one envisaged by him: it has two values *with respect to materialized labour*. In the determination of the value of commodities it has the same value, in the capital/labour exchange it has a different value, than materialized labour.

The solution to this contradiction is provided by Marx in Chapter XIX, volume I, of *Capital*, where he soon faces the problem of explaining why 'the labourer ... receives for 12 hours' labour ... less than 12 hours' labour'. He notices that one cannot 'deduce the exchange of more labour against less, from the difference of form, the one being realised, the other living'. The solution he offers is the distinction between labour and labour-power:

What the latter [the labourer] sells is his labour-power ... Labour is the substance and immanent measure of value, *but has itself no value* (Marx, 1867, pp. 502–3).

Thus, Marx seems to think that it is possible to escape the contradiction he had noticed, by distinguishing between 'labour' and 'labour-power', the former not being a commodity, but merely the 'substance' of value, which does not have itself any value. The problem of the relative value of living and materialized labour seemed therefore to disappear.

Marx had really seen a difficulty in Ricardo's theory which Ricardo had not seen – and one which had even been among the causes of the 'disintegration' of the 'Ricardian School'. The question whether 'accumulated labour' was more valuable than 'living labour', had in fact been the cause of many difficulties to the Ricardians, and had led to the abandonment of the labour theory of value. The difficulty however is not really overcome by Marx. The real issue behind it is in fact that of determining values by summing labours embodied at different times. The very fact that one must distinguish between 'antecedent' and 'present' labour in the capital/labour exchange – i.e. the very existence of profit – implies that one must also distinguish between 'antecedent' and 'present' labour when determining values. Marx's determination of the rate of profit, in his 'transformation of values into prices of production', is instead still based on the incorrect summing of labours of different dates (see also de Vivo, 1982, p. 92 ff.).

BIBLIOGRAPHY

De Vivo, G. 1982. Notes on Marx's critique of Ricardo. *Contributions to Political Economy* 1, March.

Engels, F. 1891. Introduction to K. Marx, *Wage Labour and Capital*. In Marx-Engels, *Collected Works*, Vol. 9, London: Lawrence & Wishart, 1977.

Mandel, E. 1967. *The Formation of the Economic Thought of Karl Marx*. London: New Left Books, 1971; New York: Monthly Review Press, 1971.

Marx, K. 1862–3. *Theories of Surplus Value*, Vols. I–III. London: Lawrence & Wishart, 1969–72.

Marx, K. 1867. *Capital*: *A Critique of Political Economy*, Vol. I. London: Lawrence & Wishart, 1977.

Labour Process

WILLIAM LAZONICK

The labour process is a Marxian term that refers to the ways in which labour and capital combine to produce goods and services. The emphasis on the role of labour in the production process derives from Marx's (1867) distinction between labour-power and labour. Labour-power is the capacity to work that the capitalist purchases for a wage on the labour market; labour is the effort actually expended by a unit of labour-power in the production process. Given wages and prices, the surplus-value that the capitalist extracts from the production process depends upon the amount of labour services that he can elicit from the labour-power that he has purchased.

Based upon the distinction between labour-power and labour effort, Marx's theory of surplus-value analyses the generation of productivity and profitability within the capitalist enterprise and concomitant impacts on the working conditions of the labouring population. Quite apart from the capitalist character of production, the transformation of inputs into outputs requires that human beings plan and execute the combination of their own productive capabilities with raw materials, tools and machines. Within a complex social and technical division of labour, people invest processes, design products, build plant and equipment, coordinate various productive activities, handle tools and tend machines.

Work occupies much of a person's active life, and can serve as a prime means of personal development. Marx argued, however, that capitalist control of the labour process tended to dehumanize the vast majority of workers. The social impact of capitalist development is, in his words.

> to multilate the labourer into the fragment of a man, degrade him to the level of an appendage of a machine, destroy every remnant of charm in his work and turn it into hated toil, [and] ... estrange from him the intellectual potentialities of the labour-process in the same proportion as science is incorporated in it as an independent power (Marx, [1867], 1977, p. 799).

The only reward that the worker can hope to receive for his or her long hours of labour is a wage that just suffices for sustenance at a social acceptable standard.

Within the capitalist labour process, the alienating nature of work brings to the fore the conflict over the relation between effort and earnings. For a given wage, workers want to exert themselves as little as possible while capitalists want them to work as long and hard as possible. Marx's theory of surplus-value depends critically on the assumption that the capitalist has a degree of privileged access to the workers that he employs, permitting him to extract unremunerated effort from them.

Under competitive market assumptions, the capitalist takes all prices, including wages, as given, and technology is quickly diffused so that a particular capitalist cannot retain privileged access to process or product innovations for any appreciable period of time. But the workers' need to make a basic living, the deskilling of the labour force through technological change, and the existence of a homogeneous and hence interchangeable reserve army of labour all render the worker dependent on a particular capitalist employer. As a result, the capitalist is not entirely subject to the dictates of market forces in dealing with the worker in the labour process. The more dependent the worker is upon his or her particular employer, the more power the capitalist has to demand longer and harder work in return for a day's pay. The resultant unremunerated increase in the productivity of the worker per unit of time is the source of surplus-value.

Marx drew upon the historical experience of Britain's industrial revolution to develop his analysis of the labour process. He correctly emphasized the heavy reliance of the textile factories on the relatively low-waged labour of women and children, who, lacking social power to resist, were made to work long and hard (see Pollard, 1965; Thompson, 1967; Marglin, 1974; Berg, 1985; Lazonick, 1986a). The hours of work were so extended that workers as well as more far-sighted members of the propertied classes organized for government legislation to limit the exploitation of labour. By the 1840s British factories were subject to a regulated working day, so that, for a given wage, exploitation within the labour process depended upon the amount of effort expended per unit of time rather than increases in the units of time that prolonged the working day.

Marx understood, also quite correctly, that the main obstacle confronting capitalists of the industrial revolution in attaining unremunerated intensification of labour was the resistance of skilled workers. In his view, the capitalist solution to worker opposition was the introduction of machinery into the labour process. According to Marx, machinery not only makes the capitalist less reliant on particular workers by superseding the strength and skills required of human beings in the labour process, but also displaces workers, adding to the reserve army of labour and rendering those who remain in employment all the more fearful of losing their jobs if they do not work long and hard enough. Marx recognized that, by overcoming the strength and skill limitations of humans, machinery is potentially *effort-saving*. But citing John Stuart Mill's contention that '[i]t is questionable if all the mechanical inventions yet made have lightened the day's toil of any human being' (Marx [1867], 1977, p. 492), Marx argued that capitalists were able to use machinery as a powerful weapon against workers to increase effort levels and extract surplus-value.

In historical perspective, however, Marx misperceived the impact of technology in shaping the relations between capitalists and adult male workers in 19th-century Britain. Because of the limited managerial capabilities of relatively small firms in highly competitive industries, key groups of adult-male workers maintained considerable control over the technical division of labour, the flow of work on the shop floor and the relation between effort and pay, even on the new technologies that gave rise to what Marx called 'modern industry'. During the long mid-Victorian boom, these workers consolidated their positions of job control as atomistic firms opted for collective accommodation with unions rather than let industrial conflict jeopardize the profits that were waiting to be made (Lazonick, 1979; Harrison and Zeitlin, 1985; Elbaum and Lazonick, 1986).

So long as British industry dominated world markets, as it did in the last half of the 19th century, cooperation between capitalists and workers promoted productivity growth, permitting real wages to rise without cutting into profits. Organized workers who entered into stable relations with capitalists had the power to extract a share of productivity gains and could be enticed to invest in the development of specialized productive capabilities and work harder and longer for the sake of higher earnings.

In failing to see the sustained sources of power that key groups of British workers exercised over the relation between work and pay in the 19th century, Marx ignored the positive impact that cooperative industrial relations could have on productivity growth and the simultaneous increase in both wages and profits. He also overemphasized the deskilling of the labour force as a logical consequence of technological change, neglecting the ability of workers to influence the direction of technological change, both indirectly as new technologies were adapted to make use of available skills and directly as workers received training as technical specialists to develop and implement new technologies (Samuel, 1977; Lazonick, 1981; Wood, 1982; Lazonick and Mass, 1984; Lazonick, 1986b).

In Britain, shop-floor control persisted into the second half of the 20th century, and has only recently been challenged seriously by the anti-labour policies and rapid deindustrialization of the Thatcher era. In historical perspective, Marx's analysis of the subjugation of labour to capital in the labour process would appear to be more applicable to the 20th-century experience of American capitalism, in which from the late 19th-century, craft unionism and shop-floor control of the labour process were eradicated in the mass-production industries (Montgomery, 1979; Brody, 1980).

Indeed, Baran and Sweezy's (1966) influential analysis of US monopoly capitalism follows Marx in viewing the problem of surplus extraction as solved within the modern enterprise, focusing instead on the macroeconomic problems of surplus absorption. Integrating Marx's analysis of the British labour process of the 19th-century with the Baran and Sweezy analysis of US monopoly capitalism in the 20th-century, Braverman (1974) argued that degradation of work has remained the predominant social characteristic of the modern capitalist economy.

Braverman emphasizes the role of Taylorism or 'scientific management' – by which he means the separation of the conception of work within the managerial bureaucracy from the execution of work on the shop floor – in ensuring the triumph of capital over labour in 20th-century United States. He does not, however, recognize the vast development of skills among a considerable proportion of the labour force – albeit to a considerable extent on the part of workers who are segmented from shop-floor workers and integrated into managerial bureaucracies – required to operate within an evolving high-technology environment. Nor does he analyse how the divide between management and labour within the corporate enterprise – a phenomenon that occurred between 1880 and 1920 (Chandler, 1977; Noble, 1977) – enhanced capitalists' ability to extract unremunerated effort from workers.

In fact, as a method for increasing effort through piece-rate incentive schemes, Taylorism was largely unsuccessful because 'scientific' managers sought to impose 'scientific' standards on non-unionized workers without giving them any assurance that they would share in the resultant productivity gains. In the absence of the countervailing power of craft unions that could bargain over the relation between effort and pay, management could be expected to subject workers to speed ups and stretch outs, while perhaps cutting piece rates, even in the presence of potentially effort-saving technological change. In response, even *unorganized* workers sought to restrict output by shop-floor solidarity to control the pace of work and defend themselves against unremunerated intensification of labour (Lazonick, 1983 and 1984).

Braverman (1974, p. 85) argues : 'Logically, Taylorism belongs to the chain of development of management methods and the organization of labor, and not to the development of technology, in which its role was minor.' But to dissociate Taylorism from technology is to miss the essence of the problem that the managers of mass production faced. The movement towards what was called more generally 'systematic management' arose at a time when capitalists were making large fixed investments in new mass production technologies (Litterer, 1963). The profitability of these investments depended upon the achievement of high rates of throughput, which would not be forthcoming if operatives saw fit to restrict output. Effort-saving technology held out the prospects for simultaneously lightening the physical strain of work and increasing productivity. But workers had to have some assurance that they would be able to appropriate a share of increased productivity if they were to cooperate in the actual generation of those gains (Lazonick, 1984).

During the early decades of the 20th century, American capitalists searched for methods of labour management that would increase productivity without granting the workers any formal control over the determination of the relation between effort and pay. One widely used method was close supervision of the pace of work, but its success was limited during periods of prosperity by the ability of workers to exit from undesirable workplaces.

A complementary means of both reducing labour turnover and eliciting high levels of effort from workers was the offer of high wages – a method made famous by Henry Ford's five-dollar day, instituted in 1914 in conjunction with the introduction of the automated assembly line. There are those who see 'Fordism' as the ultimate achievement in mass production prior to the computer revoluton begun in the 1970s (for example, Piore and Sabel, 1984). In fact, Ford had only short-lived success with the high-wage strategy because, in the face of a growing used-car market and demand for more luxurious cars, the competitive advantage that the company had gained from mass producing the Model T slipped away. By the early 1920s, wages paid by Ford were no higher than his competitors, and the company had the worst labour relations in the industry (Chandler, 1962; Meyer, 1981; Hounshell, 1984).

The longer-run solution to the problem of labour extraction was for corporations to hold out the promise of job security and upward mobility within the firm as the reward for hard and diligent work. During the 1920s, mass-production corporations instituted a dramatic change in labour relations as they began to make use of internal job ladders, not only within the burgeoning managerial bureaucracies but also among blue-collar workers. The erection of vertical job and wage structures represented a managerial strategy to discourage workers as individuals from seeking to better their lot by mobility via the external labour market. Instead workers who proved themselves dependable, loyal and hardworking were offered opportunities for better work conditions, security and pay within the firm (Slichter, 1929; Lazonick, 1983; Jacoby, 1984; Lazonick, 1986b).

The effective use of internal job ladders is dependent on the growth of the firm. Internal job ladders will only induce hard work if employees observe that the higher level rungs of the ladders remain in place – a promise that many US mass production corporations could make by the 1920s by virtue of their oligopolistic market control. In turn, the ability of dominant firms to extend their market power was due in part to their ability to deal with the problem of labour effort by strategies such as internalizing the labour exchange.

For dominant firms, a dynamic of rapid corporate growth was set in motion, only to be cut short as the Great Crash and its aftermath created macroconditions that even the corporate giants could not control. Unencumbered by debt, and hence immune from external pressures to produce at any cost, the response of the corporate mass-producers to the Great Depression was to cut back production and employment dramatically. The internal job structures erected in the 1920s collapsed. Significantly enough, IBM, a corporation that remains well-known for its permanent employment system, was able to keep its labour force fully employed during the 1930s by supplying 'business' machines to the expanding government sector under the New Deal (Sobel, 1983, ch. 4).

During the 1930s, however, most large manufacturing corporations were unable to provide steady employment. Workers organized, the state intervened, and by the 1940s, workers had won seniority protection and the right to bargain over wage levels and differentials for management-determined job structures. Management had to share power over the determination of wage structures with unions. But the newly acquired union prerogatives meshed well with the strategy of erecting internal job ladders that the mass production corporations had been pursuing in the non-union era before the Great Depression. That strategy once again became viable in the 1940s, 1950s and 1960s as the US economy entered a long boom characterized by expansion and diversification of the large corporations and American domination of world markets (Doeringer and Piore, 1971; Edwards, 1979).

In recent decades, however, the rise of international competition has made it more difficult for many US firms to promise job security and upward mobility to their workers. At the same time, the consolidation of social security systems has increased the level of the available 'social wage' and reduced the cost of job loss to many workers, making it more difficult for capitalists to enforce discipline in the workplace, with adverse impacts on productivity (Schor and Bowes, 1984; Bowles, 1985).

Recognizing the relation between alienated labour and low levels of effort, management has sought to deal with the problem of labour extraction by altering the technical and hierarchical division of labour in ways that 'humanize' work. These experiments often result in productivity increases on the shop floor. But, in the United States at least, they have been typically short-lived because, in redefining the hierarchical division of labour, the experiments inevitably infringe on traditional managerial prerogatives (Zimbalist, 1975; Marglin, 1979). In the late 20th century, American corporations are again searching for new methods of labour management that will yield profits without sacrificing hierarchical control.

A prime impetus for attempts to restructure the labour process in Western capitalist economies is the rise of Japanese competition over the past two decades. After World War II, many Japanese firms replaced militant labour unions by company unions that served to develop cooperative relations between labour and management characterized in part by vertical job structures that permit substantial mobility from the one into the other (see, for example, Cusumano, 1985). Within dominant firms, internal job structures and permanent employment systems give many workers long-term stakes in the firm and assure them of shares of productivity gains. As a result of the integration of particular workers into the structure of the enterprise, Japanese managers can delegate authority over day-to-day decisions to workers on the shop floor without undermining hierarchical control much more readily than is the case in US or British firms, with apparently beneficial impacts on productivity.

The development of the labour process in dominant capitalist economies such as Britain, the United States and Japan over the past century, therefore, reveals a quite different evolution of capital–labour relations from that envisioned by Marx. Exploitation of labour based upon highly intensified work for low pay certainly remains an important source of surplus-value in advanced capitalist economies. But, as research into labour-market segmentation argues, such Marxian-type exploitation characterizes 'secondary', not 'primary' relations of production in modern capitalist economies (Gordon, Edwards and Reich, 1982; Wilkinson, 1981; Osterman, 1984).

Marx's insights into conflicts of interest between capital and labour in the production process remain invaluable as points of departure for analysing the socioeconomic evolution of capitalism. The history of *successful* capitalist development demonstrates, however, the capacity for the economic system to transform conflict into cooperation so that, in fact, many if not most workers perceive that, in attacking institutions of private enterprise and accumulation, they may have much more to lose than their chains.

BIBLIOGRAPHY

Baran, P. and Sweezy, P. 1966. *Monopoly Capital*. New York: Monthly Review Press.

Berg, M. 1985. *The Age of Manufactures, 1700–1820*. London: Fontana; New York: Barnes & Noble.

Bowles, S. 1985. The production process in a competitive economy: Walrasian, Neo-Hobbesian, and Marxian models. *American Economic Review* 75(2), March, 16–36.

Braverman, H. 1974. *Labor and Monopoly Capital*. New York: Monthly Review Press.

Brody, D. 1980. *Workers in Industrial America*. New York: Oxford University Press.

Chandler, A.D., Jr. 1962. *Strategy and Structure: Chapters in the History of American Industrial Enterprise*. Cambridge, Mass.: MIT Press.

Chandler, A.D., Jr. 1980. *Giant Enterprise: Ford, General Motors, and the Automobile Industry*. New York: Harcourt, Brace & World.

Chandler, A.D., Jr. 1977. *The Visible Hand*. Cambridge, Mass.: Harvard University Press.

Cusumano, M. 1985. *The Japanese Automobile Industry*. Cambridge, Mass.: Harvard University Press.

Doeringer, P. and Piore, M. 1971. *Internal Labor Markets and Manpower Analysis*. Lexington, Mass.: D.C. Heath.

Edwards, R. 1979. *Contested Terrain*. New York: Basic Books.

Elbaum, B. and Lazonick, W. (eds) 1986. *The Decline of the British Economy*. Oxford: Clarendon.

Gordon, D., Edwards, R. and Reich, M. 1982. *Segmented Work, Divided Workers*. Cambridge and New York: Cambridge University Press.

Harrison, R. and Zeitlin, J. (eds) 1985. *Divisions of Labour*. Brighton: Harvester.

Hounshell, D. 1984. *From the American System to Mass Production, 1800–1932*. Baltimore: Johns Hopkins University Press.

Jacoby, S. 1984. The development of internal labor markets in American manufacturing firms. In *Internal Labor Markets*, ed. P. Osterman, Cambridge, Mass.: MIT Press.

Lazonick, W. 1979. Industrial relations and technical change: the case of the self-acting mule. *Cambridge Journal of Economics* 3, September, 231–62.

Lazonick, W. 1981. Production relations, labor productivity, and choice of technique: British and US cotton spinning. *Journal of Economic History* 41(3), September, 491–516.

Lazonick, W. 1983. Technological change and the control of work: the development of capital–labor relations in US mass production industries. In *Managerial Strategies and Industrial Relations*, ed. H. Gospel and C. Littler, London: Heinemann.

Lazonick, W. 1984. Work, pay, and productivity: theoretical implications of some historical research. Photocopy, Harvard University.

Lazonick, W. 1986a. Theory and history in Marxian economics. In *The Future of Economic History*, ed. A. Field, Hingham: Kluwer-Nijhoff.

Lazonick, W. 1986b. Strategy, structure, and mangement development in the United States and Britain. In *Development of Managerial Enterprise*, ed. K. Kobayashi and H. Morikawa, Tokyo: University of Tokyo Press.

Lazonick, W. and Mass, W. 1984. The performance of the British cotton industry, 1870–1913. *Research in Economic History* 9, 1–44.

Litterer, J. 1963. Systematic management: design for organizational recoupling in American manufacturing firms. *Business History Review* 37, Winter, 369–91.

Marglin, S. 1974. What do bosses do?: the origins and functions of hierarchy in capitalist production. *Review of Radical Political Economics* 6(2), Summer, 60–112.

Marglin, S. 1979. Catching flies with honey: an inquiry into management initiatives to humanize work. *Economic Analysis and Workers' Management* 13.

Marx, K. 1867. *Capital*, Vol. I. New York: Vintage, 1977.

Meyer, S. 1981. *The Five Dollar Day*. New York: State University of New York Press.

Montgomery, D. 1979. *Workers' Control in America*. Cambridge and New York: Cambridge University Press.

Noble, D. 1977. *America by Design*. New York: Oxford University Press.

Osterman, P. (ed.) 1984. *Internal Labor Markets*. Cambridge, Mass.: MIT Press.

Piore, M. and Sabel, C. 1984. *The Second Industrial Divide*. New York: Basic Books.

Pollard, S. 1965. *The Genesis of Modern Management*, Harmondsworth: Penguin.

Samuel, R. 1977. Workshop of the world: steam power and hand technology in mid-Victorian Britain. *History Workshop Journal* 3, Spring, 6–72.

Schor, J. and Bowles, S. 1984. The cost of job loss and the incidence of strikes. Harvard Institute of Economic Research Discussion Paper No. 1105.

Slichter, S. 1929. The current labor policies of American industries. *Quarterly Journal of Economics* 43, May, 393–435.

Sobel, R. 1983. *IBM: Colossus in Transition*. New York: Bantam Books.

Thompson, E.P. 1967. Time, work-discipline, and industrial capitalism. *Past and Present* 38, December, 56–97.

Wilkinson, F. (ed.) 1981. *The Dynamics of Labour Market Segmentation*. London: Academic Press.

Wood, S. (ed.) 1982. *The Degradation of Work?: Skill, Deskilling, and the Labour Process*. London: Hutchinson.

Zimbalist, A. 1975. The limits of work humanization. *Review of Radical Political Economics* 7(2), Summer, 50–59.

Labour Theory of Value

FERNANDO VIANELLO

The only instance in which Adam Smith makes the value of commodities depend on the quantity of labour required to produce them is where 'the whole produce of labour belongs to the labourer' (Smith, 1776, vol. I, p. 54; see ibid., p. 72). 'In that early and rude state of society which precedes both the accumulation of stock and the appropriate of land', he asserts 'the proportion between the quantities of labour necessary for acquiring different objects seems to be the only circumstances which can afford any rule for exchanging them for one another' (ibid., p. 53).

This contention is illustrated by the famous example of the beaver and the deer:

> If among a nation of hunters, for example, it usually costs twice the labour to kill a beaver which it does to kill a deer, one beaver should naturally exchange for or be worth two deer. It is natural that what is usually the produce of two days or two hours labour, should be worth double of what is usually the produce of one day's or one hour's labour (ibid., p. 53).

According to Smith, when profit and rent make their appearance alongside the labourer's income, the above rule is no longer applicable. The price of a commodity is then obtained by adding up its 'component parts': wage, profit and rent. These revenues, which Smith calls 'the three original sources... of all exchangeable value' (ibid., p. 59), enter into the 'natural price' of each commodity at their respective 'natural risks', such that 'the natural price itself varies with the natural rate of each of its component parts, of wages, profit and rent' (vol. I, p. 71).

The 'adding-up' theory of prices must be distinguished from Smith's claim that the price of every commodity 'resolves itself' entirely into wage, profit and rent (see vol. I, p. 57). The latter was accepted by Ricardo and rejected by Marx. The former was rejected by both.

1. Against the 'adding-up' theory Ricardo sets the labour theory of value extended to the capitalist mode of production:

233

All the implements necessary to kill the beaver and deer might belong to one class of men, and the labour employed in their destruction might be furnished by another class; still their comparative prices would be in proportion to the actual labour bestowed, both on the formation of the capital, and on the destruction of the animals (Ricardo, 1821, p. 24).

The value of the product would go partly to the labourers and partly to the capitalists; yet

this division could not affect the relative value of these commodities, since whether the profits of capital were greater or less, whether they were 50, 20 or 10 per cent or whether the wages of labour were high or low, they would operate equally on both employments (ibid.).

As gold, the standard of value, is a commodity like any other, the above argument makes the price of commodities – the exchange-ratio between each of them and gold – independent of the level of the wage, a change in which is exactly offset by a change in the opposite direction of the rate of profits: the relative weight of the two 'component parts', wages and profits, varies, but their sum remains the same.

According to Ricardo the value of a commodity produced from natural resources in short supply is regulated by the quantity of labour expended to produce it 'under the most unfavourable circumstances... under which the quantity of produce required, renders it necessary to carry on the production' (ibid., p. 73). Thus the quantity of labour governing the value of the entire quantity produced of a commodity is not that actually expended on its production, but that which would need to be expended if the entire production took place under the most unfavourable circumstances. That portion of the value which is absorbed by rent corresponds to the difference between this fictitious quantity of labour and the one actually expended on the production of the commodity. The portion of value corresponding to the quantity of labour actually expended is split up into wages and profits.

Thus the labour theory of value enables Ricardo to conceive the different revenues as resulting from the breakdown of a known magnitude, rather than that magnitude (value) as resulting from the adding up of 'component parts' (the different revenues) determined independently of each other. The contrast between these two conceptions is fixed by Marx in a highly effective image:

If I determine the lengths of three different straight lines independently, and then form out of these three lines as 'component parts' a fourth straight line equal to their sum, it is by no means the same procedure as when I have some given straight line before me and for some purpose divide it, 'resolve' it, so to say, into three different parts. In the first case, the length of the line changes throughout with the lengths of the three lines whose sum it is; in the second case, the lengths of the three parts of the line are from the outset limited by the fact that they are parts of a line of given length (Marx, 1885, p. 387).

2. If gold is produced by an unchanging quantity of labour, a rise in the price of a commodity can only stem from a process of 'extensive' or 'intensive' diminishing returns (only the former, however, will be considered in what follows). In discussing the consequences of an increasing 'difficulty of procuring the necessaries on which wages are expended', Ricardo takes the quantities consumed by each labourer as given. It follows that, as the price of corn (a typical necessary) rises, the wage in terms of gold also rises, and the profits of the manufacturers fall:

> suppose corn to rise in price because more labour is necessary to produce it; that cause will not raise the prices of manufactured goods in the production of which no additional quantity of labour is required. If, then, wages continued the same, the profits of manufacturers would remain the same; but if, as is absolutely certain, wages should rise with the rise of corn, then their profits would necessarily fall (Ricardo, 1821, pp. 48, 110–11).

Let us assume that the entire production of corn is initially obtained from land of uniform quality, and that thereafter, in order to increase the quantity produced, land of an inferior quality be brought into cultivation. The value of the quantity of corn produced on the second quality of land is governed by the quantity of labour actually expended on its production and 'is divided into two portions only: one constitutes the profits of stock, the other the wages of labour' (ibid., p. 110). The increase in the value of the quantity of corn obtained from the first quality of land is wholly swallowed up by the rent, which now begins to be paid for the use of this quality of land.

In the production of corn both expenses and proceeds per unit of produce increase. But the result is the same as in manufacturing (where only expenses increase) since the farmer 'will not only have to pay, in common with the manufacturer, an increase of wages to each labourer he employs, but he will be obliged either to pay rent, or to employ an additional number of labourers to obtain the same produce; and the rise in the price of raw produce will be proportioned only to that rent, or that additional number, and will not compensate him for the rise of wages' (ibid., p. 111).

What causes the ratio of profits to wages to fall is not the rise of rent, but – in agriculture as well as in manufacturing – the increase in wages consequent upon the increased expenditure of labour required to produce necessaries in the most unfavourable circumstances. If the commodities which increase in value are not among those purchased by labourers, the ratio of profits to wages remains unchanged (even though a part of the capitalist's purchasing power is transferred to the landowners).

3. What is true of the ratio of profits to wages is also true, in Ricardo's opinion, of the rate of profits, which forms his main concern. Indeed, what he does is simply to refer to the latter his conclusions regarding the former, so that the two concepts appear to shade into one another. 'In his observations on profit and wages, says Marx, taking up a remark of G. Ramsay's (1836, p. 174n.), 'Ricardo ...

treats the matter as though the entire capital wer laid out directly in wages'
(Marx, 1905–10, vol. II, p. 373). Marx traces this confusion back to 'the absurd
dogma pervading political economy since Adam Smith, that in the final analysis
the value of commodities resolves itself completely into ... wages, profit and rent'
(Marx, 1894, p. 841).

Smith's teaching is that, while the price of a commodity includes – along with
the revenues derived from its direct production – the value of its means of
production, the latter value can be broken down in the same way, and so on,
going backwards, until an *initial stage of production* is reached, in which the
means of production of the stage following are produced without the aid of any
other means of production. Only the value of the output in the initial stage of
production resolves itself immediately into wage, profit and rent. But the output
in each stage, whose value equals the sum of the revenues obtained in that stage
as well as in all the preceding ones, supplies the means of production for the next
stage, so that 'whole price still resolves itself either immediately or ultimately
into the same three parts of rent, labour, and profit' (Smith, 1776, vol. I, p. 57;
here 'labour' obviously stands for 'wages').

Marx's criticism of Smith's thesis of complete 'resolution' of prices into
revenues is made up of two parts, which should be kept strictly distinct. The first
is of a factual nature. In moving back from a commodity to its means of
production, and from these to their own means of production, and so on, one
will never – in Marx's view – reach an initial stage of production, since sooner
or later one is bound to encounter commodities that, either directly or indirectly,
participate in the production of themselves. Since one can never get rid of these
commodities, however far back one goes, 'it is [of] no avail for Adam Smith to
send us from pillar to post' (Marx, 1905–10, vol. I, p. 99).

The conception according to which commodities are produced in a finite
number of stages does not, of itself, lead to a confusion between the rate or profits
and the ratio of profits to wages. Since, however, in this conception the value of
the means of production employed in each stage resolves itself into the revenues
obtained in all the previous stages, 'one may ... imagine along with Adam Smith'
– this being the second part of Marx's criticism – 'that constant capital is but
an apparent element of commodity-value, which disappears in the total pattern'
(Marx, 1894, p. 845; by 'constant capital' Marx means the value of the means
of production).

That in dealing with the economy as a whole Smith and Ricardo fall into this
error emerges clearly, for example, from Smith's statement, repeated almost
verbatim by Ricardo, according to which 'what is annually saved is as regularly
consumed as what is annually spent, and nearly in the same time too; but it is
consumed by a different set of people' (Smith, 1776, vol. I, p. 359; see Ricardo,
1821, p. 151n.). The funds devoted to accumulation are here treated as wholly
employed in producing the necessaries for the labourers. This may help explaining
how, when Ricardo approaches the problem from the point of view of the economy
as a whole, he does not seem to make any distinction between the rate of profits
and the ratio of profits to wages, referring to the former as depending only on

the 'proportion of the annual labour of the country [which] is devoted to the support of the labourers' (Ricardo, 1821, p. 49; see Sraffa, 1951, p. xxxiii).

4. Although it is the labour theory of value that makes it possible for Ricardo to determine the rate of profits, his adherence to this theory appears anything but firm. Indeed, 'the principle that the quantity of labour bestowed on the production of commodities regulates their relative value' turns out to be, as Ricardo puts it, 'considerably modified' (ibid., p. 30) by the influence of other factors.

To show this Ricardo makes use of a numerical example which deserves to be quoted in full:

Suppose I employ twenty men at an expense of £1,000 for a year in the production of a commodity, and at the end of the year I employ twenty men again for another year, at a further expense of £1,000 in finishing or perfecting the same commodity, and that I bring it to market at the end of two years. If profits be 10 per cent, my commodity must sell for £2,310; for I have employed £1,000 capital for one year, and £2,100 capital for one year more. Another man employs precisely the same quantity of labour, but he employs it all in the first year; he employs forty men at an expense of £2,000, and at the end of the first year he sells it with 10 per cent profit, or for £2,200. Here then are two commodities having precisely the same quantity of labour bestowed on them, one of which sells for £2,310 – the other for £2,200 (ibid., p. 37).

Let w be the wage (equal in the example of £50 per labourer) and r be the rate of profits (equal to 10 per cent). For the sake of simplicity, we shall further suppose that the quantity produced of each of the two commodities be one unit. The price of commodity a, the first commodity in the example, is then

$$20w(1 + r)^2 + 20w(1 + r) = P_a$$

The price of the second commodity, b, is instead

$$40w(1 + r) = P_b$$

Although Ricardo does not deal systematically with the subject, here, as well as in other numerical examples, he does offer a theory in embryo, which – for any given rate of profits – makes natural prices depend not only on the quantity of labour directly or indirectly expended on each commodity, but also on what we may call the *distribution over time* of that quantity of labour.

5. Since in the foregoing example the prices of the two commodities are determined on the basis of prior knowledge of the wage and the rate of profits, one may be inclined to think, with Marshall, that according to Ricardo value is regulated by the cost of production, which includes 'Time or Waiting as well as Labour'; and that Marx wrongly interpreted his doctrine 'to mean that interest does not enter into that cost of production which governs ... value' (Marshall, 1920, p. 672 and pp. 672–3, n. 1). That this is not the case will emerge clearly if we look at Ricardo's approach to the problem of relative price variation as set

forth in a numerical example contained in his 1823 paper on *Absolute Value and Exchangeable Value* (Ricardo, 1823, pp. 383–4), an example which closely follows the one we have just examined (the only differences, which we shall ignore, being that the prices of commodities *a* and *b* corresponding to $r = 10$ per cent are said to be £231 and £220 respectively, rather than £2,310 and £2,200, and that a third commodity is also considered).

Ricardo supposes 'labour to rise in value and profits to fall – that from 10 pc' they fall to 5 pc''. He further supposes that commodity *b* be the standard of value. Making the two examples into a single one, we shall suppose that gold is produced in a single stage. If, then, the price of commodity *b* is £2,200, that is not because the wage is £50 and the rate of profits 10 per cent, but rather because it has been produced, like gold, in a single stage, employing a quantity of labour equal to 2,200 times that required to produce the quantity of gold corresponding to £1. The fall in the rate of profits from 10 to 5 per cent will thus leave the price of commodity *b* unchanged; which amounts to saying that in its production (as in that of gold) the increase in wages and the fall in profits offset each other.

However, the same increase in *w* and fall in *r* cannot bring about a smaller offsetting in the case of commodity *a*, whose price must fall from £2,310 to £2,255 (from £231 to £225.5 in Ricardo's 1823 example). This result is obtained by applying the rate of profits of 5 per cent (instead of 10 per cent) to the value of the means of production employed in the second stage of production of commodity *a*. The latter value, £1,100, does not vary, since the means of production are produced, like gold (and commodity *b*), in a single stage. The value of the term $20w(1 + r)^2$ in the equation of commodity *a* falls, therefore, from £1,210 to £1,155. The value of the second term in the sum, $20w(1 + r) = £1,100$, can be assimilated to the unchanging value of a commodity produced in a single stage.

It is evident that, if gold were produced in two years, with the same proportional distribution of labour between the two corresponding stages of production as commodity *a*, the new ratio P_a/P_b would emerge from a rise in P_b with P_a constant. It is also evident that, if all commodities were produced with the same proportional distribution of labour over time, they would all be in the same situation as gold, in whose production an increase (fall) in wages is exactly offset by the corresponding fall (increase) in profits, and the labour theory of value would stand in no need of 'modification'.

The 'modifications' have, therefore, nothing to do with the alleged necessity of adding to the labour what is depicted as a second element of the cost of production. The misunderstanding may be traced back to Malthus, who ascribes to Ricardo the very fault that Marshall seeks to acquit him of, shifting the blame onto Marx. 'We have the power indeed', Malthus remarks,

'arbitrarily, to call the labour which has been employed upon a commodity its real value, but in so doing, we use words in a different sense from that in which they are customarily used; we confound at once the very important distinction between *cost* and *value*; and render it almost impossible to explain with clearness, the main stimulus to the production of wealth, which in fact depends upon that distinction'. ·

To which Ricardo counters:

Mr Malthus appears to think that it is part of my doctrine, that the cost and value of a thing should be the same; – it is, if he means by cost, 'cost of production' including profits. In the above passage, this is what he does not mean, and therefore he has not clearly understood me (Ricardo, 1821, p. 47n.).

What Ricardo makes clear in this passage (which, surprisingly enough, Marshall quotes as evidence in support of his reading of the matter: see Marshall, 1920, p. 672) is that the labour theory of value, in its 'unmodified' as well as its 'modified' form, takes full account of 'the very important distinction between cost and value'; that is, of the existence of profits ('the main stimulus to the production of wealth'). What equals value according to this theory is not, Ricardo argues, 'cost' as commonly understood, but 'cost of production including profits', profits being what is left of the value of a commodity once wages have been deducted. (Reference to the most unfavourable circumstances under which production is carried on has been dropped since the preceding section, land being now supposed to be abundant and all of the same quality.)

6. The reader will perhaps have noted how Ricardo omits to specify by how much the wage must increase in order to cause a fall from 10 to 5 per cent in the rate of profits (elsewhere, again when dealing with the problem of relative price variation, he postulates 'such a rise of wages as should occasion a fall of one per cent, in profits'; Ricardo, 1821, p. 36). Even though Ricardo continues to express himself as if, in the relation between w and r, the independent variable were represented by the wage, in actual fact he reverses the roles, and makes w depend on r. The value of w when $r = 10$ per cent is, as we know, $w = £50$. Its value when $r = 5$ per cent can be calculated from the equation of commodity b (whose price remains £2,200). This value is slightly less than $w = £52$. 8s. 0d.

As a matter of fact, Ricardo's argument is made up of two distinct stages. In the first of these the rate of profits is determined on the basis of the 'unmodified' labour theory of value; in this stage the necessaries consumed by each labourer are taken as given (see section 2 above). The second stage takes the rate of profits as given, the problem being now to determine the prices which make the rate of profits uniform throughout the economy. These prices, as Ricardo realizes, are not regulated by the quantities of labour expended on the production of the commodities, as they were assumed to be for the purpose of determining the rate of profits. And the wage (the £52. 8s. 0d or so of the example) will in general turn out to be different from the value of the necessaries it was assumed to purchase in the first stage of the argument.

It does not escape Ricardo that the rate of profits should be determined on the basis of the 'modified' theory, and therefore of prices which, in turn, cannot be determined before the rate of profits is known. But he is unable to provide a theoretical construction capable of coping with this interdependence. Thus he does not see any other solution but that of continuing to base his analysis of income distribution on the 'unmodified' labour theory of value, which he defends as 'the nearest approximation to truth as a rule for measuring relative value, as any I have ever heard' (Letter to Malthus of 9 October 1820, in Ricardo, 1951–73, vol. VIII, p. 279).

7. A major difference between the Ricardian version of the labour theory of value and its Marxian version, to which we must now turn, lies precisely here: that the former can be described as an approximation, whereas the latter cannot. According to Marx the values of commodities exactly (not approximately) reflect the quantities of labour expended on their production, although this is not true, in general, of the 'prices of production' (Marx's name for 'natural prices'), which coexist with values.

In discussing Marx's position we shall reckon the value of commodities directly in units of labour (say, man-years). The value of the means of production which assist one labourer in the annual cycle of production of any particular commodity, or *constant capital* per unit of labour (c), and the value of one labourer's necessaries, or *variable capital* per unit of labour (v), are thus made equal to the quantities of labour expended on the production of those means of production and of those necessaries respectively.

If only circulating capital is used, the value of the output per unit of labour of any commodity is ($c + 1$), or c plus the value added per unit of labour. Since v is uniform throughout the economy (each labourer being assumed to consume the same bundle of commodities), the *surplus-value* per unit of labour ($1 - v$) will also be uniform. The same is obviously true of the ratio of surplus-value to variable capital (the *rate of surplus-value*), but not, in general, of the ratio of surplus-value to total (i.e. constant plus variable) capital. The latter ratio will be the higher, in any particular branch of production, the lower the ratio c/v (the *organic composition of capital*).

Competition, however, redistributes the overall surplus-value of the economy among the various branches of production in such a way as to render it proportional not to the variable, but to the total capital. Thus a general rate of profits comes to be established, equal to the weighted average of the ($1 - v$) to ($c + v$) ratios in the different branches of production – or, which amounts to the same thing, to the ratio of the overall surplus-value of the economy to the overall capital employed. The same mechanism establishes the prices of production, which make that rate of profits uniform throughout the economy.

Unlike Ricardo's, Marx's argument is *explicitly* framed in two stages. Since the prices of production differ from the values only on account of the different distribution of the overall surplus-value of the economy, according to Marx the rate of profits is accurately determined, for the economy as a whole, on the basis of the labour theory of value. The prices of production are then obtained from the values by replacing the surplus-value produced in each branch of production with the part of the overall surplus-value of the economy belonging to that branch according to the general rate of profits.

8. 'Surplus-value and the rate of surplus-value', says Marx, 'are, relatively, the invisible and unknown essence that wants investigating, while rate of profit and therefore the appearance of surplus-value in the form of profit are revealed on the surface of the phenomenon' (Marx, 1894, p. 43). To reveal the invisible: herein lies the task of science. But Marx's theoretical programme also involves explaining just *why* the intimate essence of thins is invisible, why it does not reveal itself 'on the surface of the phenomenon'. Marx's explanation is that those 'who are entrapped in bourgeois production relations' (ibid., p. 817) witness the *result* of the redistribution of surplus-value – the profit proportional to capital – but not the *process* leading up to this result:

The actual difference of magnitude between profit and surplus-value... in the various spheres of production now completely conceals the true nature and origin of profit not only from the capitalist, who has a special interest in deceiving himself on this score, but also from the labourer (ibid., p. 168).

Thus it comes about that

the splitting of the value of commodities after subtracting the value of the means of production consumed in their creation; the splitting of this given quantity of value, determined by the quantity of labour incorporated in the produced commodities into three component parts... appears in a perverted form on the surface of capitalist production,

wage, profit and rent taking on the aspect of 'independent revenues in relation to one another, and as such related to three very dissimilar production factors, namely labour, capital and land', from which 'they seem to arise' (ibid., pp. 867–8; we shall, however, continue to assume the absence of rent). 'To have destroyed this false appearance and illusion' represents 'the great merit of [classical] political economy' (ibid., p. 830). Against classical political economy – of which Ricardo is the 'last great representative' (Marx, 1873, p. 24) – Marx sets 'vulgar' economy: the first of these studied 'the real relations of production in bourgeois society', whereas the second 'deals with appearances only' (Marx, 1867, p. 85, n. 1).

But even Ricardo cannot be completely acquitted, in Marx's opinion, of having taken as the *starting-point* of the argument the *result* of the redistribution of surplus-value. Indeed, it is the natural prices themselves that Ricardo claims are regulated (even if only approximately; but, as will be remembered, it is 'the nearest approximation to truth' among those available; see section 6 above) by the quantities of labour expended on the production of commodities. Hence Marx's allegation that Ricardo confuses values and prices of production.

If Ricardo is compelled to presuppose what he should explain (the profit proportional to capital, as it emerges from the redistribution of surplus-value), this is – according to Marx – because his unsatisfactory treatment of non-wage capital (see section 3 above) blinds him to the distinction between surplus-value and profit:

> Ricardo wrongly identifies surplus-value with profit... these are only identical in so far as the total capital consists of variable capital or is laid out directly in wages... Ricardo evidently shares Smith's view that the *total value* of the annual product resolves itself into revenues. Hence also his confusion of value with cost-price (Marx, 1905–10, vol. II, p. 426; as so often in *Theories of Surplus-Value*, 'cost-price' here stands for 'price of production').

Here, in Marx's opinion, lies the origin of the analytical difficulties with which Ricardo had to wrestle and which Marx himself claims to have overcome, thanks to his discovery of the redistribution mechanism.

9. On 24 August 1867, a few days after correcting the proofs of the first volume of *Capital*, Marx wrote to Engels:

> The best points in my book are: (1) the *double character of labour*, according to whether it is expressed in use value or exchange value (*all* understanding of the facts depends upon this...) (2) the treatment of *surplus-value independently of its particular forms* as profit, interest, ground rent, etc. (Marx and Engels, 1942, pp. 226–7).

The second of these two contributions has been dealt with in sections 7 and 8 above (and something more on the subject will be said in section 11 below), within the limits of the hypothesis that all surplus-value is received in the form of profit. We must now turn to the first contribution – the one on which '*all* understanding of the facts' is based: the 'double character of labour'.

In the production of commodities the distribution of labour in a society among its various productive activities is not regulated *a priori*, through some form of agreement or coercion, but only *a posteriori*, through the exchange of products (Marx, 1867, p. 336). The labour of individuals is therefore not, immediately, the labour *of society* – as is the case in, say, a peasant family, within which 'the labour-power of each individual, by its very nature, operates... merely as a definite portion of the whole labour-power of the family' (Marx, 1867, p. 82; see Marx, 1859, p. 33). On the contrary, we are dealing here with 'the labour of private individuals or groups of individuals who carry on their work independently of each other'; this labour 'asserts itself as a part of the labour of society, only by means of the relation which the act of exchange establishes directly between the products, and indirectly, through them, between the producers' (Marx, 1867, pp. 77–8). It is only when the social division of labour takes this particular form that the products of labour become commodities, or acquire the quality of possessing value.

In the first chapter of *Capital* (as well as in the first chapter of *A Contribution to the Critique of Political Economy*) Marx emphasizes how in the eyes of producers commodities count not for their ability to satisfy this or that human want, but rather for their ability to find a purchaser: not for their use-value but for their (exchange-) value. Of these two qualities of commodities, use-value is the one abstracted from in the exchange, which cancels the difference between the products, in the sense that in the exchange different products are equated, or treated as equal, and reduced to their quality of possessing value.

Labour participates in the two-fold character of commodities, as useful things and things possessing value. On the one hand, 'it must, as a definite useful kind of labour, satisfy a definite social want, and thus hold its place as a part and parcel of the collective labour of all, as a branch iof a social division of labour' (Marx, 1867, p. 78). On the other hand, just as 'in viewing the coat and linen as values, we abstract from their different use-values, so it is with the labour represented by those values: we disregard the difference between its useful forms, weaving and tailoring' (ibid., p. 52); which is what producers themselves actuall do, production of commodities being *production for value* production, therefore, of abstract wealth, indifferent to its material content. What remains is a uniform, undifferentiated labour, which 'counts only quantitatively', having been 'reduced to human labour, pure and simple' (p. 52), to 'abstract human labour' (p. 81). Such is the labour which, embodied in commodities, figures as their value.

'Whenever, by an exchange', Marx writes, 'we equate as values our different products, by that very act, we also equate, as human labour, the different kinds of labour expended upon them. We are not aware of this, nevertheless we do it' (ibid., pp. 78–9). The reduction of a commodity to its mere quality of possessing value and the reduction of labour to abstract labour are thus in Marx's conception the outcome of one and the same real process (see Colleti, 1968, sect. 8). And it is only by being reduced to abstract labour and assuming the form of a quality of commodities, their value, that the *private* labour of the weaver and the *private* labour of the tailor enter into relation with each other, becoming part of a *social* division of labour. This is, in Marx's words, 'the specific manner in which the social character of labour is established' (Marx, 1859, p. 32) in the production of commodities. 'But what is the value of a commodity?', Marx enquires. 'The objective form of the social labour expended on its production' (Marx, 1867, p. 501). Or, to put it another way, abstract labour (social only in so far as abstract) represents 'the substance of value' (ibid., p. 46).

10. The picture is now complete, and we can attempt to gather together the threads of Marx's position. As we have just seen, the thesis of the reduction of labour to abstract labour is put forward by Marx in close connection with his theory of value. Indeed, the two merge into one, abstract labour being indicated as the substance of value and value as the form that labour must assume in order to acquire a social character. It remains to be added that the conception of abstract labour as the substance of value presupposes the sort of redistribution mechanism described in section 7 above. What constitutes the substance of value cannot, in fact, but consitute the substance of revenues, as the latter stem from the breakdown of the value of a given set of commodities,. It follows that the conception of abstract labour as the substance of value necessitates that the whole of this substance be found in the prices of production, having merely been partly

243

diverted away from some commodities and channeled into others (see the enlightening comparison with the 'conservation of energy' in Lippi, 1976, pp. 50–52). If this is not the case, then the aforesaid substance is not the 'substance' of anything real, and 'value' is merely a name for the quantity of labour directly and indirectly expended on the production of a commodity.

11. In the Afterword to the second (German) edition of *Capital* we read that 'the method of presentation' must differ in form from that of inquiry' (Marx, 1873, p. 28). We are, now in a position to understand this celebrated (as much as hermetic) warning. If we attend to the 'method of inquiry', the theory of the rate of profits and of the prices of production' (contained in the manuscripts published posthumously as the third volume of *Capital*) represents – as stated in the preceding section – a premise for the conception of abstract labour as the substance of value, and the cornerstone of the whole theoretical structure of *Capital*. (From a chronological point of view, it has been remarked that 'once Marx had attained – at the beginning of 1858 – what he regarded as the correct solution of the problem of how to determine the rate of profit, various elements in his thinking seem to have found an organic unity in the concept of value – the concept of a "substance" to be redistributed' (Ginzburg, 1985, pp. 105–6); the 'various elements' being basically Marx's analysis of the social division of labour and his theory of income distribution and prices.)

But if, instead, we attend to the 'method of presentation', things take on a rather different aspect. Marx calls his own presentation of the argument 'genetical', meaning by this that it consists in 'elaborating how the various forms come into being' (Marx, 1905–10, vol. III, p. 500), proceeding from the form of value that labour assumes in the act of acquiring a social character, to arrive at surplus-value, the redistribution mechanism and the establishment of a general rate of profits.

The two 'methods', or procedures, reflect the two different aims mentioned in section 8 above: the aim (proper to scientific analysis) of tearing away the veil of appearances, and the aim (proper to genetical presentation) of showing how that veil is woven together. The latter aim is not regarded by Marx as less important than the former, to explain how appearances are produced being in his opinion the only sure way of evading their deceptions.

As we have already seen, Ricardo himself is believed by Marx to be partly the victim of such deceptions, even while he contributed so greatly towards dispelling them. In conceiving the labour theory of value as a theory of natural prices, Ricardo 'omits some essential links and *directly* seeks to prove the congruity of economic categories with one another' (Marx, 1905–10, vol. II, p. 165). He does so by taking 'the rate of profits as something pre-existent which, therefore, even plays a part in the determination of *value*' (ibid., p. 434), thus missing the inner connection of forms which is reflected in Marx's genetical presentation, and according to which 'the determination of value is the primary factor, antecedent to the rate of profits and to the establishment of production prices' (ibid., vol. III, p. 377; see Gajano, 1979, ch. 3).

12. If, however, the presentation must proceed from value to the rate of profits and the prices of production, it must assume (at least provisionally) that the foundation of value be independent of what comes after, as a result of the redistribution of surplus-value. Marx thus finds himself in an *impasse*, no such independent foundation being provided by his analysis.

So it comes as no surprise that value is introduced in *Capital* in a rather sketchy way. Marx starts by declaring, as something self-evident, that in two commodities equated in exchange 'there exists in equal quantities something common to both' (Marx, 1867, p. 45). He then goes on to enquire wherein this common element consists. It is at this point that we meet the argument according to which exchange involves an abstraction from the use-value of the commodities exchanged ('the exchange of commodities is evidently an act characterised by a total abstraction from use-value': ibid., p. 45; see section 9 above). But, Marx pursues, 'if then we leave out of consideration the use-value of commodities, they have only one common property left, that of being products of labour' (ibid., p. 45). Thus he does his best to lead the reader into thinking that the prices of commodities are regulated by the quantity of labour expended on their production (otherwise the common element would not be 'in equal quantities'). Only later on does Marx put the reader on his guard with sporadic and obscure hints. ('Average prices do not directly coincide with the values of commodities, as Adam Smith, Ricardo, and others believe': ibid., p. 163n.; see ibid., p. 212n., where the reader is referred to vol. III – unpublished – and ibid., p. 290, where Marx mentions the 'many intermediate terms' wanted to resolve the 'apparent contradiction' between the labour theory of value and the existence of a uniform rate of profits.)

'Analysis', writes Marx, 'is the necessary prerequisite of genetical presentation' (Marx, 1905–10, vol. III, p. 500). But it is a prerequisite which cannot be openly declared if presentation is to remain genetical.

This limitation has given birth to two opposite and equally wrong interpretations. The one holds that Marx's theory of value has no foundation whatsoever, and treats that theory and the theory of prices of production as two mutually incompatible theories of prices (this is the thesis of the 'contradiction' between the first and the third volumes of *Capital*, put forward in Böhm-Bawerk, 1896). The other interpretation tries to defend the labour theory of value on the basis of Marx's analysis of the social division of labour, making no appeal to the redistribution mechanism and maintaining, in the last analysis, that labour forms the substance of value because it is through the exchange of commodities that the various labours, performed outside any conscious coordination, enter into relation with one another (this traditional Marxist reply to Böhm-Bawerk's criticism first appears in Hilferding, 1904, and finds its best expression in Colletti, 1968).

Obviously the labour theory of value cannot be defended on the grounds indicated by Hilferding and Colletti (as the latter has acknowledged: see Colletti, 1979). But, just as obviously, Böhm-Bawerk's grounds for dismissing it are not good ones. Actually, the reason why the labour theory of value must be rejected is not that it is devoid of foundation, but rather that what in Marx's view represents its foundation – his theory of the rate of profits and of prices of production – proves untenable in the light of the subsequent work of Tugan-Baranovsky (1905), Bortkiewicz (1907) and others, up to Sraffa (1960).

BIBLIOGRAPHY

Böhm-Bawerk, E. von. 1896. *Karl Marx and the Close of His System*. In Sweezy (1949).

Bortkiewicz, L. von 1907. *On the Correction of Marx's Fundamental Theoretical Construction*. In Sweezy (1949).

Colletti, L. 1968. Bernstein and the Marxism of the Second International. In L. Colletti, *From Rousseau to Lenin: Studies in Ideology and Society*, London: New Left Books, 1972.

Colletti, L. 1979. *Tra marxismo e no*. Bari: Laterza.

Gejano, A. 1979. *La dialettica della merce. Introduzione allo studio di 'Per la critica dell'economia politica' di Marx*. Napoli: il Laboratorio.

Ginzburg, A. 1985. A journey to Manchester: a change in Marx's economic conceptions. *Political Economy* 1.

Hilferding, R. 1904. Böhm-Bawerk's criticism of Marx. In Sweezy (1949).

Lippi, M. 1976. *Value and Naturalism in Marx*. London: New Left Books, 1979.

Marshall, A. 1920. *Principles of Economics*. 8th edn. London: Macmillan, 1964.

Marx, K. 1859. *A Contribution to the Critique of Political Economy*. Moscow: Progress Publishers, 1978.

Marx, K. 1867. *Capital: A Critique of Political Economy*, Vol. I. London: Lawrence & Wishart, 1977.

Marx, K. 1873. Afterword to the 2nd German edition. In Marx (1867).

Marx, K. 1885. *Capital: A Critique of Political Economy*, Vol. II. London: Lawrence & Wishart, 1974.

Marx, K. 1894. *Capital: A Critique of Political Economy*, Vol. III. London: Lawrence & Wishart, 1974.

Marx, K. 1905–10. *Theories of Surplus-Value*. Moscow: Progress Publishers, Vol. I, 1978; Vol. II, 1975; Vol. III, 1975.

Marx, K. and Engels, F. 1942. *Selected Correspondence 1846–1895*. New York: International Publishers.

Ramsay, G. 1836. *An Essay on the Distribution of Wealth*. Edinburgh.

Ricardo, D. 1821. *On the Principles of Political Economy and Taxation*. 3rd edn, in Ricardo (1951–73), Vol. I.

Ricardo, D. 1823. *Absolute Value and Exchangeable Value*. In Ricardo (1951–73), Vol. IV.

Ricardo, D. 1951–73. *The Works and Correspondence of David Ricardo*. Ed. P. Sraffa with the collaboration of M.H. Dobb, Cambridge: Cambridge University Press.

Smith, A. 1776. *An Inquiry into the Nature and Causes of the Wealth of Nations*. Ed. E. Cannan. London: Methuen, 1961.

Sraffa, P. 1951. Introduction. In Ricardo (1951–73). Vol. I.

Sraffa, P. 1960. *Production of Commodities by Means of Commodities: Prelude to a Critique of Economic Theory*. Cambridge: Cambridge University Press.

Sweezy, P.M. (ed.) 1949. *Karl Marx and the Close of His System* by Eugen von Böhm-Bawerk & 'Böhm-Bawerk's Criticism of Marx' by Rudolf Hilferding, together with an appendix consisting of an article by Ladislaus von Bortkiewicz on the Transformation of Values into Prices of Production in the Marxian System. New York: Augustus M. Kelley, 1966.

Tugan-Baranovsky, M. 1905. *Theoretische Grundlagen des Marxismus*. Leipzig: Duncker & Humblot.

Rosa Luxemburg

TADEUSZ KOWALIK

Rosa Luxemburg was born on 5 March 1870 in Zamosc (Polish territory under the Russian occupation), and died, murdered during the revolution, on 15 January 1919 in Berlin. Rosa Luxemburg was a socialist thinker and writer, one of the leaders of Polish and German Social Democracy and an economist. She studied in Zurich, first philosophy and natural sciences (for two years), then she graduated from the Faculty of Law and Economics. In 1897 she received her PhD for a book *Die industrielle Entwicklung Polens* (The Industrial Development of Poland) (1898). In 1898 she contracted a marriage of convenience (with G. Luebeck) to obtain German citizenship and from then, until the end of her life, she lived in Berlin. She was one of the founders of the Social Democratic Party in the Kingdom of Poland (under the Russian occupation). The main area of her activity was German Social Democracy, in which she became one of the leading intellectuals. Her articles in which she opposed the revisionism of Eduard Bernstein and defended revolutionary Marxism won her European popularity. (They were subsequently published in a book *Sozialreform oder Revolution?* [1900].)

In the period 1907–14 Luxemburg lectured in political economy, then in economic history in the Party School of German Social Democracy (her predecessor lecturing in political economy was Hilferding). Towards the end of that period Luxemburg elaborated her lectures notes in order to publish them in the form of a manual, but in view of the theoretical problems she encountered, she left the manuscript unfinished. Half the chapters were lost during the war, and the remainder were published under the title *Einführung in die Nationaloekonomie* (1925).

She aimed at producing an orthodox, popularizing manual. In the process of doing this she was still convinced that political economy found its 'peak and climax' in Marx's works and that it could be developed by his followers 'only in details'. Attempting to give an outline of the general tendencies of the capitalist economy however, she faced insurmountable problems, previously unsuspected.

She could find no satisfactory answer in Marx to the question 'what are the objective historical limits to capitalism?' Excited by her own hypothesis, she wrote 'wie im Rausch': in a period of four months she produced over five hundred pages and 'without even once reading the draft' turned it over to the publisher. This was the genesis of her *opus magnum* – *Die Akkumulation des Kapitals* (1913; English trans., 1951).

One could make a figurative comparison of her four-month effort to the activity of a volcano ejecting a flow of ideas, with its trains of thought picked up and abandoned, its questions left with no answer, its contradictory contentions. Hence there are tremendous problems in interpreting the results.

One of several possible interpretations is as follows: The evolution of her ideas, and particularly the 'illumination of 1912' exemplifies a more general trend in the development of Marxian economic thought after Marx's death. One can distinguish in the trend two rather different currents. The first is based on Marxian theory of value and surplus-value. This current has been developed mainly by the first generation of Marxists, such as Karl Kautsky. The second current came to the fore rather later. The most representative figures are Hilferding and Rosa Luxemburg in Germany, and Lenin and Tugan-Baranovsky in Russia. They undertook the task of developing those aspects of Marx's theory that deal with the dynamics of modern capitalist economy. The year 1912 marks the border between Rosa Luxemburg the 'orthodox' and Rosa Luxemburg the 'revisionist', if we use this label in a theoretical rather than a political sense. Rosa Luxemburg's changed attitude toward the Marxian theory of capitalism manifests itself in a change in her methodology. In the *Einführung* she used the method that Marx applied in the first volume of *Das Kapital*, where the starting point was an analysis of the individual commodity and individual capital. The very essence of the turning-point in her later economic theorizing consists in grasping the importance of a macroeconomic approach. She became fascinated by Marx's concept of global reproduction and accumulation, developed in the second volume of *Das Kapital* (Marx's schemes of reproduction). In this construction she now saw the perfect embodiment of Marxist political economy and the most powerful analytical tool. Francois Quesnay was now advanced, in her eyes, to the rank of a founder of economics as an exact science, while she blamed the English line of classical economy for completely obscuring the eternal and universal functions of the means of production in the labour process.

In Rosa Luxemburg's thinking, fascination with the Marxian schemes of reproduction as a promising tool of analysis of the capitalist system as a whole goes together with the argument that the decisive part of *Das Kapital* (the last part of the second volume) was unfinished and underdeveloped. In the form left by Marx, and published posthumously by Engels, the model of accumulation has been constructed, in her opinion, on several drastic assumptions which make it impossible to understand the nature of capitalist development and of its limits.

The model assumes an identity of production and realization, which means that capitalist production creates a sufficiently large sales market for itself. This assumption contradicts not only the spirit of Marx's theory but also many statements in the first and third volumes of *Das Kapital* about a tendency on the part of total demand to lag behind rapidly increasing production.

Moreover, this assumption is related to the next great disadvantage of Marx's scheme: disregard of the circulation of money. As a consequence of this, Marx could not draw any satisfactory analytical conclusions from his rejection (in the first volume of *Das Kapital*) of Say's Law. In modern terms we could say that in disregarding money Marx identified savings with real accumulation (investment).

Marx analysed the accumulation of capital within a framework of society composed only of the capitalist and the working class. In Luxemburg's opinion, this assumption of pure capitalism rendered impossible the discovery of which class benefits from the expansion of capitalist production. Approached from this angle the Marxian model of reproduction can only be understood as a vision of production for production's sake.

Another disadvantage of the Marxian concept is the assumption of unchanged organic composition of capital and constant productivity of labour. As was the case with many Marxists of her day, Luxemburg recognized only one type of technical progress, what is now called 'capital-intensive'. She was convinced that technical progress must manifest itself in an increasing organic composition of capital, i.e. increasing share of constant capital in the value of the product, or, what was for her only another way of expressing the same phenomenon, in an increasing share of Division I (the production of the means of production) in the total social product.

Luxemburg promised much more than she was able to deliver. At different stages of her analysis she tried to overcome Marx's shortcomings. However, she did not succeed in transforming the schemes of reproduction into a form which would suit her purpose. For example, the criticism of Marx's concept of pure capitalism runs through the whole of her book, but whenever she resorts to the schemes of reproduction she uses them in the original (Marx's) form. The only correction made by her to the Marxian construction was that she allowed for an increase in the productivity of labour: in her schemata of reproduction the organic composition of capital (c/v) increases from period to period. On this ground she argued that expanded reproduction inevitably brings an increasing deficit of the means of production and an increasing surplus of the means of consumption. Disproportions arising because of that could be, according to her conviction, liquidated or dampened only outside the framework of pure capitalism – by exchange between capitalist and pre-capitalist systems.

This conclusion was based not only on her general law of increase of organic composition of capital, but also on the erroneous conviction that accumulation must be allocated to the division in which it has been obtained. Thus, in her only attempt to introduce corrections in the Marxian schemata of expanded reproduction, Luxemburg cannot claim any visible theoretical achievements in the analysis of capitalist accumulation. No conclusions resulted from this attempt concerning her main contention (lack of sufficient demand as the crucial obstacle of capitalist development). In this sense the book is disappointing.

However, her work cannot be neglected. The significance of *The Accumulation of Capital* lies in the fact that it is an attempt at a theoretical solution of the known Marxian statement that the conditions of production are not identical with the conditions of realization. By rejecting Say's law she tried to prove that accumulation is affected to a large extent by the prospect of a growing market which, in turn, is determined primarily by the existing sales situation. Thus, pure capitalism provides by itself too weak a basis for rapid economic growth. Saving does not transform itself automatically into real investment. This was the direction of development of a theory of capitalist dynamics in the following decades. Michal Kalecki (1971) was the most successful in taking up problems posed by Rosa Luxemburg and solving them effectively. But, due to some special historical conditions. Marxists for a long time treated Kalecki's theory with suspicion or indifference.

An attempt by Luxemburg to include the monetary system in the theory of capitalist reproduction and accumulation also deserves attention. It can be seen from numerous passages in the second volume of *Das Kapital* that Marx tried, but failed, to solve this tremendously difficult question. It is true that Rosa Luxemburg did not solve it either. But in contrast to many other disciples of Marx she did not neglect the problem and formulated it in a much more lucid and precise way than all her predecessors and contemporaries.

Why did Rosa Luxemburg raise again the problem of the incentives to accumulation, investment and technical progress in the capitalist system? What led her to the conviction that Marx's analysis is not sufficient? One can suppose that there were historical reasons, as well as theoretical issues. Her discussion with Eduard Bernstein at the turn of this century may provide one possible explanation. She then expressed the following view:

> In the general development of capitalism small capital ... plays the part of the pioneer of technical revolution. ... If small capital is the champion of technical progress and if technical progress is the pulse of a capitalist economy then small capital is a phenomenon inseparable from capitalist development ... The gradual disappearance of medium-sized firms would not mean, as Bernstein seems to think, that the development of capitalism is revolutionary, but on the contrary, it would indicate, that is is stagnant and drowsy (*Social Reform or Revolution?*, part I:2 Adaptation of Capitalism).

Some dozen years later it was clear to her that the capitalist economy was entering the era of industrial giants and that the individual entrepreneurs of the period of free competition and the corresponding mechanisms were beginning to fade away. Rosa Luxemburg must have asked herself: 'Why does capitalism not show signs of stagnation despite this process of structural transformation?' The explanation given by Marx that the capitalist strives incessantly to maximize his profits, and in the conditions of free competition this striving becomes for each individual capitalist the 'external law of compulsion', was not valid for the new conditions.

We already know the general tenor of her theoretical answer: neither the consumption fund of the working class nor the consumption expenditures of the capitalists can provide sufficiently strong incentives to accumulation. A large part of the incentive to accumulation in a capitalist system is due to a steady and uninterrupted economic exchange between capitalist and non-capitalist environments.

Historical studies led Rosa Luxemburg to the conviction that there was no 'Chinese Wall' between classical capitalism and the phase of imperialism. This was so because political violence was for her 'nothing but a vehicle for the economic process' ([1913], 1951, p. 452). Seeing ever more clearly the importance of non-economic factors for capitalist accumulation in the past and in the future, she advanced to a broader interpretation of the process of the development of capitalism than the interpretation given by Marx in *Das Kapital*. Capital is not only born 'soaked in blood and dirt' (Marx), but grows later in very much the same way, until the moment of its collapse. Thus Rosa Luxemburg's interpretation of the essence and character of imperialism is very broad. First, a period of wars and revolutions arising from the exhaustion of the non-capitalist system provides external markets for capitalist accumulation, areas for the profitable investment of capital and basic raw materials. Without this environment as a 'feeding ground', accumulation would be, in her opinion, impossible. The main achievement of *Accumulation of Capital* probably lies in locating the problem of underdeveloped countries as a central issue in the debate on the further development or collapse of the capitalist system.

The title of the last chapter of *The Accumulation of Capital* is 'Militarism as a sphere of the accumulation of capital'. Rosa Luxemburg makes an attempt to analyse the importance of armaments production – as production and not as a tool of external expansion – for stimulating economic growth in capitalism.

She rejected the conviction prevailing at that time that the bourgeois state can merely redistribute profits and incomes, without changing anything in the conditions of reproduction of total social capital. Government expenditures for armament production resulted in the state creating 'by sleight of hand' new demand, new purchasing power, and thus influencing the magnitude of the total accumulation of capital. The demand created in this way by the state has the same effect as a newly opened market. In the era of imperialism, armament production becomes one of the important ways of solving difficulties in the realization of growing production. The attractiveness of expanding this sphere of accumulation consists, in addition, in the fact that expenditure by the state in military equipment 'free of the vagaries and subjective fluctuations of personal consumption, it achieves almost automatic regularity and rhythmic growth' ([1913], 1951, p. 466). Moreover, military expenditure places a lever with automatic and rhythmic movement in the hands of capitalist state, so that it seems at first capable of infinite expansion.

Needless to say, from today's point of view Rosa Luxemburg's approach with regard to the general role of the state is rather narrow. She also did not perceive the possibility of credit creation by budget deficits. The multiplier effect of the armament sector was hardly noticed. It is not clear whether she assumed unused productive capacity. Too much stress was laid on wages and individual incomes of small producers, as main sources of government revenue.

But the mere fact of raising the problem, considered very important today, and of showing the fundamentally correct direction in which its solution should go, elevates her to the rank of the precursors of contemporary economic thinking.

The question of the collapse of the capitalist system plays an important part in Rosa Luxemburg's thinking. The desire to grasp theoretically the objective historical limits of the mode of production was one of her motives in dealing with the problem of accumulation. In *The Accumulation of Capital*, and in her *Anti-Critique* she often returns to this problem. As an historical process the accumulation of capital, according to her, depends 'in every respect upon the non-capitalist social strata and forms of social organization' (1951, p. 366). In this way, the solution of the problem that had been a subject of controversy since the time of Sismondi, according to whom the accumulation of capital is altogether impossible, and the naive optimism of Say and Tugan-Baranovsky, in whose opinion capitalism can fertilize itself *ad infinitum*, is in dialectical contradiction: the environment of non-capitalistic social formations is essential for the accumulation of capital; only by the exchange with them can it progress and last as long as this environment exists.

This last thought, and her contention that accumulation internationalizes the capitalist mode of production by eliminating the traditional modes of production and, at the same time, cannot survive in pure capitalism, is repeated several times. However, this is only an abstract point, not a comprehensive concept of the breakdown of the capitalist system; only a 'theoretical formulation' showing a tendency in the development of capitalism – and nothing else. She made her abstract thesis on the impossibility of the existence of capitalism without the pre-capitalist environment more specific by her historical analysis of economic and socio-political conflicts of interests between the 'imperialist' and 'colonial' countries as a primary source of wars and revolutions.

SELECTED WORKS

1898. *Die Industrielle Entwicklung Polens*. Leipzig.

1900. *Sozialreform oder Revolution?* Leipzig.

1913. *Die Akkumulation des Kapitals. Beitrag zur ökonomischen Erklärung des Imperialismus*. Berlin. Trans. by Agnes Schwarzschild as *The Accmulation of Capital*, London: Routledge & Kegan Paul, 1951 (with a foreword by Joan Robinson); New Haven: Yale University Press.

1921. *Die Akkumulation des Kapitals, oder was die Epigonen aus der Marxschen Theorie gemacht haben. Eine Antikritik*. Berlin.

BIBLIOGRAPHY

Kalecki, M. 1971. *Selected Essays on the Dynamics of the Capitalist Economy 1933–1970*. Cambridge: Cambridge University Press.

Kowalik, T. 1964. Rosa Luxemburg's theory of accumulation and imperialism. In *Problems of Economic Dynamics and Planning, Essays in honour of Michal Kalecki*. Warsaw: Państowowe Wydawnictwo Naukowe, 1964. (A summary of a work available in Polish, Italian and Spanish.)

Nettl, J.P. 1966. *Rosa Luxemburg*. 2 vols, London and New York: Oxford University Press.

Market Value and Market Price

ANWAR SHAIKH

Marx defines the labour value of a commodity as the total (direct and indirect) abstract labour time required for its production. It is his contention that under capitalism the movements of commodity prices are dominated by changes in labour value magnitudes. This thesis, which he calls the law of value, requires him to connect labour values to the different *regulating prices* which act as centres of gravity of market prices under various assumed conditions of production and sale. He therefore undertakes to systematically develop the category of regulating price by introducing successively more complex factors into the analysis, linking it at each step to its foundation in labour value. It is only near the end of this developmental chain, when he begins to analyse the manner in which differences among conditions of production within an industry influence the process of regulating market prices, that we encounter the concept of *market value* (Marx, 1984, ch. X). To grasp its significance, we must first consider the steps which precede it.

The simplest expression of the law of value is when exchange is directly regulated by labour values. If we define direct price as a money price proportional to a commodity's labour value, then the simple case corresponds to the situation in which the direct price of a commodity is the regulating price (i.e. centre of gravity) of its market price. Marx begins with this premise in Volume I of *Capital*, concretizes it in Volume II to account for turnover time and circulation costs, transforms it in Volume III into the notion of prices of production (prices reflecting roughly equal rates of profit) as regulating prices, and then goes on to develop even this concept further, to account for rental payments, trading margins and interest flows. It is important to note that throughout this whole process of developing the various forms of regulating price, the aim is not only to encompass the complexity of the determinants of market prices, but also to show their connection to labour values.

The above path focuses on the complex character of the centres of gravity of various types of market prices. But the very concept of a gravitational centre

254

itself requires some discussion of the forces of supply and demand, because it is through their variation that the market price of a commodity is made to orbit around its (generally moving) centre of gravity. Accordingly, Marx also engages in a second, parallel, discussion of the manner in which a regulating price exerts its influence over market price. And here, the basic idea is that when (for instance) the growth of demand exceeds that of supply, market price will rise above regulating price, and the resulting rise in profitability above its regulating level (as embodied in the assumed regulating price) will induce capitalists to accerate supply relative to demand. The original gap between supply and demand will thereby be reduced or even reversed, thus driving the market price back towards or even below the regulating price. In this way, the dynamic adjustment of supply to demand serves to keep market price oscillating around the regulating price. Note that the whole argument is cast in terms of the relative *growth rates* of supply and demand rather than merely in terms of their (implicitly static) levels, and that market prices continually oscillate around regulating prices without ever having to converge to them in any mythical 'long run equilibrium' (Shaikh, 1982).

The preceding analysis implicitly ignores any variations in unit production costs and unit labour values, so that the regulating price itself is assumed to be unchanged during the regulation process. This is adequate as long as we abstract from differences among conditions of production within a given industry, because then each individual producer in effect embodies the average conditions and the whole story can be told simply in terms of the average producer. Under these circumstances, it is the *social* (i.e. average) unit labour value which ultimately regulates the movements of market prices, through the mediation of a particular regulating price. As Marx puts it, it is the social value of the commodity which functions here as the labour value which is regulative of market price, i.e. as the *market value*.

The obvious next step is to introduce the issue of differences among producers within an industry. Accordingly, Marx examines the situation which there are three types of production conditions in use, ranked in order from lowest efficiency (1), to medium (2), to best (3). The ranking of individual unit labour values (and unit production costs, other things being equal) will of course be in reverse order. As before, the social unit value is the total labour value of the total product divided by the amount of this total product. But this average now represents not only 'the average [unit] value of commodities produced' in this industry, but also the unit 'individual value of the ... average conditions' in the industry. Note that although the unit social value will be 'midway between the two extremes', it can nevertheless differ from the medium (2) unit value precisely because the average of existing conditions can differ from the medium (2) condition according to the weights of low (1) and high (3) conditions in total output.

The important thing at this juncture is to identify the specific conditions of production which operate to regulate market price through the ebb and flow of supply, *because it is the labour value of these particular conditions which will*

255

therefore function as the market value. This leads him to identify three types of response to a deviation of market price from some pre-existing regulating price. The first case is when all three conditions of production are able to adjust their respective rates of supply, so that the average production condition continues to regulate the market. Here, the regulating price still rests upon the average unit production cost, and the unit social value is still the market value. The only new consideration is that the regulating price and market value may vary within certain strict limits, because the functioning average condition of production may itself change insofar as the weights of its three constituent types of production conditions alter over the adjustment process. To the extent that better conditions accelerate more in the up phase and worse conditions decelerate more on the down side, even this effect will more or less cancel out over a given oscillation of market price around regulating price.

At the other extreme, Marx considers situations where the deviation of market price from regulating price goes so far as to bring either the worst or best production to the fore as the foundation of new regulating prices and market values. It is plausible, for instance, that the utilization of capacity is usually inversely correlated with the efficiency of production. Then, if demand rises sufficiently, the bulk of the slack will be taken up at first by the best, then by the intermediate and finally by the worst conditions of production. A situation may therefore arise in which the unit production costs of the worst conditions of production will come to determine the regulating price, so that the individual unit labour value of these conditions becomes the market value. Conversely, a sufficiently rapid fall in demand relative to supply may precipitate just the opposite situation, in which only the best conditions survive to regulate the market price and thus determine the regulating price and market value. It should be noted, incidentally, that while the shift of regulating conditions to one extreme or the other is precipitated here by 'extraordinary combinations' of supply and demand, this need not be the case when we consider technical change (in which the regulating conditions will be the best *generally accessible* methods of production) or production in agriculture and mining (in which the regulating conditions are often the ones on the margin of cultivation and location, hence among the worst of the lands and locations in use). From this point of view, Marx's initial discussion of Market Value is merely prelude to the much broader question of regulating value and conditions of production.

BIBLIOGRAPHY

Itoh, M. 1980. *Value and Crisis: Essays on Marxian Economics in Japan.* London: Pluto Press, ch. 3; New York: Monthly Review Press.

Marx, K. 1894. *Capital*, Vol. III, ch. X. New York: International Publishers, 1967.

Shaikh, A. 1982. Neo-Ricardian economics: a wealth of algebra, a poverty of theory. *Review of Radical Political Economy* 14(2), Summer, 67–83.

Marxian Value Analysis

J.E. ROEMER

For Marx, the labour theory of value was not a theory of price, but a method for measuring the exploitation of labour. The exploitation of labour, in turn, was important for explaining the production of a surplus in a capitalist economy. In a feudal economy, the emergence of a net product, surplus to the consumption of producers and to the inputs consumed in production, was palpable. For the serf reproduced himself on his family plot of land during part of the week, and then worked for the lord, doing demesne or corvée labour during the other part. There was a temporal and physical division between production for subsistence or reproduction, and production which generated an economic surplus and was appropriated by the lord. Under capitalism, with the division of labour, such a demarcation no longer existed. If capitalism is characterized by competitive markets, where each factor is paid its true 'value', and no one makes a windfall profit by cheating his partner in exchange, how could a surplus emerge? In what manner could a sequence of equal exchanges transform an initial set of inputs into a larger quantity of outputs, with the surplus being appropriated systematically by one class, the capitalists? Marx's project was to explain the origin of profits in a perfectly competitive model, where each factor, including labour, received its competitive price in exchange.

Marx thought he had discovered the answer to this apparent economic sleight of hand by tracing what happened to labour as it passed from the workers who expended it, to the products in which it became embodied, and eventually to the profits of capitalists who sold these commodities. In some of his writings, notably in *Capital*, Volume I, he simplified the argument by assuming that the prices of goods were equal to the amounts of labour they embodied. The embodied labour in a good is the amount of labour necessary to produce that good, and to reproduce all inputs used up in its production. (Assume the only non-produced input is labour.) In particular, this is true also for the good 'labour power'; the embodied labour in a week's labour supplied by a worker is the amount of labour necessary to produce the goods which that worker consumes to reproduce himself for work the following week. If all goods exchange at their embodied labour values (the simplifying assumption) then, in particular, the worker receives a wage in consumption commodities (say, corn) which is just necessary to reproduce himself (which includes the reproduction of the working-class family). The secret of accumulation, for Marx, lay in the discovery that the embodied labour value of one week's labour was, let us say, four days of labour. In four days of socially expended labour, given the existing technology and stock of capital, the consumption commodities necessary to reproduce the worker could be produced. Thus the worker was paid an amount of corn which required four days to produce, his wage for seven days' labour. The surplus labour of three days became embodied in commodities which were the rightful property of the capitalist who hired the worker. Why would the worker agree to such a deal? Because he had no access to the means of production necessary for producing his consumption goods on any better terms. Those means of production were owned by the capitalist class. (Although the simplifying assumption, that equilibrium prices are equal to or proportional to embodied labour values, is rarely true. Marx conjectured that the deviation of prices from labour values was not crucial to understanding the origin of profits. On this point he was correct. Much ink has been spent on the 'transformation problem', which tries to relate embodied labour values to equilibrium prices in general. As will be shown below, prices need not be proportional to embodied labour values for the theory of class and exploitation to be sensible. Hence the study of the transformation problem is a pointless detour.)

Imagine a corn economy, where there are two technologies for producing corn, a Farm and a Factory:

—Farm: 3 days' labour produces 1 corn output
—Factory: 1 days' labour + 1 corn (seed) produces 2 corn output.

On the Farm, corn is produced from labour alone, perhaps by cultivating wild corn on marginal land. In the capital-intensive Factory technology, seed corn is used as capital. One unit of seed capital reproduces itself and produces one additional corn output with one day of labour. Suppose both techniques require one week for the corn to grow to maturity. Let there be 1000 agents, ten of whom each own 50 units of seed corn. The other 990 peasants own only their labour power. Suppose a person requires one corn per week to survive; his preferences are to consume that amount, and then to take leisure. Assume that if he owns a stock of seed corn, he is not willing to run it down: he must replenish the inputs which he uses up before consuming. What is an equilibrium for this economy, which is guaranteed to reproduce the stocks with which it begins?

Since there are only 500 bushels of seed corn, the required consumption of 1000 corn cannot be reproduced using only the Factory technology, since the seed capital of 500 must be replaced. Capital is scarce relative to the labour which is available for it to employ. The wage which the 'capitalists', who own the seed corn, will offer at equilibrium to those whom they employ will therefore be bid down to the wage which peasants can earn in the marginal Farm technology: 1/3 corn per day labour. At any higher wage, all peasants will wish to sell their labour to the capitalists, and there is insufficient capital to employ them all. (It is assumed peasants have no preference for life on the Farm over life in the Factory. All they care about is rate at which they can exchange labour for corn.) At the wage of 1/3 corn per day, 500/3 peasants become workers in the Factory, each working for three days, planting three units of seed corn, and earning a wage of one corn. This exhausts the capital stock. The remaining peasants stay on the Farm, and also earn one corn with three days' labour. The ten capitalists each work zero days; altogether, they make a profit of $(500 - 500/3) = 333.3$ corn, after paying wages and replenishing their seed stock.

In the Factory technology, the embodied labour value of one corn is one day's labour; that amount of labour produces one corn output and reproduces the seed capital used. But the worker, at equilibrium, must work three days to earn one corn. This is so because he does not own the capital stock required for operating the efficient Factory method. His alternative it to eke out a subsistence of one corn by doing three days' labour on the Farm. The worker is said to be *exploited* if the labour embodied in the wage goods he is paid is less than the labour he expends in production. This is the case here, and it is evidently what makes possible the production of a surplus, in an economy where all agents wish only to work long enough to reproduce themselves (and their capital stock). Note this last statement characterizes, as well, the capitalists: in this story, they get 333 corn profits and expend no labour, a result consistent with their having subsistence preferences, where each desires to work only so long as he must to consume his own corn per week.

Contrast this capitalist economy, where three classes have emerged – capitalists, workers and peasants – to the following subsistence, peasant economy. Everything is the same as above, except the initial distribution of corn: let each of the 1000 persons own initially 0.5 corn. At equilibrium, each agent will work two days and consume one corn. First, he uses the Factory to turn his 0.5 seed corn into 0.5 corn net output, which costs him 0.5 days of labour; then he must produce another 0.5 corn for consumption, for which he turns to the Farm, where he works for 1.5 days. Each agent consumes one corn with two days' labour, an egalitarian society, which is classless. (There are other ways of arranging the equilibrium in this economy, in which one group of agents hires another group to work up its capital stock, while they, in turn work on the Farm. But the final allocation of corn and labour is the same as in the equilibrium just described.) There is a fine point here: perhaps one should say, in both economies, that the amount of labour socially embodied in one corn is two days (not one, as written above), for that is what is required to produce society's necessary corn consumption given the capital stock and available techniques. This will not change the verdict that the workers in the capitalist economy are exploited, while no one is exploited in the egalitarian society.

Contrast these two economies, which differ only in the initial distribution of the capital stock. Inequality in the distribution of the means of production gives rise to: (1) the production of a surplus above subsistence needs, or accumulation;

(2) exploitation, in the sense that some agents expend more labour than is embodied in the goods they consume and others expend less labour than is embodied in what the consume; and (3) classes of agents, some of whom hire labours, some of whom sell labour, and some of whom work for themselves. The exploitation of labour emerges with the unequal ownership of capital, or the 'separation' of workers from the means of production. The existence of an industrial reserve army (here, the peasantry) who have access to an inferior technology to reproduce themselves explains the equilibration of the wage at a level below that which exhausts the product of labour in the capitalist sector. Moreover, exploitation may be an indicator of an injustice of capitalism. If it does not seem fair that a serf must work three days a week for the lord perhaps it is not fair either that a wage labourer must expend more labour than is embodied in the wage goods he receives. That verdict, however, is not obvious and requires further analysis. Although the story can be made complicated, these simple models demonstrate the main features of the Marxian theory of labour exploitation.

CLASS, EXPLOITATION AND WEALTH. Consider an economy of N agents, with n produced commodities and labour. The input–output matrix which specifies the linear technology is A, and the row vector of direct labour inputs needed to operate the technology is L. Agent i has an initial endowment vector of goods w^i and one unit of labour power. For simplicity, assume subsistence preferences are as above: each agent wishes to earn enough income to purchase some fixed consumption vector b, and not run down the value of his initial endowment, valued at equilibrium prices. After working enough to earn that amount, he takes leisure. It is clear that each agent will only operate activities, at a given price vector, which generate the maximum rate of profit. Normalize prices by setting the wage at unity. For all activities to operate at equilibrium, the commodity price vector p must satisfy:

$$p = (1 + \pi)(pA + L). \tag{1}$$

Prices p obeying (1) generate a uniform and hence maximal rate of profit π for all activities. (The only activities we observe are the ones reported in A and hence without loss of generality, we may assume the profit rate must be equalized for all sectors of production, since agents only operate maximal profit rate activities.)

The vector of embodied labour values in commodities is Λ:

$$\Lambda = L(1 - A)^{-1}. \tag{2}$$

A worker, whose initial endowments are none except his labour power, must earn wages sufficient to purchase the subsistence vector b, which requires:

$$pb = 1. \tag{3}$$

From these three equations, it can be demonstrated (see Morishima, 1973; Roemer, 1981) that:

$$\pi > 0 \quad \text{if and only if} \quad \Lambda b < 1. \tag{4}$$

Equivalence (4) was coined by Morishima the 'fundamental Marxian theorem', as it shows that profits are positive precisely when labour is exploited (for the second inequality says that the labour embodied in the wage bundle is less than one unit of labour).

An agent in this model minimizes the labour he expends, subject to earning revenues sufficient to buying his consumption b, and to replace the finance capital he uses. Suppose, for simplicity, there is no borrowing and all production must be financed from initial wealth. In general, an agent will optimize by hiring some labour, selling some of his own labour, and/or working on his own capital stock. Let x^i be the vector of activity levels which agent i operates himself, financed with his wealth; let y^i be the vector of activity levels he hires others to operate, which he finances; let z^i be the amount of labour he sells to other operators. His problem is to choose vectors x^i, y^i and z^i to:

$$\min Lx^i + z^i$$

subject to

(i) $$pAx^i + pAy' \leqslant pw^i$$

(ii) $$p(1 - A)x^i + p(1 - A)y^i - Ly^i + z^i \geqslant z^i \geqslant pb.$$

The first constraint requires him to finance the activities operated out of his endowment, and the second requires that his revenues, net of wages paid and replacement costs, suffice to purchase the consumption bundle b. As well as the price vector satisfying (1), equilibrium requires that the markets for production inputs, consumption goods and labour must clear. It can be proved that at such a 'reproducible solution', society is divided into five classes of agents, characterized by their relation to the hiring or selling of labour, as follows. There is a class of *pure capitalists*, who only hire labour (y^i is non-zero, but x^i and z^i are zero vectors); there is a class of *mixed capitalists*, who hire labour and work for themselves as well ($y^i \neq 0 \neq x^i$, $z^i = 0$); there is a class of *petty bourgeoisie*, who only work for themselves, and neither hire nor sell labour ($x^i \neq 0$; $y^i = 0 = z^i$); there is a class of *mixed proletarians*, who work for themselves part-time, and also sell their labour power on the market ($x^i \neq 0 \neq z^i$, $y^i = 0$); and there are *prolterians*, who only sell their labour power ($z^i \neq 0$, $x^i = 0 = y^i$). It is clear, from consulting the agent's programme, that this last class comprises those agents who own nothing but their labour power. More generally, the *Class–Wealth Correspondence Theorem* states that the five classes named, in that order, list agents in descending order of wealth. This verifies an intuition of classical Marxism.

There is, as well, a relation of class to exploitation. The *Class–Exploitation Correspondence Principle* states that the agents who hire labour are exploiters and the agents who sell labour are exploited. The exploitation status of agents in the petty bourgeoisie is ambiguous. Exploitation is defined as before: an agent is exploited if he expends more labour than is embodied in the vector b, and he is an exploiter if he expends less labour than that. It is important to note that this relationship of class to exploitation is a theorem of the model, not a postulate. Both the class and exploitation status of an agent emerge in the model as a consequence of optimizing behaviour, determined by the initial distribution of endowments, technology and preferences. These aspects of agents which in classical Marxism were taken as given (their class and exploitation status) are here proved to emerge as part of the description of agents in equilibrium, from initial given data of a more fundamental sort (endowments, etc.). For this reason, the model described provides microfoundations for classical Marxian descriptions. Generalizations and discussion of the model are pursued in Roemer (1982, 1985a). See Wright (1985) and Bardhan (1984, ch. 13) for empirical applications. For a general evaluation of the Marxian theory of exploitation and class, see Elster (1985, ch. 2, 4 and 5).

From the viewpoint of modern capitalism, many criticisms can be levelled against these stories. Foremost among them, perhaps, is the assumption of subsistence preferences. What happens if agents have more general preferences of income and leisure? The Class–Exploitation Correspondence Principle continues to hold, but the correspondence between class and wealth may fail. It fails, however, only for preference orderings which are unusual: the Class–Wealth Correspondence is true if the elasticity of labour supplied by the population, viewed cross-sectionally with respect to its wealth, is less than or equal to unity. There can, therefore, be no general claim that exploitation corresponds to wealth, in the classical way – that the poor are exploited by the rich. Whether the exploitation–wealth correspondence holds depends on the labour supply behaviour of agents as their wealth changes.

EXPLOITATION AS A STATISTIC. Note that the fundamental conclusions of classical Marxian value analysis – the association of exploitation with class, in a certain way, and the association of exploitation with profits and accumulation – hold even when equilibrium prices are not proportional to labour values. For the prices of equation (1) are not, except in a singular case, proportional to the labour values of equation (2). Therefore, the usefulness of exploitation theory need not rest upon the false labour theory of value. It is for this reason that the transformation problem, for so long a central concern in Marxian economics, is unimportant.

That usefulness, instead, depends on how good a statistic exploitation is for the phenomena it purports to represent. Does the exploitation of labour explain accumulation? The 'fundamental Marxian theorem' would seem to say so. But, in fact, it can be shown that in an economy capable of producing a surplus, every commodity can be viewed as exploited, not just labour power. If corn is chosen as the value numeraire, then the amount of corn value embodied in a unit of corn is less than one unit of corn, so long as profits are positive. Thus labour power is not unique, as Marx thought, in regard to its potential for being exploited, and it is a false inference that the exploitation of labour 'explains' profits any more than the exploitation of corn or steel or land does. (For versions of this 'generalized commodity exploitation theorem', see Vegara (1979), Bowles and Gintis (1981), Samuelson (1982) and Roemer (1982).)

Is exploitation a good statistic for the injustice of capitalist appropriation of the surplus? Only if the initial distribution of endowments, which gives rise to such appropriation, is unjust. Marx claimed this was so, by arguing that initial capitalist property was established by plunder and enclosure (*Capital*, Volume 1, Part 8). But suppose there were a clean capitalism, in which initial inequalities in the ownership of capital were generated by differential hard work, skills, risk-taking postures and perhaps luck of the agents. Would the ensuing class structure, exploitation and differential wealth indicate an injustice, or would it reflect the consequences of persons exercising traits which are rightfully theirs, and from which they deserve differentially to benefit? These topics are pursued in Cohen (1979) and Roemer (1985b).

In sum, the Marxian theory of exploitation is liberated from the labour theory of value. The link between class and exploitation is robust; but Marx's claim that the exploitation of labour is the unique explanans of accumulation is false. If one's class, defined above as one's relation to hiring or selling of labour, is important sociologically in determining behaviour (such as collective action against another class) and preferences, then the positive theory of class determination described is of use. Exploitation remains a statistic, of some value, for the inequality in the distribution of productive assets. But in this role, exploitation may not correspond to wealth as in the classical story: if the labour supplied by agents responds with excessive enthusiasm to increases in their wealth, then the rich can be 'exploited' by the poor. The ethical conclusion from an observation of exploitation is in this case unclear.

Even aside from this peculiar case, exploitation is a circuitous proxy for differential wealth in productive assets, and one's normative evaluation of exploitation depends on one's view of the process that generates that inequality. If agents are the rightful owners of their alienable means of production, because they accumulated them through the exercise of their rightfully owned talents and preferences then exploitation does not represent unjust expropriation. If agents are not entitled to own alienable productive assets, either because they have no right to their talents and preferences (whose distribution is morally arbitrary), or because they came to possess those assets in some other unjustifiable way, then exploitation represents an expropriation. Inheritance, for example, might be an unjust way of acquiring assets which were originally acquired in an untainted manner. The essential question which lies behind the theory of exploitation concerns the fairness of a system of property allowing private ownership of alienable productive assets. The concept of exploitation based on the calculation of surplus labour accounts is, in this writer's view, a circuitous route towards the discussion of that central issue.

Ethical views concerning what kinds of asset may justifiably be privately appropriated change through history. Property in other persons, as in slavery, or more limited rights over the powers of other persons, as in feudalism, are no longer viewed as legitimate. The Marxian theory of exploitation is associated with a call for the abolition of private property in the productive assets external to persons. (Marx himself did not explicitly base his call for the abolition of such property on grounds of fairness, but on grounds of efficiency, despite the clear ethical tone of his attacks on capitalism. For an evaluation of the debate surrounding this question, see Geras (1985).) The cogency of that call must be established independently of the theory of exploitation.

BIBLIOGRAPHY

Bardhan, P. 1984. *Land, Labor and Rural Poverty: Essays in Development Economics*. New York: Columbia University Press.

Bowles, S. and Gintis, H. 1981. Structure and practice in the labor theory of value. *Review of Radical Political Economics* 12(4), 1–26.

Cohen, G.A. 1979. The labor theory of value and the concept of exploitation. *Philosophy and Public Affairs* 8(4), Summer, 338–40.

Elster, J. 1985. *Making Sense of Marx*. Cambridge and New York: Cambridge University Press.

Geras, N. 1985. The controversy about Marx and justice. *New Left Review* No. 150, March–April, 47–85.

Marx, K. 1867. *Capital: A Critique of Political Economy* Vol. 1. London: Lawrence and Wishart, 1977.

Morishima, M. 1973. *Marx's Economics*. Cambridge and New York: Cambridge University Press.

Roemer, J.E. 1981. *Analytical Foundations of Marxian Economic Theory*. Cambridge: Cambridge University Press.

Roemer, J.E. 1982. *A General Theory of Exploitation and Class*. Cambridge, Mass.: Harvard University Press.

Roemer, J.E. 1985a. *Value, Exploitation, and Class*. London: Harwood Academic Publishers.

Roemer, J.E. 1985b. Should Marxists be interested in exploitation? *Philosophy and Public Affairs* 14(1), Winter, 30–65.

Samuelson, P. 1982. The normative and positivistic inferiority of Marx's values paradigm. *Southern Economic Journal* 49(1), July, 11–18.

Vegara, J.M. 1979. *Economia politica y modelos multisectoriales*. Madrid: Editorial Tecnos.

Wright, E.O. 1985. *Classes*. London: New Left Books. Distributed in U.S.A. by Schocken Books.

Marxism

ANDREW ARATO

The term 'Marxism' is much overused today: the category is deemed applicable by all sides of political divides unable to agree on anything else. No taxonomic sense, however, can be given to the conceptual chaos behind the wide variety of identifications. Only the historical reasons can be explored in the present context. Here *Marxism* will signify a *tradition* combining two related, originally 19th-century, intellectual complexes: (1) a particular, philosophically materialist, comprehensive world view seeking to give a unified, this-worldly explanation to all dimensions of human existence and (2) a 'theory of movement' (R. Koselleck, 1989) oriented to the struggles of the industrial working class designed to accelerate historical time, to help bring a (logically, normatively or historically) necessary future closer to the present by 'linking theory and practice'. Both of these complexes are derived from the philosophy of history (or one of the philosophies of history) of Karl Marx, but the founder had little interest in working out a general *Weltanschauung*. In this respect Friedrich Engels was, in works such as *Herr Eugen Dühring's Revolution in Science* and the posthumous *Dialectics of Nature*, the founder of Marxism. Those who look back to the original work of Marx as against the tradition founded by Engels should be identified by the adjective '*Marxian*', as in Marxian philosophy, economics, social theory or anthropology, etc. Nevertheless Marx's relation to Marxism is too complex to allow a neat division between the two. As Lukács first demonstrated in 1923, Engels's interpretation of Marx's oeuvre in the sense of a generalized worldview and a unified science missed the actual philosophical depth of the latter's theory of history, social theory and critique of political economy. The cost was the elimination, misunderstanding or de-emphasis of fundamental concepts like alienation, reification, fetishism, praxis, subject, etc. Nevertheless, the great power and influence of Engels's synthesis came from Marx's own marriage of science and philosophy of history, bringing together the intellectual prestige of enlightenment with the motivating power of the concepts of romanticism. In another respect as well, Marx, despite having supposedly declared that he was not a 'Marxist', contributed to the foundations of Marxism. He *did* interpret his own thought in all of its phases as providing a theory of movement based on a philosophy of history whose major concepts included (typically) historical stage, transition, revolution and progress. The specific content of this theory was meant to be both an interpretation of *the meaning* of the movement of the industrial working class, and contribution to its enlightenment. No doubt, Marx understood scientific commun*ism* or social*ism* not only as the diagnosis of the crisis of this time, but also as its resolution in anticipation and acceleration of a desired future. This future was conceived in different ways in his various works, but always involved the abolition of differentiated economic and political institutions and the creation of conscious, planned, collective control over economic life as well as direct, democratic participation in all 'political' processes. It is important to note on the one hand that Marx's views of the transition to such a condition were heterogeneous and at different times involved authoritarian étatistic forms (*Communist Manifesto*), the direct democratic (*Civil Wars in France*) and even parliamentary democratic forms (various addresses, and possibly *Class Struggles in France* as well as *The 18th Brumaire of Louis Bonaparte*). Common to all these forms on the other hand was the postulate of the abolition of the division of state and civil society, i.e. an independent civil society with its mediating institutions. The plurality of forms of transition worked out by Marx points to the different politics of later Marxisms, the underlying hostility between civil society and the state strengthening the logic of all the politically significant varieties.

The historical influence of Marxism had been nothing short of spectacular. Until World War II and in some countries until the 1970s, it was the dominant ideology of the various European continental labour movements in Social Democratic, Communist, Socialist and Euro-Communist forms. The theoretical works oriented to these movements were often of the highest quality; it is enough to mention only the best works of Kautsky, Bernstein, Hilferding, Luxemburg, the Austro-Marxists, Lukács, Gramsci and countless others. Secondly, from 1905 or so to as late as the 1970s, another version of Marxism eclipsed even nationalism as the dominant revolutionary ideology of 'underdeveloped' or 'peripheric' agrarian societies. Again significant intellectual output accompanied this process, from Lenin, Parvus, Trotsky and Bukharin to Mao, Guevera and Cabral. Finally, from 1917 but more globally from 1945, an increasing number of regimes have used a version of Marxism as their 'science of legitimation', their official state cult. While the early phases of this process even here involved serious intellectual work – for example, the 1920s soviet debates about economic development (Preobrazhensky, Bukharin and others) and the problems of law and politics (Pashukanis, Stukha, et al.) – from the 1930s Marxism in power always meant tremendous simplification and even falsification of the doctrines of classical Marxism (not to speak of Marxian theory). However, this intellectual reduction was for a time amply compensated by the prestige of successful revolutions. Thus Communist movements outside the powers of Communist regimes continued to attract an astonishing number of philosophers, scientists, economists, historians, social theorists, legal scholars, writers, poets and plastic artists, even as their counterparts were suppressed in the Soviet Union, and later Eastern Europe and China.

Today one senses an ever deepening exhaustion of Marxism in all of the areas of its greatest historical influence. Among the mass parties and unions of European labour only an ever smaller minority remains or even calls itself Marxist. The official Marxisms of the established regimes are increasingly ritualized, the operating beliefs of the leaders and ideologists themselves have been shifting toward other doctrines: nationalism, authoritarian technocracy, pragmatism, great power politics, small nation *raison d'état*. Even among third world movements, the remaining area of dynamic influence, Marxism today has more powerful competitors than never before.

The idea of the 'crisis of Marxism' is almost as old as Marxism itself. There are, nevertheless, deep-seated reasons today why the epoch of Marxism as defined here (and not the rich and varied influence of the thinker Karl Marx) is over. As a world-view Marxism has certainly been shaken by the general secularization, decentralization, differentiation and pluralization of world-views that is for better or worse the hallmark of modernity. More importantly, as a theory of movement it was paradoxically the very successes of Marxism that have undermined it. It is this second aspect that is decisive, because it inhibits the often attempted transformation of Marxism in a direction no longer bound to a comprehensive, metaphysical worldview, i.e. toward a 'critical theory' or a 'philosophy of praxis' in the sense of the early theorists of Western Marxism: Lukács, Korsch, Gramsci, Horkheimer and Marcuse.

In most general terms then, politically failed attempts can be described as breaks with the tradition of Engels in order to build a new *Marxism* around the *Marxian* legacy itself. This implied in each case not only a return to the Hegelian foundations of Marx's thought, a revival of the key concepts of alienation, reification, consciousness of subjectivity, but also a primary emphasis on the theory of movement dimension and in particular the mediation of theory and praxis. The latter emphasis however depended on an intellectually adequate and politically favourable response on the part of those to be addressed by theory, an impossibility in the case of the actually successful regimes and movements. In the case of the Soviet regime it hardly mattered that the very first Western Marxists sought to give it a new philosophical justification. The abandonment of the metaphysical world-view of Marxism could not be contemplated first of all because Lenin in his *Materialism and Empiriocriticism* helped to canonize it. More fundamentally it was just such a world-view, along with the deterministic and closed structure it lent to the Marxian philosophy of history that allowed the ritualization of the doctrine as a new state cult. The anti-authoritarian biases of Western Marxism, formulated in a much repeated critique of bureaucracy, expressed well the incompatibility of Western and Soviet Marxism, whatever the particular political choices of individual Western Marxists. In the case of Social Democracy the problem was not so much the abandonment of the general world-view of Engels et al.; after all the Austro-Marxists and other Kantian

267

socialists were able to do this *within* the existing organizational frameworks. The renewed stress on a theory of movement emphasizing revolutionary rupture and future orientation was understood by Social Democrats (except the Austro-Marxists) as expressing the spirit of the rival Bolshevism, with which some of the founders of the Western Marxism at least were associated. Again more fundamentally the clash was between present and future orientation, bureaucratic organization and movement, (welfare) statism and anti-statism.

In world-historical terms Marxism represented a set of ideological and political responses to the epoch of classical capitalism, to the first stage of K. Polanyi's 'Great Transformation' (1949): the self-regulating market. Both of the two major types of outcomes with which 'successful' Marxist movements had an 'elective affinity' were powerfully state strengthening: the emergence of étatist forms of modernization-industrialization where private capital could not or could no longer promote economic development (A. Gerschenkron) and the construction of democratic, interventionist, welfare states in already developed capitalist countries where the 'normal' operation of the self-regulating market produced disastrous consequences not only for the substratum of human life but also for the market economy itself (K. Polanyi). In both cases versions of Marxism were dynamic and influential as ideologies of the process ('revolution' and 'reform') and were made gradually irrelevant by the results. The issue was not only that Soviet-type societies and democratic welfare states are not the Marxist 'utopia' or even the 'transitional society'. More damaging was the fact that the Marxian philosophy of history in any of its original versions had no place for a new, industrial form of domination; neither capitalism or socialism, or even a hybrid of the two, while the Marxian critique of political economy had no concepts to deal with the 'primacy of the political' and tended to exclude the possibility of a reconstructed, capitalist society involving a good deal of state interventionism and redistributive activity built upon the institutionalization and integration of the working class and class-based conflict.

Neither the formidable attempts of Trotsky (*Revolution Betrayed*, etc.) and of historians to depict the Soviet Union as a deformed workers' state, nor bureaucratic collectivism or state capitalism, nor the various theories of state-organized monopoly or state monopoly capitalism could successfully address the new contexts. The reason was of course that all these attempts involved a desperate desire to stay within the historico-philosophical framework of Marxism that was deeply enmeshed within the ideological counter-attack of the modern state, or more properly of state-strengthening elites, against the apparently more powerful (under classical capitalism) institutional complex of the modern economy. For this reason above all Marxism has found it hard to remain or to become a critical theory where a version of the modern bureaucratic state became the centre of societal steering and control (Soviet-type societies) or even where modern state and capitalist economy shared steering and control functions in historically unprecedented combinations (welfare states).

The failure of Marxism in the face of the modern state has been manifested most openly in the context of the emergence of new types of social movements.

The problem was not simply that these movements have now been forced to oppose the state (something hardly unprecedented) but, rather the very goals were now reconceived as ·'society strengthening'. As a result of important historical learning experiences, victory was no longer seen in terms of inclusion in state power ('Reform') or even as smashing the state ('Revolution') but, in the case of the most advanced segments of movements, as rebuilding civil society and controlling (rather than abolishing) market economy and bureaucratic state. Unlike the Social Democracy the state was found not to be a neutral force that could be simply occupied and used by different classes. But as against Bolshevism and even the older Western Marxism (both more orthodox here than Social Democracy) the programme of smashing the state and the utopia of the withering away of the state were now implicitly recognized as powerfully étatistic. If the modern state does not simply express the power of a class in society but of an independent structure, then, contrary to the claim of Engels in *Anti-Dühring*, the project of the withering away of the state by way of the abolition of classes and the nationalization of the means of production cannot be successful. On the contrary the very attempt presupposes enormous concentration of state power feeding on the continued social division which it itself constitutes. The actual experience of Marxist revolutionary states (as all previous revolutions according to the judgement of Marx in *The 18th Brumaire*) was a dramatic confirmation of this process, the results representing the most serious challenge to all who seek to defend Marxism in the face of the projects of the new movements.

Of course we cannot yet speak of the actual death of Marxism. In Soviet-type societies as well as in various third world adaptations of this model, Marxism–Leninism still exists as the official state doctrine and cult. However, in a period of the crisis of this model and the failure (winter 1968) of bloc-wide reform strategies, the rational elements of any Marxism (e.g. the project and the expectation of dysfunction and crisis free incremental economic development) had to be eliminated. The result is a ritualized, de-intellectualized doctrine increasingly cynically held. This affects Third World contexts, where under Western hegemony and/or right-wing authoritarian domination something like earlier revolutionary versions of the Leninism are still upheld. Here the future orientation of Marxian theory is increasingly determined by the actual outcome of the Soviet model which is known and which is decreasingly attractive as against a utopia drawn from Western sources, presupposing Western tradition, one that was nowhere realized. Third World Marxism increasingly reduces to a merely present orientation that involves primarily the assumption of a specific position in world conflicts, or (less attractively) to a conscious preparation for future power positions of the Soviet type. Since the mid-1970s neither of these orientations seems to be able to match more dynamic and radical ideologies where these are available, in particular national self determination and religious fundamentalism. Paradoxically, Marxism in the Third World is at its most influential where it is allied with the cultural and political forces of its old enemies: nationalism and radical Catholicism.

The intellectually most significant attempts to renew Marxism in our time (mid-1950s and after) occurred in its historical homeland: Western and Central Europe. The goals of all the relevant trends were to work out critical theories of Soviet type and/or advanced capitalist socialist societies, for the orientation of new types of opposition. What is common among all of them was the attempt, once again, to break with Marxism as a general, metaphysical world-view, while the dimension of a theory of movement was held on to and built upon. Three (and a possible fourth) stages or types can be distinguished in this whole development – each with a relatively different relationship to actual movements.

(1) *Revisionism* was the first of those, primarily of East Central European origins, but radiating to the communist parties of the West as well as the Soviet Union. Revisionism involved the recovery of the democratic socialist stress of turn of the century revisionism (E. Bernstein et al.), and the corresponding abandonment of Marxian doctrines deemed especially anti-democratic, e.g. the dictatorship of the proletariat. The political high point of revisionism was the preparation of 1956 in Poland and Hungary. The intellectual foundations of revisionism were, however, rather shallow and eclectic; on the one hand non-objectionable features and even the style of Marxism–Leninism were adhered to (at times for pragmatic reasons) and on the other there were attempts to make the very same set of doctrines vehicles for 'socialist legality', industrial democracy, market socialism and at times party pluralism. Thus the failure of revisionism was not only political but also theoretical, and all subsequent attempts to renew Marxism involved far greater efforts at genuine theory building.

(2) The *Renaissance* of Marxism (Lukács) otherwise called the philosophy of praxis (partially overlapping with Revisionism) was of simultaneously Western European, East European and Yugoslav origins. Its return was not only to Marx's own philosophy and social theory, but also to its real predecessor: the Western Marxism of the 1920s and 1930s. However, unlike Western Marxism, the Renaissance of Marxism involved at least some attempts to apply Marxian theory to the critique of Soviet type societies. The Renaissance of Marxism, in spite of its common intellectual style was oriented to different political projects in East and West. In East Europe it became the ideology of the internal democratization of communist parties and of reform from above, culminating in the Czech events in 1968. In the West the relevant political streams were the New Left and in some countries movements of working class youth, culminating in the French 1968 uprisings as well as the Italian 'hot autumn' one year later. Almost all major trends in the Renaissance of Marxism, like their Western Marxism forerunners, were open to at least some elements of non-Marxist thought: Husserl and Heidegger, Freud and Weber, structural linguistics and anthropology, Keynes and the neo-Keynesians were of major influence. The classical intellectual products included the works of Polish, Yugoslav, Czech and Hungarian praxis philosophers, Modzelewski and Kuron's *Open Letter*, Sartre's *Critique*, the early *Socialisme ou Barbarie*, Baran and Sweezy's *Monopoly Capital*, Marcuse's *Soviet Marxism* and *One-Dimensional Man*, the revivals of the older critical theory in West Germany and the United States, of Gramsci in Italy and finally a good deal of Marx scholarship in France and West Germany. The

purely intellectual achievements of the Renaissance of Marxism were significant; to it we owe the present availability of all dimensions of the ouevre of Marx. Politically, however, the Renaissance of Marxism was doomed when established regimes turned away from internal reform in the East, and when the New Left dissipated or proceeded to imitate authoritarian Marxisms imported from the Third World.

The last two stages of the attempted renewal of Marxism, its *Reconstruction* (3) and *Transcendence* (4), are to be located first of all in the changed contexts of movements: the new social movements of the West and the democratic opposition of the East. Each of the two types of attempts is to be found in both world contexts, but the *Reconstruction* of Marxism has its centre in the West while the *Transcendence* of Marxism is primarily Eastern, even if there has been very strong French participants. Interestingly enough the movements addressed by both trends are those that reflectively incorporate and criticize the experience of the étatist response to the capitalist economy – thus in a sense they are all 'post-Marxists'. Nevertheless, both the Reconstruction and Transcendence of Marxism seek to address post-Marxist movements in ways residually continuous with the tradition. In the case of the first, associated primarily with younger members of the Frankfurt School (Habermas, Offe, Wellmer et al.) the aim was (at least until the mid-1970s) to serve the normative project of human emancipation inherited from Marx and Western Marxism with entirely new theoretical instruments: linguistic philosophy, hermeneutics, systems theory, symbolic interactionism, structural functionalism, social scientific conflict theory, developmental psychology, etc. The Marxian critique of political economy preserved a certain model character for this trend, but only for a non-economistic crisis theory. In the early 1980s it has become clear that the new movements of ecology, feminism, youth and peace (rather than some intellectual new class as some have charged) were the projected addresses of this theoretical strategy.

The Transcendence of Marxism, anticipated by Merleau-Ponty's *Adventures of the Dialectic*, is represented by thinkers such as Castoriadis, Lefort, Touraine and Gorz in France, and above all a whole series of East European writers, publicists and philosophers like Kolakowski, Juron, Michnik, Kis, Bence and Vajda. In the United States this position is represented by *Telos*, a journal of radical social thought. The figures of this intellectual topos are not simply non-Marxists or anti-Marxists: they declare their rejection of both dimensions of Marxism as defined here (and especially their foundation: Marx's philosophy of history) while continuing to rely on some key categories of the tradition (theory and practice, state and civil society). This preservation, however, involves some characteristic twists: in particular the normative project of the radical democratic unification of state and society is rejected in the name of an independent civil society and its mediating institutions.

The specific achievement of the Transcendence of Marxism, and of the East European opposition addressed by it, is the thematization of a self-limiting radical democracy seeking to rebuild or democratize independent societal institutions, seeking to control rather than to absorb modern state and economy. Such a model also seems to correspond to the project of the non-fundamentalist wings of new social movements in the West (the French CFDT and second left, the *Realpolitiker* fraction of the German Greens, etc.) even if the great rhetorical presence of fundamentalists tends to occlude this fact. Furthermore, the project corresponds also to the programmes of present day democratizing movements under Latin American dictatorships: in particular in Argentina, Brazil and Chile. The increasing universality of self-limiting radical democracy or the democratization of civil society has had, since the mid-1970s, an apparently decisive effect even on the theorists of the Reconstruction of Marxism, in particular the work of Habermas in the 1980s.

On the other side of the achievement of the Reconstruction of Marxism has been above all the creation of a social theory that has surpassed the best in the Marxism tradition in complexity, scope and self-reflection. Unfortunately we cannot yet speak of the post-Marxist generation either equalling or fully appropriating this social theory. Thus a synthesis of the normative concerns of the transcendence of Marxism with the analytical power of the works of the Reconstruction of Marxism has occurred more in the West than the East, more in Germany than in France. At the same time the politically most advanced expression of such a synthesis took place in the East, in the Polish democratic movement, and was better understood in France than in Germany. Thus it is the paradox of the present situation of even the illegitimate offsprings of Marxism (reminiscent of one described by Marx in 1843) that there is a geopolitical disjuncture between the most advanced version of theory and the most self reflective form of political action. It is too early to tell if theory and praxis can be brought closer together and if any version of Marxism can serve as a bridge between them. The archaeological link between all versions of Marxism and the strengthening of the state speaks against such a possibility in the epoch of the offensive of different models of civil society against the state. The popular understandings of Marxism cannot be easily liberated from previous experience. It may also be the case that the incorporation of the critique of the state in any reconstructed Marxism is destined to burst all conceivable forms that would guarantee even a tenuous continuity with the tradition.

BIBLIOGRAPHY

Arato, A. and Breines, P. 1979. *The Young Lukacs and the Origins of Western Marxism.* New York: Continuum Press.

Bottomore, G.T. et al. 1983. *A Dictionary of Marxist Thought.* Oxford: Basil Blackwell; Cambridge, Mass.: Harvard University Press.

Cohen, J.L. 1982. *Class and Civil Society. The Limits of Marxism Critical Theory.* Amherst: University of Massachusetts Press.

Habermas, J. 1976. *Communication and the Evolution of Society.* Boston: Beacon Press.

Kolakowski, L. 1978. *Main Currents of Marxism*. 3 vols, Oxford and New York: Oxford University Press.
Koselleck, R. 1985. *Past Futures. On the Semantics of Historical Time*. Cambridge, Mass.: MIT Press.
Piccone, P. 1983. *Italian Marxism*. Berkeley: University of California Press.
Polanyi, K. 1944. *The Great Transformation*. New York: Rinehart.

Marxist Economics

ANDREW GLYN

By Marxist economics we mean the work of those later economists who based their methodology and approach on the work of Karl Marx. Excluded from discussion here is the enormous body of exegetical literature seeking to amplify the genesis of and development of Marx's own thinking (Rosdolsky, 1968). Before discussing three areas where the contribution of Marxists has been most striking and important, it is helpful to bear in mind certain features of their approach which could be said to separate them off from other traditions in economic theory.

Marxist economists view the capitalist system as essentially *contradictory*, in the sense that its malfunctions derive in an essential way from its structure, rather than representing 'imperfection' in an otherwise harmonious mechanism. At the heart of this structure is the relationship between capital and labour, which is necessarily an exploitative one. The conflict which results has a crucial influence on the way the capitalist system develops in every respect, from the form of technologies developed to the pattern of state policies adopted. Capital accumulation, the motor of the system, cannot therefore be analysed simply in quantitative terms: the structural changes in the economy which it brings are influenced by, and in turn help to shape, relations between the classes. So while the underlying logic of capitalism has remained unchanged, its history can be divided into different periods characterized by particular sets of class relations, technologies, state policies and international structures.

If some of these ideas would seem practically self-evident to economists with any interest in economic history, this underlines the powerful confirmation which the past century has provided for many of Marx's central ideas. It cannot, unfortunately, be said that mainstream economic theory has caught up with this, hiding, under ever more powerful formal techniques, an unchanging conceptual superficiality in its approach.

The body of Marxist economics which underpins the approach of Marxist economists to the analysis of particular phases and aspects of capitalist development may be divided into three main parts: (1) the labour process; (2)

value, profits and exploitation; (3) capital accumulation and crises. What follows represents a brief survey of debates around and developments of these aspects of Marx's work; it is necessarily narrowly 'economic' (excluding work on the theory of the state and of classes) and concentrates on theoretical debate rather than on historical application.

THE LABOUR PROCESS. Marx's most fundamental criticism of his Classical predecessors, and especially of Ricardo, was that they failed to analyse how the capitalist system emerged as a specific mode of production resulting from a particular historical process. The dispossession of previously independent producers led to a division of society into workers, with only their labour power to sell, and employers who owned and controlled the means of production. This ownership was the basis of the profit appropriated by the capitalists, for it gave them control over the process of production itself. It allowed the capitalist class as a whole to force the working class to work longer than was required to produce their means of subsistence. Marx paid special attention to this control over the labour process, analysing in great detail how the development of machinery qualitatively increased the depth of this control by literally taking the pace of work out of the hands of the workers. This stress on the process of production as a *labour* process is arguably the most important distinguishing feature of Marxist economics as compared to other schools, which analyse production solely in technical terms (Rowthorn, 1980, ch. 1).

It was not, however, until more than 100 years after the publication of volume 1 of *Capital* that his analysis of capitalist control over the labour process was applied to subsequent developments. Harry Braverman's *Labour and Monopoly Capital* (1972) had as its central theme the striving of employers to separate the conception of tasks from their execution, in order to preserve and enhance their control over the process of work. Frederick Taylor's system of Scientific Management, for example, analysed the operations required of skilled machine tool operatives so that 'scientific' timings could readily be allocated for new types of work. Ford's introduction of the assembly line was similarly intended to force a certain pace of work. Subsequent writers have extended this analysis to describe systems of 'bureaucratic' control exercised in large modern corporations, where effort is secured by payment systems allowing a steady progression of earnings for loyal employees (Edwards, 1979).

This more recent work is a revision, as well as an extension, of Marx's own analysis. In his conception of 'modern industry' control over the pace of work was exercised by the machine itself, which carried out the operations on the materials automatically, leaving the worker as a simple machine minder who fed the machine and dealt with minor malfunctions. This pattern, which Marx saw in contemporary developments in the textile industry, has not become the universal one. For in many types of production the worker still carries out operations on the materials. This has made it necessary for the employers to attempt to gain control over the speed of work by mechanical contrivance (the production line which obliges the worker to carry out tasks at a set speed) or organizational means (scientific management). Moreover, it has been more recently argued that 'Fordist' systems of mass production, where there is a minute division of labour, are giving way to more flexible systems where workers perform a greater range of tasks (Aglietta, 1979). This reflects the trend towards more sophisticated consumer goods, which demand shorter production runs and more model changes, and also the problems of overcoming the employee dissatisfaction with mindless and repetitive work which exploded in a number of countries at the end of the 1960s.

Marx's fundamental insight remains, however, the inspiration of this whole body of work, focusing on an issue of tremendous contemporary significance as employers struggle with the necessity of restructuring production in the fiercely competitive conditions of the 1980s (see as an example Willman and Winch, 1985). Only very recently has mainstream economics begun to address the problem of controlling work, and even here, as argued by Bowles (1985), from a less compelling perspective.

VALUE, PROFITS AND EXPLOITATION. Critics of Marx, from Böhm-Bawerk (1896) onwards, have always contended that his theory of profits and exploitation was fatally flawed by his reliance on a simplistic 'labour theory of value' – that commodities exchange in proportion to the amount of labour time required to produce them. If the price of a commodity was determined directly by this 'embodied labour', then the wage would directly measure the labour time required to produce the goods which workers bought in order to maintain themselves (the *value of labour power* in Marx's terminology). Profit, being the difference between the value added by the worker and the wage, would similarly measure directly the excess of time worked over the value of labour power, that is the surplus value produced by the worker while under the employer's control. At the level of society as a whole, total profits would be a direct measure of the surplus labour performed by the whole working class, that is the time worked beyond that necessary to reproduce the means of subsistence. Marx's *rate of exploitation*, the ratio of surplus value to the value of labour power, would be directly reflected in the ratio of profits to wages. Marx's insistence that the source of profit was the capitalist's ability to control the labour process, and thus force the working class to perform surplus labour, would receive a clear expression.

Marx himself was quite aware that the assumption he employed in *Capital*, Volume I, that commodities exchange at their values, that is, in proportion to the labour required to produce them, was a simplification designed to highlight the overall relation between capital and labour. In Volume III he explains that this assumption will only hold when the *organic composition of capital*, that is the ratio between the value of outlays on machinery and materials (*constant capital*) and on wages (the value of variable capital), is equal across industries. Where the organic composition differs across industries, then the surplus value produced by workers in a particular industry would represent a greater or lesser rate of profit on total capital employed depending on whether the organic composition was low or high. But exchange in proportion to labour time would inevitably mean that the capitalists within an industry received surplus value equal to that produced by their workers. This is because the commodities they received in exchange would be of equal value to those produced, thus leaving a surplus value for the capitalists, after setting aside what was required to pay for constant and variable capital, just equal to the surplus value their workers produced. Accordingly exchange in proportion to labour time would imply unequal profit rates across sectors, which is impossible under competitive conditions.

Marx's own solution was to propose that commodities exchange not at their values, but at their prices of production. These represented a modification or transformation of values in order to ensure equal rates of profit across sectors despite unequal organic compositions of capital. It was simple for him to show that such prices of production implied that industries with a high organic composition, and which therefore needed to appropriate more surplus value than its workers produced to compensate for the bigger outlays on constant capital, would have to have a higher than average ratio of price of production to value (and vice versa for low organic composition sectors). So Marx's solution to the transformation problem involved a simple redistribution of total surplus value away from labour intensive industries.

As von Bortkiewicz (1906) was the first to point out, Marx's solution to the transformation problem was incorrect. When constructing his prices of production Marx adds the average rate of profit applied to the values of the inputs. But if commodities do not sell at their values then capitalists are not purchasing their inputs at their values but at their prices of production. So correct prices of production have to be calculated on the basis of a simultaneous transformation of inputs *and* outputs from values to prices of production. Marx was actually aware that this further step was necessary but thought, not unreasonably, that it would make no important difference. Unfortunately he was wrong.

For the 'correct' solution to the transformation problem makes it impossible to maintain Marx's equality between such value aggregates as surplus value and the total value of output on the one hand, and their prices correlates, profits and total output in money prices. Much subsequent literature (see von Bortkiewicz (1906) and the later generalization by Seton (1957)) concentrated on describing the circumstances under which at least one of the 'invariances' between the price and value systems would hold. It can be argued, however, following the Uno school of Japanese Marxists (see Itoh, 1980), that this search for numerical equality between surplus value and profit is wholly misconceived, stemming from Marx's failure to maintain consistently his Volume I distinction between the *substance* of value (labour time) and its *form* (money prices). Any attempt to force numerical equality is artificial and thus misleading.

Even so this does not dispose of the 'problem'. For the correct, simultaneous solution also makes the rate of profit on capital employed different from Marx's general rate of profit, calculated as the ratio of surplus value to the value of capital employed (see von Bortkiewicz, 1906, and Steedman, 1977). What might

277

seem more damaging still is that the rate of exploitation in value terms is not in general equal to the ratio of profits to wages. So Marx's basic expression of the extent of capitalist domination does not find a direct reflection in the money aggregates.

This in fact does not damage Marx's theory at all. The ratio of profits to wages reflects the ratio of surplus product to the bundle of wage goods as manifested in the exchange process (aggregate wages must represent the price of production of all wage goods and aggregate profits the price of production of the surplus product). The rate of exploitation is the ratio of the work done to produce the two bundles. These two ratios will only be equal when the organic compositions in the sectors producing the wage goods and surplus products are equal. Clearly there is no theoretical necessity for this to hold, though empirical estimates by Woolf (1979) suggest that the deviation of relative prices from relative values for these bundles of commodities may be rather small.

This divergence between the form of exploitation (the ratio of profits to wages) and its real substance (the ratio of surplus value to the value of labour power) can be readily accepted. Using Sraffa's construction of a standard commodity to show what pattern of industries would ensure equality between the two ratios seems to add rather little (see Medio, 1972). Retreating to the rather grandly named Fundamental Marxian Theorem, that positive profits require positive surplus value (Morishima, 1973), also seems unnecessarily defensive in that it fails to explain clearly the relationship between the price and value dimensions. It is important to emphasize that this interpretation of the transformation problem does not establish the case *for* analysis in terms of values. It merely shows how the value categories can be reconciled with the surface phenomena of profits and prices.

Further controversy over the adequacy and usefulness of Marx's theory of value has revolved around two further issues. The whole 'transformation problem' assumed that the values of commodities can be unambiguously defined as the labour time socially necessary for the production of a commodity at prevalent degrees of mechanization, skill and intensity of work. But critics from Böhm-Bawerk onwards have disputed that difference types of labour can be 'reduced' to simple labour (see Rowthorn, 1980, ch. 6). It has further been argued (Steedman, 1977) that, in situations of joint production, labour values may not be determinable at all. If the output of shepherds is mutton and wool, how can their labour be allocated between the two products? If the employers used the wool and the shepherds ate the mutton it would not be possible to divide the shepherds' total working day into the necessary labour worked to produce the means of subsistence and the surplus labour worked for the employers. More generally, where there are different methods of joint production, the standard method of deriving labour values can lead to their being negative. Negative surplus value has been shown to coexist with positive profits (Steedman, 1977), though not uncontroversially (King, 1982).

These criticisms have at least made Marxists accept that there are real analytical difficulties in drawing up consistent value schema. The riposte of some (e.g.

Himmelweit and Mohun, 1981 drawing on the work of I.I. Rubin, 1928) that the whole project of deducing values prior to their reflection in market prices is a misguided 'neo-Ricardian' exercise has not found much favour. It seems to abandon any *quantitative* aspect to value theory, leaving simply a *qualitative* emphasis on understanding exchange as an exchange of labours (see Hilferding's reply in Böhm-Bawerk [1896]; Sweezy, 1942; Rubin, 1928).

The conceptual problems in formalizing value theory hardly differentiate it from other theoretical constructs. The most serious attack on it has come from those claiming that it is *redundant*, that it adds nothing to the conceptualization of equilibrium prices and profits based on physical quantities. This criticism goes back at least to Joan Robinson (1942), was formalized by Samuelson (1971) and re-emphasized by Steedman (1977). Following Sraffa (1960), it is argued that prices and profits can be derived directly from knowledge of the real wage and the requirements of labour and means of production required to produce commodities, and that values can only be derived from the same data. Thus it is said that it is unnecessary to go via values to reach profits (even assuming values can be unambiguously defined). This attack has confronted Marxists with the question – what precisely is it that values are designed to do?

The justifications for using labour as the central conceptual category, and thus analysing exchange and exploitation in terms of embodied labour time, have ranged from rather abstract statements of the fundamental role played by labour in Marx's whole theory of society (Shaikh, 1981), to the claim that working with values focuses the analysis on labour's part in production (Dobb, 1937). Sen (1978) points out that we naturally focus on the human contribution to production just as we focus on an artist's part in a sculpture. Indeed, critics of value theory never stop to question why they are perfectly happy to regard labour productivity as a vital concern (over time, across countries etc.) but object to the concept of value (which is just the inverse of labour productivity). Certainly for those who accept the central role of the economic surplus produced by the working class in the development of society, and the relations on the factory floor as the key to the production of this surplus, then analysis in terms of labour time is clear and simple. If we want a vivid and forceful way of analysing the relation between capital and labour then labour time seems the obvious category to use. After all what capitalists make workers do is *work*.

ACCUMULATION AND CRISES. Marx's *Capital* was aimed not only at uncovering the basis of capitalist exploitation but above all at revealing capitalism's 'laws of motion'. Marx argued that competition between capitalists was fought out by their investing in new, more efficient techniques of production and that the economies of scale which this brought acted as a pressure forcing individual capitalists to accumulate (a very different conception from the neoclassical idea of accumulation as trading off present for future consumption – see Marglin, 1984). The outcome of this process was the increased concentration of industry (termed centralization by Marx), which was further accelerated by the development of the credit system. Many Marxist writers, from Hilferding (1910) to post-war Marxists (Mandel, 1962) have documented this trend, with the conclusion being drawn on occasions that the extent of monopolization was actually destroying the pressure to accumulate (Baran and Sweezy, 1966). This seemed to be contradicted, however, by the great boom of the 1950s and 1960s in Europe and Japan, and the spread of international competition which it brought.

For Marx the impact of accumulation, both on the working class and on profits, was dominated by its presumed labour-saving form. Marx argued that higher productivity required an increased volume of constant capital per worker (what later economists have called the capital–labour ratio). While this is not necessarily the case, since new techniques may economize on constant capital, subsequent experience has entirely vindicated Marx's view. What has been more controversial are the implications of this for employment, wages and the rate of profit.

A rising mass of constant capital per worker implies that employment grows more slowly than the capital stock. But whether or not this leads to a rising or falling *reserve army of labour* depends on the strength of accumulation, the rate of which technical progress is labour saving and the growth of the labour force. In the advanced countries at least, the trend has indeed been for the capitalist sector to overcome pre-capitalist sectors like peasant agriculture, but for those 'set free' to be absorbed into wage labour. It is important here to distinguish the impact of the trend of accumulation on employment (at full utilization of capacity), from periods of 'cyclical' unemployment, which may be of extended duration of course, resulting from the under-utilization of capacity during crises. The mass unemployment of the 1970s and 1980s in Europe, for example, is obviously due mainly if not wholly to the crisis of accumulation (that is, the lack of it), rather than to the form accumulation has been taking.

Despite periodic bouts of unemployment there has been a tendency for real wages to grow in line with labour productivity in the advanced countries, that is, for the profit share to be roughly constant over time or even to decline. Despite measurement complications concerning the treatment of self-employment, this suggests that Marx's rate of exploitation has not shown the tendency to increase which he expected would be ensured by the reserve army of labour. Some authors (Gillman, 1957) have sought to verify a rising rate of exploitation by reference to Marx's concept of unproductive labour (supervisory staff, bank employees etc.). If these workers are regarded as being paid out of surplus value, rather than as constituting a cost of production which reduces surplus value, and if their relative importance in the labour force has been rising (which it has), then a rising rate of exploitation is consistent with a rising share of wages in national income. But to argue that the surplus value available to the capitalists for accumulation has declined because, given the growth of productivity of productive workers, there has been a growth in the proportion of unproductive workers, does not seem to add much to the simpler idea that the growth of productivity of all workers has been insufficiently fast relative to real wages.

The rising trend of real wages has raised the issue as to whether Marx's concept of the value of labour power, dependent on the time required to produce the 'necessaries' is still valid. The usual answer has been for Marxists to stress the 'moral and historical' element in the value of labour power as defined by Marx. Periods of strong demand for labour and the development of trade unions have allowed a widening of workers' 'needs', including the provision of more extensive state services. The difficulties that employers have found in cutting real wages, and governments in seriously eroding the welfare services despite the mass unemployment in the 1970s and 1980s, have added conviction to the idea that the current standard of living is, socially, *necessary* (Rowthorn, 1980, ch. 7).

Marx argued that the trends towards a rising organic composition would allow the rate of exploitation to be increased, but would nevertheless lead to a falling *rate* of profit on total capital employed as outlays on constant capital would grow. Despite the fact that Marx regarded this Law of the Tendency of the Rate of Profit to Fall as the 'most important law of political economy' it played only rather a background role in the classic works of Marxism (Luxemburg, 1913; Hilferding, 1910). With the revival of interest in Marxist economics in the late 1960s it received prominence in the works of writers such as Mandel (1975). The main controversy has surrounded whether or not there is a fundamental tendency for the value of constant capital per worker to rise as the Law requires. Marx himself recognized that this was the outcome of a two-sided process. The increased mass of constant capital per worker tended to drag the value of capital up. On the other hand the productivity growth which was part and parcel of the process tended to reduce the value of constant capital per worker. Whether the value of constant capital per worker rises or falls depends on whether productivity grows slower or faster than the increased mass of capital per worker. Marx himself gave no convincing reasons why productivity growth should be the slower of the two, and it has long been argued that there is no such reason (Robinson, 1942; Sweezy, 1942; van Parijs, 1980). Attempts to argue that in some sense the rise in the mass of constant capital per worker is more fundamental and that there is a Law of the Tendency of the Rate of Profit to Fall even if it was manifested in a upward trend in the profit rate (Fine and Harris, 1978) have not been found convincing. Marxists who have attempted to provide empirical evidence in support of the Law have typically confused the mass of constant capital with its value: the capital–output ratio, which is the price correlate of the value of capital per worker, has not shown an upward trend.

If this objection makes a falling profit trend contingent on the strength of productivity growth (an empirical matter), the second line of objection (originated by Okishio, 1961) argues in fact that the techniques willingly introduced by capitalists will never, in and of themselves, result in a lower profit rate for the capitalist class. It can be shown that new techniques which raise the profit rate for the innovating capitalist will also imply, contrary to Marx's belief, a cost saving and thus a higher profit rate for the capitalist class. For the average profit rate to fall with the introduction of new techniques, therefore, there must have been, in addition, some increase in real wages. All this is not to say that the value of constant capital may not rise in some periods, and that it may not be associtated with a falling profit rate (both were true of many countries in the early 1970's), but only that there must also be rising wages (as was also the case). It has been argued by Shaikh (1978) that oligopolists might not maximize the profit rate; but even if this were so it could not establish any necessity for the profit rate to fall.

Discussion of the Law of the Tendency of the Rate of Profit to Fall has emphasized the importance of the course of real wages for the development of capitalism. The two main schools of Marxist crisis theory have indeed placed real wages at the centre, but in very different ways. Underconsumptionist theorists (Luxemburg in the classic period, Sweezy amongst later writers) have argued that insufficient growth in real wages depresses the incentive to invest by restricting the market for consumer goods. As Tugan-Baranovsky (summarized by Sweezy, 1942) pointed out with the help of Marx's reproduction schemes, it is not possible to prove the *necessity* of a crisis of underconsumption from a rising rate of surplus value. As Marx explained, whether or not surplus value was realized depends entirely on capitalists' spending decisions (on investment and consumption). The capitalists could realize a growing share of surplus value provided they were prepared to invest more and more in the capital goods sector (Dept I), even though this investment was destined just to produce more capital goods (Bukharin, 1924). So crises of underconsumption, which would arise when capitalists failed to increase their investment in line with the potential surplus value, rely on the behavioural assumption that capitalists will actually not keep up their investment spending. The most influential postwar analysis along these lines, Baran and Sweezy's *Monopoly Capital* (1966, which acknowledges its theoretical debt to Steindl, 1952), saw the growing monopolization of US capitalism enhancing the tendency for the share of surplus value to rise, while at the same time relaxing the pressure to invest.

It was something of an irony that just at the time that *Monopoly Capital* was written, Europe and Japan were enjoying a phenomenal boom. Many Marxist economists in these countries favoured an overaccumulation theory of crisis (Glyn and Sutcliffe, 1972; Rowthorn, 1980, chs 4–6; Itoh, 1980). The strength of the boom eroded the reserve army of labour and caused tight labour markets, rising wages and thus falling profits, inflation and a recession (Armstrong, Glyn and Harrison, 1984). Also emphasized by these theories has been the role of stronger trade unions in pressing for higher state welfare spending and the difficulties that full employment brought for employers attempting to reorganize production to increase productivity (Bowles, Gordon and Weisskopf, 1983).

Why these difficulties should lead to a crisis, rather than simply slower growth, again depends on the central question of capitalists' investment behaviour. Precisely why and when a fall in profits leads to a precipitate decline in investment is notoriously difficult to model. Japanese Marxists (Itoh, 1980) have made an important contribution by emphasizing the importance of the credit system in both prolonging a boom and initiating a collapse. Kalecki, who immortalized Marx's insight in the dictum 'workers spend what they get, capitalists get what they spend', wrote near the end of his life that the determination of investment 'remains the great *pièce de résistance* of economics' (1971, p. 165).

The recuperative role of crises in restoring the conditions for renewed accumulation has always been stressed by Marxists. It is more plausible in the case of crises due to overaccumulation (where the problem is rising wages) than for underconsumption crises (where wages have been rising too slowly). Indeed, Keynesian policies of demand expansion seem designed to meet the latter, and political difficulties have to put forward at blocking such an obvious solution (Baran and Sweezy, 1966). In crises of overaccumulation Keynesian policies are more likely to be used in reverse, in order to speed up the impact of unemployment in reducing labour's bargaining position over wages and productivity. Some French Marxists, known as the 'Regulation School' have recently emphasized the necessity for the whole pattern of institutions, state policies, technologies etc. to be reformed if a major structural crisis is to be overcome (Aglietta, 1979; Boyer, 1979; de Vroey, 1984). Whether the microchip, decentralization of production, internationalization of production and capital markets, Japanese-style industrial relations, more freedom for market forces and so forth provide a new 'way out' for capitalism in the 1990s is currently under intense discussion.

If this review of Marxist economics has concentrated on debates about, revisions to and extensions of Marx's own ideas it is to emphasize that the days of Stalinist orthodoxy and dogmatic repetition of the texts are gone. Marxist economics is again making a forceful and imaginative contribution to the analysis of contemporary society.

BIBLIOGRAPHY

Aglietta, M. 1979. *A Theory of Capitalist Regulation.* London: New Left Books. Distributed in U.S.A. by Schocken Books.

Armstrong, P., Glyn, A. and Harrison, J. 1984. *Capitalism Since World War II.* London: Fontana.

Baran, P. and Sweezy, P. 1966. *Monopoly Capital.* New York: Monthly Review Press.

Böhm-Bawerk, [1896] 1948. *Karl Marx and the Close of his System.* Ed. P. Sweezy, New York: Kelly. (First published in German.)

Bortkiewicz, L. von. 1906. On the correction of Marx's fundamental theoretical construction in the third volume of Capital. In Böhm-Bawerk, 1948. (First published in German.)

Bowles, S. 1985. The production process in a competitive economy. *American Economic Review* 75(2), March, 16–36.

Bowles, S., Gordon, D. and Weisskopf, T. 1983. *Beyond the Wasteland.* New York: Anchor Press.

Boyer, M. 1979. Wage formation in historical perspective: the French experience. *Cambridge Journal of Economics* 3(2), June, 99–118.

Braverman, H. 1972. *Labor and Monopoly Capital.* New York: Monthly Review Press.

Bukharin, N. 1924. *Imperialism and the Accumulation of Capital.* Ed. K. Tarbuck, London: Allen Lane, 1972. (First published in German.); New York: Monthly Review Press.

Dobb, M. 1937. *Political Economy and Capitalism.* London: Routledge & Kegan Paul; New York: International Publishers, 1945.

Edwards, R. 1979. *Contested Terrain*. London: Heinemann.

Fine, B. and Harris, L. 1978. *Rereading Capital*. London: Macmillan.

Gillman, J. 1957. *The Falling Rate of Profit*. London: Dobson.

Glyn, A. and Sutcliffe, B. 1972. *British Capitalism, Workers and the Profit Squeeze*. Harmondsworth: Penguin.

Gough, I. 1979. *The Political Economy of the Welfare State*. London: Macmillan. Distributed in U.S.A. by Humanities Press.

Hilferding, R. 1910. *Finance Capital*. London: Routledge & Kegan Paul, 1981. (First published in German.)

Himmelweit, S. and Mohun, S. 1981. Real abstractions and anomalous assumptions. In I. Steedman et al., *The Value Controversy*, London: Verso.

Itoh, M. 1980. *Value and Crisis*. London: Pluto Press: New York: Monthly Review Press.

Kalecki, M. 1971. *Selected Essays on the Dynamics of the Capitalist Economies*. Cambridge and New York: Cambridge University Press.

King, J. 1982. Value and exploitation: some recent debates. In *Classical and Marxian Political Economy*, ed. I. Bradley and J. Howard, London: Macmillan; New York: St. Martin's Press.

Luxemburg, R. 1913. *The Accumulation of Capital*. London: Routledge & Kegan Paul, 1951; New Haven: Yale University Press. (First published in German.)

Mandel, E. 1962. *Marxist Economic Theory*. London: Merlin.

Mandel, E. 1975. *Late Capitalism*. London: New Left Books.

Marglin, S. 1984. *Growth, Distribution and Prices*. Cambridge, Mass.: Harvard University Press.

Medio, A. 1972. Profits and surplus value. In *A Critique of Economic Theory*, ed. E. Hunt and J. Schwartz, Harmondsworth: Penguin.

Morishima, M. 1973. *Marx's Economics*. Cambridge and New York: Cambridge University Press.

O'Connor, J. 1973. *The Fiscal Crisis of The State*. New York: St. Martin's Press.

Okishio, N. 1961. Technical change and the rate of profit. *Kobe University Economic Review* 7, 85–99.

Parijs, P. van. 1980. The falling-rate of profit theory of crisis. *Review of Radical Political Economics* 12(1), Spring, 1–16.

Robinson, J. 1942. *An Essay on Marxian Economics*. London: Macmillan; 2nd edn, New York: St. Martin's Press, 1966.

Rosdolsky, R. 1968. *The Making of Marx's Capital*. London: Pluto Press, 1977. (First published in German.)

Rowthorn, R. 1980. *Capitalism, Conflict and Inflation*. London: Lawrence & Wishart. Distributed in U.S.A. by Humanities Press.

Rubin, I. 1928. *Essays on Marx's Theory of Value*. Detroit: Black & Red, 1972. (First published in Russian.)

Samuelson, P. 1971. Understanding the Marxian notion of exploitation. *Journal of Economic Literature* 9, June, 399–431.

Sen, A. 1978. On the labour theory of value. *Cambridge Journal of Economics*, June, 175–180.

Seton, F. 1957. The transformation problem. *Review of Economic Studies* 24, June, 149–60.

Shaikh, A. 1978. Political economy and capitalism. *Cambridge Journal of Economics* 2(2), June, 232–51.

Shaikh, A. 1981. The poverty of algebra. In I. Steedman et al., *The Value Controversy*. London: Verso.

Sraffa, P. 1960. *Production of Commodities by Means of Commodities*. Cambridge: Cambridge University Press.

Steedman, I. 1977. *Marx After Sraffa*. London: New Left Books.

Steindl, J. 1952. *Maturity and Stagnation in American Capitalism*. Oxford: Blackwell.

Sweezy, P. 1942. *The Theory of Capitalist Development*. New York: Monthly Review Press.

Vroey, M. de. 1984. A regulation approach interpretation of the contemporary crisis. *Capital and Class* 23, Summer, 45–66.

Willman, P. and Winch, G. 1985. *Innovation and Management Control*. Cambridge: Cambridge University Press.

Woolf, E. 1979. The rate of surplus value, the organic composition of capital and the general rise of profit in the US economy 1947–67. *American Economic Review* 69(3), June, 329–41.

Ronald Lindley Meek

ANDREW SKINNER

Meek (1917–1978) was born in Wellington, New Zealand, where he received his early education at both school and university. He went to Cambridge in 1946 to take a PhD under the supervision of Piero Sraffa (1949). Meek was appointed to a Lectureship in Glasgow University in 1948, during A.L. Macfie's tenure of the Adam Smith Chair.

Meek was translated to the Tyler Chair of Economics in Leicester University in 1963, where he did much to develop the Department. But it is as a lecturer that Ronald Meek is and was remembered by all those fortunate enough to have been taught by him. An admirable expositor, always prepared to an extent which included circulation of abstracts of the text, Meek's physical presence, allied to a stylish delivery, were admirably suited to the didactic tradition, especially in its Scottish form.

The high regard in which he was held by colleagues in Leicester is tangibly expressed in a volume of essays, edited by I. Bradley and M. Howard, entitled *Classical and Marxian Political Economy* (1982). This volume, and the attached bibliography, give some idea of Meek's output and range of interest. He wrote, for example, a series of articles in the field of Soviet Studies in the 1950s. These were followed in the 1960s by nine, highly technical, contributions to the study of the electricity industry. Meek's grasp of technique in this field of study may explain his later interest in quantitative methods; an interest which resulted in *Figuring Out Society* (1971). His last work would have been a book on matrix algebra.

In the 1960s Meek also found time to celebrate a life-long passion and a favourite place, in publishing what he always claimed to be his best-seller, *Hill Walking in Arran* (1963, 2nd edn, 1972).

But it is as an historian of economic thought that Meek will best be remembered; remembered for his contribution to the understanding of the classical period before Marx as well as for his essays on Marxian economics. Meek's position as a Marxist also helps to explain his *Studies in the Labour*

Theory of Value (1956, 2nd edn, 1973) which owed 'its origin to a long correspondence which the author had in 1951 with Mrs. Robinson' regarding the validity of the labour theory of value (1956, p. 7). In this work, Meek sought to trace the historical development of the theory, before examining its restatement by Marx and its possible 're-application'.

Of the earlier writers, Meek's work on the French Oeconomists or Physiocrats is particularly noteworthy. The *Economics of Physiocracy* (1962) was followed by a variorum edition of Quesnay's *Tableau Oeconomique* (1972) and that in turn by translations of A.R.J. Turgot's historical essays (1973) which include the *Reflections on the Formation and Distribution of Riches*, written in 1766.

In translating these works, Ronald Meek did more than any other scholar to make them accessible to an English-speaking public. His extensive works of commentary also did more than any others to expose the purpose behind Quesnay's macroeconomic model of the 'circular flow' and threw a unique light on the still more sophisticated work of 'revisionists' such as Baudeau and Turgot – with the latter producing a model of a capital-using system with distinct factors of production and categories of return. It is access of this kind which permits the modern scholar to form some estimate of the impact which such work must have had on Adam Smith when he visited Paris in 1766; a time when the intellectual output of the School had arguably reached its zenith (1962, pp. 31–3).

Meek's interest in Marx is also reflected in his identification of the historical and sociological (in addition to the economic) dimension of the work done by Quesnay and Turgot. This aspect of Meek's commentary also reflects his identification of what he called a 'Scottish Contributin to Marxist Sociology' (1954; 1967). The argument gave prominence to the 'four stages' theory of socio-economic development as it appeared especially in the work of Adam Smith and John Millar. Meek worked on this theme for the twenty years which preceded the publication of his *Social Science and the Ignoble Savage* (1976); the most complete statement of his position. The anthropological dimension reflects the content of his first published work (1943).

Meek's interest in the field is important of itself, but also for his appreciation of Adam Smith. Without suggesting that it is '*too* misleading' to imply that Smith was the author of a 'liberal' position (1977, p. 3) he felt it more important to note that:

> Smith, like Marx, was a wholeman, who tried to combine a theory of history, a theory of ethics, and a theory of political economy into one great theoretical system.... There is no doubt that Marx can properly be said to be the heir of the basic ideas of the Scottish Historical School (1967, p. 50).

Such an appreciation of Smith helps to explain Meek's commitment to the planning of the Glasgow edition of the *Works and Correspondence*, following as it did on J.M. Lothian's discovery of new lecture notes in 1958. The same appreciation is evident in his meticulous preparation of the *Lectures on Jurisprudence* (Report dated 1762/63), for which he assumed the major responsibility.

Ronald Meek had a profound knowledge of Marx which informs and illuminates his works of commentary.

SELECTED WORKS

1943. *Maori Problems Today*. Wellington: Progressive Publishing House.

1956. *Studies in the Labour Theory of Value*. London: Lawrence & Wishart,2nd edn, 1973.

1962. *The Economics of Physiocracy*: *Essays and Translations*. London: Allen & Unwin. This volume contains an introduction to the work of the school, and in Part 2 five essays, the first four of which appear in amended form. They are: 'Problems of the Tableau Economique' (1960); 'The Physiocratic Concept of Profit' (1959); 'Physiocracy and the Early Theories of Under-Consumption' (1951); 'Physiocracy and Clasicism in Britain' (1951), and 'The Interpretation of Physiocracy' (1962).

1963. *Hill Walking in Arran*. Isle of Arran Tourist Association. 2nd edn, 1972.

1967. *Economics and Ideology and Other Essays*: *Studies in the Development of Economic Thought*, London: Chapman & Hall. This Volume contains 12 essays which appear in amended form. They are: 'The Rehabilitation of Sir James Steuart' (1958); 'Adam Smith and the Classical Concept of Profit' (1954); 'The Scottish Contribution to Marxist Sociology' (1954); 'The Decline of Ricardian Economics in England' (1950); 'Thomas Joplin and the Theory of Interest' (1950–51); 'Karl Marx's Economic Method' (1959); 'The Falling Rate of Profit' (1960); 'Marx's Doctrine of Increasing Misery' (1962); 'Some Notes on the Transformations Problem' (1956); 'Mr. Sraffa's Rehabilitation of Classical Economics' (1961); 'The Place of Keynes in the History of Economic Thought' (1950–51); 'Economics and Ideology' (1957).

1971. *Figuring Out Society*. London: Collins.

1972. (With M. Kuczynski.) *Quesnay's 'Tableau Economique'*. London: Macmillan.

1973. *Turgot on Progress, Sociology and Economics*. Cambridge: Cambridge University Press.

1976. *Social Science and the Ignoble Savage*. Cambridge and New York: Cambridge University Press.

1977. *Smith, Marx and After*: *Ten Essays in the Development of Economic Thought*. London: Chapman & Hall. This vol. includes: 'Smith and Marx' (1977); 'Smith, Turgot and the Four Stages Theory' (1971); 'The Development of Adam Smith's Ideas on the Division of Labour' (with A.S. Skinner, 1973); 'New Light on Adam Smith's Glasgow Lectures on Jurisprudence' (1976); 'A Plain Person's Guide to the Transformation Problem' (1977); 'From Values to Prices: Was Marx's Journal Really Necessary?' (1976); 'The Historical Transformation Problem' (1976); 'Value in the History of Economic Thought' (1974); 'Marginalism and Marxism' (1972); 'The Rise and Fall of the Concept of the Economic Machine' (An Inaugural Lecture, 1965).

1978. (With D.D. Raphael and P.G. Stein.) *Adam Smith*: *Lectures on Jurisprudence*. Oxford, Clarendon Press; Vol. V in the Glasgow edn of the *Works and Correspondence*.

A complete bibliography of R.L. Meek's writing will be found in *Classical and Marxian Political Economy*: *Essays in Honour of Ronald L. Meek*, ed. I. Bradley and M. Howard, London: Macmillan (1982), xi–xiv; New York: St. Martin's Press.

Mode of Production

R. JESSOP

This concept was first introduced by Karl Marx in his efforts to theorize the overall structure and dynamic of capitalism. It has since been widely used, mainly in Marxist political economy and historical studies, to analyse various economic systems. Although there is broad agreement on its general field of application, different approaches exist towards defining and distinguishing particular modes of production. Some of the resulting problems are considered below.

Marx used the concept of mode of production in two main ways; to analyse the economic base and to describe the overall structure of societies. Thus he employed it to specify the particular combination of *forces* and *relations* of production which distinguished one form of labour process and its corresponding form of economic exploitation from another. He also employed it to characterize the overall pattern of social reproduction arising from the relations between the economic base (comprising production, exchange, distribution and consumption) and the legal, political, social and ideological institutions of the so-called superstructure. The latter usage is particularly problematic. Its conceptual basis is fuzzy and it encourages monocausal economic analyses of whole societies. But even the more rigorously defined and carefully theorized analysis of production proper involves problems. For Marx concentrated on the *capitalist mode of production*, discussed it in relatively abstract terms, and considered pre-capitalist modes largely in terms of their differences from capitalism. Many of these ambiguities and lacunae survive today so that the meaning and scope of the concept are still contested.

MODE OF PRODUCTION DEFINED. Marx analysed modes of production in terms of the specific economic form in which the owners of the means of production extracted unpaid surplus labour from the direct producers. For him this form always corresponded to a definite stage of development of the methods of labour and their social productivity. He also described this economic form as 'the innermost secret, the hidden basis of the entire social structure' (*Capital*, III, ch.

47, sect. II). For it provides 'the real foundation on which rise legal and political superstructures and to which correspond definite forms of social consciousness' (1859, Preface). Orthodox Marxists have generally focused on three modes of production: ancient society based on the direct exploitation of slave labour, feudalism with its serf labour and appropriation through ground rent, and capitalism with its free wage-labour and appropriation through surplus-value (see below).

In general terms a mode of production can be defined as a specific combination of forces and relations of production so organized that it can sustain a distinctive mode of appropriating surplus labour. Forces of production include not only the means and objects of labour but also labour-power itself. They are never purely technical in character but are always shaped by the prevailing social relations of production. The latter can be divided analytically into relations *in* production and relations *of* production (cf. Burawoy, 1985). Relations *in* production comprise the working relations between classes within a productive entity, for example, between capital and labour in the factory; relations *of* production are grounded in the capacities to allocate resources to diverse productive activities and to appropriate surplus-labour in determinate forms. It is the combination of these forces and relations which defines the basic pattern of class relations and determines the overall pattern of production, distribution and consumption in its articulation with the appropriation of surplus.

For a distinct mode of production to exist, the forces and relations of production must complement each other so that together they sustain the economic basis of the relevant mode of appropriation. This does not mean that modes of production can somehow reproduce themselves autonomously. There are always extra-economic preconditions (such as law, the state, or specific systems of ideas) which must be secured for economic reproduction to exist. In turn, economic activity is an essential precondition of other activities and its form has its own effects thereon. This mutual presupposition and reciprocal causality have encouraged the extension of the 'mode of production' concept to societies as a whole. Where the forces and relations of production are not usually supportive and/or their essential extra-economic conditions are not secured, various situations can exist short of an economic collapse. Most studies have examined transitions from one mode of production to another. But is also possible that an *ad hoc*, contingent and temporary economic system could emerge combining elements from different modes of production.

SOME BASIC QUESTIONS. Almost all the basic questions involved in discussions of modes of production are grounded in the Marxian legacy. Can there be a general theory of modes of production or does each mode have to be examined in its own right? Does a general theory (or even the very concept of mode of production) commit one to an economic reductionist analysis of societies and their succession? How does capitalism differ from (a) pre-capitalist modes and (b) any future communist mode of production? How should one identify the nature and differences among pre-capitalist modes and, in particular, can one follow Marx in positing a distinctive Asiatic mode of production? Moreover, given that there are different modes of production and forms of labour, how are they to be articulated? How should one periodize the development of particular modes of production? Only some of these issues can be discussed here. Thus no reference will be made to the complex problems involved in defining the modes of production in actually existing or future socialist or communist societies. Likewise only indirect reference will be made to problems of periodization.

A GENERAL THEORY OF MODELS OF PRODUCTION? Orthodox Marxists have followed Marx in dividing economic development into different epochs and in establishing causal links between their economic bases and other social relations. Underpinning this approach there is often a philosophy of history which ascribes an inherent teleogical drive to the sequence of modes of production. This drive is generally attributed to the emergence of a contradiction between the productive forces and the extant relations of production. Whenever the latter hinder the further development of the productive forces, they are overturned through a revolutionary transition to a more progressive mode (cf. Cohen, 1978). In addition to its technological determinism, this approach also suffers from its assumption that only a few pre-capitalist modes existed.

An alternative approach to a general theory was attempted by French structuralists (notably Balibar) in the 1960s and 1970s. Balibar (1970) emphasized the determining role of the relations rather than forces of production and also tried to avoid teleology. He outlined three basic elements and two relations of production to be found in all modes of production and also introduced the concept of a 'transitional mode of production'. Alternative combinations of these constituent elements and relations generated different modes of production. Unfortunately this produced a simplistic and formal taxonomy. It reduced differences among modes to how their constituent elements are combined and thereby implied that the elements themselves are invariant. This ignored the changing social character of both the forces and relations of production. Moreover, whereas the concept of 'transitional' modes is inherently teleological, the idea that all other modes could always reproduce themselves left the problem of historical change unresolved. Thus neither historical materialist orthodoxy nor structuralist taxonomy suggests that a general theory of modes of production is worthwhile.

ARE MODES OF PRODUCTION PURELY ECONOMIC? This conclusion does not invalidate studies concerned with the structures, genealogies or dynamics of particular modes of production. It means only that these cannot be subsumed under a master theory which explains their specific forms, their succession and their laws of motion. Particular studies must, of course, define the mode of production under investigation.

There are three main approaches to this task. Firstly, a mode of production can be defined wholly in economic terms, identifying its constituent productive forces and relations of production. Secondly, the forces and relations of production can also be considered in their political and ideological aspects. And, thirdly, the definition can be extended to include the totality of economic, poltical and ideological relations necessary for social reproduction as well as economic production. This first definition is unsatisfactory. Pre-capitalist exploitation typically involved extra-economic relations: in turn these could involve direct compulsion (e.g. slavery or the levy of tribute or taxes) and/or political or ideological mechanisms (e.g. a legal monopoly of land or kinship relations). Moreover, not even capitalist production can be reduced to a purely technical process unencumbered by political and ideological considerations. Indeed recent studies have shown the extent to which even the forces of production can embody political and ideological relations by constraining the activities of workers and by maintaining the separation between mental and manual labour. The third definition is also unsatisfactory. For it is equally wrong to include all the political and ideological factors involved in its social reproduction when defining a given mode. This would eliminate the distinction between a mode of production and its extra-economic conditions of existence and thereby encourage neglect of the different ways in which these conditions can be secured. Thus neither a narrow nor a broad definition of modes of production is acceptable.

It is best to consider relations of production as having economic, political and ideological moments without claiming that they thereby exhaust all social relations. Thus one could study the labour process as involving (a) socio-technical process of transformation of nature, (b) patterns of coordination, surveillance and control over workers, and (c) a particular division between mental and manual labour. This does not subsume all political and ideological relations under the mode of production. For, beyond it, there are specific legal, political, social and ideological institutions. How these are articulated with the relations of production (notably through the medium of property relations) will vary from one mode to another. Nor is there any reason to believe that these institutions will always contribute to securing the extra-economic preconditions of a given mode. Finally, nothing in this approach entails the argument that the forces and/or relations of production determine (whether alone or predominantly) the form and/or content of other social spheres. This has important implications for analysing the unity and coherence of pre-capitalist social formations as well as for the dynamic of class relations more generally.

HOW ARE MODES OF PRODUCTION ARTICULATED? Granted that different modes of production exist and can be combined, how are they articulated? This question has generated arcane disputes concerning whether two distinct modes of production could co-exist in the same economic space (cf. Wolpe, 1982). But it has also led to interesting analyses of the articulation of different forms of social and private labour with a dominant mode of production. These include studies of tribal societies; the impact of capitalism on pre-capitalist societies more generally; the relations between metropolitan and peripheral capital; and the periodization of metropolitan capitalism itself into distinct stages which can be variously combined.

A recent and related topic concerns domestic labour. Some feminists have argued that there is a separate and autonomous domestic mode of production in which women are exploited by a dominant class of men. Others have argued that there is a client domestic mode of production through which capital exploits women because their unpaid domestic labour helps to lower the reproduction costs of all wage-labour. What is clear, such disputes aside, is that domestic labour (as opposed to a domestic mode of production) both contributes to capital accumulation and yet lies beyond it. This highlights the need to examine how modes of production are articulated with other forms of labour.

PRE-CAPITALIST MODES. Marx and Engels considered pre-capitalist modes of production in several works, most notably in Marx's *Grundrisse* (1857–8). Here Marx suggested an evolutionary schema comprising a tribal stage (with three successive sub-stages, viz. hunting, nomadic pastoralism and sedentary agriculture); then an ancient slave-holding system based on city-states; then a feudal stage; and then capitalism. He also mentioned Germanic and Slavonic forms of tribalism and outlined an 'Asiatic mode of production'. In all cases he focused on the various forms of agrarian property involved in different modes of production. Marxist economic historians and anthropologists have built on these arguments and have also described other pre-capitalist modes of production.

ANCIENT SOCIETY AND FEUDALISM. Marxists conventionally argue that ancient society was based on slave labour. But slaves can be found in many different economic and political systems so that slavery as such cannot be the defining characteristic of one particular mode of production. It is equally clear that not all the productive labour in ancient societies was performed by slave labour. A better approach emphasizes that ancient societies were organized around city-states and considers how politics intervened in the appropriation of surplus in the ancient mode of production.

Under feudalism a landlord class exploits serf labour. Serfs are tied to the land through political and legal mechanisms and cultivate it on payment of feudal ground rent. Because they actually occupy the land and can determine how it is worked, surplus must be appropriated through customary forms of extra-economic coercion. The particular political shell within which feudal exploitation occurs has often been neglected by Marxist scholars. Yet this makes it difficult to distinguish one form of pre-capitalist rent and its accompanying mode of production from another. It is important to connect more general historical approaches to feudalism (which emphasize such factors as parcellized sovereignty, vassal hierarchy and the system of economic and military fiefdom) with the analysis of feudal economies. Only thus can one understand the particular forms and dynamic of feudalism in Europe and Japan as compared with the other agrarian modes of production (cf. Anderson, 1974b).

AN ASIATIC MODE OF PRODUCTION? Marx provided several different accounts of the Asiatic mode but always emphasized the absence of private property in land.

In general he noted that Asiatic societies had autarchic village communities which combined crafts with cultivation; but they were also dominated by an overarching state which claimed absolute title to the soil and appropriated the bulk of economic surplus in the form of tax or labour levies.

The scope of this concept seems to vary inversely with that of 'feudalism'. For, given the limited number of modes of production traditionally considered, one or other concept must subsume the most widely divergent economic systems. However, whereas feudalism is generally agreed to be a valid concept and to have been instantiated in the West, neither the concept nor the existence of an Asiatic mode are universally accepted. This partly reflects political disputes concerning the 'semi-Asiatic' character of pre-revolutionary Russia and polemical suggestions that the Soviet system (especially under Stalin) is an Asiatic despotism (e.g. Wittfogel, 1957). More generally the concept is theoretically contradictory in Marxist terms (states are not supposed to develop in otherwise classless societies) and also historically inadequate (Asiatic systems were diverse and dynamic rather than homogeneous and stagnant). The history of the concept suggests that there is still much work to be done in analysing pre-capitalist modes of production.

CAPITALISM. Capitalism involves the generalization of the commodity form to labour-power and the appropriation of surplus-labour in the form of surplus-value. Economic exploitation and capital accumulation both depend upon economic exchange mediated through market forces. This relative separation between economic and extra-economic relations and the dominance of the economic in the dynamic of capital accumulation has encouraged the belief that capitalism can be understood purely as an economic phenomenon. But there are important extra-economic preconditions of capital accumulation (in law, the state, specific forms of family, ideology etc.) and they always intervene in the economic realm. In addition the economic relations themselves have political and ideological moments (cf. above).

Recent studies of relations in production have emphasized how the labour process has important extra-economic aspects. Key concepts here have been the 'politics of production', 'factory regimes' and the mental–manual division of labour (e.g., Burawoy, 1985; Thompson, 1983). Likewise there have been important non-economistic analyses of capitalist relations of production more generally. Worth noting here are studies concerned with 'regimes of accumulation' and patterns of 'regulation'. These aim to provide a more concrete and conjunctural analysis of capitalist periodization than do more orthodox studies which posit a unilinear and mechanical succession of capitalist stages. They recognize that structural changes and institutional innovation are essential for long-term accumulation and that each national economy has its own specificity within the international system. They emphasize the periodic structural and strategic reorganization of the social relations in and of production. Particular attention has been paid to the shift from regimes based on extensive accumulation to those based on intensive accumulation (especially Fordism). Such studies consider the ensemble of conditions governing the use and reproduction of labour-power, the dynamic of investment and forms of competition, changes in the monetary system, and so on. They also consider changing accumulation strategies and patterns of institutional regulation intended to secure the cohesion of different national systems and their stable insertion into the international economy (e.g., Aglietta, 1979; and de Vroey, 1984).

FURTHER RESEARCH. The concept of mode of production is clearly both complex and problematic. This is particularly true for pre-capitalist modes. Studies here have frequently adhered too rigidly to Marx's own typologies and also find difficulty in handling the intimate connections between their pre-capitalist relations of production and extra-economic relations. But there is enormous scope for further research on pre-capitalist modes. In dealing with capitalist economies, the most promising areas of research comprise: (a) the politics of production and associated 'factory regimes'; (b) regimes of accumulation and patterns of regulation; and (c) the articulation of capitalism with other modes of production and/or forms of social or domestic labour. In each case this means paying more careful and systematic attention to the articulation between the economic, political and ideological moments of production. Without progress in this direction the spectres of teleology, technological determinism and monocausal economic explanations will continue to haunt Marxist analyses.

BIBLIOGRAPHY

Aglietta, M. 1979. *A Theory of Capitalist Regulation*. London: New Left Books. Distributed in U.S.A. by Schocken Books.

Anderson, P. 1974a. *Passages from Antiquity to Feudalism*. London: New Left Books; New York: Schocken.

Anderson, P. 1974b. *Lineages of the Absolutist State*. London: New Left Books; New York: Schocken.

Balibar, E. 1970. The basic concepts of historical materialism. In L. Althusser and E. Balibar, *Reading Capital*, London: New Left Books; New York: Pantheon.

Banaji, J. 1977. Modes of production in a materialist conception of history. *Capital and Class* 3, Autumn, 1–44.

Bloch, M. 1961. *Feudal Society*. 2 vols, London: Routledge & Kegan Paul; Chicago: University of Chicago Press.

Bloch, M. 1982. *Marxism and Anthropology*. London: Oxford University Press.

Burawoy, M. 1985. *The Politics of Production*. London: New Left Books. Distributed in U.S.A. by Schocken Books.

Cohen, G.A. 1978. *Karl Marx's Theory of History*. Oxford: Oxford University Press; Princeton, N.S.: Princeton University Press, 1979.

Edwards, R. 1979. *Contested Terrain*. New York: Basic Books.

Finley, M. 1982. *Economy and Society in Ancient Greece*. London: Chatto & Windus.

Harvey, D. 1982. *The Limits of Capital*. Oxford: Blackwell; Chicago: Chicago University Press.

Hindess, B. and Hirst, P.Q. 1975. *Pre-Capitalist Modes of Production*. London: Routledge & Kegan Paul.

Hobsbawm, E. 1964. Introduction: In. K. Marx, *Pre-Capitalist Economic Formations*, London: Lawrence & Wishart; New York: International Publishers, 1965.

Kula, W. 1976. *Economic Theory of the Feudal System*. London: New Left Books.

Marx, K. 1859. Preface to *A Contribution to the Critique of Political Economy*. London: Lawrence & Wishart, 1971.

Marx, K. 1867–94. *Capital*. 3 vols, Harmondsworth: Penguin.

Marx, K. 1957–8. *Grundrisse der Kritik der politischen Oekonomie*. Berlin: Dietz. Trans., Harmondsworth: Penguin, 1973.

Molyneux, M. 1979. Beyond the domestic labour debate. *New Left Review* No. 116, July–August, 3–27.

Padgug, R.A. 1976. Problems in the theory of slavery and slave society. *Science and Society* 40(1), 3–27.

St. Croix, G. de 1982. *The Class Struggle in the Ancient Greek World*. London: Duckworth; Ithaca: Cornell University Press.

Thompson, P. 1983. *The Nature of Work*. London: Macmillan.

Turner, B.S. 1978. *Marx and the End of Orientalism*. London: Macmillan.

Vroey, M. de. 1984. A regulation approach interpretation of the contemporary crisis. *Capital and Class* 23, Summer, 45–66.

Wittfogel, K.A. 1957. *Oriental Despotism: a comparative study of total power*. New Haven; Yale University Press.

Wolpe, H. (ed.) 1982. *The Articulation of Modes of Production*. London: Routledge & Kegan Paul.

Monopoly Capitalism

PAUL M. SWEEZY

Among Marxian economists 'monopoly capitalism' is the term widely used to denote the stage of capitalism which dates from approximately the last quarter of the 19th century and reaches full maturity in the period after World War II. Marx's *Capital*, like classical political economy from Adam Smith to John Stuart Mill, was based on the assumption that all commodities are produced by industries consisting of many firms, or capitals in Marx's terminology, each accounting for a negligible fraction of total output and all responding to the price and profit signals generated by impersonal market forces. Unlike the classical economists, however, Marx recognized that such an economy was inherently unstable and impermanent. The way to succeed in a competitive market is to cut costs and expand production, a process which requires incessant accumulation of capital in ever new technological and organizational forms. In Marx's words: 'The battle of competition is fought by cheapening of commodities. The cheapness of commodities depends, *ceteris paribus*, on the productiveness of labour, and this again on the scale of production. Therefore the larger capitals beat the smaller.' Further, the credit system which 'begins as a modest helper of accumulation' soon 'becomes a new and formidable weapon in the competitive struggle, and finally it transforms itself into an immense social mechanism for the centralization of capitals' (Marx, 1867, ch. 25, sect. 2). Marx, and even more clearly Engels when preparing the second and third volumes of *Capital* for the printer two decades later, concluded, in the latter's words, that 'the long cherished freedom of competition has reached the end of its tether and is compelled to announce its own palpable bankruptcy' (Marx, 1894, ch. 27).

There is thus no doubt that Marx and Engels believed capitalism had reached a turning point. In this view, however, the end of the competitive era marked not the beginning of a new stage of capitalism but rather the beginning of a transition to the new mode of production that would take the place of capitalism. It was only somewhat later, when it became clear that capitalism was far from on its last legs that Marx's followers, recognizing that a new stage had actually arrived, undertook to analyse its main features and what might be implied for capitalism's 'laws of motion'.

The pioneer in this endeavour was the Austrian Marxist Rudolf Hilferding whose magnum opus *Das Finanzkapital* appeared in 1910. A forerunner was the American economist Thorstein Veblen, whose book *The Theory of Business Enterprise* (1904) dealt with many of the same problems as Hilferding's: corporation finance, the role of banks in the concentration of capital, etc. Veblen's work, however, was apparently unknown to Hilferding, and neither author had a significant impact on mainstream economic thought in the English-speaking world, where the emergence of corporations and related new forms of business activity and organization, though the subject of a vast descriptive literature, was almost entirely ignored in the dominant neoclassical orthodoxy.

In Marxist circles, however, Hilferding's work was hailed as a breakthrough, and its pre-eminent place in the Marxist tradition was assured when Lenin strongly endorsed it at the beginning of his *Imperialism, The Highest Stage of Capitalism*. 'In 1910,' Lenin wrote, 'there appeared in Vienna the work of the Austrian Marxist, Rudolf Hilferding, *Financial Capital* .... This work gives a very valuable theoretical analysis of "the latest phase of capitalist development", the subtitle of the book.'

As far as economic theory in the narrow sense is concerned, Lenin added little to *Finance Capital*, and in retrospect it is evident that Hilferding himself was not successful in integrating the new phenomena of capitalist development into the core of Marx's theoretical structure (value, surplus value and above all the process of capital accumulation). In chapter 15 of his book ('Price Determination in the Capitalist Monopoly. Historical Tendency of Finance Capital') Hilferding, in seeking to deal with some of these problems, came up with a very striking conclusion which has been associated with his name ever since. Prices under conditions of monopoly, he thought, are indeterminate and hence unstable. Wherever concentration enables capitalists to achieve higher than average profits, suppliers and customers are put under pressure to create counter combinations which will enable them to appropriate part of the extra profits for themselves. Thus monopoly spreads in all directions from every point of origin. The question then arises as to the limits of 'cartellization' (the term is used synonymously with monopolization). Hilferding answers:

> The answer to this question must be that there is no absolute limit to cartellization. What exists rather is a tendency to the continuous spread of cartellization. Independent industries, as we have seen, fall more and more under the sway of the cartellized ones, ending up finally by being annexed by the cartellized ones. The result of this process is then a *general cartel*. The entire capitalist production is consciously controlled from one center which determines the amount of production in all its spheres .... It is the consciously controlled society in antagonistic form.

There is more about this vision of a future totally monopolized society, but it need not detain us. Three quarters of a century of monopoly capitalist history has shown that while the tendency to concentration is strong and persistent, it is by no means as ubiquitous and overwhelming as Hilferding imagined. There are powerful counter-tendencies – the breakup of existing firms and the founding of new ones – which have been strong enough to prevent the formation of anything even remotely approaching Hilferding's general cartel.

The first signs of important new departures in Marxist economic thinking began to appear toward the end of the interwar years, i.e., the 1920s and 1930s; but on the whole this was a period in which Lenin's *Imperialism* was accepted as the last word on monopoly capitalism, and the rigid orthodoxy of Stalinism discouraged attempts to explore changing developments in the structure and functioning of contemporary capitalist economies. Meanwhile, academic economists in the West finally got around to analysing monopolistic and imperfectly competitive markets (especially Edward Chamberlin and Joan Robinson), but for a long time these efforts were confined to the level of individual firms and industries. The so-called Keynesian revolution which transformed macroeconomic theory in the 1930s was largely untouched by these advances in the theory of markets, continuing to rely on the time-honoured assumption of atomistic competition.

The 1940s and 1950s witnessed the emergence of new trends of thought within the general framework of Marxian economics. These had their roots on the one hand in Marx's theory of concentration and centralization which, as we have seen, was further developed by Hilferding and Lenin; and on the other hand in Marx's famous Reproduction Schemes presented and analysed in Volume II of *Capital*, which were the focal point of a prolonged debate on the nature of capitalist crises involving many of the leading Marxist theorists of the period between Engels' death (1895) and World War I. Credit for the first attempt to knot these two strands of thought into an elaborated version of Marxian accumulation theory goes to Michal Kalecki, whose published works in Polish in the early 1930s articulated, according to Joan Robinson and others, the main tenets of the contemporaneous Keynesian 'revolution' in the West. Kalecki had been introduced to economics through the works of Marx and the great Polish Marxist Rosa Luxemburg, and he was consequently free of the inhibitions and preconceptions that went with a training in neoclassical economics. He moved to England in the mid-1930s, entering into the intense discussions and debates of the period and making his own distinctive contributions along the lines of his previous work and that of Keynes and his followers in Cambridge, Oxford and the London School of Economics. In April 1938 Kalecki published an article in *Econometrica* ('The Distribution of the National Income') which highlighted differences between his approach and that of Keynes, especially with respect to two crucially important and closely related subjects, namely, the class distribution of income and the role of monopoly. With respect to monopoly, Kalecki stated at the end of the article a position which had deep roots in his thinking and would henceforth be central to his theoretical work:

The results arrived at in this essay have a more general aspect. A world in which the degree of monopoly determines the distribution of the national income is a world far removed from the pattern of free competition. Monopoly appears to be deeply rooted in the nature of the capitalist system: free competition, as an assumption, may be useful in the first stage of certain investigations, but as a description of the normal stage of capitalist economy it is merely a myth.

A further step in the direction of integrating the two strands of Marx's thought – concentration and centralization on the one hand and crisis theory on the other – was marked by the publication in 1942 of *The Theory of Capitalist Development* by Paul M. Sweezy, which contained a fairly comprehensive review of the pre-war history of Marxist economics and at the same time made explanatory use of concepts introduced into mainstream monopoly and oligopoly theory during the preceding decade. This book, soon translated into several foreign languages, had a significant effect in systematizing the study and interpretation of Marxian economic theories.

It should not be supposed, however, that these new departures were altogether a matter of theoretical speculation. Of equal if not greater importance were the changes in the structure and functioning of capitalism which had emerged during the 1920s and 1930s. On the one hand the decline in competition which began in the late 19th century proceeded at an accelerated pace – as chronicled in the classic study by Arthur R. Burns, *The Decline of Competition*: *A Study of the Evolution of American Industry* (1936) – and on the other hand the unprecedented severity of the depression of the 1930s provided dramatic proof of the inadequacy of conventional business cycle theories. The Keynesian revolution was a partial answer to this challenge, but the renewed upsurge of the advanced capitalist economies during and after the war cut short further development of critical analysis among mainstream economists, and it was left to Marxists to carry on along the lines that had been pioneered by Kalecki before the war.

Kalecki spent the war years at the Oxford Institute of Statistics whose Director, A.L. Bowley, had brought together a distinguished group of scholars, most of them emigrés from occupied Europe. Among the latter was Josef Steindl, a young Austrian economist who came under the influence of Kalecki and followed in his footsteps. Later on, Steindl recounted the following:

> On one occasion I talked with Kalecki about the crisis of capitalism. We both, as well as most socialists, took it for granted that capitalism was threatened by a crisis of existence, and we regarded the stagnation of the 1930s as a symptom of such a major crisis. But Kalecki found the reasons, given by Marx, why such a crisis should develop, unconvincing; at the same time he did not have an explanation of his own. I still do not know, he said, why there should be a crisis of capitalism, and he added: Could it have anything to do with monopoly? He subsequently suggested to me and to the Institute, before he left England, that I should work on this problem. It was a very Marxian problem, but my methods of dealing with it were Kaleckian (Steindl, 1985).

Steindl's work on this subject was completed in 1949 and published in 1952 under the title *Maturity and Stagnation in American Capitalism*. While little noticed by the economics profession at the time of its publication, this book nevertheless provided a crucial link between the experiences, empirical as well as theoretical, of the 1930s, and the development of a relatively rounded theory of monopoly capitalism in the 1950s and 1960s, a process which received renewed impetus from the return of stagnation to American (and global) capitalism during the 1970s and 1980s.

The next major work in the direct line from Marx through Kalecki and Steindl was Paul Baran's book, *The Political Economy of Growth* (1957), which presented a theory of the dynamics of monopoly capitalism and opened up a new perspective on the nature of the interaction between developed and underdeveloped capitalist societies. This was followed by the joint work of Baran and Sweezy, *Monopoly Capital: An Essay on the American Economic and Social Order* (1966), incorporating ideas from both of their earlier works and attempting to elucidate, in the words of their Introduction, the 'mechanism linking the foundation of society (under monopoly capitalism) with what Marxists call its political, cultural, and ideological superstructure'. Their effort, however, still fell short of a comprehensive theory of monopoly capitalism since it neglected 'a subject which occupies a central place in Marx's study of capitalism', that is, a systematic inquiry into 'the consequences which the particular kinds of technological change characteristic of the monopoly capitalist period have had for the nature of work, the composition (and differentiation) of the working class, the psychology of workers, the forms of working-class organization and struggle, and so on.' A pioneering effort to fill this gap in the theory of monopoly capitalism was taken by Harry Braverman a few years later (Braverman, 1974) which in turn did much to stimulate renewed research into changing trends in work processes and labour relations in the late 20th century.

Marx wrote in the Preface to the first edition of Volume 1 of *Capital* that 'it is the ultimate aim of this work to lay bare the economic law of motion of modern society'. What emerged, running like a red thread through the whole work, could perhaps better be called a theory of the accumulation of capital. In what respect, if at all, can it be said that latter-day theories of monopoly capitalism modify or add to Marx's analysis of the accumulation process?

As far as form is concerned, the theory remains basically unchanged, and modifications in content are in the direction of putting even greater emphasis on certain tendencies already demonstrated by Marx to be inherent in the accumulation process. This is true of concentration and centralization, and even more spectacularly so of the role of what Marx called the credit system, now grown to monstrous proportions compared to the small beginnings of his day. In addition, and perhaps most important, the new theories seek to demonstrate that monopoly capitalism is more prone than its competitive predecessor to generating unsustainable rates of accumulation, leading to crises, depressions and prolonged periods of stagnation.

The reasoning here follows a line of thought which recurs in Marx's writings, especially in the unfinished later volumes of *Capital* (including *Theories of Surplus Value*): individual capitalists always strive to increase their accumulation to the maximum extent possible and without regard for the ultimate overall effect on the demand for the increasing output of the economy's expanding capacity to produce. Marx summed this up in the well-known formula that 'the real barrier of capitalist production is capital itself'. The upshot of the new theories is that the widespread introduction of monopoly raises this barrier still higher. It does this in three ways.

(1) Monopolistic organization gives capital an advantage in its struggle with labour, hence tends to raise the rate of surplus value and to make possible a higher rate of accumulation.

(2) With monopoly (or oligopoly) prices replacing competitive prices, a uniform rate of profit gives way to a hierarchy of profit rates – highest in the most concentrated industries, lowest in the most competitive. This means that the distribution of surplus value is skewed in favour of the larger units of capital which characteristically accumulate a greater proportion of their profits than smaller units of capital, once again making possible a higher rate of accumulation.

(3) On the demand side of the accumulation equation, monopolistic industries adopt a policy of slowing down and carefully regulating the expansion of productive capacity in order to maintain their higher rates of profit.

Translated into the language of Keynesian macro theory, these consequences of monopoly mean that the savings potential of the system is increased, while the opportunities for profitable investment are reduced. Other things being equal, therefore, the level of income and employment under monopoly capitalism is lower than it would be in a more competitive environment.

To convert this insight into a dynamic theory, it is necessary to see monopolization (the concentration and centralization of capital) as an ongoing historical process. At the beginning of the transition from the competitive to the monopolistic stage, the accumulation process is only minimally affected. But with the passage of time the impact grows and tends sooner or later to become a crucial factor in the functioning of the system. This, according to monopoly capitalist theory, accounts for the prolonged stagnation of the 1930s as well as for the return of stagnation in the 1970s and 1980s following the exhaustion of the long boom caused by World War II and its multifaceted aftermath effects.

Neither mainstream economics nor traditional Marxian theory have been able to offer a satisfactory explanation of the stagnation phenomenon which has loomed increasingly large in the history of the capitalist world during the 20th century. It is thus the distinctive contribution of monopoly capitalist theory to have tackled this problem head on and in the process to have generated a rich body of literature which draws on and adds to the work of the great economic thinkers of the last 150 years. A representative sampling of this literature, together with editorial introductions and interpretations, is contained in Foster and Szlajfer (1984).

BIBLIOGRAPHY

Baran, P.A. 1957. *The Political Economy of Growth.* New York: Monthly Review Press.

Baran, P.A. and Sweezy, P.M. 1966. *Monopoly Capital: An Essay on the American Economic and Social Order.* New York: Monthly Review Press.

Braverman, H. 1974. *Labor and Monopoly Capital: The Degradation of Work in the Twentieth Century.* New York: Monthly Review Press.

Burns, A.R. 1936. *The Decline of Competition: A Study of the Evolution of American Industry.* New York: McGraw-Hill.

Foster, J.B. and Szlajfer, H. (eds) 1984. *The Faltering Economy: The Problem of Accjmulation Under Monopoly Capitalism.* New York: Monthly Review Press.

Hilferding, R. 1910. *Das Finanzkapital.* Trans. M. Watnick and S. Gordon as *Finance Capital,* ed. T. Bottomore, London: Routledge & Kegan Paul, 1981.

Kalecki, M. 1938. The distribution of the national income. *Econometrica,* April.

Lenin, V.I. 1917. *Imperialism, The Highest State of Capitalism.*

Marx, K. 1867. *Capital,* Vol. 1. Moscow: Progress Publishers.

Marx, K. 1885. *Capital,* Vol. 2. Moscow: Progress Publishers.

Marx, K. 1894. *Capital,* Vol. 3. Moscow: Progress Publishers.

Steindl, J. 1952. *Maturity and Stagnation in American Capitalism.* Oxford: Blackwell.

Steindl, J. 1985. The present state of economics. *Monthly Review,* February.

Sweezy, P.M. 1942. *The Theory of Capitalist Development.* New York: Monthly Review Press.

Sweezy, P.M. 1966. See Baran and Sweezy (1966).

Veblen, T. 1904. *The Theory of Business Enterprise.* New York: Charles Scribners' Sons.

Organic Composition of Capital

ANWAR SHAIKH

The distinction between labour value transferred and labour value added is crucial to Marx's theory of value. For the capitalist system as a whole, the abstract labour-time previously materialized in machinery and materials (c) merely reappears in the total product. The capital expended for the purchase of c is therefore constant-in-value. On the other hand, whereas the capital expended for the engagement of workers is determined by the labour value of their means of consumption (v), their actual employment results in a quantity of abstract labour-time (l) which is generally different from v. Thus capital expended for the purchase of labour-power is intrinsically variable-in-value. Indeed, the secret of capitalist production is contained precisely in this variability, since surplus value ($s = 1 - v$) only exists to the extent that l is greater than v. It follows from this that for any given total capital expended ($c + v$), its *composition* between c and v is the utmost importance, because only v expands total capital value from $c + v$ to $c + l = c + v + s$ (Marx, 1867, pp. 421, 571).

The ratio c/v, the *value composition*, is the immediate measure of the composition of capital. But since c represents the value of machines and materials and v the value of labour-power, the (vectors of) technical proportions in which various machines and materials combine with labour (the *technical composition* of capital) clearly stand behind the value composition c/v (Marx, 1863, ch. 33; and Marx, 1894, ch. 45). That is to say, the technical composition is the inner measure of the composition of capital. Similarly, since $c + v$ materializes itself as $c + l$, we can view the ratio c/l as the outer measure of the composition of capital – the *materialized composition* of capital (Marx, 1894, ch. 8). At a more concrete level each of the above value-measures acquires a corresponding price counterpart, and each element of any price/value pair is in turn differentiated into stock/flow measures. We shall see that that distinctions can play an important role at times. None the less, because the value relations are so fundamental to the basic argument, we will concentrate our attention on this level.

It is evident that the technical, value and materialized compositions of capital

304

are intrinsically related. Indeed, it was one of Marx's central claims that the *movements* of all three are dominated by one overriding force: the mechanization of labour process, which is 'the distinguishing historic feature' of the capitalist mode of production.

To see how this works, we begin by reducing the technical composition vector to a scalar measure TC by valuing the current vector elements at time t in terms of the unit values of means of production in some base year t_0. Suppressing the current time subscript t, let $k^j =$ the jth means of production per worker, λ_1, $\lambda_2 =$ indexes of the unit values of means of production and wage goods respectively, $w =$ an index of the real wage per worker, $h =$ the number of hours worked by each worker, all at time t; while λ_{jo}, $\lambda_{io} =$ the unit values of means of production and wage goods, respectively, and $v_0 =$ a constant representing the labour value of a unit of labour-power, all in the base year t_0. Then

$$k = [k_j] = \text{the technical composition}$$

$$= \text{a vector of means of production per worker} \tag{1}$$

$$TC = \text{a scalar measure of the technical composition of capital}$$

$$= \sum_j \lambda_{jo} k_j. \tag{2}$$

Next, note that $c/v = c'/v'$ and $c/l = c'/h$, where c' and v' are per worker, and h is th length of the working day. Then

$$c' \equiv \sum_j \lambda_j k_j = \left[\frac{\sum_j \lambda_j k_j}{\sum_j \lambda_{jo} k_j} \right] \sum_j \lambda_{jo} k_j = \lambda_1 TC$$

where $\lambda_1 =$ the term in brackets $=$ an index of the current unit value of means of production. Similarly,

$$v' \equiv \sum_i \lambda_i w_i = \left[\frac{\sum_i \lambda_i w_i}{\sum_i \lambda_{io} w_i} \right] \left[\frac{\sum_i \lambda_{io} w_i}{\sum_i \lambda_{io} w_{io}} \right] \left[\sum_i \lambda_{io} w_{io} \right] = \lambda_2 w v_0$$

where the terms in brackets are respectively:

$\lambda_2 =$ an index of the current unit value of means of production

$w =$ an index of the real wage

$v_0 =$ the base year value of labour-power

$$c/v = (TC/v_0)(\lambda_1/\lambda_2)(1/w) \tag{3}$$

$$c/l = (TC/v_0)(\lambda_1)(v_0/h). \tag{4}$$

Now, according to Marx's argument, mechanization is a continual process of increasing the productivity of labour through the use of ever greater quantities of machines and materials per worker. In a mathematical sense, this means a secular rise in most but not necessarily all of the elements of the technical composition vector (which will itself grow in dimension). It is therefore easy to see why the technical composition measure TC will tend to rise secularly, and why, other things being equal, this in turn will transmit an upward tendency to both c/v and c/l through their common term TC/v_0 (equations (3)–(4)). Because this latter term is both the direct gauge of the effect of a rising technical composition on c/v and c/l and also itself a constant-value measure of the current year's value composition, Marx calls it the *organic composition* of capital (Fine and Harris, 1976; Shaikh, 1978; Weeks, 1981). Accordingly, we write

$$OC = TC/v_0 = \text{the organic composition of capital.} \qquad (5)$$

The organic composition OC is evidently the critical link between the technical composition and the value and materialized compositions. But since the latter two have other determinants as well, we need to consider the specific influence of these other factors. In this regard, Marx argues that these other factors act as counter-tendencies which may slow down, but do not negate, the basic upward trend produced by the tendency toward a rising technical composition of capital (Rosdolsky, 1977, part V, appendix).

Consider the above expression for the value composition c/v (equation (3)). Here, we see that in addition to the organic composition OC, it depends also on the ratio λ_1/λ_2, and on the real wage w. But the former factor will serve primarily to create fluctuations around the basic trend produced by the rising organic composition, because the diffusion of technical change will tend to confine the variations in λ_1/λ_2 within a fairly narrow range. Therefore, it is only a secularly rising real wage which can cause the trend of the value composition to lag systematically behind that of the organic composition (though at the same time it accelerates the growth of organic composition by enhancing the scope of mechanization) (Marx, 1867, ch. 15). The trend of the organic composition is thus an upper bound to that of the value composition. A corresponding lower bound can then be found by noting that the value composition is related to the materialized composition through the rate of surplus value:

$$c/v = (c/l)(l/v) = (c/l)[(v + s)/v] = (c/l)(1 + s/v). \qquad (6)$$

On the question of the rate of surplus value, Marx argued that workers could not generally capture all of the gains in productivity achieved through mechanization, so that over time real wages would normally rise more slowly than productivity and the rate of surplus value would tend to rise (Rosdolsky, 1977). In the equation (6) above, this in turn immediately implies that the trend of c/l will be the lower bound to that of c/v.

This brings us to the trend of c/l itself. Here, the central theme of Marx's argument is that for individual capitalists the principal purpose of mechanization is to lower their unit production costs and thereby raise their profitability. But the gain of reduced units (flow) costs generally carries with it a corresponding requirement of the increased *capitalization* of production, i.e. a corresponding increase in the scale of investment required per unit of output (and hence in unit fixed costs). This familiar tradeoff between unit variable and unit fixed costs (Pratten, 1971, pp. 306–7; Weston and Brigham, 1982, pp. 145–7) turns out to be a sufficient condition for the rise in the organic composition OC to dominate the falling unit value of means of production (λ_1), so that the net result is a secularly rising c/l (Shaikh, 1978, pp. 239–40). And once it has been established that c/l rises over time, it follows from our earlier discussion concerning equation (6) that c/v also rise secularly. We can therefore say that under the conditions Marx sees as characteristic of capitalist industrialization, the resulting mechanization and capitalization of production expresses itself in a rising technical and hence organic composition OC, a less rapidly rising materialized composition c/l, and a value composition c/v which rises more slowly than the organic composition but more rapidly than the materialized composition.

All of this brings us to the implications of levels and movements of the various measures of the composition of capital. Marx distinguishes three major domains in which these factors are of critical importance. First, there is the domain of price/value relations, in which he uses the inter-industrial dispersion of organic compositions in any given period to derive the principal difference between prices of production and prices proportional to labour values. Here, the cross-sectional dispersion in organic compositions is initially taken to reflect the underlying variations in (the vectors of) technical compositions. Marx notes (but does not pursue) the fact that his results would undoubtedly be somewhat modified by the additional complications which arise when one distinguishes the dispersion of value compositions from that of the technical compositions, and the further dispersion of the price (transformed) compositions from that of the value (untransformed) compositions (Marx, 1894, chs 9, 45). Much of the subsequent debate surrounding the relations between values and prices of production (the Transformation Problem) has in fact centred around the complexity of the latter set of differences, with the dominant position being that such considerations effectively negate Marx's original formulations (Steedman, 1977, chs 1–2). Yet recent work shows that the empirical differences between Marx's prices of production and the conventional (Bortkiewicz–Sraffa) 'correct' ones are generally very small, that both are good predictors of actual market prices (as are labour values also, all with R^2's between 93–6 per cent), and that there are sound mathematical reasons why the basic value categories dominate the overall results – as Marx quite correctly perceived from the start (Shaikh, 1984; Ochoa, 1984).

The second domain in which the composition of capital plays a central role is in the maintenance of a reserve army of labour. Marx points out that while the accumulation of total capital $c + v$ increases the demand for labour, the attendant growth in the value composition of capital c/v in turn decreases the demand for labour. Where the net effect is negative, the reserve army grows. And where it is positive, the resulting shrinkage in the reserve army eventually puts pressure on the labour market and accelerates the growth in real wages. This rise in real wages then slows down accumulation on one hand, while on the other it accelerates the pace of mechanization and hence the growth of c/v. In this way, the growth of the value composition automatically adjusts so as to maintain a reserve army of labour. When capitalism is viewed on the world scale, this phenomenon assumes great significance.

The third, and perhaps most important application of the concept of the composition of capital arises in connection with what Marx calls 'one of the most striking phenomena of modern production', which is the tendency of the rate of profit to fall. The central variable in this case is the stock/flow materialized composition of capital C/l, because any sustained rise in C/l can be shown to give rise to an actual falling rate of profit, *no matter how fast the rate of surplus is rising*. Writing the rate of profit r in terms of s, v, $l = v + s$, and $C = $ total (constant and circulating) capital advanced, we get

$$r = \frac{s}{C} = \frac{s/v}{C/v} = \frac{s/v}{(C/l)(l/v)} = \frac{s/v}{1 + (s/v)} \cdot \frac{1}{(C/l)}. \tag{7}$$

It is evident from equation (7) that as the rate of surplus value rises, the term $s/l = (s/v)/(1 + s/v)$ rises at an ever decreasing rate, since in the limit it approaches 1. Thus, no matter how fast the rate of surplus value rises, the rate of profit eventually falls at a rate asymptotic to the rate of fall of l/C (Rosdolsky, 1977, chs. 16. 17, 26 and part V, appendix).

But the matter does not end there, because this issue recently sparked a fresh round of debates. On one side was an argument based on the (essentially neoclassical) theory of perfect competition, in which capitalists are assumed to invest in new methods only if these raise their own rate of profit, on the grounds that they would otherwise prefer to continue using their existing plant and equipment; and on the opposite side, an argument based on Marx's notion of competition-as-war, in which capitalists are driven to invest in those methods which lower their unit production costs, because the first ones to do so can cut prices and thereby expand their total profits through larger market shares. In the former case, the result is that the general rate of profit will necessarily rise, other things being equal; in the latter, the general rate of profit will tend to fall (as outlined above), provided that the new methods generally embody higher unit fixed costs.

In the original debates, the focus was on the differing implications of two apparently contradictory investment criteria; profit rate maximizing versus unit cost minimizing (profit margin maximizing). However, a subsequent contribution by Nakatani effectively dissolved this apparent opposition by showing that *both criteria are equivalent to selecting the highest projected rate of profit*. The principal difference then arises from the fact that in the case of perfect competition it is assumed that firms neither anticipate nor engage in price-cutting behaviour, while in the cases of competition-as-war, firms are assumed to necessarily do both (Nakatani, 1979). With this step, the issue reverts back to the two opposing conceptions of capitalism which lie behind these different notions of competition.

BIBLIOGRAPHY

Fine, B. and Harris, L. 1976. Controversial issues in Marxist economic theory. In *Socialist Register*, ed. R. Milibrand and J. Saville, London: Merlin. Distributed in U.S.A. by Humanities Press.

Marx, K. 1858. *Grundrisse*, London: Penguin.

Marx, K. 1863. *Theories of Surplus Value*, Part I. Moscow: Progress Publishers.

Marx, K. 1867. *Capital*, Vol. I. London: Penguin, 1976.

Marx, K. 1894. *Capital*, Vol. III. New York: Vintage, 1981.

Nakatani, T. 1979. Price competition and technical choice. *Kobe University Economic Review* 25, 67–77.

Ochoa, E. 1984. Labour values and prices of production: an inter-industry study of the US economy, 1947–1972. PhD dissertation. Graduate Faculty, New School for Social Research.

Pratten, C.F. 1971. *Economies of Scale in Manufacturing Industry*, Cambridge: Cambridge University Press.

Rosdolsky, R. 1977. *The Making of Marx's Capital*. London: Pluto Press.

Shaikh, A. 1978. Political economy and capitalism: notes on Dobb's theory of crisis. *Cambridge Journal of Economics* 2(2), 233–51.

Shaikh, A. 1984. The transformation from Marx to Sraffa. In *Ricardo, Marx, Sraffa*, ed. E. Mandel. London: Verso.

Steedman, I. 1977. *Marx After Sraffa*. London: New Left Books.

Weeks, J. 1981. *Capital and Exploitation*. Princeton: Princeton University Press.

Weston, J.F. and Brigham, E.F. 1982. *Essentials of Managerial Finance*. 6th edn, Chicago: Dryden Press.

Georgii Valentinovich
Plekhanov

M. FALKUS

Plekhanov (1856–1918) was a major figure in the development of Marxist economic and political philosophy during the late 19th century. His importance springs from four principal sources. He was the first Russian intellectual to apply Marxist theory to Russian conditions. In so doing, he undermined the intellectual foundations of the Populists (*Narodniki*) and showed the relevance of Marxist economic determinism to Russia. Secondly, he exerted a profound influence upon the Russian revolutionary intelligentsia, persuading many of them to abandon Populism in favour of Marxism. Plekhanov was one of the founders of the Marxist Russian Social Democratic Party. Thirdly, the originality and perception shown in Plekhanov's own voluminous and wide-ranging writings show him to be an outstanding Marxist theoretician. Finally, the approval given Plekhanov's writings by Marx and, especially, Lenin (despite their later disagreements) has assured Plekhanov of an honoured place in Soviet histories of the development of socialist philosophy. Indeed, Plekhanov was one of the two figures whose writings were specifically acknowledged by Lenin as leading to his own conversion to Marxism; the other was Marx.

Plekhanov was born on 29 November 1856 in the village of Gudalovka in what was then the province of Tambov (Lipetsk Oblast). He was the son of a wealthy nobleman and attended military college in Voronezh and the Konstantin Cadets' College in St Petersburg in 1973–4 before entering the St Petersburg Institute of Mines. Here he became influenced by the revolutionary movements of the time and was eventually expelled in 1876 for his part in such activities. In 1875 he had joined the *Narodniki* and in the following year he joined the newly-formed *Zemlya i Volya* (Land and Liberty) *Narodnik* organization – Russia's first political party. This group believed that Russia's future lay with the peasant masses, and that the peasants should be given land. Plekhanov soon became one of the leading *Narodnik* writers and activists, and took part in the 'going to the people' movement. He also gave a speech at a major demonstration organized in 1876 by *Zemlya i Volya* in front of St Petersburg's Kazan Cathedral.

In 1879 the *Narodnik* movement split, the majority faction advocating the use of terrorist tactics. Plekhanov favoured a more moderate approach, and together with a small group of other leading *narodniks* (including Pavel Axelrod and Leo Deutsch) formed the non-violent *Cherny Peredel* movement (Black Repartition – i.e. the movement wanted repartition of the fertile Black Soil lands to the peasantry).

In January 1880 Plekhanov emigrated to Europe to escape persecution from the tsarist authorities. He remained in exile until 1917, living in Switzerland, France, Italy and elsewhere, travelling widely throughout the continent. In western Europe he made contact with numerous other Russian revolutionary exiles and also became deeply interested by Marxist thought. From about 1882 he became a fervent advocate of Marxism, and in his writings he now sought to establish the relevance of Marxism to Russian conditions and to undermine the intellectual foundations of Russian populism. In 1883 Plekhanov founded in Geneva Russia's first Marxist Social Democratic organization, the Liberation of Labour. The group translated into Russian and published many workers by Marx and Engels, Plekhanov himself translating the *Communist Manifesto*.

During the 1880s and 1890s Plekhanov wrote his most influential works, denouncing not only the populists but the Legal Marxists and the Economists (Marxist factions which developed after 1895), and he put forward his own interpretation of the path towards socialism which Russia was to follow. The root of his philosophy was in what he termed 'scientific' historical materialism, exposing the *narodniks* as 'unscientific'. In Plekhanov's view, revolution could not succeed unless it has the support of the class-conscious masses. Revolution could not come from the agrarian peasantry, and must come from the urban proletariat. As he argued in *Socialism and the Political Struggle* (1883) and *Our Differences* (1885), the utopian socialists (Blanquists) were mistaken in their reliance on intellectual conspiracy alone: revolution could succeed only as a result of a class struggle emanating from the working classes. It therefore became important for Plekhanov to demonstrate that Russia's path towards socialism could not come, as the *narodniki* argued, from the village-based commune (*mir*) and the peasantry. Capitalism in Russia was a necessary phase of historical development and was not 'accidental' or 'non-Russian'. Indeed, in Russia of the 1880s capitalism was already a reality.

To be sure, Plekhanov's theories contained many obscurities and contradictions. Fundamental were the dichotomies between economic determinism and the role of the revolutionary, and also between the reliance on the class-conscious urban masses and the evident industrial backwardness of Russia. Plekhanov 'solved' the problems, albeit unsatisfactorily, by arguing that the Russian revolution could be accelerated by the role of the revolutionary intelligentsia, whose activities were to compensate for the lack of a middle class. He wrote in *Our Differences*: 'Our capitalism will fade without ever having flowered.'

311

Particularly influential was Plekhanov's *On the Question of the Development of the Monistic View of History*, which was brought to Russia by the Marxist publisher Potresov in 1894. Here Plekhanov elevated the 'objectivism' of Marx in contrast to the subjective values of the *Narodniki*. He wrote, 'the criterion of truth lies not in me, but in the relations which exist outside of me'. Thus, objectivity was possible in social theory. Plekhanov drew from Marx, and from the traditions of the English economists and German historicists, the fundamental principle that economic forces determine social development.

Plekhanov was active in the Second International (1889) and attended its Congresses in Zurich (1893), Amsterdam (1904) and Copenhagen (1910). Together with Lenin, Martov and Potresov, Plekhanov founded *Iskra* (The Spark) in 1900 – the first Russian Marxist newspaper. In 1903 he worked jointly with Lenin to draw up the programme adopted at the famous Second Congress of the Social Democratic Party, but it was shortly after this that Plekhanov broke with Lenin and the Bolsheviks and sided with the Mensheviks. During the Revolution of 1905 Plekhanov advocated an 'opportunist' alliance with the liberals, while in 1914 he supported the war against Germany for the defence of Russia (in opposition to Lenin and the Bolshevik position). In that year he formed the *Yedinstvo* (Unity) group, which was designed to bring together the Mensheviks and the anti-Lenin Bolsheviks, but its influence was negligible.

After the Revolution of February 1917 Plekhanov returned to Russia, supporting the Provisional government and the continuation of the war. He denounced the Bolshevik coup of October 1917, and shortly afterwards fell ill with tuberculosis. Ostracized by Lenin and terrorized by the Cheka, Plekhanov's wife took him to Finland, where he died on 30 May 1918.

Despite his differences with Lenin and the Bolsheviks after 1903, Plekhanov's writings have continued to be highly regarded and widely studied in the Soviet Union. During the 1920s his library and archives were gathered from a number of European centres and taken to Leningrad, where the Plekhanov Library was established, and his complete writings were published.

SELECTED WORKS

1883. *Socialism and the Political Struggle*.

1885. *Our Differences*.

1895. *Anarchism and Socialism*. Trans. by Eleanor Marx Aveling, Chicago: C.H. Kerr.

1897. *Contributions to the History of Materialism*. Trans. by Ralph Fox as *Essays in the History of Materialism*, London: Lane, 1934.

1923–7. *Sochineniya* (Works). 24 vols, Moscow. *Selected Works*, 5 vols, Moscow: Progress Publishers.

BIBLIOGRAPHY

Baron, S. 1963. *Plekhanov: the Father of Russian Marxism*. London: Routledge & Kegan Paul; Stanford, California: Stanford University Press.

Chagin, B.A. 1963. *G.V. Plekhanov i ego rol' v razvitii Marksistskoi Filosofii*. Moscow and Leningrad: Akademii Nauk.

Keep, J.L.H. 1963. *The Rise of Social Democracy in Russia*. Oxford: Clarendon Press.

Primitive Capitalist Accumulation

ROSS THOMSON

The primitive (or original) accumulation of capital is a concept developed in Karl Marx's *Capital* and *Grundrisse* to designate that process which generates the preconditions of the ongoing accumulation of capital. The character of these preconditions is derived from the concept of capital, understood to be the process whereby money is invested in the purchase of means of production and labour-power (the worker's capacity to labour) which in turn produce commodities embodying surplus-value. Capital therefore presupposes money amassed to be accumulated, labour-power as the property of labourers separated from ownership of the means of production, and markets in which commodities can be sold. Primitive accumulation therefore must involve more than Adam Smith's notion that 'The accumulation of stock must, in the nature of things, be previous to the division of labour' (1776, p. 260), whether the stock consists of money, means of production or means of subsistence. For this notion ignores the need for a proletariat, the importance of which is shown by settler colonies which have wealth but, insofar as the availability of land precludes the emergence of a market for labour-power, no capital.

To grasp the process generating the preconditions of capital entails historical investigation, which for Marx focused principally on the first industrial capitalist power, England, during the historical period, extending from the mid-16th century through 1770, called the stage of manufacturing. Primitive accumulation consisted of several distinct processes which transformed each of the elements of the inherited division of labour between the towns and the countryside: landed property which combined common with private rights of landlords and free peasant proprietors, merchant capital in wholesale trade, and craft centred in the urban trades. We will identify and evaluate Marx's account of these processes and will then consider whether this account helps understand the rise of English industrial capitalism and the processes of primitive accumulation elsewhere. Partly to remedy misunderstandings brought about by Marx's intentionally one-sided emphasis on the role of force, we will emphasize the economic mechanisms at work.

THE AGRICULTURAL REVOLUTION. For Marx (1890, chs 27, 29), the first and foremost effect of the 'agricultural revolution' of the 16th through 18th centuries was to expropriate the peasant from the soil and establish capitalist agriculture. Marx argues that a new, money-oriented nobility and gentry forcibly enclosed desmesne, common and waste land, consolidated small farms into larger ones and at times converted to pasturage. Capitalist farmers grew from a differentiation of the peasantry. By 1800, both yeoman and communal rights had been eliminated.

While Marx did overemphasize both the coerciveness and the significance of enclosures, his basic point that a landless proletariat and capitalist agriculture had become widespread in the manufacturing period remains valid. Enclosures converted property characterized by shared rights into private property. Although enclosures usually accorded with the custom of the manor and were undertaken by agreement of those with property rights, they did rely on the local power of landlords and, especially in the second half of the 18th century, the centralized power of the state. As Tawney emphasized (1912), they were an important means of expropriation of those without legally enforceable rights to their land, notably leaseholders, squatters and cottagers.

But other factors may have been more important in separating peasants from the land. Engrossment combined many small farms into few larger farms and therefore replaced small leaseholders by larger capitalist tenants. The differentiation of the peasantry led to land sales by some (Lenin, 1908; Dobb, 1947). This process was facilitated by the presence of a land market and the growth of population from 1500 to 1640 and again after 1750. Demographic expansion among the landless further increased the numbers of proletarians (Tilly, 1984).

Marx (1890, ch. 30) maintained that the transformation of agriculture had the significance of creating a proletariat for industry as well as agriculture. The supply of both agricultural goods and labour-power for other sectors of the economy increased as a result of growing labour productivity, a second facet of the agricultural revolution, combined with more intense work and lower consumption by workers compared to smallholders. This argument has received support from recent agrarian history, which points to productivity growth coming from convertible husbandry, new rotations including grasses and the turnip and greatly improved animal husbandry (Chambers and Mingay, 1966; Kerridge, 1967; Jones, 1974). Such innovation may have been aided by the accumulation of capitalist farmers and by the control and scale afforded by enclosure and engrossment. Moreover, enclosures were often depopulating, especially when they led to convertible husbandry or pasturage. Such changes allowed the share of nonagricultural population to rise from 40 per cent in 1688 to 64 per cent in 1801 in a period when England was largely self-sufficient in foodstuffs.

Finally, Marx correctly contended that with the decline of subsistence production, wage-labourers contributed to the expansion of the home market. But especially in periods of rising prices like the 16th century, the growing rural middle class may have added even more to market expansion, particularly for industrial products. Growing productivity may also have supported the home market by causing relative agricultural prices to fall, so that incomes in the industrial sector could rise while the income of farmers need not decline (John, 1965; Jones, 1974).

COMMERCIAL ACCUMULATION AND MARKET EXPANSION. The genesis of capitalist agriculture contrasts sharply with the birth of capitalist industry. While agriculture generated both its own capitalists and workers, the urban crafts played a distinctly secondary role in forming either pole of industry. Rather, the agricultural revolution inadvertently supplied the labourers, and merchants advanced much of the money to employ them and shaped markets in which their products were sold. To grasp the birth of industrial capital, we must first look at merchants.

The question is how merchant activity fostered primitive accumulation. In the genesis of capitalism, Marx held that merchants played a decisive, independent role: 'Today, industrial supremacy brings with it commercial supremacy. In the period of manufacture it is the reverse: commercial supremacy produces industrial predominance' (1890, p. 918). Of course market growth need not stimulate either industry or wage-labour; it led to the development of grain-producing serfdom in Poland and slave sugar and tobacco plantations in much of the Americas. But even these might have contributed to capitalist development if trade with peripheral areas using these labour forms financed industrial production in England (Wallerstein, 1976; cf. Brenner, 1977).

Merchants could foster primitive accumulation by expanding markets, by providing employment, or by investing profits. While Marx emphasizes domestic causes of proletarianization, he focuses primarily on international commerce in accounting for the genesis of the industrial capitalist (1890, ch. 31). This interpretation stresses the forcefulness and unevenness of primitive accumulation; it was through servile labour in the colonies, the slave trade and commercial wars that the English prospered and replaced the Dutch as the dominant mercantile power by 1700.

No doubt international commerce had a central role in industrial expansion. Growing exports stimulated domestic output; particularly for the textile industries, something like half the output of which was exported. In most of the 18th century, industrial exports grew more rapidly than industrial output, increasing their share of that output from about a fifth to a third from 1700 to 1800. Imports of industrial raw materials, like silk, cotton, dyestuffs and iron, also supported English industry. Marx's stress on the colonial system is warranted by the expansion of the share of domestic exports shipped to the American colonies from 11 per cent in 1700 to 37 per cent in 1772, as well as by its growing significance for imports and reexports (Davis, 1962; Minchinton, 1969; Cole, 1981).

Merchant services and profits also stimulated domestic output. The ascendency of British merchants in world trade led to the expansion of the ports. Commerce was the principal factor in London's growth, and consumption spending by merchants, related professionals and labourers fostered both industrial and agricultural expansion in much of England. Lesser ports had similar effects.

315

Purchases of ships, armaments and connected products likewise supported industry. While large and growing, the reinvested profits of the international merchant community remained principally in the same lines of business and, except for a few industries in the ports, offered little industrial financing.

Marx's stress on international commerce is surely one-sided; others, including Lenin (1908), have shifted the focus to the home market. For this market, which in England regularly consumed some nine-tenths of the national product, grew with the perhaps 80 per cent increase of that product from 1700 to 1780.

But the home market had significance beyond its share of national output. As Hobsbawm argues (1954), capitalism involves production for a mass market, and the combination of traditional local and export markets could not supply the necessary scale. During the manufacturing period, an integrated, mass market was born. This transformation was not of course confined to the home market; Hobsbawm underscores the importance of new markets in the colonies. But the home market was primary. It became much more spatially integrated. For food, fuel and many industrial products, the great expansion of London was central to this process. Expanding national markets were accompanied by growing regional specialization of production. The mass market was supported by the emerging class structure, especially the prosperous middle class of farmers, modest merchants, manufacturers, and some professionals and tradesmen. Particularly in times of falling agricultural prices, workers added to this market. Finally, a series of new commodities spread through sections of the home market, including the new textiles, stockings, new tools, and a host of housewares made of metal, pottery and glass. For most of these, the home market was decisive (Eversley, 1967; Thirsk, 1978).

The reinvested profits of domestic merchants, like their international counterparts, remained preponderantly within the commercial sphere. They expanded their working capital, deepened their wholesale marketing network, and helped form the clearing-house and bill-discounting mechanisms through which the market worked. They were the principal investors in transportation improvements like the expansion of coastal shipping, turnpike construction, river deepening, and, from the second half of the 18th century, canal construction. Domestic merchants could also finance industry, but even if they did not, their investment created conditions where others would.

THE BIRTH OF INDUSTRIAL CAPITAL. In his well-known discussion of paths to capitalism, Marx identified two ways that industrial capitalists were formed; producers could become capitalists and merchants, or merchants could enter production and employ wage-labourers (1894, ch. 20; see also Dobb, 1947). At stake is not just the genesis of industrial capital but also its dynamic. For Marx, the merchant path separates the worker from ownership of the product but retains inherited techniques and social organization of production. It is ultimately conservative; 'however frequently this occurs as a historical transition ... it cannot bring about the overthrow of the old mode of production by itself, but rather preserves it and retains it as its own precondition' (1894, p. 452). By

316

contrast, producers-turned-capitalists comprise 'the really revolutionary way' since they grow by transforming the organization and techniques of production.

Two quite different kinds of wholesale capitalist production were formed: manufacturing in the narrow sense and domestic industry. Manufacturing had the more innovative organization of the production process. It grouped craft workers specialized by task in the capitalist's workshop and often entailed economies of scale and significant capital costs. It was not solely the creation of producers; the funds, organizational abilities and market knowledge of merchants and even landlords also played a part. Manufacturing most commonly arose in industries which were new (alum, gunpowder, glass, cane sugar), used new techniques (salt, pig iron, heavy iron products), or produced for newly integrated markets(coal). Marx is ambiguous about its significance; he calls manufacture 'a characteristic form of the capitalist process of production' which 'prevails throughout the manufacturing period' yet recognizes that it never dominated the system (1890, pp. 455, 911).

Domestic industry was far more widespread. Born earlier in the textile trades, domestic industry expanded across many industries in the manufacturing stage. Spurred by relatively high wages and inelastic labour supply in the organized urban trades, both merchants and producers put out work to be done in the homes of outworkers. Some domestic industry arose in urban areas, especially London, but more was proto-industrial – household production of wholesale industrial goods by those retaining ties to land and rural communities (Mantoux, 1928; Mendels, 1972; Kriedte, et al., 1981).

This proto-industry had distinctive patterns of development. It generally originated in pastoral regions and declining or large-scale agricultural areas. Over time, outwork by independent producers declined and wage-labour rose. Through the efforts of both merchants and producers, proto-industry spread within and between localities. Immigration and a distinctive proto-industrial family structure which encouraged earlier marriages and rising birth rates gave an elasticity to employment in existing areas, but ties to the land meant that rapid expansion could not only achieved by the geographic spread of industry. Much of this growth was undertaken by the formation of new firms holding advantages of knowledge of and proximity to the local population.

By themselves or with others, producers were instrumental in changing the production process and its products. Both from the Continent and within England, craftsmen diffused techniques to make pig iron, paper, saltpetre, and brass and copper products. They also made a few advances in coal mining, iron making and civil engineering. No doubt the division of labour was refined in manufacturing and learning in the proto-industrial regions improved skills. But the circumscribed technical knowledge of most crafts, and the personal interactions required to transmit skills, formed barriers which limited the scope and importance of technical innovations and rendered their diffusion slow and uneven.

Changes in products were far more general. The largest of the rural industries, textiles, maintained its position in the world market by developing the new, lighter fabrics called the new draperies, as well as introducing cotton, fustian, linen and silk. Pots, pans, nails, pins, knives, buttons, stockings, ribbon, lace, glass bottles and earthen pots all developed for the home market in the late 16th and early 17th centuries (Thirsk, 1978). Merchants and craftsmen were both active in developing and diffusing these product innovations.

These changes in techniques and products formed a dynamic in production which gave competitive advantages to innovating firms and regions. The use of these advantages helped replace the inherited pattern of local and external markets by a new kind of market, called by Polanyi the internal market (1944). The products of innovators substituted for imports and also extended the market absolutely, particularly among middle and lower class consumers. The internal market grew with market integration and the increased per capita income and consumption resulting from productivity increases and transportation improvements. As its share of national product grew, industry came to create more of its own demand. Success in the internal market provided the basis from which some commodities entered export markets. In the international economy, as well as in England, industrial advance was leading to commercial success.

PRIMITIVE ACCUMULATION AND THE STAGES OF THE CAPITALIST ECONOMY. In England, more than in any country before or since, the manufacturing stage realized the preconditions of capitalist production. This stage also created conditions for the distinctive kind and pace of accumulation characteristic of the stage of large-scale industry. It thus satisfies the criterion that Gerschenkron employed to assess the usefulness of the concept of primitive accumulation: whether this prior accumulation aided the rapid growth associated with the onset of industrialization (1963, pp. 31–51).

Manufacturing did this not so much in the way Gerschenkron stresses, by the transfer of previously accumulated wealth to industrialists. The model capital requirements of early factories and the primary role of producers in founding industrial firms – Marx's revolutionary path to capitalism – makes it difficult to justify the role of the prior accumulation of wealth in this way (Crouzet, 1985). Far more important were marketing and transportation investments, which together with the agricultural revolution developed markets wide enough to warrant the extensive factory investment and the formation of a capital goods sector characteristic of the Industrial Revolution (Hobsbawm, 1954). Moreover, the manufacturing period generated the proletariat to work in the factories and – through the development of milling techniques, new products like the clock, the printing press, firearms and the Newcomen engine, and the great expansion of the tool-making sector – supplied agents willing and able to solve the technological problems of industrialization.

But even in England, primitive accumulation was by no means identical to the processes of the manufacturing stage. It involved processes prior to this stage, like the growth of towns and the elimination of serfdom. Nor was it completed within the manufacturing stage. For the persisting ties to the land, the structure of income distribution, and the inherited forms of labour limited the supply of labour-power, the extent of the market, and the growth of productivity (Levine, 1975). It was left to the dynamic of the next stage to complete the 'dissolution of the old economy relations of landed property', since 'only with the development of modern industry to a high degree does this dissolution at individual points acquire its totality and extent' (Marx, 1973, p. 277).

Still, the extent to which the conditions of capitalist production were created within the stage of manufacturing made England unique. In it alone had the agricultural revolution taken 'the classical form' (Marx, 1890, p. 876). The success of its industrialization reinforced its uniqueness by altering the process of primitive accumulation. Growing productivity and falling prices undercut the viability of proto-industrial and town craft producers at home and, through the growth of an export economy, abroad. The steamship and railroad overcame locational limits to competition. Separation from the means of production had become a consequence of the industrial stage of capitalism.

Moreover, for latecomers the prior generation of a supply of money capital and labour-power within their countries had less importance than in England. Primitive accumulation was internationalized; capital and labour-power both migrated more readily. New credit institutions and state policies could supply capital during the course of industrialization (Gerschenkron, 1962). On the Continent, large-scale industry was often born while peasantries persisted. More extreme was the United States, which was already a major industrial power at the time its frontier closed, and which, in the absence of widespread separation of agricultural producers from the land, sold principally in the home market.

Capitalism is for Marx a world-historical system, not a set of autarkic national units. There can therefore be no stage of primitive accumulation which uniformly prepares the way for capitalism in each of these units. The very success of the kinds of processes which brought large-scale, industrial capitalism in England changed both the process of primitive accumulation elsewhere and the relation of these processes to capitalist expansion. By tying the concept of primitive accumulation to a periodization of capitalist development, Marx provides insight into both the classical case of the genesis of capitalism and the necessarily different forms this genesis took elsewhere.

BIBLIOGRAPHY

Brenner, R. 1977. The origins of capitalist development: a critique of neo-Smithian Marxism. *New Left Review* No. 104, July–August, 25–92.

Chambers, J. and Mingay, G. 1966. *The Agricultural Revolution: 1750–1880*. London: Batsford.

Cole, E. 1981. Factors in demand 1700–80. In *The Economic History of Britain Since 1700*, ed. R. Floud and D. McCloskey, Cambridge: Cambridge University Press.

Crouzet, F. 1985. *The First Industrialists: The Problem of Origins*. Cambridge: Cambridge University Press.

Davis, R. 1962. *The Rise of the English Shipping Industry in the Seventeenth and Eighteenth Centuries*. London: Macmillan.

Dobb, M. 1947. *Studies in the Development of Capitalism*. New York: International.

Eversley, D. 1967. The home market and economic growth in England, 1750–80. In *Land, Labour and Population in the Industrial Revolution*, ed. E. Jones and G. Mingay, London: Edward Arnold.

Gerschenkron, A. 1962. *Economic Backwardness in Historical Perspective*. Cambridge, Mass.: Harvard University Press.

Hobsbawm, E. 1954. The general crisis of the European economy in the 17th century. *Past and Present* 54(4), May, 33–53; 54(6), October, 44–65.

John, A. 1965. Agricultural productivity and economic growth in England, 1700–1760. *Journal of Economic History* 25, March, 19–34.

Jones, E. 1974. *Agriculture and the Industrial Revoluton*. New York: Wiley.

Kerridge, E. 1967. *The Agricultural Revolution*. London: George Allen & Unwin; New York: A.M. Kelley, 1968.

Kriedte, P., Medick, H. and Schlumbohm, J. 1981. *Industrialization before Industrialization*: *Rural Industry in the Genesis of Capitalism*. Cambridge and New York: Cambridge University Press.

Lenin, V.I. 1908. *The Development of Capitalism in Russia*. 2nd edn. In Lenin, *Collected Works*, Vol. 3. Moscow: Progress, 1964.

Levine, D. 1975. The theory of growth of the capitalist economy. *Economic Development and Cultural Change* 24(1), October, 47–74.

Mantoux, P. 1928. *The Industrial Revolution in the Eighteenth Century*. New York: Macmillan, 1961.

Marx, K. 1890. *Capital: A Critique of Political Economy*, Vol. I. New York: Vintage, 1977.

Marx, K. 1894. *Capital: A Critique of Political Economy*, Vol. III. New York: Vintage, 1981.

Marx, K. 1857–8. *Grundrisse: Foundations of the Critique of Political Economy*. Harmondsworth: Penguin, 1973.

Mendels, F. 1972. Proto-industrialization: the first phase of the industrialization process. *Journal of Economic History* 32(1), March, 241–61.

Minchinton, W. 1969. *The Growth of English Overseas Trade in the Seventeenth and Eighteenth Centuries*. London: Methuen.

Polanyi, K. 1944. *The Great Transformation: The Political and Economic Origins of Our Time*. Boston: Beacon, 1957.

Smith, A. 1776. *An Inquiry into the Nature and Causes of the Wealth of Nations*. Ed. E. Cannan, New York: Random House, 1965.

Tawney, R. 1912. *The Agrarian Problem in the Sixteenth Century*. New York: Harper, 1967.

Thirsk, J. 1978. *Economic Policy and Projects: The Development of a Consumer Society in Early Modern England*. Oxford: Clarendon Press; New York: Oxford University Press.

Tilly, C. 1984. Demographic origins of the European proletariat. In *Proletarianization and Family Life*, ed. D. Levine, New York: Academic Press.

Wallerstein, I. 1976. *The Modern World System: Capitalist Agriculture and the Origins of the European World-Economy in the Sixteenth Century*. London: Academic Press.

Rate of Exploitation

FABIO PETRI

According to Karl Marx, the proletariat, i.e. wage labourers, is exploited by the capitalists: behind the apparent freedom and equality of the partners in the wage contract, Marx sees a power inequality which results in the workers being exploited by the capitalists in the same sense in which the serfs were exploited by their feudal landlords, or slaves by their masters. The capitalists are able to compel the workers to produce a surplus product, which they appropriate as profit, not by virtue of any productive contribution of theirs, but simply owing to their superior bargaining position vis-à-vis the workers, deriving from their collective monopoly of the means of production. Much the same (although without using the term 'exploitation') had already been said by Adam Smith, who also anticipated Marx on the importance of the repressive state apparatus's support for the institution of private property.

This general perspective explains Marx's occasional use of the term 'rate of exploitation' as synonymous with 'rate of surplus value', the latter being the more frequently used term, whose meaning will now be clarified. The labour value of, or labour embodied in, a commodity is defined by Marx as the sum of the direct and indirect labour necessary to its production, i.e. of the live labour expended in its direct process of production plus the labour embodied in the means of production used up (according to the socially necessary conditions of production) in that same process. If the socially necessary live labour performed in the whole economy is L, and the labour embodied in the means of production used up to produce the total social product is C, then the labour value of the total social product is $L + C$, and of the net social product is again L (because the net social product is defined as the total social product minus that part of it which replaces the means of production used up, a part whose labour value is clearly C). If now V is the labour embodied in the part of the net social product going to the workers, then $S \equiv L - V$, the surplus labour, or surplus value, is the labour embodied in the surplus product. Under constant returns to scale, only V, instead of L, would be necessary to produce a net product equal to the

321

workers' share only; hence Marx calls V the 'necessary' or 'paid' labour, and S the surplus or 'unpaid' labour, and divides in the same proportions the average working day into a 'paid' and an 'unpaid' part. The ratio S/V is what he calls 'rate of surplus value' or 'rate of exploitation'.

Given the techniques in use, S/V depends on the average wage basket, and its changes reflect changes in the balance of power between classes. Its importance for Marx lies in its being one of the two proximate determinants of the rate of profits, the other one being the average 'organic composition of capital', i.e. the ratio of what Marx called 'constant capital' (the labour value of the capital goods employed in the production process) to what Marx called 'variable capital' (the labour value of the wage goods, which for Marx are part of capital because he considered wages to be advanced, rather than paid at the end of the production period as is usually assumed nowadays), in other words the ratio C/V (assuming for simplicity that all the capital goods utilized in the economy are circulating capital). The rate of exploitation and the organic composition of capital can also be defined for each industry: then $s + v$ is the live labour performed in that industry; s/v, the rate of exploitation, is the ratio of the surplus or 'unpaid' labour to the labour value of the real wages obtained by the workers in that industry, c the value of the capital goods employed; c/v the organic composition of capital; and the rate of profits is given by $r = s/(c + s)$ which can also be re-written as $r = (s/v)/[(c/v) + 1]$. If – as Marx assumes in Volume I of *Capital* – commodities exchanged at prices proportional to labour values, then the rate of profits (assuming prices proportional to labour values) could be uniform across the different industries only if – what observation shows not to be true – c/v were uniform (s/v is, on the other hand, uniform if the hourly wage is uniform or, as Marx assumes, heterogeneous or differently paid labour is reduced to homogeneity on the basis of relative wages). Marx was thus able to understand, more clearly than anyone before him, why the tendency of profit rates towards uniformity will cause relative prices to deviate from relative labour values. He nonetheless thought that in the economy as a whole the deviations cancel out, and that the uniform rate of profits is therefore the same as the average rate of profits which would obtain if commodities did exchange at labour values, i.e. $r = S/(C + S)$, or $r = (S/V)/[(C/V) + 1]$.

Thus, he thought, the influences on the rate of profits can be better understood by studying the way they affect the two ratios S/V and C/V. This he thought to be a useful distinction because it allowed one better to separate the effects on the rate of profits of various types of technological change (effects which could be seen to be important in so far as they affected C/V or – e.g. speedups – S/V) from the effects of the workers' struggles over the wage level or, given the *daily* wage, over the length of the working day (affecting S/V).

This role of the rate of exploitation as defined by Marx has been undermined by the subsequent analytical advances in the theory of prices of production, association with the names of Dmitriev, Bortkiewicz, Sraffa and now many others. It has been seen that Marx's basic insight was correct in that the *data* (the technological conditions, i.e. the matrix of physical and labour inputs, and the average wage basket), from which individual labour values and the aggregate magnitudes S, V, C are derived, do suffice to determine the rate of profits and relative prices; but it has also been seen that Marx's formula $r = S/(C + V)$ is incorrect except in very special cases, and that, although it would be possible to find algorithms to determine the correct rate of profits and prices from individual labour values, the calculation of labour values is anyway superfluous, a direct determination of the rate of profits and prices from those data being possible and easier. New analytical instruments, e.g. the wage-profit frontier, allow a more rigorous study of the effects of changes in technology or in the real wage on the rate of profits than S/V and C/V (e.g. it has been seen that technical change may in some cases cause r to move in a direction opposite to what Marx's formula would lead to to expect), relegating – for the study of these problems – labour value magnitudes to historical importance only, in that they allowed Marx to determine prices and the rate of profits, and the effects of the main forces acting on them, in the only (imperfect) way concretely possible at the time (Garegnani, 1984).

Many marxists (e.g. Sweezy, Hunt, Nuti) defend the importance of labour values by arguing that these allow one to show that workers are exploited. It is often claimed, in this connection, that central to Marx's analysis was the so-called Fundamental Marxian Theorem, stating that the rate of profits is positive if and only if the rate of exploitation is positive (Morishima, 1974). This is a doubtful claim, since the theorem re-states, in terms of labour embodied, the obvious fact – accepted by all critics of Marx as well – that profits can only be positive if wages do not absorb the entire net product. To call the S/V ratio 'rate of exploitation' is not a *demonstration* that workers are exploited: e.g. the marginalist, or neoclassical, approach would have no quarrel with the Fundamental Marxian Theorem and yet would argue that workers are not exploited, because they receive their marginal products, i.e. as much as each of them is contributing to production, and in the same way a positive rate of profits does not emerge from domination but rather corresponds to the marginal product of capital, and is therefore a just reward to the sacrifice of postponed consumption which, through savings, creates the capital: the marginalist explanation of distribution thus implies that capitalists (i.e. in the marginalist approach, savers) do contribute to production. The required demonstration of the existence of exploitation appears rather to lie in the validity of Marx's different explanation of why the surplus product does not go to the workers, referred to above, now supported by the criticisms directed at the marginalist theory of distribution (Eatwell and Milgate, 1983).

The existence of exploitation is therefore not endangered by the demonstration, due to Steedman (1975), that the Fundamental Marxian Theorem cannot be generalized to the case of joint production, so long at least as labour values are defined as usual, i.e. as the prices (in terms of the wage) at a zero rate of profits (if A and B are the square matrices of input and output coefficients respectively, and l the labour input vector, then the vector of labour values k is determined by $kA + l = kB$; this expression is what the price equations $(pA + wl)(1 + r) = pB$

collapse to if $r = 0$ and $w = 1$; without joint production one has $B = I$, the identity matrix, and hence $kA + l = k$). With joint production, some labour values may be negative, and the surplus product may then have a negative labour value, implying a negative rate of exploitation. An intuitive explanation is as follows. The labour value of a commodity is an employment multiplier, indicating by what amount total employment would change if (with constant returns) the net product of that commodity increased by 1 unit, the other net products remaining constant. If several commodities are jointly produced by several processes, an increase in the net product of only one commodity may require expanding some processes but contracting some others (no contraction would be necessary in the absence of joint products): the resulting total variation in employment need not be positive. If the rate of exploitation is negative, total employment would have to increase in order not to produce the surplus product at all. But, it would seem, there still is exploitation, because the surplus product is not going to the workers, while it would if the capitalists' domination were not preventing the wage from rising.

Morishima and others have counter-argued that the idea of a negative labour embodied in a (single or composite) commodity makes no sense, and have proposed to re-define (via linear programming) the labour embodied in a commodity as the minimum labour time necessary, with the known techniques, to produce a net product containing at least that commodity (but possibly other commodities as well; individual labour values are then no longer additive, the labour value of a bundle of wool and mutton is no longer the sum of the labour values of the wool and of the mutton). The surplus labour S^* is then the difference between L and the minimum labour V^* necessary to produce, with the available technical knowledge, a net product containing at least the total wage basket. The rate of exploitation is then re-defined as S^*/V^*: a notion, it would seem, only interesting for purposes of comparison of reality with possible utopias ('how much less workers could afford to work if the social goal were the minimization of their working time, given their consumption'). It is not impossible, anyway, that in extreme cases S^*/V^* be zero in spite of a positive surplus product, as shown by the following example: the economy produces only, and jointly, wool and mutton from sheep, the surplus product consists of all the wool and the real wages of all the mutton; the rate of profits might be positive too (Petri, 1980).

This and other recent attempts at re-defining labour values and the rate of exploitation cannot, it would seem, find support in Marx, where the role of labour values appears to have been only the determination of prices and of the rate of profits, as shown for example by the way labour values are determined: Marx, like Ricardo, determines labour values on the no-rent land, and reduces heterogeneous labour to homogeneity on the basis of relative wages (implying a rate of exploitation uniform for all kinds of labour; see Steedman, 1985): which is what he must do in order to argue that prices would be proportional to labour values were it not for the non-uniformity of the organic composition of capital. Nowadays, ethical aims, for example some measurement of the degree of suffering imposed upon workers by capitalism, are often implicit in the search for re-definitions of the rate of exploitation. This is not necessarily illegitimate, but should be clearly stated and distinguished from Marx's own project.

BIBLIOGRAPHY

Bortkiewicz, L. von. 1907. Value and price in the Marxian system. Trans. in *International Economic Papers* Nol 2, 5–60, 1952.

Dmitriev, V.K. 1974. *Economic Essays on Value, Competition and Utility*. Ed. D.M. Nuti, Cambridge: Cambridge University Press.

Eatwell, J. and Milgate, M. (eds) 1983. *Keynes's Economics and the Theory of Value and Distribution*. London: Duckworth.

Garegnani, P. 1984. Value and distribution in the classical economists and Marx. *Oxford Economic Papers* 36(2), June, 291–325.

Hunt, E.K. and Schwartz, J.G. (eds) 1972. *A Critique of Economic Theory*. Harmondsworth: Penguin.

Marx, K. 1867–94. *Capital*, Vols. I–III. Moscow: Progress Publishers, 1965–6.

Mainwaring, L. 1984. *Value and Distribution in Capitalist Economies. An Introduction to Sraffian Economics*. Cambridge: Cambridge University Press.

Morishima, M. 1974. Marx in the light of modern economic theory. *Econometrica* 42(4), July, 611–32.

Morishima, M. and Catephores, G. 1978. *Value, Exploitation and Growth*. London and New York: McGraw-Hill.

Petri, F. 1980. Positive profits without exploitation: a note on the generalized fundamental marxian theorem. *Econometrica* 48(2), March, 531–3.

Sraffa, P. 1960. *Production of Commodities by Means of Commodities*. Cambridge: Cambridge University Press.

Steedman, I. 1975. Positive profits with negative surplus value. *Economic Journal* 85, March, 114–23.

Steedman, I. 1985. Heterogeneous labour, money wages, and Marx's theory. *History of Political Economy* 17(4), 551–74.

Steedman, I., Sweezy, P. et al. *The Value Controversy*. London: New Left Books. Distributed in U.S.A. by Schocken Books.

Realization Problem

P. KENWAY

The realization problem was first considered by classical economists such as Ricardo and Sismondi. Keynes's theory of effective demand has a bearing on it too. But it was Marx who gave it its most rounded – and controversial – treatment. At its simplest, the realization problem amounts to this: is there sufficient monetary demand for the commodities which have been produced to be sold, and sold at their value?

It is by no means obvious that there is really any problem at all. Why is the very act of production itself not enough to guarantee that there will be sufficient demand to ensure that all commodities will be sold? This was the view held strongly by Ricardo. His argument amounted to this: nobody produces except to sell and nobody sells except to buy something else. Marx showed that such arguments were wrong because they overlooked the specific nature of capitalist production (*see* CRISES).

The realization problem arises therefore because production under capitalism is but a phase within the circulation of capital, $M - C \ldots P \ldots - C' - M'$. Here, money is firstly converted into means of production and labour-power $(M - C)$. Production then takes place $(C \ldots P \ldots C')$. The produced commodities must then be sold $(C' - M')$, they must be reconverted into money, their value must be realized (Marx, 1885, p. 709). This must happen if the circuit of capital is to be complete. That this must happen, and yet that it may not, is the realization problem.

Some of the features of the problem must be emphasized. The commodity has a value before it arrives on the market, this value being made up of the constant and variable capital consumed in its manufacture, along with the surplus value produced. By the time the question of realization arises, a certain level of output is presupposed, which depends particularly on the amount of capital thrown into production; and for the realization problem to be overcome, a certain level of monetary demand must be found in the sphere of circulation.

These aspects are derived from an analysis of the individual capital only. Whilst an investigation of the realization problem must take all of them into account. the problem can only fully be analysed in the context of the reproduction of the total social capital. This Marx did in his discussion of the reproduction schemes, in part three of Volume Two of *Capital*.

THE REPRODUCTION SCHEMES. The reproduction schemes can be viewed as abstract, two-sector models of the production and circulation of capital. Department one produces means of production. The value of its output is made up of $C_1 + V_1 + S_1$, where C_1 is the constant capital and V_1 the variable capital used up in production. S_1 is the surplus value produced. Department two produces means of consumption and the value of its product is likewise made up of $C_2 + V_2 + S_2$.

Marx considered two situations, simple and expanded reproduction. Simple reproduction is where capitalists devote all their surplus value to the purchase of consumption goods and seek only to produce in the next period at the same level as this. Expanded reproduction is where capitalists must accumulate some of their surplus value in order to obtain a larger stock of constant and variable capital, for use in the next period.

The point of the schemes was to investigate how the circulation must proceed in order for capital successfully to reproduce itself. This involves circulation within and between the two departments. For example, simple reproduction requires that capitalists in department two acquire means of production to the value C_2 from department one in order to be able to produce again.

Two points should be noted. Firstly, when considering the reproduction of the total social capital, account must be taken of both value and use-value. This had not been necessary when considering the individual capital only. There, Marx had simply assumed that within the sphere of circulation would be found all the commodities necessary both to transform the capital value into new elements of production and commodities to satisfy workers' and capitalists' consumption (Marx, 1885, p. 470).

Secondly, the scheme for expanded reproduction requires capitalists to accumulate (rather than consume) value out of this year's surplus value. It is important to emphasize that the amount accumulated must be a sufficient value to cover the *entire* amount of extra capital needed, both the extra constant capital and the extra variable capital.

This means that in department one $(1 - a_1)S_1$ must be equal in value to $dC_1 + dV_1$. Likewise, in department two $(1 - a_2)S_2$ must be equal in value to $dC_2 + dV_2$. (*a* denotes the portion of surplus value devoted by capitalists to consumption whilst the prefix *d* denotes the additional capital required).

These, combined with the requirement that the supply of means of production must equal the demand for them:

$$C_1 + V_1 + S_1 = C_1 + C_2 \text{ (replacing what has been used up)}$$

$$+ dC_1 + dC_2 \text{ (the extra required for next year)}$$

327

are sufficient to construct workable examples of capitalist reproduction. (See, for example, the numerical examples given in Marx, 1885, pp. 586–91.)

Other relationships can be derived from these which must hold if reproduction is to proceed successfully. One such, the 'Bukharin condition' for expanded reproduction (Rosdolsky, 1968, p. 449) is:

$$C_2 + dC_2 = V_1 + dV_1 + a_1 S_1.$$

In other words, what department two needs to buy from department one $(C_2 + dC_2)$ must equal what department one needs to buy from department two $(V_1 + dV_1 + a_1 S_1)$. In the case of simple reproduction this reduces to the more familiar expression: $C_2 = V_1 + S_1$.

INTERPRETATION OF THE REPRODUCTION SCHEMES. Analysis of the schemes shows that accumulation and the circulation of values and use-values can take place in such a way as to permit the successful resolution of the realization problem. The expansion of capital is shown to be possible. The theory must demonstrate this in view of the history of capitalist development. In so doing, Marx was refuting economists such as Sismondi who thought that expanded reproduction was impossible.

But one must be careful not to conclude too much from this result. The 'Austrian Marxists' for example concluded that the schemes showed that the reproduction cycle of capital need never break down. Hilferding went so far as to argue that the schemes proved that Marx had never been a supporter of the breakdown theory (cited in Rosdolsky, 1968, p. 451).

This view is mistaken. The schemes cannot just be interpreted as if they are a model of the 'real world'. They are at a particular level of abstraction and leave out of account, for example, not only technical progress but also any impact of changes in either the organic composition of capital or the rate of surplus value.

More importantly however, the fact that the simultaneous consideration of value, use-value and accumulation does not uncover insurmountable difficulties is by no means the same thing as proving that the circuit of capital need never be broken or that the realization problem is never going to manifest itself as a real difficulty.

What the schemes show – or more properly illustrate, for it is a result of the *method* of Marx's argument – is something rather different: the realization problem can be solved this year, but that solution creates anew all the conditions which will ensure that the problem arises again next year. To solve the problem this year, values must once more be tied-up as capital which must next year be put to use to produce surplus value. These values must subsequently be realized. This year's solution is the seed from which next year's problem springs.

THE REALIZATION PROBLEM AND GLUTS. The schemes also show the close connection between the realization problem and the potential, within the reproduction of capital, for general gluts of capital and commodities.

From the formulation of the reproduction schemes, it is easy to see that this year finishes up with a stock of means of production to be carried over to next year. This is not all that is carried over, however. For the value of output in department two $(C_2 + V_2 + S_2)$ exceeds the value of consumption out of this year's income, wages $(V_1 + V_2)$ plus capitalist consumption $(a_1 S_1 + a_2 S_2)$. The excess amounts to the value of the additional variable capital to be accumulated $(dV_1 + dV_2)$. This result is caused by the requirement that value be produced and accumulated to cover the *entire* amount of additional capital needed for production on an expanded scale, not just to cover the additional constant capital alone.

Thus both stocks of means of production and means of consumption are carried forward. Both grow in an orderly way if production grows smoothly and their value can be realized so long as this continues. But these stocks bear testimony to the fact that the process of reproduction contains the potential for a general glut, which in the first place can take the form of unused means of production and unsold consumption goods. This potential will not manifest itself so long as the realization problem is overcome. But the constant recurrence of the realization problem means that the potential of the general glut is constantly renewed.

THE REALIZATION PROBLEM AND THE THEORY OF EFFECTIVE DEMAND. Finally, what is the relationship between this analysis and Keynes's theory of effective demand? The schemes certainly include the result that the level of output at which all output can be sold is the one at which net investment equals that part of surplus value not devoted to capitalist consumption (assuming that workers do not save). This comes over clearly, for example in the discussion of the difficulties posed for simple reproduction by depreciation, that is, where capital is not fully exhausted within the one year (Marx, 1885, p. 528 et seq.).

There is, however, a significant difference between Marx and Keynes here. Whereas Keynes was investigating the 'theory of what determines the *actual employment* of the available resources' (Keynes, 1936, p. 4), Marx was concerned with the '"theory" of what enables a given level and structure of output to be realized, to be sold, in order that production may begin anew'.

The theory of effective demand certainly sheds an interesting light on the realization problem. But Marx's investigation of the realization problem is part of a coherent whole. The fact that his analysis is firmly rooted in a theory of value shows this. In contrast, Keynes's theory was developed in opposition to the orthodox theory of value and output (which are of course one and the same theory). The theory of effective demand is beset with the difficulty of explaining *why* the monetary level of demand matters. Marx's analysis of the nature of capitalist production provides this (see Kenway, 1980).

An explanation of what determines the actual employment of the available resources is most pertinent, especially during a slump. But the investigation of how, why and whether capitalism can produce and reproduce itself is surely the more profound and more general question.

Marxian economics

BIBLIOGRAPHY

Kenway, P. 1980. Marx, Keynes and the possibility of crisis. *Cambridge Journal of Economics* 4(1), March, 23–36.

Keynes, J.M. 1936. *The General Theory of Employment, Interest and Money*, London: Macmillan, 1973; New York: St. Martin's Press.

Marx, K. 1885. *Capital*, Vol. II. Harmondsworth: Penguin, 1978.

Rosdolsky, R. 1968. *The Making of Marx's 'Capital'*. London: Pluto, 1977. Distributed in U.S.A. by Humanities Press.

Regulation

ROBERT BOYER

During the debates of the 1980s, the term '*régulation*' suggested state intervention in the name of economic management, though its opposite, '*dérégulation*', was more widely used. In the area of economic policy and in accordance with Keynesian precepts, regulation indicates the adjustment of macroeconomic activity by means of budgetary or monetary contracyclical interventions.

This term is also used in physics and biology, but with different meanings. In mechanics, a regulator is a means to stabilize the rotary speed of a machine. In biology, regulation corresponds to the reproduction of substances such as DNA. In general terms, the theory of systems involves the study of the role of a set of negative and positive feed-back loops in relation to the stability of a complex network of interactions.

Here, a third meaning of the term will be more thoroughly developed. While it is not completely disconnected from the preceding meanings, it is nevertheless distinct from them. Theories of *régulation* constitute an area of research which has focused on analysing long-term transformations in capitalist economies. Initially, this work was mainly French; but related studies can be found in various OECD as well as Third World countries (Hausmann, 1981; Ominami, 1985). These combine Marxian intuitions and Kaleckian or Keynesian macroeconomics in order to revive institutionalist or historicist studies.

At a primary level, a form of *régulation* denotes any *dynamic process of adaptation* of production and social demand resulting from a conjunction of economic adjustments linked to a given configuration of social relations, forms of organization and structures (Boyer, 1979 and 1986a). On a secondary, more ambitious level, this problematic aims at describing, and where possible at explaining, the transition from one mode of *régulation* to another in a long-term historical perspective (Aglietta, 1982; G.R.E.E.C., 1981). So the aim of this problematic is far-reaching and of a general character but its field is defined by three essential questions: How can we explain the *transition* from periods of high and relatively regular growth to periods of relative stagnation and instability?

331

Why, *during the passage of time* do crises take different directions? Can one assume that growth and crises assume significantly different *national forms*?

Most economic theories – neoclassical, Keynesian, or even Marxist – emphasize the general invariables of eminently abstract systems, in which history serves merely as a confirmation, or failing that, as a perturbation. In contrast, the *régulation* approach seeks a broader interaction between history and theory, social structures, institutions and economic regularities (de Vroey, 1984).

As a starting point we consider the hypothesis of the *central role of accumulation* as the driving force of capitalist societies. This necessitates a clarification of factors that reduce or delay the conflicts and disequilibria inherent in the formation of capital, and which allow for an understanding of the *possibility* of periods of sustained growth (Boyer and Mistral, 1978). These factors are associated with particular regimes of accumulation, namely the form of articulation between the dynamics of the productive system and social demand, between the distribution of income between wages and profits on the one hand; and on the other hand the division between consumption and investment. It is then useful to explain the *organizational principles* which allow for a mediation between such contradictions as the extension of productive capacity under the stimulus of competition, and downward pressure on wages which inhibits the growth of demand. The notion of *institutionalized form* – defined as a set of fundamental social relations (Aglietta, 1982) – enables the transition between constraints associated with an accumulation regime and collective strategies; between economic dynamics and individual behaviour. A small number of key institutional forms, which are the result of past social struggles and the imperatives of the material reproduction of society, frame and channel a multitude of partial strategies which are decentralized and limited in terms of their temporal horizon. Research on the United States (Aglietta, 1982) and France (Boyer, 1979, 1986a) distinguish between five main institutional forms.

The forms of competition describe by what mechanisms the compatibility of a set of decentralized decisions is ensured. They are competitive while the ex post adjustment of prices and quantities ensure a balance; they are monopolist if the ex ante socialization of revenue is such that production and social demand evolve together (Lipietz, 1979). *The type of monetary constraint* explains the interrelations between credit and money creation: credit is narrowly limited in terms of movement of reserves when money is predominantly metallic; the causality is reversed when, on the contrary, the dynamics of credit conditions the money supply in systems where the external parity represents the only constraint weighing upon the national monetary system (Benassy et al., 1979). *The nature of institutionalized compromises* defines different configurations of relations between the State and the economy (Andrew and Delorme, 1983): the State-as-Arbiter when only general conditions of commercial exchange are guaranteed; as the interfering State when a network of *régulations* and budgetary interventions codify the rights of different social groups. *Modes of support for the international regime* are also derived from a set of rules which organize relations between the Nation-State and the rest of the world in terms of commodity exchange, capital movements and monetary settlements. History goes beyond the traditional contrast between an open and a closed economy, free trade and protectionism; it makes apparent a variety of configurations spaced out between the hegemonic economy constituting the axis of the international system, and countries at the periphery of this system (Mistral, 1982; Lipietz, 1986a). Finally, *forms of wage relations* indicate different historical configurations of the relationship between Capital and Labour, i.e. the organization of the means of production, the nature of the social division of labour and work techniques, type of employment and the system of determination of wages, and finally, workers' way of life. If, in the first stages of industrialization, wage-earners are defined first of all as producers, during the second stage, they are simultaneously producers and consumers. Hence the contrast between 19th-century wage relations and the Fordist relations corresponding to the contemporary period (Coriat, 1978; Aglietta and Brender, 1984; Boyer, 1979 and 1987).

On the basis of these forms, one can analyse the logic of the behaviour of social groups and of individuals ensuring the relative coherence and stability of the current accumulation regime. At this point appears the notion of *régulation*, as a conjunction of mechanisms and principles of adjustment associated with a configuration of wage relations, competition, State interventions and hierarchization of the international economy. Finally, a distinction between '*small*' and '*big*' *crises* is called for (Billaudot and Granou, 1985; Lorenzi et al., 1980; Boyer, 1986a; Mazier et al., 1984). The former, which are of a rather cylical nature, are the very expression of *régulation* in reaction to the recurrent imbalances of accumulation. The latter are of a structural nature: the very process of accumulation throws into doubt the stability of institutional forms and the *régulation* which sustains it. The partial rupture in the functioning of the system paves the way to social struggles and political alternatives.

If the relevance of a theoretical model derives from the scope of its conclusions, it is imperative to point out some of the major findings in research pursued during the last decade. According to this problematic, in long-term dynamics as well as in short-term development *institutions are important*. Historical research confirms that sometimes institutional forms make an impression on the system in operation; at other times they register major changes in direction. At the end of a period which can be counted in decades, the very mode of development – i.e. the conjunction of the mode of *régulation* and the accumulation regime – is affected: there will be changes in the tendencies of long-term growth and eventually in inflation, specificities of cyclical processes (coexistence of recessions and deflations or marked stagflationist character) (CEPREMAP-CORDES, 1977).

So a periodization of advanced capitalist economies emerges which is not part of the traditional Marxist theory (Lorenzi et al., 1980). Despite the rise in monopoly, the interwar period is still marked by competitive regulation. After World War II an accumulation regime without precedent is instituted – that of intensive accumulation centred on mass consumption (Bertrand, 1983) – known as *Fordist* and channelled through *monopolist* type regulation.

In fact, the alteration in wage relations – in particular the transition to Fordism

(Coriat, 1978), i.e. the synchronization of mass production and wage-earners' access to the 'American way of life' – and in monetary management, i.e. transition to internally accepted credit money – seems to have played a greater role than the change in modes of competition or conjunctural stabilization policies *à la* Keynes (Aglietta, 1982; Aglietta and Orlean, 1982; Boyer, 1978).

Since the Sixties, we have allegedly been experiencing a big crisis without historical precedent; corresponding to an altogether original form of development (Boyer and Mistral, 1978; Mazier et al., 1984). This explains the absence, at least at the present, of cumulative depression and persistent, if more moderate, inflation (Lipietz, 1985).

In consequence, it is logical that former economic policies lose their efficacy (Boyer, 1986a). First, because the crisis is not cyclical but structural; this invalidates the policy of fine-tuning; second, because the structural changes which permitted the 1929 crisis to be overcome have become blocked (Lipietz, 1986b). They can therefore not be repeated in order to find a way out of the accumulated contradictions and imbalances.

There is no economic or technological determinism in the strictest sense. The multiplicity of past variants of Fordism and the diversity of strategies now deployed point to an opening, however partial, to ways out of crisis (Boyer, 1986b, 1986c). New problems are emerging which relate to an original articulation between industry and the service sector (Petit, 1986).

Moreover, research on social formations other than France, the United States and the old industrialized countries shows the extreme relativity of institutional forms, accumulation regimes and forms of regulation which cannot be reduced to a cardinal opposition between Taylorism and Fordism, competitive versus monopolist capitalism, etc. Rather than irrefutable results and a perfected theory, the regulation approach sets out general notions and a method of work. It is up to future research to turn these premises into a more complete theory.

BIBLIOGRAPHY

Aglietta, M. 1982. *Regulation and Crisis of Capitalism.* New York: Monthly Review Press.

Aglietta, M. and Brender, A. 1984. *Les métamorphoses de la société salariale.* Paris: Calmann-Levy.

Aglietta, M. and Orlean, A. 1982. *La violence de la monnaie.* Paris: PUF.

André, Ch. and Delorme, R. 1983. *L'état et l'économie.* Paris: Seuil.

Benassy, J.P., Boyer, R. and Gelpi, R.M. 1979. Régulation des économies capitalistes et inflation. *Revue économique* 30(3), May.

Bertrand, H. 1983. Accumulation, régulation, crise: un modèle sectionnel théorique et appliqué. *Revenue économique* 34(6), March.

Billaudot, B. and Granou, A. 1985. *Croissance et crises.* 2nd edn, Paris: La Découverte.

Boyer, R. 1979. Wage formation in historical perspective: the French experience. *Cambridge Journal of Economics* 3, March, 99–118.

Boyer, R. 1986a. *Théorie de la régulation: une analyse critique.* Paris: La Découverte.

Boyer, R. 1986b. New technologies and employment in the Eighties. In *Barriers to Full Employment*, ed. J.A. Kregel, London: Macmillan.

Boyer, R. (ed.) 1986c. *Capitalismes fin de siècle*. Paris: PUF.

Boyer, R. (ed.). 1987. *Labour Flexibility in Europe*. Oxford: Oxford University Press.

Boyer, R. and Mistral, J. 1978. *Accumulation, inflation, crises*. Paris: PUF.

CEPREMAP-CORDES, 1977. Approches de l'inflation: l'exemple français. Convention de recherche No. 22, December.

Coriat, B. 1978. L'atelier et le chronomètre. Paris: C. Bourgois.

De Vroey, M. 1984. A regulation approach interpretation of the contemporary crisis. *Capital and Class* 23, Summer, 45–66.

G.R.E.E.C. 1981. *Crise et régulation*. Grenoble: PUG, DRUG.

Hausmann, R. 1981. State landed property, oil rent and accumulation in Venezuela: an analysis in terms of social relations. PhD Thesis, Cornell University, August.

Lipietz, A. 1979. *Crise et inflation, pourquoi?* Paris: Maspéro.

Lipietz, A. 1985. *The Magic World. From Value to Inflation*. London: Verso.

Lipietz, A. 1986a. New techniques in the international division of labor: regimes of accumulation and mode of regulation. In *Production, Work, Territory*, ed. Scott and Storper, London: Allen & Unwin.

Lipietz, A. 1986b. Behind the crisis: the exhaustion of a regime of accumulation. A 'regulation school' perspective some French empirical works. *Review of Radical Political Economics* 18(1–2), Spring-Summer.

Lorenzi, J.H., Pastre, O. and Toledano, J. 1980. *La crise du XXe siècle*. Paris: Economica.

Mazier, K., Basle, M. and Vidal, J.F. 1984. *Quand les crises durent* ... Paris: Economica.

Mistral, J. 1982. La diffusion internationale de l'accumulation intensive et sa crise. In *La recherche en économie internationale*, ed. J.L. Reiffers, Paris: Dunod, 205–37.

Mistral, J. 1986. Régime international et trajectoires nationales. In Boyer (1986c). 167–202.

Ominami, C. 1985. *Les transformations dans la crise des rapports nord-sud*. Paris: La Découverte.

Petit, P. 1986. *Slow Growth and the Service Economy*. London: Frances Pinter; New York: St. Martin's Press.

David Ryazanov

D.J. STRUIK

Ryazanov (1870–1938) was born David Borisovich Goldendach on 10 March 1870, in Odessa. Because of his connections, first with the Narodniks, then with the budding social democracy, he spent several years in prison. In 1898, he joined the new Russian Social Democratic Party, belonging after 1903 to the Menshevik wing. Between 1900 and 1905, he did research abroad on the labour movement and contributed to Kautsky's *Neue Zeit*. He participated in the Revolution of 1905, and by 1907 was again in Germany, doing that research on Marx and Engels on which his fame is mainly based.

By this time Franz Mehring and others had started the publication of works of Marx and Engels hidden in archives, private collections and often obscure periodicals. Ryazanov contributed two volumes, *Gesammelte Schriften von K. Marx und F. Engels, 1852 bis 1862* (1920, published in Stuttgart and translated into German by Luise Kautsky), which contain among others the writings on the Crimean War and on Palmerston. The war intervened with a study on the First International, which was only published in 1926 as *Die Entstehung der Internationalen Arbeiter Assoziation* (Marx–Engels Archiv I, Frankfurt am Main).

The revolution of 1917 brought Ryazanov back to Russia, where he joined the Bolsheviks, who formed the Communist Party in 1918. He placed all his knowledge at the service of the Soviet State, and in 1920 became director of the new Marx–Engels Institute. His main purpose was the preparation of the collected works of Marx and Engels. To this end, Ryazanov went travelling abroad, collecting, copying, buying whatever he could find, including material from the rich archives of the German Social Democratic Party. The Institute bought up whole libraries on economic and labour conditions in various countries. Starting from scratch, the Institute in 1930 possessed 55,000 pages of photostats, 32,000 pamphlets, 450,000 books and periodicals, and was growing.

The Russian edition of the works of Marx and Engels came out between 1931 and 1951 in 28 volumes. The edition in the original languages included only seven volumes, containing works up to 1848. It is known as the MEGA, short for *Marx–Engels Gesamtausgabe* (published in Berlin, Moscow and Leningrad, 1927–35). It made available the *Deutsche Ideologie* and the *Economic–Philosophic Manuscripts of 1844*. The *Dialectics of Nature* came out in *Marx–Engels Archiv* II (1927, 117–395). The Institute also published many other works of Marxist authors, such as Plekanov and Liebknecht.

Ryazanov's lectures on Marx and Engels, published in 1923 and 1928 in Russian, were published in English as *Karl Marx and Friedrich Engels* (1927) and republished with a new preface in 1973. His remarkable edition of *The Communist Manifesto* appeared in English in 1930.

Because of his involvement in Menshevik activity, Ryazanov lost his position in 1931, and was succeeded by V.V. Adoratskilz (1878–1945). He spent some time in Saratov and Leningrad, doing research. He died in Saratov in 1938.

SELECTED WORKS

1917. (ed.) *Gesammelte Schriften von Karl Marx und Friedrich Engels 1852 bis 1862*. 2 vols. Trans. L. Kautsky, Stuttgart: J.H.W. Dietz.

1926. (ed.) *Die Entstehung der Internationalen Arbeiter Assoziation*. Marx–Engels Archiv I, Frankfurt am Main.

1927a. (ed.) *Dialectics of Nature*. Marx–Engels Archiv II, 117–395.

1927b. *Karl Marx and Friedrich Engels*. New York: International Publishers. Republished with new preface by D.J. Struik, New York and London: Monthly Review Press, 1973.

1927–35. (ed.) *Marx–Engels Gesamtausgabe* (full title: *Karl Marx, Friedrich Engels, Historisch-Kritische Gesamtausgabe, Werke Schrifte, Briefe*). 7 vols. Berlin and Moscow-Leningrad: Marx–Engels Institute.

1930. *The Communist Manifesto of Karl Marx and Friedrich Engels*. Introduction and explanatory notes by D. Ryazanov. Trans. from the Russian edn of 1922. London: Martin Lawrence.

Simple and Extended Reproduction

MEGHNAD DESAI

The schemes for Simple Reproduction and for Extended Reproduction refer to Marx's pioneering formulation of a two-sector general equilibrium growth model. Quesnay's *Tableau économique* is their forerunner: Leontief's Input–Output model and the Fel'dman–Mahalanobis planning model could be claimed among their progeny.

The two sectors (Departments) reproduce capital goods (Dept I) and consumption goods (Dept II). Marx's accounts are written in terms of labour values, i.e. after physical inputs and outputs have been converted into the direct and indirect labour time required for their production. Total value produced is divided into value of capital goods used up (constant capital), the value of the wage goods purchased by the workers who spend their entire wage bill on them (variable capital) and surplus value.

Thus for the two Departments we have

$$c_1 + v_1 + s_1 = Y_1$$
$$c_2 + v_2 + s_2 = Y_2$$
$$C + V + S = Y$$

where c_i is the input of constant capital, v_i variable capital and s_i surplus value in the ith Dept. Now in simple reproduction, we assume zero growth. This requires $Y_1 = C$, i.e. output of constant capital, to equal the inputs required to sustain the given level of total output Y. Then the consumption goods output must satisfy the condition $V + S = Y_2$. These two conditions together imply an intersectoral balance of trade requirements

$$c_2 = v_1 + s_1$$

that is the demand for capital goods input by Dept II (and hence implicitly its

338

projected output level, given linear technology) must match the wage bill and capitalists' consumption requirement in Dept I.

In chapter XX of *Capital* Vol. 2, where Marx formulates simple reproduction, much attention is devoted to the problem of accounting for constant capital, which is consumed within the production process. Marx was groping here for a distinction between gross output and net output and the relation between income and output. Thus V and S represent incomes received respectively by workers and capitalists. To this corresponds as net output Y_2. But what, Marx puzzled, happens to the payments corresponding to C, the constant capital? The national income and accounting categories implicit in simple reproduction were brought out by Shigeto Tsuru in an appendix to Sweezy (1942).

It was the scheme for a growing economy – for extended reproduction – that was the origin of a long debate and could also be said to have encouraged the formulation of business cycle theory. In this case, the formal scheme was as above but it was allowed that $Y_1 > C$, i.e. more capital goods were produced than were required for reproduction of output at the level Y. Let us denote each production period by subscript t. So we have $Y_{1t} > C_t$ and by implication $Y_{2t} < V_t + S_t$. To allow continued reproduction of the economy without causing excess supply of capital goods or excess demand for consumption goods, there had to be some diversion of demand away from Y_2 towards Y_1. This of course implies net investment. Marx proposed that capitalists of Dept I would accumulate one half of the surplus value they received and spend the other half on consumption goods. The capitalists of Dept II would then absorb the remaining capital goods so as to clear the market for Y_1. This automatically clears the market for Y_2.

Despite such seemingly arbitrary rules for accumulation behaviour, i.e. a fixed proportion of surplus value to be invested by Dept I capitalists, the passive adaptive behaviour of Dept II capitalists, no flow of investment across Departments etc., Marx was able to arrive at a remarkable result. Starting from seemingly arbitrary numerical values, the economy would settle down to balanced growth between the two Departments by the second period. Morishima (1973) has characterized this as the fastest converging two-sector growth model in economic literature.

The result given in *Capital* 2/XXI aroused a long debate among Marxists. How could one reconcile this picture of an economy in perpetual balanced growth with Marx's prediction elsewhere in his work of a capitalist economy riddled with crises and liable to breakdown as a result of increasing contradictions including a falling rate of profit despite growth and accumulation? Was Marx portraying the improbability of this outcome in absence of a planning mechanism that could order capitalists to invest a given proportion? Was this another example of a glaring inconsistency between different parts of *Capital*, as had been argued in the case of the value–price relationship by Böhm-Bawerk?

In the long debate that followed the publication of *Capital* Vol. 2, many attempts were made to alter the numerical magnitudes of Marx's example to generate business cycles. The notion that disproportionality in the investment in and/or growth of the two sectors could cause cycles was developed by Tugan–Baranovsky. The centrality of Dept I investment decisions, although arbitrarily imposed by Marx, led to the development of theories of business cycle emphasizing the capital–goods industries as the source of these fluctuations (Aftalion, Spiethoff). But the most searching critical analysis of Marx's scheme came from Rosa Luxemburg. *The Accumulation of Capital* offers both a survey of the pre-1914 debate in this area and an attempt to probe the reasons for the puzzle of a balanced growth equilibrium in a Marxian model.

Luxemburg raises questions about the reasons for capitalists to invest in the absence of any strong demand signals. Could investment be indefinitely sustained by capitalists buying from each other? Should there not be some examination of the markets for the products of the two Departments? In this respect, Luxemburg proposed that such a model should be put in the context of a world economy with exports to 'less developed' areas playing a crucial role in providing markets, especially for capital goods. This export relation could be part of an imperial relation between the developed country at the core and the periphery but need not be so. Another source for products of Dept I could be state expenditure on armaments.

As far as Dept II was concerned, Luxemburg saw that perpetual balanced growth required unlimited supplies of labour or some other condition to guarantee the constancy of real wages. If not, the expansion in Dept II would slow down, thus disrupting the balanced growth equilibrium. Here again the role of the less developed sectors in the economy (agriculture, small business) and of the less developed countries in the periphery as sources of reserve labour and of supplies of cheap foodstuffs were articulated by her.

Despite her insights, Luxemburg cannot be said to have integrated growth and cycles in a Marxian framework. There was a tension in such an enterprise for a Marxist, since a cyclical economy could perpetuate itself. It was thought necessary for a Marxist to demonstrate not only that cycles occurred but that they got increasingly severe and led eventually to a breakdown of capitalism. Subsequent discussion of schemes for expanded reproduction became involved with the breakdown controversy (surveyed in Sweezy, 1942; see also Brewer, 1980).

The analytical problem of the likely coexistence of growth and cycle within the schemes of extended reproduction was not tackled till Morishima (1973). He formulates the schemes of extended reproduction as a matrix difference equation and considerably generalizes the assumptions. Thus he assumes a constant propensity to save on part of all capitalists and allows capitalists to invest in either Department. He shows that under such conditions growth is accompanied by oscillations of increasing amplitude if Dept II has a higher organic composition of capital ($c_i/(c_i + v_i)$) than Dept I. Otherwise growth is explosive without oscillations. Note that this contrasts strongly with Uzawa's two-sector growth model where the relatively higher capital labour intensity of the consumption goods sector is required for stability. Thus Morishima's result would indicate that by allowing unequal propensities to save (and invest) in the two Departments and restricting capitalists to invest within the Department, Marx was able to obtain a balanced growth outcome. This may lead to a conclusion that restrictions in capitalists' investment behaviour may be necessary to stabilize an otherwise unstable economy.

The schemes of extended reproduction can be further reduced to a single nonlinear difference equation in which the differential in the growth rates between the two sectors $\Delta \ln (y_1/y_2)$ depends on the proportion of output levels (y_1/y_2). This is done while retaining all the original assumptions in the schemes of extended reproduction. For a suitable choice of the propensity to save of Department I capitalists, convergence to balanced growth can be immediate, i.e. even faster than in the original (Desai, 1979).

An offshoot of the schemes of extended reproduction has been their influence on the Soviet planning practice. Fel'dman used the extended reproduction scheme framework to tackle the question of investment priorities of the Soviet First Five Year Plan. The priority accorded in Soviet planning to Dept I can be said to have some roots in the Marx–Fel'dman extended reproduction scheme. Independently of Fel'dman, Mahalanobis used a similar two sector model for India's Second Five Year Plan (see Desai, 1979, for detailed references).

The intimate connection required between profits (surplus value) and investment to clear markets and sustain growth in an economy that the extended reproduction scheme illustrates could also be said to have influenced Kalecki's formulation of the macroeconomic model, which he arrived at independently of Keynes.

Thus the reproduction schemes have usefulness both in the understanding of static macroeconomic equilibrium and of multisectoral growth equilibrium. The fruitfulness of extended reproduction schemes for a theory of growth cycles could be said to be underexplored even today.

BIBLIOGRAPHY
Brewer, A. 1980. *Marxist Theories of Imperialism*. London: Macmillan.
Desai, M. 1979. *Marxian Economics*. Oxford: Basil Blackwell; Totawa, N.J. Rowman & Littlefield, 1980.
Luxemburg, R. 1913. *Die Akkumulation des Kapitals. Ein Beitrag zur ökonomischen Erklärung des Imperialismus*. Berlin: Vereinigung Internationaler, Verlag-Austalten, 1922. Trans. by A. Schwarzschild as *The Accumulation of Capital*, London: Routledge & Kegan Paul, 1951; New Haven: Yale University Press.
Marx, K. 1885. *Das Kapital*, Vol. II. Ed. F. Engels, Hamburg: Otto Meisner.
Morishima, M. 1973. *Marx's Economics: A Dual Theory of Value and Growth*. Cambridge and New York: Cambridge University Press.
Sweezy, P.M. 1942. *The Theory of Capitalist Development*. New York: Monthly Review Press.

Socially Necessary Technique

JOHN EATWELL

The typical representation of the problem of choice of technique involves the selection of a desired combination of production methods from a 'book of blue-prints' which contains the set of all available methods. In a competitive economy the cost-minimizing combination of techniques is chosen, and it is this 'efficient' set of techniques which is relevant to the analysis of price determination.

The representation does not accord with the manner in which techniques are invented and introduced. Typically, the enterpreneur does not face a wide range of technological options (and certainly not an indefinitely large range of input combinations). And changes in the method of production most typically incorporate innovations – in other words, rather than turning the pages of the book of blue-prints, new pages are added.

Marx (1867) attempted to capture these processes of technological innovation inherent in technical choice in his concept of the 'socially necessary technique'. The socially necessary technique or 'dominant' technique is that which is used by those producers whose activities constitute the determination of 'normal' costs-of-production and hence, normal prices; which producers and so which technique this might be will differ according to market structure, which may in turn be affected by the relationship between technology, entry and competition. In a highly competitive sector in which entry is easy and techniques easily acquired, then most producers will use the socially necessary technique and most pay the same cost of production and receive the same price. In more concentrated sectors, in which entry is limited and access to techniques is difficult or even restricted, then a small group of dominant firms will tend to be price leaders, and it is the technique used by these firms which is relevant in analysing the determination of normal cost and normal price.

The technique which is 'dominant' in the determination of prices is not necessarily dominant technologically. A superior technique may be used by a limited number of producers, yielding them 'super-profits', yet be insufficiently generalized in use to affect current price determination.

342

Conversely, some 'fossils', embodying out-of-date methods, are also used. These are not reproduced since they would yield a rate of return on their supply price lower than the general rate of profits, but they nonetheless yield positive quasi-rents, and are worth retaining so long as there is demand for their services.

Neither 'superior' technique nor 'fossils' are relevant to the determination of value and distribution.

The idea of socially necessary technique, 'the conditions of production normal for a given society' (Marx, 1867, p. 129) is thus not a technological, but an economic concept. It must be related to conditions of competition and accumulation. And in a changing economy it is inevitably imprecise. Nonetheless, Marx's discussion should alert us against a too facile representation of technology, and of the relationship between conditions of production and normal cost of production.

BIBLIOGRAPHY
Marx, K. 1867. *Capital*, Vol. I. Harmondsworth: Penguin Books, 1976.

Surplus Value

ANWAR SHAIKH

Profitability regulates the health of capitalist society. In this regard, Marx identifies *two* distinct sources of profit: profit on transfer (or even forcible appropriation) of wealth, which dominates the Mercantilist period; and profit on production of surplus value, which comes into prominence under Industrial Capital. Since trading activities can be linked to either source of profit, it is useful to begin with trading profits.

Individual trading profit arises whenever a commodity is re-sold at a profit. To the merchant who acquires a commodity of £100 and resells it for £200, it is his entrepeneurial ability to 'buy cheap and sell dear' which determines his gain (which covers trading costs and profit). But from the perspective of the system as a whole, the chain of transactions from initial to final sale simply serves to share out the total selling price among the various transactors, including the merchant. This holds true whether or not the transactions are fair or unfair, free or forced.

The merchant's gain is his 'balance of trade surplus'. But it is crucial to distinguish between a situation in which the overall 'balance of trade' is zero because the merchant's surplus is offset by a corresponding deficit somewhere else in the chain; and one in which the total balance is positive because the merchant's gain is merely his particular share in some overall surplus *whose origin therefore lies outside of trading activities themselves*. The former case corresponds to profit on the transfer of wealth, and the latter to profit on the production of surplus value. We will consider each in turn.

PROFIT ON TRANSFER OF WEALTH. A system-wide profit on the transfer of wealth appears mysterious because the surplus of the merchant does not seem to be counterbalanced by any corresponding deficit. Suppose merchant capitalists barter goods costing them £100 for those of a non-capitalist community or tribe,

344

which they then resell for £200. This swap leaves the combined wealth of the participants unchanged. Yet it gives rise to a profit on the capitalist side without any corresponding loss on the non-capitalist side, so that a net profit appears *for the system as a whole*. How is that possible?

The tribe's participation in trade may be motivated by fear, by ceremonial considerations, or by the hope of gaining objects which are socially more desirable. In all cases, it is a social assessment which stands behind the trade. But for the merchants, the important thing is that the tribal objects they acquire can be resold for a monetary gain. In Marx's terminology, the tribe is operating within the simple commodity circuit $C-C'$, in which one set of use-values C is exchanged for another useful set C'; while the merchants are operating within the capital circuit $M-C-C'-M'$, where a sum of money $M = £100$ is ultimately transformed into a larger sum $M' = £200$, through the exchange of one set of use-values C for a more valuable set C'.

The above circuits form the two poles of the transaction. However, because only one of these poles is assessed in monetary terms, any monetary gain recorded there has no counterpart at the other pole. A net monetary gain can thus appear for the system as a whole. Note that this would not be the case if both poles were treated in the *same* terms. If the tribe's goods were valued at their final selling price of £200, it would be obvious that the tribe had exchanged a set of commodities worth £200 for another worth only £100, thereby losing in monetary value exactly as much as the merchants gain. In the end, it is *inequality of exchange* which underlies profit on transfer of wealth (profit on alienation) (Marx, 1863, ch. 1).

Interestingly enough, neoclassical economics tends to treat profit as simply profit on alienation. This is why the analysis of 'pure exchange' occupies so prominent a position within the theory. For instance, a classic illustration depicts a prisoner-of-war camp in which all prisoners receive equal (Red Cross) packages of commodities. An entrepeneur among the prisoners then mediates a more desirable distribution of the total mass of commodities, a part of which he pockets as his own reward. Since the other prisoners all gain in terms of their respective subjective (and hence non-comparable) utilities, that portion of their collective endowment which is gained by the entrepreneur is not treated as their loss. On the other hand, for the entrepreneur it is precisely this transferred wealth which is counted as his profit. With one pole of the transaction in subjective utility and the other in material gain, profit seems to be created out of thin air. Instead of attempting to dissolve this false appearance, neoclassical economics concentrates on presenting profit as the just reward of the capitalist class (Alchian and Allen, 1969, chs. 1–4).

PROFIT ON PRODUCTION OF SURPLUS VALUE. With the rise of industrial capital, it became increasingly clear that industrial profit was quite different from profit on alienation. The latter was dependent on trade and unequal exchange, while the former was tied to production, wage labour and apparently equal exchange (Meek, 1956, Ch. 1). It is exactly in order to locate the fundamental difference

345

between the two that Marx insists on explaining industrial profit even when all exchanges are essentially equal (Marx, 1867, Ch. 5).

Marx begins by noting that every society must somehow direct the labour time at its disposal toward the production of the goods and services necessary to sustain and reproduce itself. In the case of class societies, the reproduction of the ruling class requires that it be able to extract a surplus product from the subordinate classes. This means that every ruling class must somehow get the subordinate classes to work beyond the time necessary to produce their own means of consumption, for it is this *surplus labour time* which creates the requisite surplus product (*see* EXPLOITATION).

The same basic process operates in capitalist society, but it is hidden under the surface of exchange relations and money magnitudes. To show this, Marx starts by assuming that the money price of each commodity is proportional to the total abstract labour time socially necessary for its production (its labour value). In the case of wage-labour, this means that money wages are proportional to the number of hours (v) workers must put in a given day in order to produce their collective daily means of consumption. Under the above circumstances, all commodities, including labour power (the capacity to work), exchange in proportion to the labour time socially necessary for their reproduction. All exchanges are therefore equal in a fundamental social sense, so that (for the moment) profit on alienation is ruled out of consideration.

During the production process a particular quantity of means of production (raw materials and machines) is used up each day. The abstract labour time (c) which was previously required to reproduce them is thereby transferred to the product. If we add to this the labour time worked by workers in a given day (l), the resultant sum ($c + l$) represents the total abstract labour time socially necessary to produce the daily product.

If exchange is proportional to labour times, then the price of the total social product is proportional to $c + l$. But the corresponding money cost of producing this product is proportional to $c + v$, since c represents the abstract labour cost of the means of production used up and v represents the corresponding costs of the workers employed. It follows from this that aggregate profits will exist only if $c + l > c + v$, which implies $l > v$. In other words, when prices are proportional to labour values (equal exchange), profit is the direct monetary expression of surplus labour time $s = l - v > 0$. This surplus labour time, performed by workers who produce commodities for capitalists (i.e. who produce commodity-capital), is what Marx calls *surplus value*.

Even when exchange is no longer proportional to labour value, the connection between profit and surplus value continues to hold, but in a more complex manner. In effect, when prices deviate from proportionality with labour values, this can give rise to transfers of value from one set of transactors to another. Now total profits can depart from proportionality with total surplus value – even though in the aggregate the gains and losses due to transfers of value exactly cancel out! This apparent paradox, which has long bedevilled the extensive literature on the so-called Transformation Problem, is easily resolved once one

346

recognizes that the profit is a measure which only picks up a portion of the overall transfers of value involved. By definition, aggregate profit is simply the difference between the price of aggregate output and the price of that portion of this output which corresponds to the *flows* of commodities used up as 'inputs' into production, either directly as means of production or indirectly as wage goods. Thus, insofar as value is transferred between total output and these particular inputs, what capitalist producers as a whole may gain in revenues through a higher selling price is at the same time what they thereby lose through higher input costs. Total profits are therefore unchanged, because feedback between the price of outputs and the prices of these particular inputs prevents any overall transfer of surplus value. But the same cannot be said for those transfers involving the remaining portions of aggregate output, which enter respectively into the capital stock of the firm (as inventories, plant and equipment) or into the possession of the capitalists themselves as consumption goods. In the former case, any transfers are reflected in the balance sheets of the firms and are at best only partially transmitted to costs; whereas in the latter case, any gain in profits through a higher selling price of capitalist consumption goods is reflected in a corresponding loss in the personal accounts of the capitalists themselves, rather than in increases in business costs. Because the measure of profit only picks up a subset of the value transfers, total profit can end up departing from proportionality with surplus value – within strict limits. *This is merely the same principle which underlies mercantilist profit.* It was well known to Marx himself (Shaikh, 1984).

FURTHER ISSUES. First of all, it is important to note that only at an abstract level of analysis is money profit (with or without the equalization of the rate of profit) the sole expression of surplus value. At a more concrete level, surplus value appears as producers' profits, gross trading margins, rents, interest, taxes and dividends. Similarly, one can develop the analysis to account for profits across industries, across firms within industries, across regions, and across nations. Contained within this movement from the abstract to the concrete is a subtle and powerful theory of competition and pricing, on whose basis this analysis can be developed (see the essay on Market Value and Market Price).

Secondly, our earlier discussion of profit on alienation should alert us to the fact that surplus value is not the only source of profit. This understanding is one of the great strengths of Marx's analysis of the determinants of profit. It is also an important historical and empirical issue in its own right. Even in the modern capitalist world, where surplus value is clearly the dominant basis for profit, one must be careful to account for transfers of wealth and value from non-capitalist spheres (petty commodity and non-commodity production) to capitalist ones – particularly in analysing the so-called Third World.

Thirdly, it should be noted that the very concept of the *transfer* of wealth and value is predicated on a distinction between those activities which produce the goods and services (use-values) comprising the annual wealth, and those which serve to transfer this wealth from one set of hands to another. This distinction

347

is in turn merely part of a more general one between production and non-production activities. In the latter camp we find not only the familiar category of personal consumption activities, but also the classical notion of *social consumption* activities such as those involved in the exchanging of goods, services and money; general administrative activities in both the private and public sectors; and various other social activities such as defence, etc. Production uses up use-values in order to produce more use-values. Personal and social consumptions use up use-values in order to achieve some other desired end. As such, the distinction between them has nothing to do, *per se*, with other distinctions such as those between necessary/unnecessary, desirable/undesirable and basic/non-basic activities. More importantly, the distinction between production and non-production activities has profound implications for the manner in which the wealth of capitalist nations is measured and analysed (Shaikh, 1978, section IV.C).

Fourthly, within the general category of production activities, a further difference arises between those which produce surplus value (i.e. produce surplus labour for a capitalist employer), and those which either produce value (petty commodity producers) or produce use-values for direct use (households, non-commodity producing communities). Though all these labours are productive of social wealth, only the first is directly productive of surplus value. This is why Marx singles out this particular form of labour as that labour which is productive-of-capital – i.e. which is 'productive labour' from the point of view of capital. As a corollary to the above, it is then necessary to distinguish between the rate of exploitation (which applies to all workers employed by capital) and the rate of surplus value (which is the rate of exploitation of 'productive labour', since it alone produces surplus value) (Marx, 1867, Appendix, part II).

Lastly, it is important to recognize that the preceding categories interact in complex ways. For example, surplus value is simply the difference between the length of the working day (l) of productive workers, and that portion of it (v) which is required to produce the commodities they and their families consume. But the quantity of social labour time represented by v is not at all the same as the total social labour time required to reproduce productive workers, because the latter generally includes household and community labour involved in the reproduction of labour-power. To the extent that these non-capitalist labours are responsible for the bulk of the use-values consumed by productive workers, only a small amount of *commodities* will be involved. But since capitalists need only pay workers just enough to acquire the commodity portion of their standard of living, v will be low and s correspondingly high. Then, as capitalist production erodes village and/or household production, commodities will begin to comprise an ever greater portion of the standard of living of workers even as this overall standard may itself decline. To the capitalists, workers will be getting progressively more 'expensive' as their commodity requirements rise. Yet the workers themselves may be getting ever poorer if their overall standard of living is declining. Over certain periods, a rising real wage is perfectly compatible with a falling standard of living – as the history of many a developing capitalist country demonstrates. All this goes to show that no analysis of a concrete social formation can afford to ignore the *interrelationships* between profit on transfer of wealth and profit on production of surplus value, between production and non-production activities and between capitalist and non-capitalist labour.

BIBLIOGRAPHY

Alchian, A.A. and Allen, W.A. 1969. *Exchange and Production Theory in Use.* Belmont, California: Wadsworth.

Marx, K. 1863. *Theories of Surplus Value*, Part I: Moscow: Progress Publishers.

Marx, K. 1867. *Capital*, Vol. I. London: Penguin, 1976.

Meek, R.L. 1956. *Studies in the Labour Theory of Value.* New York: Monthly Review Press.

Shaikh, A. 1978. An introduction to the history of crisis theories. In *U.S. Capitalism in Crisis.* New York: Union for Radical Political Economics.

Shaikh, A. 1984. The transformaton from Marx to Sraffa. In *Ricardo, Marx, Sraffa*, ed. E. Mandel, London: Verso.

Paul Malor Sweezy

JOHN BELLAMY FOSTER

One of the leading figures in Western Marxism and co-editor (with Harry Magdoff) of *Monthly Review*, Sweezy is known both for his contributions to economics and his influence on the development of socialist thought. Born on 10 April 1910 in New York, the son of an officer of the First National Bank of New York, he obtained his early education at Exeter and Harvard University, from which he received his BA in 1931. In 1932 he left Cambridge, Massachusetts for a year of graduate study at the London School of Economics. Awakened by the Great Depression, and responding to the intellectual ferment in Britain, during what was to be a turning point in world history, Sweezy quickly gained sympathy for the Marxist perspective to which he was introduced for the first time. Returning to the US in 1933 to do graduate studies at Harvard, he found the academic climate much changed, with Marxism becoming a topic of intense interest in some of the larger universities. As he recalled many years later,

> It was under these circumstances that I acquired a mission in life, not all at once and self-consciously but gradually and through a practice that had a logic of its own. That mission was to do what I could to make Marxism an integral and respected part of the intellectual life of the country, or, put in other terms, to take part in establishing a serious and authentic North American brand of Marxism (Sweezy, 1981a, p. 13).

In pursuing this goal at Harvard, Sweezy received much direct help and indirect inspiration from the great conservative economist Joseph Schumpeter, whose analysis of the origins, development and imminent decline of capitalism revealed a complex, critical appreciation of the Marxian schema. Sweezy's 1943 essay on 'Professor Schumpeter's Theory of Innovation', which compared Schumpeter's analysis of enterpreneurial development to Marx's theory of accumulation, was to be one of the pathbreaking studies in this area.

Receiving his PhD in 1937, Sweezy assumed a position as instructor at Harvard until 1939, when he rose to the rank of assistant professor. During these years he played a central role in two of the major areas of debate in economics: (1) the theory of imperfect competition, and (2) the issue of secular stagnation. Sweezy's interest in the monopoly question began early in his career, as shown by his first book (winner of the David A. Wells prize), *Monopoly and Competition in the English Coal Trade, 1550–1850* (1938). His 1939 article, 'Demand Under Conditions of Oligopoly', in which he presented the kinked demand curve analysis of oligopolistic pricing, remains one of the classic essays in modern price theory. Along with a small group of Harvard and Tufts economists, Sweezy was one of the authors and signatories of the influential Keynesian tract, *An Economic Program for American Democracy* (1938), which provided a convincing rationale for a sustained increase in public spending during the final years of the New Deal. While continuing to carry out his teaching responsibilities at Harvard, Sweezy worked for various New Deal agencies (including the National Resources Committee and the Temporary National Economic Committee) investigating the concentration of economic power. His study, 'Interest Groups in the American Economy', published as an appendix to the NRC's well-known report, *The Structure of the American Economy* (1939), was to be an important guide to later research.

From the lecture notes to his Harvard course on the economics of socialism, Sweezy produced his seminal work, *The Theory of Capitalist Development* (1942). Containing a comprehensive review of Marxian economics up until the time of World War II, this study also did much to determine the character of later Marxian theory through its advocacy of Laudislau von Bortkiewitz's solution to the 'transformation problem', its presentation of a logically acceptable 'underconsumptionist' model of accumulation and crisis, and its elaboration of Marxian views on monopoly capitalism. Rapidly translated into several languages, *The Theory of Capitalist Development* soon established Sweezy's reputation as the foremost Marxian economist of his generation.

During World War II Sweezy served in the Office of Strategic Services (OSS) and was assigned to the monitoring of British plans for postwar economic development. With a number of years still remaining in his Harvard contract when the war ended, he opted to resign his position rather than resume teaching, recognizing that his political and intellectual stance would hinder his receiving tenure. In this period, Sweezy authored numerous articles on the history of political economy and socialism, some of which were reprinted in his book, *The Present as History* (1953), and edited a volume containing three classic works on the 'transformation problem': *Karl Marx and the Close of His System* by Eugene Böhm-Bawerk, *Böhm-Bawerk's Criticism of Marx* by Rudolf Hilferding, and 'On the Correction of Marx's Fundamental Theoretical Construction in the Third Volume of *Capital*' by Bortkiewicz (which Sweezy translated into English). His 1950 critique of Maurice Dobb's *Studies in the Development of Capitalism*, in which Sweezy, following his interpretaton of Marx, emphasized the role of the world market in the decline of feudalism, launched the famous debate over the transition from feudalism to capitalism which has played a key role in Marxian historiography ever since.

With the financial backing of literary critic F.O. Matthieson, Sweezy and the Marxist historian Leo Huberman founded *Monthly Review* (subtitled 'An Independent Socialist Magazine') in 1949 as an intellectual resource for an American left threatened by anti-Communist hysteria. Two years later they began publishing books under the imprint of Monthly Review Press, when it came to their attention that in the repressive climate of the times even such celebrated authors as I.F. Stone and Harvey O'Connor were unable to find publishers for their book manuscripts.

In 1953, at the height of the McCarthyite period in the US, the state of New Hampshire conferred wide-ranging powers on its attorney general to investigate 'subversive activities'. On this basis, Sweezy was summoned to appear before the state attorney general on two occasions in 1954. Adopting a principled opposition to the proceedings, he refused to answer questions regarding: (1) the membership and activities of the Progressive Party, (2) the contents of a guest lecture delivered at the University of New Hampshire, and (3) whether or not he believed in Communism. As a result, he was declared in contempt of court and consigned to the county jail until purged of contempt by the Superior Court of Merimack County, New Hampshire. On appeal, this decision was upheld by the New Hampshire Supreme Court. In response to a further appeal, the US Supreme Court overturned the verdict of the state court in 1957, on the grounds that there was no legal evidence that the New Hampshire legislators actually wanted the attorney general to obtain answers to these questions; and that the obvious violation of Sweezy's constitutional liberties could not be justified on the basis of political activities only 'remotely connected to actual subversion' (US Supreme Court, 1957).

Despite the adverse ideological climate, Sweezy continued to author articles on all aspects of Marxian theory, adding hundreds of essays by the 1980s. The publication of Paul Baran's book, *The Political Economy of Growth* (1957), marked the beginning of Marxian dependency theory and helped to establish *Monthly Review*'s primary identity as a backer of third world liberation struggles. Visiting Cuba shortly after the revolution, Huberman and Sweezy co-authored two influential works on the transformation of Cuban economic society: *Cuba: Anatomy of a Revolution* (1960) and *Socialism in Cuba* (1969).

The appearance in 1966 of *Monopoly Capital* by Baran and Sweezy (published two years after Baran's death) represented a turning point in Marxian economics. Although described by the authors themselves as a mere 'essay-sketch', it rapidly gained widespread recognition as the most important attempt thus far to bring Marx's *Capital* up to date, as well as providing a formidable critique of prevailing Keynesian orthodoxy.

Where Sweezy himself was concerned, *Monopoly Capital* reflected dissatisfaction with the analysis of accumulation and crisis advanced in *The Theory of Capitalist Development*. His earlier study had been written when mainstream economics was undergoing rapid change due to the Keynesian 'revolution' and the rise of imperfect competition theory. Thus, he had provided a detailed elaboration of both Marx's theory of realization crisis (or demand-side constraints in the accumulation process), and of work by Marx and later Marxian theorists on the concentration and centralization of capital. As with mainstream theory, however, these two aspects of Sweezy's analysis remained separate; and hence he failed to develop an adequate explanation of the concrete factors conditioning investment demand in an economic regime dominated by the modern large enterprise. It was essentially this critique of Sweezy's early efforts that was provided by Josef Steindl in *Maturity and Stagnation in American Capitalism* (1952: 243–6), who went to show how a more unified theory could 'be organically developed out of the underconsumptionist approach to Marx' based on Michal Kalecki's model of capitalist dynamics, which had connected the phenomenon of realization crisis to the increasing 'degree of monopoly' in the economy as a whole.

In fact, it was out of this argument, as outlined by Steindl, that the underlying framework for Baran and Sweezy's own contribution in *Monopoly Capital* was derived. Thus, they suggested that Marx's fundamental 'law of the tendency of the rate of profit to fall' associated with accumulation in the era of free competition, had been replaced, in the more restrictive competitive environment of monopoly capitalism, by a law of the tendency of the surplus to rise (defining surplus as the gap, at any given level of production, between output and socially necessary costs of production). Under these circumstances, the critical economic problem was one of surplus absorption. Capitalist consumption tended to account for a decreasing share of capitalist demand as income grew, while investment was hindered by the fact that it took the form of new productive capacity, which could not be expanded for long periods of time independently of final, wage-based demand. Despite the fact that there was always the possibility of new 'epoch-making innovations' emerging that would help absorb the potential economic surplus, all such innovations – resembling the steam engine, the railroad and the automobile in their overall effect – were few and far between. Hence, Baran and Sweezy concluded that the system had a powerful tendency toward stagnation, largely countered thus far through the promotion of economic waste by means of 'the sales effort' (including its penetration into the production process) and military expenditures, and through the expansion of the financial sector. All such 'countervailing influences' were, however, of a self-limiting character and could be expected to lead to a doubling-over of contradictions in the not too distant future.

The publication of *Monopoly Capital* coincided with the rise of the New Left, largely in response to the Vietnam War. The work of Baran and Sweezy thus constituted the initial theoretical common ground for a younger generation of radical economists in the US who formed the Union for Radical Political Economics in 1968. In 1971, Sweezy delivered the Marshall Lecture at Cambridge University. Some of his most influential writings during this period were reprinted in *Modern Capitalism and Other Essays* (1972). From 1974 to 1976 he served on the executive of the American Economic Association, and in 1983 was granted an honorary doctorate of literature from Jawaharlal Nehru University in India.

Together with Harry Magdoff (who replaced Huberman as co-editor of *Monthly Review* after the latter's death in 1968), Sweezy has continued to strengthen the analysis of *Monopoly Capital* in the decades following its publication, utilizing the original framework to explain the reemergence of stagnation and the rise of financial instability, in such works as *The Dynamics of US Capitalism* (1970), *The End of Prosperity* (1977), *The Deepening Crisis of US Capitalism* (1979) and *Four Lectures on Marxism* (1981).

With the demise of detente and the appearance of a new cold war, Sweezy has grappled increasingly with the question of 'actually existing socialism' in Eastern Europe – emphasizing the class-exploitative character of these societies, as well as their advances over capitalist states at similar levels of development, and their largely defensive international posture – in such works as *Post-Revolutionary Society* (1981).

SELECTED WORKS

1938. *Monopoly and Competition in the English Coal Trade, 1550–1850.* Cambridge, Mass.: Harvard University Press.

1939a. Demand under conditions of oligopoly. *Journal of Political Economy* 47, August, 568–73.

1939b. Interest groups in the American economy. In US National Resources Committee, *The Structure of the American Economy*, Pt I, Washington, DC: US Government Printing Office.

1942. *The Theory of Capitalist Development: Principles of Marxian Political Economy.* New York: Monthly Review Press.

1943. Professor Schumpeter's theory of innovation. *Review of Economics and Statistics* 25, February, 93–6.

1949. (ed.) *Karl Marx and the Close of His System by Eugen Böhm-Bawerk and Böhm-Bawerk's Criticism of Marx by Rudolf Hilferding.* Reprinted, London: Merlin Press, 1976.

1960. (With L. Huberman.) *Cuba: Anatomy of a Revolution.* New York: Monthly Review Press.

1966. (With P.A. Baran.) *Monopoly Capital: an Essay on the American Economic and Social Order.* New York: Monthly Review Press.

1969. (With L. Huberman.) *Socialism in Cuba.* New York: Monthly Review Press.

1970. (With H. Magdoff.) *The Dynamics of US Capitalism.* New York: Monthly Review Press.

1972. *Modern Capitalism and Other Essays.* New York: Monthly Review Press.

1976. (With others.) *The Transition from Feudalism to Capitalism.* London: New Left Books.

1977. (With H. Magdoff.) *The End of Prosperity.* New York: Monthly Review Press.

1981a. *Four Lectures on Marxism.* New York: Monthly Review Press.

1981b. *Post-Revolutionary Society.* New York: Monthly Review Press.

BIBLIOGRAPHY

Foster, J.B. 1986. *The Theory of Monopoly Capitalism.* New York: Monthly Review Press.

Gilbert, R. et al. 1938. *An Economic Program for American Democracy.* New York: Vanguard.

Steindl, J. 1952. *Maturity and Stagnation in American Capitalism.* Oxford: Blackwell. Reprinted, New York: Monthly Review Press, 1976.

US Supreme Court 1957. Sweezy *v.* New Hampshire. *US Reports.* October Term, 1956.

Transformation Problem

E.K. HUNT AND MARK GLICK

The 'transformation problem' is at the heart of the Marxian labour theory of value. The topic has always been the subject of sharp controversy. The controversy reflects not only the general ideological conflicts that surround all Marxist ideas, but also the disagreement among Marxists themselves about the nature of the labour theory of value. After defining the problem in Marx's terms, we first present Marx's solution and the claims which he makes regarding its properties. This discussion is then followed by a brief critical review of the various solutions which have been proposed since Marx.

THE 'TRANSFORMATION PROBLEM'. To Marx, the value of a commodity consisted of the labour embodied in the means of production that were used up in the production of the commodity (dead labour) and the labour expended in the current production period (living labour).

$$W = L_d + L_l \tag{1}$$

where W is value, L_d is dead labour, and L_l is living labour. Living labour can be separated into necessary labour L_n and surplus labour, L_s. Necessary labour is that proportion of living labour that creates the value equivalent of the worker's wages, and surplus labour is the remaining living labour time during which the value equivalent of surplus value is created. Thus, the following equation holds:

$$W = L_d + L_n + L_s \tag{2}$$

In actual pricing processes, Marx believed that capitalists summed up the costs of production and then added a percentage markup, which was determined by the average rate of profit. Thus, the formula for equilibrium prices is:

Price of Prod = cost of commodities + cost of labour + Profit markup or, using p for the prices of production, c for constant capital, v for variable capital, and

356

r for the rate of profit, we have:

$$P = c + v + r(c + v)$$

where $r + s/c + v$ and $r(c + v) = s/c + v(c + v) = s$.

The general correspondence between the various types of labour and the cost-components of price is obvious:

$$W = L_d + L_n + L_s$$
$$\updownarrow \quad \updownarrow \quad \updownarrow \quad \updownarrow$$
$$P = c + v + r(c + v).$$

Price corresponds to value, constant capital corresponds to dead labour; variable capital corresponds to necessary labour; and profit corresponds to surplus value.

The most important reason why this correspondence is not proportional or one-to-one, however, is that the production of different commodities involves unequal organic compositions of capital (defined as either c/v or L_d/L_1). The exchange of commodities at values is thus incompatible with equal rates of profit. Given two industries which exchange at values, their rates of profit can only be equal if their organic compositions are equal:

$$r_1 = \frac{s_1/v_1}{c_1/v_1 + 1} = \frac{s_2/v_1}{c_2/v_2 + 1}.$$

Since the rates of surplus will be equalized through competition between workers, it follows that equal rates of profit imply equal organic compositions $(c_1/v_1) = (c_2/v_2)$. Marx argued that this would not be the case in general and that (c/v) varied significantly from sector to sector.

MARX'S SOLUTION. Marx's solution to the problem was to transform values into prices of production which correspond to equalized rates of profit. In chapter 9 of Volume III of *Capital* he presents a table with five sectors and transforms values to prices of production by the following procedure. First he calculates the average rate of profit as:

$$\frac{\sum S_i}{\sum (c_i + v_i)}$$

Once given the average rate of profit, r, he recalculates all of the prices according to the formula:

$$(1 + r)(c_i + v_i)$$

Marx was anxious to show that the essence of the labour theory of value and the theory of surplus value can be preserved when the transition is made from values to prices. Prices, he argued, are merely transformed values and profit is redistributed surplus value. In order to show the consistency of this view he made the following two claims concerning the aggregates in his transformation solution: 1. The sum of values = the sum of prices; 2. The sum of surplus value = the sum of profit.

The sum of the profits for all the different spheres of production must accordingly be equal to the sum of surplus values, and the sum of prices of production for the total social product must be equal to the sum of its values (Marx [1867], 1981, p. 273).

The equality of these aggregates was used by Marx to argue that only a redistribution has occurred and nothing has actually been created or destroyed in the transformation from values to prices.

THE REPRODUCTION SCHEME ARGUMENT: BORTKIEWICZ, SWEEZY, SETON. Following the publication of Marx's solution to the transformation problem, a number of critics pointed out that Marx had not completely solved the transformation problem. In his solution, Marx had transformed the output prices while the input prices remained in values. This was an inadequate solution, it was argued, since capitalists buy inputs at prices and not values. In addition, the output price of one commodity is the input price of another. In his famous 1907 article, Bortkiewicz attempted to solve the transformation problem by simultaneously transforming both inputs and outputs (Bortkiewicz, 1907). But in his result he found that he could obtain only one of the two claims made by Marx. Either total prices were equal to total values or total surplus value was equivalent to total profit, but not both. He considered this as an important criticism of the labour theory of value.

In 1942, Sweezy build on the Bortkiewicz result using a three sector reproduction scheme. Although Bortkiewicz used this apparatus as a matter of convenience, Sweezy argued that the transformation procedure should 'not result in a disruption of the conditions of simple reproduction' (Sweezy, 1942, p. 114). Sweezy went beyond Bortkiewicz, and claimed that his solution would satisfy both of Marx's claims. He obtained such a result by assuming that the output of the luxury sector is equal to unity, and assuming that this sector also has the average organic composition. He argued that these two assumptions are reasonable since the output of the luxury sector can be considered the money commodity, and to avoid price/value deviations in the money commodity, its organic composition must be set equal to the average of the first two sectors. Seton later provided a proof of Sweezy's example.

Unfortunately, Sweezy's success is a result of his assumptions. First, since surplus value is equal to the output of the luxury sector, setting this output equal to one in both prices and values ensures that total surplus value will equal total profit. The assumption of a socially average organic composition in the third sector obtains the second condition. If the sum of the organic compositions of department I and department II is equal to that of department III, and department III's output is set equal in prices and values, then the sum of prices and values in departments I and II must also be equal. Not only are Sweezy's results true by definition, but these two assumptions are unnecessarily restrictive for a convincing solution to the transformation problem.

NORMALIZATION BY SRAFFA'S STANDARD COMMODITY: MEDIO. In general, it can be said that, lacking an invariant measure of value, it has proven impossible to obtain a transformation solution in which the equalities between values and prices as well as profit and surplus value can be simultaneously maintained without the aid of extremely restrictive assumptions. When Sraffa's standard commodity became widely known there was initially some hope that it might provide such an invariant measure. This hope was quickly abandoned, however, when it was realized how restrictive the nature of the invariance of Sraffa's standard commodity is.

Marx, however, suggested a third method for linking prices to labour values. It is within the context of this third method that Alfredo Medio (1972) demonstrated that Sraffa's standard commodity could provide an important analytical tool for the Marxist labour theory of value. Marx realized that if a commodity could be found that was produced with the socially average organic composition of capital, then the rate of profit which could be obtained in the production and sale of that commodity would be identical whether all commodities were sold at their labour values or at their transformed money prices. Therefore, the rate of profit on that commodity would be determined entirely by labour values. Moreover, since competition tended to equalize all profit rates, it could be shown that the socially average rate of profit (by virtue of which all price calculations could be made with a cost-of-production theory of prices) would correspond to the rate of profit on the average commodity – a rate determined entirely by labour value calculations. If a numeraire that equates aggregate profit and aggregate surplus value (or equates the aggregate of values and prices) cannot be found, then an average industry whose rate of profit is determined by labour values suffices to connect the labour value analysis and the price analysis.

Medio demonstrated that in the industry producing Sraffa's standard commodity, the Marxian formula for the rate of profit, $r = (s/v)/(c/v + 1)$, always holds true. In Medio's demonstration the profit rate (r) is the money rate of profit by which capitalists mark up their money costs to arrive at prices. The rate of exploitation, or rate of surplus value (s/v), is defined in labour value terms. It is the rate at which surplus value is created in the sphere of production, and hence it is equal in all industries. The organic composition of capital (c/v), however, has a special meaning in Medio's formulation. It is determined by labour values alone, and is a weighted average of all of the production processes that make up the industry that produces the standard commodity.

Medio's solution has been criticized by the observation that a standard commodity does not actually exist, and that a hypothetical form of measurement is a weaker claim than that sought by Marx.

THE ITERATIVE METHOD AND BALANCED GROWTH: SHAIKH. Anwar Shaikh's popular solution to the transformation problem has been published in two important papers with a seven year gap (Shaikh, 1977; 1984). In his 1977 paper on the transformation problem. Shaikh is concerned with establishing a link between Marx's method and what he considers the 'correct' prices obtained by Bortkiewicz. Instead of developing a new mathematical apparatus, all one had to do, according to Shaikh, is to iterate Marx's procedure. If one takes Marx's prices of production and uses them as inputs, and then uses Marx's procedure again to obtain new prices of production, and so on, one converges on the set of Bortkiewicz prices. Shaikh's actual procedure, however, makes a number of assumptions which are found in Bortkiewicz but may not be in Marx. He sets the sum of prices equal to the sum of values in each step, and adjusts the money wage at every step so that the workers consume a certain bundle of commodities at the previous period's prices. Shaikh's procedure does obtain the set of prices consistent with the Bortkiewicz method, but also like Bortkiewicz, he obtains only one of Marx's aggregates. In Shaikh's solution total surplus value is not equal to total profit. Why not? This is the issue discussed in his 1984 paper.

In his 1984 paper, Shaikh argues that the transformation solution should not adopt ad hoc assumptions to obtain both of Marx's aggregates. Instead, he reasons, we should actually expect total surplus value and total profit to differ. This difference is due to the price-value deviations and the size of the luxury sector. When price-value deviations exist in the luxury sector, surplus value can be gained or lost through the circuits of revenue. His proof of this argument utilizes the assumption of balanced growth. In a situation of balanced growth he shows that the difference between surplus value and profit can be shown to be proportional to the price-value deviation in the sector producing luxury products. Such a result is very close to the well known property of von Neumann systems that when an economy is at maximum balanced growths and one of Marx's claims is assumed, then the other will automatically follow. Unfortunately, Shaikh's result cannot hold in a real economy where balanced growth is not satisfied.

THE 'NEW SOLUTION': DUMÉNIL, LIPIETZ AND FOLEY. What is being called the 'new solution' to the transformation problem by a small but growing group of Marxist economists was first introduced to English-speaking readers by Lipietz (1982), but the original solution was formulated by Duménil (1980) and later 'discovered' independently by Duncan Foley (1982). The new solution entails two important assumptions which are traced back to Marx. The first is that (the sum of prices equals the sum of values) should be modified to read: the sum of the prices of the net product (defined as the value added) should be the sum of the values of the net product. The second assumption is that distribution must be defined ex post, as either the value of the money wage which workers receive (Foley, 1982), or the bundle of consumption goods which the workers buy valued at prices (Duménil, 1980). Once these two assumptions are made any set of values can be transformed into any set of prices with the property that both of Marx's aggregates hold.

Duménil and Foley make two arguments for the adoption of their unique normalization procedure on the net product. First, they claim that such a normalization avoids double counting (Duménil, 1983–4, p. 442). In addition, they both argue that such a normalization conforms to Marx's view of what value is. Value 'is the linking of the total labour expended in a given period with the production associated with it, that is, the net product' (Duménil, 1983–4, p. 442). In addition, they argue that wages must be evaluated on the basis of prices and not as the value of a wage bundle. This view of distribution avoids the problem that when prices deviate from values, the rate of exploitation in price terms depends on the particular set of goods which workers buy and is not settled in the production process. They further argue that, in the previous formulations, if any part of the wage is saved the rate of surplus value becomes incaluable. Foley goes further than Duménil and argues that the wage should not be considered as a bundle at all. Wages are a sum of money, he claims, which can be used to buy any goods at the existing set of prices. In addition, unlike a wage bundle, the money wage conceals the exploitative nature of capitalist relations (Foley, 1982, p. 43).

One argument which has been posed against this view is that in the set of 'new solution' prices of production the sum of the values of constant capital does not equal the total sum of its prices. A convincing argument justifying this result must be established. In addition, the distribution assumption requires ex post knowledge. The actual set of prices must be known before the rate of wages can be established. One cannot move step by step from values into prices. The two realms must be considered separately while the new solution only provides a mapping procedure from one to the other.

SUMMARY AND IMPLICATIONS. The transformation problem arose from the attempt to show that the labour theory of value is consistent with the money prices of exchange. Marx's two claims that total prices should be equal to total values and total surplus value should be equal to total profit have traditionally been considered a prerequisite to the argument that prices are merely transformed values and profit is redistributed surplus value. We have shown that this result can be obtained by using numerous different assumptions. Some of these procedures hold total prices and values constant but require special assumptions to obtain an equality between surplus value and profit, others do the reverse. Many of these assumptions are clearly unjustifiable while others are rather more realistic. The 'new solution' of Duménil and Foley obtains both aggregates but finds a discrepancy between constant capital in price and value terms, while Medio's solution holds that equality of the rate of profit in value and money terms is more important than either of the two more traditional equalities.

It is clear from the literature on the 'transformation problem' that its resolution will not be merely a mathematical exercise. The ground of this continuing debate in the future will, instead, concern the social and economic implications of the competing assumptions which are adopted and their compatibility with the tenets of the labour theory of value. This, however, will be a complex debate since Marxists themselves have strong disagreements about the specific nature of the labour theory of value as well as its role or function within the Marxist theoretical system.

BIBLIOGRAPHY

Bortkiewicz, L. 1907. Value and price in the Marxian system. Trans. in *International Economic Papers* No. 2, 1952, 5–61.

Marxian economics

Duménil, G. 1980. *De la valeur aux prix de production.* Paris: Economica.

Duménil, G. 1983–4. Beyond the transformation riddle: a labor theory of value. *Science and Society* 47(4), Winter, 427–50.

Foley, D. 1982. The value of money, the value of labor power and the Marxian transformation problem. *Review of Radical Political Economics* 14((2), Summer, 37–47.

Lipietz, A. 1982. The so-called 'transformation problem' revisited. *Journal of Economic Theory* 26(1), 59–88.

Marx, K. 1867. *Capital.* Vol. I. Harmondsworth: Penguin, 1981.

Medio, A. 1972. Profits and surplus value: appearance and reality in capitalist production. In *A Critique of Economic Theory*, ed. E.K. Hunt and J. Schwartz, New York: Penguin.

Seton, F. 1957. The 'transformation problem'. *Review of Economic Studies* 24, June, 149–60.

Shaikh, A. 1977. Marx's theory of value and the 'transformation problem'. In *The Subtle Anatomy of Capitalism*, ed. J. Schwartz, Santa Monica: Goodyear.

Shaikh, A. 1984. The transformation from Marx to Sraffa. In *Ricardo, Marx, Sraffa*, ed. E. Mandel, London: Verso.

Sweezy, P. 1942. *The Theory of Capitalist Development.* New York: Monthly Review Press, ch. 7.

Kozo Uno

T. SEKINE

A prominent Japanese Marxian economist known especially for his rigorous and systematic reformulation of Marx's *Capital*. Born in Kurashiki in western Japan in a year of intense social unrest, Uno (1897–1977) early took an interest in anarcho-syndicalism and Marxism. Not being of an activist temperament, however, he strictly disciplined himself to remain, throughout his life, within the bounds of independent academic work. For this deliberate separation of theory (science) from practice (ideology) he was frequently criticized. After studying in Tokyo and Berlin in the early 1920s, Uno taught at Tohoku University (1924–38), the University of Tokyo (1947–58) and Hosei University (1958–68). During most of the war years he kept away from academic institutions. He authored many controversial books, especially after the war. His 11-volume *Collected Works* were published by Iwanami-Shoten in 1973–4.

The problem with Marx's *Capital*, according to Uno, is that it mixes the theory and history of capitalism in a haphazard fashion (described as 'chemical' by Schumpeter) without cogently establishing their interrelation. Uno's methodological innovation lies in propounding a stages-theory of capitalist development (referring to the stages of mercantilism, liberalism and imperialism) and using it as a mediation between the two.

Capitalism is a global market-economy in which all socially needed commodities tend to be produced as value (i.e. indifferently to their use-values) by capital. This tendency is never consummated since many use-values in fact fail to conform to this requirement. Only in theory, which synthesizes 'pure' capitalism, can one legitimately envision a complete triumph of value over use-values. The inevitable gap between history, in which use-values appear in their raw forms, and pure theory in which they are already idealized as merely distinct objects for use, must be bridged by stages-theory, which structures itself around use-values of given types (as 'wool', 'cotton' and 'steel' respectively typify the use-values of the three stages).

Uno's emphasis on 'pure' capitalism as the theoretical object has invited many uninformed criticisms. His synthesis of a purely capitalist society as a self-contained logical system follows the genuine tradition of the Hegelian dialectic, and is quite different from axiomatically contrived neoclassical 'pure' theory. Unlike the latter which takes the capitalist market for granted, Uno's theory logically generates it by step-by-step syntheses of the ever-present contradiction between value and use-values. The pure theory of capitalism is thus divided into the three doctrines of circulation, production and distribution according to the way in which this contradiction is settled. By specifically articulating the abiding dialectic of value and use-values, already present in *Capital*, Uno has given Marxian economic theory its most systematic formulation, a formulation which militates against the two commonest Marxist errors known as voluntarism and economism.

Uno's approach is not dissimilar to Karl Polanyi's in appreciating the tension between the substantive (use-value) and the formal (value) aspect of the capitalist economy. Unlike Polanyi, however, Uno ascribes more than relative importance to capitalism, in the full comprehension of which he sees the key to the clarification of both pre-capitalist and post-capitalist societies. Thus Uno's approach reaffirms and exemplifies the teaching of Hegel (and Marx) that one should 'learn the general through the particular', and not the other way round.

BIBLIOGRAPHY

Albritton, R. 1984. The dialectic of capital: a Japanese contribution. *Capital and Class* 22, 157–76.

Albritton, R. 1985. *A Japanese Reconstruction of Marxist Theory.* London: Macmillan; New York: St. Martin's Press, 1986.

Itoh, M. 1980. *Value and Crisis, Essays in Marxian Economics in Japan.* New York: Monthly Review Press.

Sekine, T.T. 1975. Uno-Riron: a Japanese contribution to Marxian political economy. *Journal of Economic Literature* 13, 847–77.

Sekine, T.T. 1984. *The Dialectic of Capital, a Study of the Inner Logic of Capitalism.* Tokyo: Toshindo Press.

Uno, K. 1980. *Principles of Political Economy, Theory of a Purely Capitalist Society.* Translated from the Japanese by T.T. Sekine, Brighton: Harvester Press.

Value and Price

MEGHNAD DESAI

The problem of the relationship between value and price – the so called Transformation Problem – is a central issue in Marxian economics. In one sense it can be posed as a technical or mathematical problem of deriving a set of prices from a given set of value equations. But it if were only a technical problem then it should have a definite answer – either a solution exists or it does not. It is surprising therefore that this problem has continued to attract succeeding generations of economists since the date of publication of Volume 3 of *Capital* in 1894 (Marx, 1894).

The debate shows no signs of abating and seems a rare example of a problem which continues to invite new solutions or versions in new mathematical language of the old solution. There can rarely have been a question in economic theory which has been solved so many times in so many different mathematical languages but yet not resolved finally. This continuing fascination of the Transformation Problem leads one to suspect that there is more than a technical issue at stake.

The *locus classicus* of the debate is chapter IX of *Capital* Vol. 3 (3/IX), which was published posthumously by Engels from notes left by Marx. There is evidence however that the material contained in this volume was written some time in the 1860s before the publicaton of *Capital* Vol. 1 (Marx, 1867). This is of more than biographical interest in the debate. In Vol. 1, Marx developed his theory on the explicit assumption that values and prices were proportional to each other. This was done in awareness of two qualifying conditions; *first* that this was a special case and generally value and prices were related systematically but not proportionally, but *second* that values and value relations were unobservable, latent or structural whereas prices were observable, actual and phenomenal. The hidden nature of value relations – commodity fetishism – is crucial to Marx's argument and hence it would have been totally uncharacteristic of Marx's approach not to have foreseen that values and prices diverge from each other.

This divergence of prices from values emerged as a central result of 3/IX and was seized upon by Böhm-Bawerk in his *Karl Marx and the Close of His System*

365

(1896; Sweezy, 1949) as a basic deficiency and disproof of Marx's theory of profits. He took it to be a complication that may have arisen in Marx's work after he had written the first volume and an impression was conveyed that the price–value divergence, being contrary to the proportionality assumed in Vol. 1, invalidated the conclusions in that volume.

If Böhm-Bawerk was able to gain and convey this impression it was because Marx's attempt at solving the Transformation Problems *looks* unfinished. Having derived a numerical solution for prices from a set of value equations, as we will see below, Marx confronts the divergence as a puzzle and then spends some pages tacking around the problem but in no way presenting it as a systematic outcome. Thus it could be thought from reading 3/IX that the Transformation Problem was left unsolved.

THE PROBLEM. Marx's theory of profit was that profits were the money form of surplus value produced by labour during the production process. The conversion of surplus value into profits was accomplished not at the level of the firm but of the whole economy. This conversion had to be effected in the context of a contractual purchase of labour by employers (i.e. no extraeconomic coercion) and secondly, the rate of profit had to be equal in all activities. The first consideration meant that the wage rate – the exchange value of the commodity sold by the labourer and bought by the employer – was determined on the same principles as any other commodity. Thus the existence of surplus value had to be reconciled with an economic determination of the exchange value of the commodity labour power.

To drive a wedge between the product of labour and its price, Marx used the accepted distinction between use value and exchange value of a commodity. The commodity in question, labour power, is the labourer's potential for production. The use-value of labour power to the purchaser of the commodity – the capitalist employer – was measured in terms of the total labour time contracted to be spent by the labourer in production – the length of the working day in hours. The exchange value of labour power, like that of any other commodity, was the amount of labour time required for its reproduction, measured by the labour time equivalent of the basket of wage goods purchasable by the given wage. Having thus obtained two commensurable measures of the use value and the exchange value of labour power, the wedge between them was identified as surplus value, produced by the labourer but retained by the purchaser of labour power, the capitalist employer.

Now the total value of a commodity comprised the value contained in the materials used up in the production process – raw materials and energy used as well as the wear and tear of the fixed means of production – which Marx labelled *constant capital* (c) and the total value contributed by labourers. The latter consists of the exchange value of the wage, i.e. of paid labour, labelled variable capital (v) by Marx, and surplus labour (value) (s) which was the remainder. Given this framework the proportion of surplus value to value paid for (constant capital plus variable capital) is defined as the (value) rate of profit. This quantity can be expressed as a product of the rate of surplus value (s/v) and the organic composition of capital ($c/c + v$). Thus, the (value) rate of profit p in the ith economic activity

$$p_i = \frac{s_i}{v_i}\left[1 - \frac{c_i}{(c_i + v_i)}\right] = r_i(1 - g_i) \tag{1}$$

where r_i is the rate of surplus value and g_i is the organic composition of capital. But if this were the basis of actual profits, activities with a higher proportion of living labour would earn a higher rate of profit (given identical rates of exploitation) relative to ones with the lesser labour intensive activity. But since we have to provide for equal rates of profit in all activities, a further step has to be taken to reconcile the theory of unequal value rates of profit with equal actual (or price) rates of profit.

Marx envisaged a pooling of surplus value from all activities at the level of economy and then its redistribution in a transformed form as profits equi-proportional to the amount of capital (fixed and variable) invested in each activity. This was done by the price of a product departing from its unit value. The ratio would be above one for activities with organic composition of capital above average and below one for those below average. This condition will reconcile the unequal value rates of profit, given equal rates of surplus value with equal (price) rates of profit. Indeed for Marx this gives a usable rule for predicting transfer of surplus value from one sector to another as he did in his chapter on Absolute Rent (3/XLV).

The problem is however that the numerical example used in 3/IX contained a conceptual error (though this is disputed as we shall see below) which gave the calculations a tentative, half-finished, unsolved appearance. This can be best explained by setting out Marx's numerical example but in a more general notation. He took five activities labelled $i = 1, \ldots, 5$, each using as inputs constant capital c_i and variable capital v_i with the g_i being different in each activity from the other. The output of the activities were not specifically identified nor was it clear whether they were of the constant capital or the variable capital category. To keep the inputs and outputs separate therefore let input prices be labelled p_c, p_v and output prices p_i.

The value of output can be expressed as

$$y_i = c_i + v_i + s_i = \{[1 + r(1 - g_i)]/(1 - g_i)\}v_i$$
$$= [(1 + \rho_i)/(1 - g_i)]v_i. \tag{2}$$

In equation (2), we have used equation (1) and assumed as Marx did that the rate of exploitation is identical in all activities. (All the variables, total value y_i as well as c_i, v_i, could be interpreted as being per unit of physical output if thought convenient.) Corresponding to (2), the price (total revenue) of output was written by Marx as

$$p_i = (1 + \pi)(c_i + v_i) = ((1 + \pi)/(1 - g_i))v_i. \tag{3}$$

367

Again but especially in this case, variables could be thought of in terms of per unit of output.

To determine π, the actual (price) rate of profit, Marx imposed the condition that the sum of surplus values in all activities was equal to the total of profits over all activities i.e.

$$\sum_i s_i = r \sum_i v_i = \pi \sum_i (c_i + v_i). \tag{4a}$$

Since however his five units were taken to be of the same size in terms of total value, he also trivially obtained an alternative normalization conditions that the total value produced equalled total revenue, that is

$$\sum y_i = \sum p_i. \tag{4b}$$

Using the normalization conditions notice that (2) and (3) together yield

$$p_i/y_i = (1 + \pi)/(1 + \rho_i) = (1 + r(1 - g))/(1 + r(1 - g_i)). \tag{5}$$

Thus strict proportionality of prices and values can only hold if either the rate of exploitation is zero, i.e. no exploitation, or for the case of identical organic compositions of capital $g_i = g$. Given (4b) it was not difficult to see that the price – value differences cancel out in the aggregate. While Marx found some positive and some negative deviations of p_i from y_i, he had no precise explanation to offer at this stage. It is obvious however, as he saw, that (5) implies

$$p_i/y_i \gtrless 1 \quad \text{as } g_i \gtrless \bar{g} \quad \text{where} \quad \bar{g} = \sum \bar{c}_i \bigg/ \sum (c_i + v_i).$$

The problem with Marx's calculation is not that prices diverge from values – that the must – but that the specification of (3) is mistaken if (5) holds. The correct way to write the price equation is to weight the inputs by their respective prices, i.e.

$$p_i = (1 + \pi)(p_c c_i + p_v v_i). \tag{3a}$$

At one level, we can see that Marx made a mistake in considering the cost of inputs in value terms rather than in price terms. It has been argued however (Shaikh, 1977; Morishima and Catephores, 1975) that (2)–(5) can be thought of as the first stage of an ergodic process. By substituting the values obtained by (5) into (3) to modify the input prices, the calculations will converge so that the prices in (5) and (3) would be consistent with each other.

But this can only be done if the physical specification of c_i and v_i is matched to one or more of the commodities produced. If this is not done then we have two more prices than we can solve for. It was Bortkiewicz's merit to have reformulated Marx's problem using Marx's Reproduction Schemes outlined in *Capital* Vol. 2 to allow for matching specification of physical outputs and inputs with constant and variable capital. This allowed him to reduce the size of the problem (the number of unknowns) and allow for aggregate availability constraints on inputs and outputs. He took a model with three commodities (industries or departments) with Department 1 'capital' good (constant capital), Department 2 'wage' good (variable capital) and Department 3 capitalists' consumption (luxury) good. Thus, two of his three commodities were inputs as well as outputs in the production process, i.e. they are basic in the sense of Sraffa, but the third one is an output to be consumed but not an input.

Let the three departments (commodities) be denoted as $j = 1, 2, 3$. The value equations are the same as in Marx but Bortkiewicz's treatment allows a clearer input–output demarcation. Thus, the value equations can be written

$$y_i = y_{1j} + (1 + r)y_{2j} \tag{6}$$

where y_{ij} is the input to good i in the output of good j etc. The price equations are

$$p_j = (1 + \pi) \sum_i p_i y_{ij}. \tag{7}$$

Bortkiewicz preserved (4a) as the normalization condition. But in addition he took care to ensure that the conditions of simple reproduction were satisfied. Thus, he imposed for the two inputs

$$y_i = \sum_i y_{ij}, \quad i = 1, 2. \tag{8}$$

But having implicitly chosen his magnitudes to satisfy (4b) as well, he imposed a condition

$$\sum_j s_j = y_3. \tag{9}$$

While (8) are conditions on total availability of inputs to sustain the required level of output, equation (9) is a 'consumption function' for the recipients of surplus value. As there is no accumulation by assumption, we require that all surplus value is spent on the 'luxury good' produced by Department 3.

Thus Bortkiewicz correctly formulated the problem and even put it in the appropriate general equilibrium framework lacking in Marx's formulation in 3/IX. The solution is straightforward and need not be given here (see Sweezy, 1942, 1949; Desai, 1979). This should have settled any debate about the problem. It emerges that prices are systematic functions of values but are not proportional to them. But the solution was published in German in 1907 and did not become generally known until Sweezy described it in his *Theory of Capitalist Development*, nor did it become available until Sweezy's translation of it in 1949. Within this forty-year interval, economists' knowledge of the linear model had advanced as a result of the works of Leontieff and von Neumann. It was obvious therefore that the problem could be reformulated in these terms. Winternitz proposed such a formulation in 1949 and a full general solution in terms of n goods was given by Morishima and Seton (1961). Roemer (1980) has shown that the linearity assumption can be dropped and a solution in the 'Arrow–Debreu language' can be obtained.

Two areas of controversy arose during the 1970s. First was whether it was necessary to go through the tranformation problem at all to solve for prices from physical intput–output data. This was raised by Samuelson (1971). Second is a more serious problem about the conditions required for solution when there is joint production in the von Neumann–Sraffa sense.

Samuelson's point can be simply made. In order to arrive at value equations such as (2) or (6), we have to translate the data, which are in terms of physical output flows and labour inputs, into the direct and indirect labour content of inputs. After such a translation, we proceed with the transformation. But as we know from input–output analysis, from the physical input data, one can directly solve for prices from the dual of the Leontieff matrix. If one thought the purpose of the exercise was to provide merely a set of prices consistent with a set of values, he is entirely right. What the criticism misses, however, is that if we were to follow Marx's purpose in providing a theory of profits, the separation of labour input into paid and unpaid components (which assumes a political economic background) and the use of the concept of the rate of exploitation are required. If one is to reject Marx's theory of profits, it can be done quite independently of the Transformation Problem, as Wicksteed was able to do even before the publication of *Capital* Volume 3 since he rejected the labour theory of value, classical or Marxian, as such (Wicksteed, 1884; see Desai, 1979, for details).

The second line of criticism is much more serious. This is because it claims that positive surplus value is neither necessary or sufficient for positive profits i.e. it denies the existence of any mapping from values to prices that can satisfy certain general conditions. The problem is with Marx's treatment of fixed capital. In his formulation of the value equations, Marx takes a flow measure of non-labour inputs. This suffices if all capital equipment has only one period life since then the stock and flow measures are equivalent. But if the capital equipment lives beyond the production period some account has to be taken of this in writing the value and prices equations. Bortkiewicz was also able to formulate this problem with different rates of turnover of capital i.e. different lengths of life in another, even lesser known, paper of his (Bortkiewicz, 1906–7). But he took the rates of turnover to be fixed and known in advance. This is less general than one wishes (see Desai (1979) for a description). Marx can be said to have used implicitly a neoclassical accounting technique whereby the rental on capital correctly measures its productive contribution. But, as Morishima (1973) points out, a von Neumann accounting scheme in a 'joint production' model is more appropriate.

It was Steedman (1977) who first constructed a numerical example in which there is negative surplus value but positive profit. This is an example of the generic case of non-convexities which are known to arise in activity analysis (Koopmans, 1951). Steedman made it however an argument for abandoning Marxian value theory in favour of a Ricardo–Sraffa formulation. This suggestion has parallels with Samuelson's suggestion, since the detour via labour values can be shown to be misleading in some cases. It has also been pointed out that the non-convexity problem can arise in the Ricardo–Sraffa scheme just as much as in the Marx scheme. Morishima (1973, 1975) has taken the view that all that is necessary is to reformulate the value–price problem under joint production with appropriate inequality constraints so that non-negativity of (surplus) values and prices are assured. This would seem the more rigorous formulation. The question does remain however of the behavioural foundations of the mechanism that will ensure that in a capitalist economy, only activities with positive surplus values are chosen.

The transformation problem thus continues to fascinate economists even as they debate its relevance. It formed the basis in Bortkiewicz's case for an early formulation of a general equilibrium problem in linear terms. It has been argued that it is more appropriate for planning calculations in a socialist economy than in a capitalist economy whose workings it was supposed to illuminate (Samuelson and Weiszacker, 1971; Morishima, 1973). To Marxists as to their opponents, more important issues such as the moral justification for capitalism seem to be at stake in the solution or non-solution of this seemingly arid technical problem. This is one reason why it will no doubt go on attracting new solutions and new attacks.

BIBLIOGRAPHY

Böhm-Bawerk, E.R. von 1896. Zum Abschluss des Marxschen System. In *Staatswissen-schaftliche Arbeiten: festgaben für Karl Knies*, ed. O.V. Boenig, Berlin. Trans. as 'Karl Marx and the close of his system' in Sweezy (1949).

Bortkiewicz, L. von. 1906–7. Wertrechnung und Preisrechnung im Marxischen System. *Archiv fur Sozialwissenschaft und Sozialpolitik*, July 1906, July and September 1907. Trans. as: Value and price in the Marxian system. In *International Economic Papers* No. 2, ed. Alan T. Peacock et al., London and New York: Macmillan, 1952.

Bortkiewicz, L. von. 1907. Zur Berichtigung der grundlegenden theoretischen konstruktion von Marx in dritten Band des 'Kapital'. *Jahrbucher für Nationalökonomie und Statistik*, July. Trans. as: 'On the Correction of Marx's Fundamental Theoretical Construction in the Third Volume of *Capital*' as Appendix in Sweezy (1949).

Desai, M. 1979. *Marxian Economics*. Oxford: Basil Blackwell; Totowa, N.J: Rowman & Littlefield, 1980.

Koopmans, T.C. 1951. *Activity Analysis of Production and Allocation*. Cowles Commission Monograph No. 13, New York: John Wiley.

Marx, K. 1894. *Das Kapital*, Volume III. Ed. F. Engels, Hamburg: Otto Meissner.

Morishima, M. 1973. *Marx's Economics: A Dual Theory of Value and Growth*. Cambridge and New York: Cambridge University Press.

Morishima, M. and Catephores, G. 1975. The transformation problem: a Markov process. In *Value Exploitation and Growth – Marx in the Light of Modern Economic Theory*, ed. M. Morishima, New York: McGraw-Hill.

Morishima, M. and Seton, F. 1961. Aggregation in Leontief matrices and the labour theory of value. *Econometrica* 29, 203–20.

Roemer, J. 1980. A general equilibrium approach to marxian economics. *Econometrica* 48, March, 505–30.

Samuelson, P.A. 1971. Understanding the marxian notion of exploitation: a summary of the so-called transformation problem between marxian values and competitive prices. *Journal of Economic Literature* 9(2), June, 399–431.

Samuelson, P.A. 1972. *The Collected Scientific Papers of Paul A. Samuelson*, Vol. 3. Ed. Robert C. Merton, Cambridge, Mass.: MIT Press.

Samuelson, P.A. and Weiszacker, C. 1971. A new labour theory of value for rational planning through the use of the bourgeois profit rate. *Proceedings of the National Academy of Sciences*, June. Also in Samuelson (1972).

Schwartz, J. 1977. *The Subtle Anatomy of Capitalism*. Santa Monica, California.

Shaikh, A. 1977. Marx's theory of value and the transformation problem. in Schwartz (1977).

Steedman, I. 1977. *Marx after Sraffa*. London: New Left Books.

Sweezy, P.M. 1942. *The Theory of Capitalist Development*. New York: Monthly Review Press.

Sweezy, P.M. (ed.) 1949. *Karl Marx and the Close of His System* by E. von Böhm-Bawerk and *Böhm-Bawerk's criticism of Marx* by Hilferding. New York: Augustus Kelly.

Wicksteed, P.H. 1884. Das Kapital: a criticism. First published in *Today*, October 1884, reprinted in P.H. Wicksteed, *The Commonsense of Political Economy* Vol. II, 1933.

Winternitz, J. 1948. Values and prices: A solution of the so-called transformation problem. *Economic Journal* 58, 276–80.

Vulgar Economy

KRISHNA BHARADWAJ

Karl Marx used the epithet 'vulgar economy' to describe certain analytical positions which, beginning in classical economy in the works of Malthus, Say, some of the post-Ricardians including John Stuart Mill, developed eventually into an 'analytical system' (as in Say) and took an 'academic form' (as in the writings of Roscher, among others) (see *Theories of Surplus Value*, Vol. III, pp. 500–502). The epithet was not simply a derogatory label but had thus a specific analytical content and significance. Marx contrasted sharply the 'vulgar' from the classical political economy, the latter comprising of 'all the economists who since the time of W. Petty have investigated the real internal framework of bourgeois relations of production' (*Capital*, Vol. I, pp. 174–5). Vulgar economy, while drawing upon the materials provided by scientific political economy – and therefore lacking in originality – ruminated instead over the 'appearances'. Marx saw, in capitalist production, 'more than in any other', a 'reality', 'the inner physiology of the system' – which was captured in scientific political economy, in its analysis locating the generation of surplus in production, in its theory explaining the manner in which surplus is appropriated by the owners of the means of production and distributed as the tripartite revenues of rents, profits and wages, and which brought to light the inevitable and endemic conflicts of class interests and thence the contradictions incipient in the processes of generation, distribution and accumulation of surplus. Marx was himself to build his theory on the rudiments provided by political economy. However, this 'reality' hides behind 'appearances' which assume forms and emerge as esoteric concepts and categories of analysis pertaining to the sphere of exchange where 'Freedom, Equality, Property and Bentham' reign supreme; exchange appears as between 'equivalents', governed entirely by competition on the market. Also, the true social relations take fetishistic forms in 'false consciousness', forming the subjectivist perceptions of the participant agents of production. Marx attacked vulgar political economy for remaining at the level of these 'appearances'; since these often reflected perceptions of the bourgeois agents of production, vulgar

373

economy tends to defend, rationalize and therefore to serve the interests of the bourgeois class. While Marx thus recognized, in vulgar political economy, an explicit or implicit ideological function, providing apologetics for the bourgeoisie, his critique was not confined only to the ideological; he painstakingly traced its analytical roots and development and criticized the logical inconsistencies and ambivalences of its theoretical positions.

For Marx, the significant achievement of scientific political economy was in tracing the source of surplus in production and identifying the role of labour as a cause of value and the source of surplus value. It grasped the 'internal interconnections' of capitalist production through recognizing the different role that the 'agents' – land, capital and labour – played in the process of production and in generating value and the different principles by which their revenues were governed. It identified the constraint binding upon the wage–profit relation. In contrast, vulgar political economy adopted the 'trinity formula' concerning the form and sources of these revenues. Treated as having a symmetric coordinate status, land was seen as the source of rent and capital of profits just as labour is of wages, it being held that the agents are all paid according to their productivity. Thus land as well as capital is as much a source of value and of surplus as labour. Thus 'we have complete mystification of the capitalist mode of production, the conversion of social relations into relations among things'; to Marx, the entitlement to surplus in the form of rents and profits, originating from the property relations, is here confounded with the creation of surplus by the material means themselves. Further, through giving a symmetric role and status to the trinity, by envisaging their revenues as determined by the same process of competitition, and independently of each other, a harmonious view of classes was constructed. This view, explaining distributive revenues in 'doctrinaire language' helped the theory to conform to the bourgeois perceptions: wages appeared as the competitive return to labour and, analogously, as Senior proposed, profits as the recompense for abstinence. The rise in distributive revenues of any one class, reflecting its enhanced productive contribution, could not interefere with others' revenues which were determined alike but independently.

Marx sees the roots of the later vulgar economy in certain 'vulgar representations' or 'elements' in classical political economy. While generously praising the masterly vision of Adam Smith for fathoming 'the inner connection' and, for the first time, describing and providing 'a nomenclature and corresponding mental concepts' for 'the external, apparent forms of its life', Marx critizes, at length, an important 'vulgar' element in Smith: when Smith constructs the natural price of a commodity from adding up wages, rents and profits, determined independently of each other and separately, they become *sources of value* instead of having 'a source *in* value'. After having revealed the intrinsic connection among wages and profits, Smith leaps into 'the connection as it appears in competition'. Marx attaches a great historical significance to Ricardo 'for science' in that he brought back 'the inner connection – the contradiction between the apparent and the actual movement of the system and brought into the open the objective basis for the inescapable antagonism of class interests'.

This apart, Marx also discusses a number of other shortcomings of classical political economy that provided scope for vulgarization, such as their inadequate recognition of the historical and transient character of the capitalist mode, of the full implication of labour-power becoming a 'commodity' and of capital as a 'social relation' apart from its 'material form'; of the process of transforming surplus value into profits and of the intervention of money into barter and the evolution of its functions over the advancing stages of capitalist accumulation. All these inadequacies were exploited by vulgar political economy in building up a sanguine and harmonious view of the functioning and growth of the capitalist system, whereas Marx found the system ridden with internal contradictions and recurrent crises.

Marx traced the growth of vulgar political economy and its ascendency over scientific political economy in terms of the concrete conditions of the historical stages of class struggle. He saw the period between 1820 and 1830 as the last decade of scientific activity when Ricardo's theory was popularized and extended and when 'unprejudiced polemics' was possible. By 1830, the bourgeoisie had conquered political power in France and England, their ascendancy over the landed interests was firmly established while the class struggle of labour was assuming threatening proportions. 'It sounded the knell of scientific bourgeois economics. It was thenceforth no longer a question whether this or that theorem was true but whether it was useful to capital or harmful, expedient or inexpedient' (Preface to the second edition, *Capital*, Vol. I).

Vulgar political economy itself passed through analytical stages in the period. Marx notices: 'Only when political economy has reached a certain stage of development and has assumed well-established forms – that is, after Adam Smith – does ... the vulgar element become a special kind of political economy.' Thus, Say separates the vulgar notions in Smith's work (such as the supply and demand determination of value) and puts them forward as a distinct system. Borrowing from the advancing political economy, vulgar economy also thrives: after Ricardo, particularly, the decline of his theory sets in; the erosion and obfuscation occurring in the hands of his own followers. The hostility to Ricardian theory was sharpened by the use made of labour theory by the utopian writers who, on the basis of their naive interpretation, advocated a radical change in social order. Vulgar political economy becomes increasingly apologetic, as in Bastiat, with the capital–labour confrontation emerging sharply in society, until it assumes a further 'academic form' where apologetics was concealed in an 'insipid erudition' (Marx refers to Roscher as a 'master of this form'!) (1861–3, Vol. III, pp. 500–502.)

What emerges from Marx's detailed critique, particularly in the *Theories of Surplus Value*, is that his attack was not only ideological but also analytical. While a fully-fledged alternative system to replace classical political economy had not yet emerged in Marx's time, the latter had been eroded and conditions become ripe for its subversion.

Marxian economics

BIBLIOGRAPHY

Marx, K. 1861–3. *Theories of Surplus Value*, Vols. I–III. London: Lawrence & Wishart, 1972.

Marx, K. 1890. *Capital*, Vol. I. 4th edn, London: Pelican Marx Library, 1976.

Marx, K. 1894. *Capital*, Vol. III. Moscow: Progress Publishers, 1974.

Contributors

Alice H. Amsden Visiting Professor, MIT, Department of Civil Engineering and Urban Studies and Planning. *International Firms and Labour in Kenya* (1971); 'The division of labour is limited by the type of market: the Taiwanese machine tool industry' in *World Development* (1977); *The Economics of Women and Work* (1980); 'The State and social development in Taiwan' in *States and Social Structures* (ed. P. Evans, 1985); *Asia's Next Giant: late industrialization in South Korea* (1989).

Andrew Arato Associate Professor, Department of Sociology, New School for Social Research, New York. *The Essential Frankfurt School Reader* (ed. with Eike Gebhardt, 1978); *The Young Lukács and the Origins of Western Marxism* (with Paul Breines, 1979); 'Civil society vs. the state: Poland 1980–1', *Telos 47*; 'Empire vs. civil society: Poland 1981–2', *Telos 50*.

Krishna Bharadwaj Professor of Economics, Jawaharlal Nehru University, Winner, William Wedderburn Fellowship; V.K.R.V. Rao Prize (1986). 'Economic growth and transport requirements: a comparative study in methods of project', *Economic Weekly* (1961); 'Structural linkages in the Indian economy', *Economic Weekly* (1962); *Production Conditions in Indian Agriculture* (1974); *Classical Political Economy and Rise to Dominance of Supply and Demand Theories* (1976/8); *Themes in Value and Distribution: classical theory Reappraised* (1978); *On Some Issues of Method in Analysis of Social Change* (1980).

Tom Bottomore Emeritus Professor of Sociology, Sussex University. *Elites and Society* (1964); *Political Sociology* (1979); *A Dictionary of Marxist Thought* (ed., 1983); *The Frankfurt School* (1984); *Theories of Modern Capitalism* (1985); *Sociology: A guide to problems and literature* (1987).

Robert Boyer Research Officer, Centre National de la Recherche Scientifique, Director of Studies, École des Hautes Études en Sciences Sociales, Paris. 'Wage formation in historical perspectives: the French experience', *Cambridge Journal of Economics* (1979); *Capitalismes fin de siècle* (ed., 1986); *The Search for Labour Flexibility: the European economies in transition* (ed. 1988); *La théorie de la régulation: une analyse critique* (1986/8); 'Technical change and the theory of "regulation"' in *Technical Change and Economic Theory* (ed. G. Dosi, C. Freeman, R. Nelson, G. Silverberg and L. Soete, 1988); 'Labour discipline and aggregate demand: a macroeconomic model', *The American Economic Review* (with S. Bowles, 1988).

Robert Brenner Professor, Department of History, University of California, Los Angeles.

G. Catephores Department of Political Economy, University of London. *An Introduction to Marxist Economics* (1988).

Ednaldo Araquém da Silva Assistant Professor, New School for Social Research, New York. Fulbright Visiting Fellow, Cedplar/UFMG (Brazil, 1985–6). 'Measuring the incidence of rural capitalism: a discriminant analysis of survey data from Northeast Brazil', *Journal of Peasant Studies* (1984); 'Wage – profit trade-offs in Brazil: an input/output analysis', *Science and Society* (1987); 'Preços e distribuição de renda no Brasil: una análise de insumo/produto', *Pesquiso & Planejamento Econômico* (1988).

Suzanne-Simone de Brunhoff Senior Research Officer, Centre National de la Recherche Scientifique, Paris. *Marx on Money* (1976); *The State, Capital and Economic Policy* (1978); *L'heure du marche, Critique de Liberalisme* (1986).

Meghnad Desai Professor of Economics, London School of Economics. 'Growth cycles and inflation in a model of the class struggle', *Journal of Economic Theory* (1973); 'Phillips curve: A revisionist interpretation', *Economica* (1975); *Applied Econometrics* (1976); *Marxian Economics* (1979); *Testing Monetarism* (1981); 'Men and Things', *Economica* (1986).

Giancaro de Vivo Associate Professor of Economics, University of Naples. 'Sul sistema di equilibrio economico generale di Walras', *Economia Internazionale* (1976); 'International integration and the balance of payments constraint: the case of Italy', *Cambridge Journal of Economics* (1980); 'Notes on Marx's critique of Ricardo', *Contributions to Political Economy* (1982); 'Robert Torrens and Ricardo's 'corn-ratio' theory of profits', *Cambridge Journal of Economics* (1985); 'Torrens on value and distribution', *Contributions to Political Economy* (1986).

John Eatwell Fellow, Trinity College, Cambridge. *Keynes's Economics and the Theory of Value Distribution* (with Murray Milgate, 1983); *Whatever Happened to Britain?* (1984).

Roy Edgley Professor of Philosophy, Sussex University (retired). *Reason in theory and Practice* (1969); 'Reason and violence', *Radical Philosophy* (1973); 'Freedom of speech and academic freedom', *Radical Philosophy* (1975); 'Education for industry', *Radical Philosophy* (1978); 'Philosophy' in *Marx: The First Hundred Years* (ed. D. McLellan, 1983); 'Sociology, social criticism and Marxism', *Social Theory and Social Criticism* (ed. W. Outhwaite and M. Mulkay, 1987).

Malcolm Falkus Professor of Economic History, University of New England. *Readings in the History of Economic Growth* (1968); 'Russia's national income in 1913: a re-evaluation', *Economica* (1968); *The Industrialization of Russia 1700–1914* (1972); *Always Under Pressure: a history of North Thames Gas since 1949* (1988).

John B. Foster Professor, Evergreen State College, Washington. *The Faltering Economy* (ed., with Henryk Szlajfer, 1984); *The Theory of Monopoly Capitalism* (1986).

John O. Foster Professor and Head of Department of Applied Social Studies, College of Technology, Paisley. *Class and the Industrial Revolution* (1973); *The Politics of the UCS Work-In* (with Charles Woolfson, 1984); *Track Record: the story of the Caterpillar Occupation* (1988).

Ernest Gellner William Wyse Professor of Social Anthropology, University of Cambridge. Fellow, British Academy; Honorary Foreign Member, American Academy of Arts and Sciences. *Relativism in the Social Sciences* (1985); *State and Society in Soviet Thought* (1988); *Plough, Sword and Book* (1988).

M. Glick University of Utah.

Andrew Glyn Lecturer, Corpus Christi College, Oxford. *British Capitalism, Workers and the Profit Squeeze* (with Bob Sutcliffe, 1972); *Capitalism Since World War II* (with P. Armstrong and J. Harrison, 1984); 'The economic case against pit closures' in *Debating Colliery Closures* (ed. D. Cooper and T. Hopper, 1988); 'The diversity of unemployment experience since 1973' (with Bob Rowthorn) in *The End of the Golden Age* (ed. S.A. Marglin, 1989).

David M. Gordon Professor of Economics, New School for Social Research, New York. Guggenheim Fellow (1984–5); Member, Institute for Advanced Study (1987–8). *Segmented Work, Divided Workers* (with Richard Edwards and E. Wiesskopf, 1982); *Beyond the Waste Land* (with Richard Edwards and Michael Reich, 1984).

R.H. Green *Development Options for Africa in the 1980's and Beyond* (ed., with P. Ndegwa and L.P. Mureithi, 1985); *Management for Development* (ed., with P. Ndegwa and L.P. Mureithi, 1987).

Donald J. Harris Professor of Economics, Stanford University, California. National Research Council – Ford Foundation Fellow (1984–5). 'Inflation, income distribution, and capital accumulation in a two-sector model of growth', *The Economic Journal* (1967); 'Income, prices, and the balance of payments in underdeveloped economies: a short-run model', *Oxford Economic Papers* (1970); 'On Marx's scheme of reproduction and accumulation', *Journal of Political Economy* (1972); *Capital Accumulation and Income Distribution* (1978); 'Profits, productivity, and thrift: the neoclassical theory of capital and distribution revisited', *Journal of Post-Keynesian Economics* (1982); 'Accumulation of Capital and the rate of profit in Marxian theory', *Cambridge Journal of Economics* (1983).

E.K. Hunt Professor of Economics, University of Utah. *Property and Profits* (1981); *History of Economic Thought* (1979); *Economics* (with Howard J. Sherman, 1981).

A. Hussain Senior Lecturer, Department of Economics, University of Keele. *Paths of Development in Capitalist Agriculture* (ed. with Keith Tribe, 1984); *Transforming China's Economy in the Eighties* (ed. with Stephan Feuchtwang and Thierry Pairault, 1988); *Marxism and the Agrarian Question* (1980).

Bob Jessop Senior Lecturer, Department of Government, University of Essex. *The Capitalist State* (1982); *Nicos Poulantzas* (1985); *Thatcherism* (1988); *The Political Economy of Post-war Britain* (1989); *Essays in State Theory* (1989).

P.M. Kenway Department of Economics, University of Reading.

Tadeusz Kowalik Warsaw. 'Rosa Luxembourg's theory of accumulation and imperialism' in *Problems of Economic Dynamics and Planning, Essays in Honour of Michal Kalecki* (1964); 'Central planning', 'Lange–Lerner mechanism', 'Oskar Ryszard Lange', *The New Palgrave* (ed. J. Eatwell, M. Milgate and P. Newman, 1987).

William Lazonick Professor of Economics, Barnard College, New York. President-Elect, Business History Conference (1990). *Value Creation on the Shop Floor* (forthcoming); *The Decline of the British Economy* (with Bernard Elbaum, 1986); 'Financial commitment and economic performance: ownership and control in the American industrial corporation', *Business and Economic History* (1988); 'Business organization and competitive advantage: capitalist transformations in the twentieth century' in *Proceedings of the Second International Conference on the History of Enterprise* (forthcoming).

Ernest Mandel Professor, Vrije Universiteit, Brussels. *An Introduction to Marxist Economic Theory* (1967); *Late Capitalism* (1975); *Ricardo, Marx, Sraffa* (1984); *The Meaning of the Second World War* (1986); *Beyond Perestroika* (1989).

Nobuo Okishio Professor, Faculty of Economics, Kobe University. 'Monopoly and the rates of profit', *Kobe University Economic Review* (1955); 'Technical changes and the rate of profit', *Kobe University Economic Review* (1961); 'A mathematical note on Marxian theorems', *Welwirtshaftliches Archiv* (1963); *The Theory of Accumulation* (1976); 'Note on technical progress and capitalistic society', *Cambridge Journal of Economics* (1977).

Fabio Petri Facoltà di Scienze Economiche a Banacarie, Instituto di Economia, Siena.

John E. Roemer Professor of Economics, University of Economics. Fellow, Econometric Society. *A General Theory of Exploitation and Class* (1982); 'Rationalizing revolutionary ideology', *Econometrica* (1985); 'Equality of resources implies equality of welfare', *Quarterly Journal of Economics* (1986); 'Axiomatic bargaining theory on economic environments', *Journal of Economic Theory* (1988); 'Public ownership of the external world and private ownership of self', *Journal of Political Economy* (with H. Moulin, 1989); *Free to lose: an introduction to Marxist economic philosophy* (1988).

Massino Salvadori Professor, Facoltà di Scienze Politiche, Catania. *The Rise of Modern Communism* (1953); *Modern Socialism* (1968); *Eurocomunismo e Socialismo Sovietico* (1978); *Karl Kautsky and the Socialist Revolution 1880–1938* (1979).

Thomas T. Sekine Professor of Economics and Social and Political Thought, York University, Canada. *The Dialectic of Capital* (2 vols., 1984/6); 'The law of market value', *Science and Society* (1983); 'The Circular Motion of Capital', *Science and Society* (1981); *Uno's Principles of Political Economy* (trans., 1980); 'Uno Riron: a Japanese contribution to Marxian political economy', *The Journal of Economic Literature* (1975).

Amartya K. Sen Drummond Professor of Political Economy, All Soul's College, Oxford; Lamont University Professor, Harvard University. President, Econometric Society 1984; Fellow, British Academy. *On Economic Inequality* (1973); *Employment, Technology and Development* (1975); *Poverty and Famines* (1981); *Resources, Values and Development* (1984); *On Ethics and Economics* (1987); *Commodities and Capabilities* (1985).

Anwar M. Shaikh Professor of Economics, Department of Economics, New School for Social Research, New York; Research grant, Jerome Levy Economics Institute of Bard College (1989); Distinguished Scholar, American Scholars to

China, National Academy of Sciences (1985). 'A simple solution to Harrod's knife-edge problem', *Kaldor and Mainstream Economics: confrontation or convergence (Festschrift for Nicolas Kaldor)* (ed. E.J. Nell and Willi Semmler, 1989); 'Accumulation, finance, and effective demand in Marx, Keynes, and Kalecki', *Financial Dynamics and Business Cycles: new prospects* (ed. Willi Semmler, 1988); 'The falling rate of profit and the economic crisis in the U.S.', *The Imperiled Economy* (ed. Robert Cherry, 1987); 'The welfare state and the myth of the social wage', *The Imperiled Economy* (with E. Ahmet Tonak, ed. Robert Cherry, 1987); 'The transformation from Marx to Sraffa: prelude to a critique of the neo-Ricardians', *Marx, Ricardo, Sraffa* (ed. Ernest Mandel, 1984); 'Laws of algebra and laws of production: humbug II', *Growth, Profits and Property: essays in the revival of political economy* (ed. E.J. Nell, 1980).

Andrew Stewart Skinner Daniel Jack Professor of Political Economy, Clerk of Senate, University of Glasgow. Fellow, Royal Society of Edinburgh. *Sir James Steuart, Principles of Political Oeconomy (1767)* (ed., 1966); *Adam Smith, The Wealth of Nations* (ed., with R.H. Campbell and W.B. Todd, 1976); *A System of Social Sciences: papers relating to Adam Smith* (1979); *Adam Smith, Essays on Philosophical Subjects* (ed., with D.D. Raphael, 1980); *Adam Smith* (with R.W. Campbell, 1982).

Gareth Stedman Jones Reader, History of Social Thought, Cambridge University; Fellow, King's College, Cambridge. *Outcast London* (1971); *Languages of Class* (1983).

Josef Steindl Honorary Professor, University of Vienna. Honorary Doctorate, University of Graz. *Maturity and Stagnation in American Capitalism* (1952); *Random Processes and the Growth of Firms: a study of Pareto law* (1965).

Dirk J. Struik Professor of Mathematics Emeritus, MIT. *Yankee Science in the Making* (1948); *A Concise History of Mathematics* (1948); *Lectures on Classical Differential Geometry* (1950); *A Source Book in Mathematics 1200–1800* (1969); *The Land of Stevin and Huygens* (1981).

Paul M. Sweezy Co-Founder and Co-Editor of *The Monthly Review*. *The Present as History* (1953); *Monopoly Capital* (with Paul A. Baran, 1968); *The Theory of Capitalist Development* (1976); *The Global Crisis of Capitalism* (1980); *Stagnation and the Financial Explosion* (with Henry Magdoff, 1987).

Ross Thomson Professor, New School for Social Research, New York.

Jim Tomlinson Senior Lecturer, Department of Economics, Brunel University. *Problems of British Economic Policy 1870–1945* (1981); *The Unequal Struggle? British Socialism and the Capitalist Enterprise* (1982); *Monetarism: is there an* *alternative?* (1985); *Employment Policy: the crucial years 1939–55* (1987); *Public Policy and the Economy Since 1900* (1989).

F. Vianello Facoltá di Economia e Commercia, Universita degli Studi di Modena. *Nitti, Francesco Saverio, Scritti di Economia e Finanze* (1969); *Il Piano del Lavoro della CGIL* (ed., 1978); *Il Profitto e il Potere* (1979).

P.J.D. Wiles Professor Emeritus, University of London. *Political Economy of Communism* (1962); *Economic Institutions Compared* (1979); *Price, Cost and Output* (1961); *Communist International Economics* (1968); *Economics in Disarray* (ed., with Guy Routh, 1984).